INSIGHT GUIDE

SOUTH AMERICA

APA PUBLICATIONS   L

Part of the Langenscheidt Publishing Group

ABOUT THIS BOOK

INSIGHT GUIDE
SOUTH america

Editorial

Project Editor
Natalie Minnis
Managing Editor
Huw Hennessy
Editorial Director
Brian Bell

Distribution

UK & Ireland
GeoCenter International Ltd
The Viables Centre
Harrow Way, Basingstoke
Hants RG22 4BJ
Fax: (44) 1256-817988

United States
Langenscheidt Publishers, Inc.
46–35 54th Road
Maspeth, NY 11378
Fax: (718) 784-0640

Worldwide
APA Publications GmbH & Co.
Verlag KG (Singapore branch)
38 Joo Koon Road
Singapore 628990
Tel: (65) 865-1600
Fax: (65) 861-6438

Printing

Insight Print Services (Pte) Ltd
38 Joo Koon Road
Singapore 628990
Tel: (65) 865-1600
Fax: (65) 861-6438

CONTACTING THE EDITORS
Although every effort is made to provide accurate information in this publication, we live in a fast-changing world and would appreciate it if readers would call our attention to any errors or outdated information that may occur by writing to us at: **Insight Guides, P.O. Box 7910, London SE1 8ZB, England. Fax: (44 171) 620-1074. e-mail: insight@apaguide.demon.co.uk**

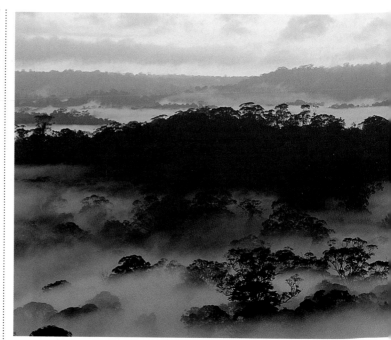

All Insight Guides are the result of teamwork, and this one is no exception. It involved an experienced group of writers and photographers, with in-depth knowledge of South America, working under the direction of Insight Guides' editorial team in London, who have produced more than 400 books since 1970.

How to use this book

This book has been carefully structured both to convey an understanding of the country, its people and its culture, and to guide readers through its sights and activities, both the famous highlights and some lesser-known attractions.

◆ To understand contemporary South America, you need to know something about its colorful history. From the Inca Empire to the Spanish Conquest and from some chilling military dictatorships through to reforming modern democracies, South America has had a dramatic and eventful history. The **Features** section covers the history and culture of the whole region in a series of lively and informative essays, focusing on the modern developments of individual countries and their common roots before the Conquest.

◆ The main **Places** section provides a complete country-by-country guide to all the sights and areas worth seeing, including opening times of museums,

Ing ¹/2000

archeological sites and art galleries. Places of special interest are coordinated by number with specially-drawn full-color maps of each country, major cities and tourist regions.

◆ The **Travel Tips** section provides a convenient reference for information on travel, accommodation, restaurants, outdoor activities, Spanish and Portuguese language tips and more. Information may be located quickly by using the index printed on the back cover flap.

◆ The **Photographs** have been carefully chosen not only to convey the beauty of the countries, the landscape, flora and fauna, but also to give an accurate impression of the people of South America and their everyday lives.

The contributors

This new edition was updated by journalist and frequent traveler **Natalie Minnis**, and builds on earlier editions by **Tony Perrottet**. The editors looked for writers who had a combination of affection for and detachment from their specialist subjects.

The chapters on South American history were contributed by **Nick Caistor**, who is the Latin America Editor at the BBC World Service. Natalie Minnis wrote about the people of South America, and the music and dance chapter was written by **Shannon Shiell**, a Glasgow-based Latin dance expert who has lived and worked in South America. The arts and architecture chapters were contributed by **Mike Gonzalez**, senior lecturer in the Department of Hispanic Studies at Glasgow University. The outdoor sports chapter and new writing on Ecuador were written by **Jane Letham** and **Mark Thurber**, based in Quito, who run their own trekking and mountaineering tours around Peru and Ecuador.

Chapters in the Places section were revised and updated by **Jasper Corbett** (Colombia), **Elizabeth Kline** (Venezuela), **Martin Symington** (The Guianas), **Diana Zileri** (Peru), **Natalie Minnis** (Bolivia), **Patrick Knight** (Brazil), **Dick Barbour-Might** (Paraguay), **Ruth Bradley** (Chile) and **Dr Jill Hedges** (Uruguay, Argentina and the Falkland Islands).

The chief photographers were **Mireille Vautier** and **Eduardo Gil**. Many photographs of Brazil were supplied by **H. John Maier**.

Map Legend

▬ ▬ ▪ ▪	International Boundary
▬ ▬ ▬ ▬	State Boundary
⊖	Border Crossing
▬ ▪ ▬ ▪	National Park/Reserve
▬ ▬ ▬ ▬	Ferry Route
Ⓜ	Metro
✈ ✈	Airport: International/ Regional
🚌	Bus Station
🅿	Parking
❶	Tourist Information
✉	Post Office
⚑ † ✝	Church / Ruins
†	Monastery
☪	Mosque
✡	Synagogue
⚑ ⌂	Castle / Ruins
∴	Archeological Site
∩	Cave
1	Statue/Monument
★	Place of Interest

The main places of interest in the Places section are coordinated by number with a full-colour map (e.g. ❶), and a symbol at the top of every right-hand page tells you where to find the map.

INSIGHT GUIDE
SOUTH AMERICA

CONTENTS

Girl from the
Bolivian
altiplano

Travel Tips

Insight on ...

Information panels

THE UNDISCOVERED CONTINENT

From the Andes to the Amazon, from dense forests to alluring beaches, South America's diversity is extraordinary

South America is a man with a moustache, a guitar and a revolver." That is how foreigners see the continent, according to the Colombian novelist Gabriel García Márquez. More perhaps than any other continent, South America has been the victim of stereotypes and misconceptions. Most people see it as one huge, mysterious jungle, a mountainous wasteland or a backward rural world languidly lost in an eternal *siesta*.

But from the moment you step out of an aircraft anywhere in South America, it's obvious that the images fail to capture even a fraction of the reality. There are mighty rivers, wilderness areas and final frontiers, but also ancient civilizations and vibrant new cultures. The Amazon basin and its remote outposts grab the imagination of novelists, screenwriters and adventure seekers, while the elegant salons of Buenos Aires and the stylish resorts along the Caribbean attract a less vocal following. Like the Amazon rainforest, the Andes are home to communities that have barely changed for centuries; unlike the enormous metropolises of Brazil and Argentina, where life is so modern and energetic it will leave you breathless.

The countries in South America share a common history – thousands of years of indigenous cultures broken by European intrusion 500 years ago; colonial rule followed by bitter wars of independence; then an unsteady progress at the fringe of world events. Despite these shared experiences, each country retains its own character.

On the north coast (*see page 85*), are Colombia and Venezuela, Guyana, Suriname and French Guiana, racially mixed and geographically divided between rugged mountains, hot equatorial coastline and dense Amazon rainforest. South of Colombia lies the Andean heartland of South America (*see page 139*): Peru, Bolivia and Ecuador, which have the highest Indian populations on the continent, clustered around the barren highlands where the mighty Inca empire once reigned and now the continent's least developed region.

The east (*see page 223*) is dominated by the giant Brazil, in a world of its own, separated from its Spanish-speaking neighbors by a Portuguese heritage – despite bordering on every single country in the continent except Ecuador and Chile. In the cooler southern zones (*see page 259*), are Paraguay, Chile, Uruguay and Argentina, the most European-influenced and prosperous of South American republics, with vast empty spaces that stretch along the spine of the Andes to the last stop before Antarctica: Tierra del Fuego.   ❏

PRECEDING PAGES: Grey Glacier, Torres del Paine National Park, Chile; the "Devil's Throat", Iguaçu Falls, Brazil; reed boat on Lake Titicaca, Bolivia; beach in Rio, Brazil.
LEFT: "El Tren a las Nubes" ("The Train to the Clouds"), northern Argentina.

20,000–4500 BC

PRE-COLUMBIAN TIMELINE

Human settlement in South America began with nomadic hunter-gatherers travelling southward, and reached its peak with the Inca Empire at the time of the Conquest

EARLIEST ORIGINS
First humans arrive in South America, around 20,000 BC, related to hunter-gatherers who crossed the Bering Straits "ice-bridge" between Asia and the Americas, following herds in search of food.

◁ *Ceramic vessel in a feline form,*

3000 BC–400 AD

POTTERY AND METAL
The first production of ceramics in South America began around 3000 BC, according to carbon dated remains found in Colombia and Ecuador. These earliest ceramics were fashioned by hand, and mostly utensils, but highly sophisticated ornamental and ceremonial items were soon being produced, from the Andes to the mouth of the Amazon.
Gold was the first metal known to be worked in the Andes, with remnants found in central Peru dating from around 2000 BC. The practice soon spread to Bolivia and later to Ecuador and Colombia. Gold and silver items of incredible beauty and technical quality were produced in huge quantities, as symbolic decorations of the ruling classes of the emerging state societies.

▷ *Silver breastplate, Chibcha culture, Colombia, c.1200 BC.*

400 BC–1100 AD

MASTER WEAVERS
The earliest textiles, found in central Peru, have been dated from as early as 8600 BC. Around 400 BC, the Nazca and Paracas cultures rose to prominence along the coastal desert of southern Peru. These people were the technical masters at weaving and pottery, much of which has survived in funeral chambers, preserved by the dry air. Some of the textiles found have more than 200 threads to the square

inch – finer than most modern materials. The Nazca culture also produced the famous lines on the desert floor, which still mystify visitors and archeologists alike – with interpretations ranging from a giant astronomical calendar to a landing strip for extraterrestrials.

◁ *Woven cotton cloth decorated with feathers, Paracas culture, Peru c.1000 BC.*

1100–1569 AD

BIRTH OF THE INCAS
c1100 AD, the legendary appearance of Manco Capac, rising out of Lake Titicaca, hailed as the Sun god and divine leader of the chosen Inca race. The city of Cuzco is founded by Manco Capac, legendary first Inca ruler. The Inca state is called *Tahuantin-suyu*, the "Land of the Four

Quarters," with Cuzco at its center, as the "Umbilicus of the Universe."
c1430 AD, Incas defeat Chancas and extend their empire across a huge area of South America, based on military efficiency, road network, terracing, irrigation and stone architecture.

◁ *Quipú knotted cords, used by Inca officials to keep an inventory of goods and produce.*

SETTLING DOWN

Cave remains and shell mounds (*sambaquis*) found in Brazil, and stone tools found in Peru, suggesting earliest humans from c.17,000–5000 BC. But the most reliable evidence of the first human settlement was at Monte Verde in central Chile, where remains have been dated at 12,500 BC.

◁ *Pottery figure of religious leader, Chavin culture, Peru, c.1200 BC*

FISHING AND FARMING

Between 7500 BC and 4500 BC Andean peoples began seasonal cultivation of crops, including the potato, maize, manioc and sweet potato; and domestication of dogs, llamas, alpacas and guinea pigs. Coastal tribes from present-day Ecuador to northern Chile harvested rich marine life of the Pacific, boosted by the Humboldt Currrent. The fishermen made hooks from shell, bone and cactus spines.

SOCIAL SKILLS

From about 2800 BC, societies began to form in the central and northern Andes. The earliest of these were the Chavín, in northern Peru; the Tiahuanaco to the south of Lake Titicaca and the San Agustín culture in southern Colombia. They built massive ceremonial urban centers in stone, produced highly sophisticated ceramics, textiles and religious artifacts in gold and other precious metals and stones. They formed large populations of up to hundreds of thousands, organized in complex social hierarchies and covering large administrative regions. Amazonian societies also flourished at about this time, if not earlier. Aruak-speaking people inhabited a region near to present-day Manaus from as early as 3000 BC.

◁ *Gold "Darien pectoral" from Colombia, 900–1200 AD. Figure has alligator-like head, thought to represent a supernatural being, a priest or a shaman.*

IMPERIAL EXPANSION

Based in the deserts of northern Peru, the Moche culture built up an empire from about 100–800 AD, that covered much of the north of the country. Their military and commercial influence was aided by their roadbuilding and irrigation works, skills later picked up by the Incas. Above all, the Moche were superb artisans, producing ceramics and fine metal and precious stone ornaments to a standard never seen before in the Americas. The Moche Empire disappeared dramatically and mysteriously, around 700 AD. From about 600–1000 AD the religious Tiahuanaco culture combined with the militaristic Huari of the central Andean highlands to form an empire that at its peak spread into present-day Bolivia.

◁ *Gold burial mask, Lambayeque culture, Peru, 1100–1400 AD.*

PEAK AND FALL

Around the mid 1400s, the Inca Empire expands rapidly, firstly under Pachacutec and, later, under his son, Topa Inca. The Chimu empire, based in northern Peru, is defeated by the Incas, c.1466 AD. **1532 AD**, The Spanish conquistadors arrive in Peru; Inca Atahuallpa is executed a year later. In 1569, Tupac Amaru, the last Inca, is killed by the Spanish and the Conquest is complete.

◁ *Gold ornament, Sinu culture, Colombia, 1100–1600 AD.*

◁ *European missionaries bring the Gospel to Amazon indians.*

THE FIRST PEOPLES

Pre-Columbian South America was a place of cultural diversity where enduring traditions and unique lifestyles were forged and great empires were built

The first colonisation of South America is shrouded in mystery, as knowledge of those early times has had to be pieced together from archaeological finds and linguistic evidence. Experts now believe that the first Americans arrived from the Asian continent, crossing the Bering Straits when they were

solid with ice during the last Ice Age, some 40,000 years ago. These bands of hunter-gatherers gradually spread down America; some sites in Patagonia show the far south was inhabited by around 9,000 BC. Remains of mastodon, sloth and other animals which have since disappeared, found together with arrowheads, demonstrate that these people were hunter-gatherers, but little else is known of their way of life or social organization.

Over several thousand years, these small groups turned from hunting to a more settled farming existence. According to archaeological evidence, some lived close to the seashores and subsisted on a diet of fish and shellfish;

some settled in the Andean highlands, and others adapted to the tropical lowlands of the Amazon. These early settlers appear to have grown beans and peppers, and to have used domesticated dogs to help them hunt small game. Maize is thought to have been cultivated from Peru down to Argentina by 3,000 BC, and some of the highland groups also began to herd llama and other camelids. The first pottery remains found date from about 3,000 years ago.

First societies

As these groups became based around seasonal agriculture, population gradually increased, and more complex societies emerged, with officials, including chieftains and priests or shamans. Some of the earliest remains discovered are from **La Tolita** in Ecuador, which date from around 2,000 years ago, but the **San Agustín** culture in southern Colombia appears to have been one of the outstanding early sites. Here, burial mounds and intricate sculptures speak of a high degree of social organization, with religious ceremonies and complex burial rites.

Over the centuries, these small population centres grew into larger regional units, with ceremonial sites that have yielded a great deal of information. In some cases, such as the **Taironas** of the northeastern highlands of Colombia, it is thought that up to 250,000 peo-

THE MYTH OF EL DORADO

One of the early Colombian cultures, the Chibcha, gave rise to perhaps the most enduring South American legend, that of El Dorado. The Chibchas were divided into two kingdoms who worshiped the sun as their chief deity, and practised human sacrifice. The ceremony for appointing a new Chibcha ruler apparently involved throwing gold statues into a lake, covering the new leader in gold dust and immersing him in the water until it had washed off. This made him "El Dorado" – the Golden One, giving rise to the legend.

ple lived on one site; by now, the main buildings were made of stone, and gold, emeralds and other precious stones were used both for ornament and for trade.

The great edifices

In Peru and in the Andean highlands of Bolivia, there is evidence that settled occupation began as early as 5,000 BC. By 2,000 BC large monumental structures were being built, by population groups estimated at around 1,000 or 1,500 people. One of the most significant of these early centres grew up around 1,000 BC in the **Moche valley** near the northern Peruvian

superseded in northern Peru by the **Moche** culture, which flourished from AD 200-700. The Moche are known for their prolific production of beautiful stirrup-spouted pottery, which depicted every aspect of their life, from violence and erotica to medical treatments. They also produced fine gold, silver and copperwork. Their imposing capital at **Moche** is dominated by two large structures – the **Huaca del Sol** and the **Huaca de la Luna** – temples of the sun and moon, built around a large plaza or central square. In around AD 500 natural disasters probably forced them to move from Moche; their later centre at **Pampa Grande** shows that

coastline. It is known as the **Chavín** culture, after the archaeological site at **Chavín de Huántar,** about 3,000 meters (10,000 ft) up in the Andean mountains, thought to date from 3,000 years ago. The most impressive structure here is a platform of earth and rock with a hollow interior, known as **El Castillo** or The Castle, probably used for religious ceremonies.

The Chavín culture, which also produced fine pottery and intricate stone stelae, is believed to have gone into a decline around 200 BC. It was

LEFT: pre-Columbian artefact from the Gold Museum, Bogotá, Colombia. **ABOVE:** the Gateway of the Sun, Tiahuanaco, Bolivia.

the culture continued to thrive until the 8th century. Later, the **Chimu** culture, based at **Chan Chan** (*see page 164*), showed a continuity of development in these coastal sites.

At the same period in the south of Peru, the **Nazca** culture came to the fore (*see page 150*). The Nazca people are best known for the extraordinary lines they drew in the desert, which from the air can be seen to represent figures such as hummingbirds, monkeys or fish, but which do not make sense from ground level. The size and complexity of the lines gave rise to the theory that extra-terrestrials must have visited South America in ancient times: although this idea is now dismissed, as yet there is no convincing explanation as to why a farming community should have spent so much time making such an immense display.

Further inland, near Lake Titicaca in northern Bolivia, the **Wankarani** people who lived by fishing, herding llama and growing potatoes, gave rise to the fascinating society known as the **Tiahuanaco** culture (*see page 181*). Their main centre, **Pukara**, was 3,600 meters (12,000 ft) up on the altiplano of the Andes. Some 40,000 people are thought to have lived in this city, with an impressive ceremonial

> ### ENORMOUS EMPIRE
>
> The Inca empire is believed to have encompassed around a third of South America's population.

and his son Topa defeated the Chimu to the north, so that in two generations the Incas succeeded in taking over the two most important Andean centers. The Incas continued to expand their rule: pushing down into northern Chile, Huayna Capac conquered what is now Ecuador, setting up a second center of empire in Quito. By 1525, the Inca empire extended 4,000 km (2,500 miles) from northern Ecuador to central Chile. Between six and 12 million people are estimated to have lived in the empire known as **Tawantinsuyu** or "Land of the Four Quarters".

complex at its heart. The people of Tiahuanaco are among the first in South America to have used stone to create large permanent buildings; about 1,200 years ago their power and influence reached down as far as the Atacama desert in Chile.

The Incas

The last and most impressive of these Andean highland cultures was the **Inca** empire. This was based in the valley of Cuzco, in what is now Peru, and only emerged around AD 1400, during the rule of the semi-mythical leader Viracocha. In 1438 his son Yupanqui defeated the Tiahuanaco people around Lake Titicaca,

At the top of the Inca hierarchy was the emperor, or Sapa Inca, thought to be a descendant of the sun god Inti. The emperor was married to his sister, but had many other wives as well. Beneath him was a complicated priestly and administrative system, designed to keep control over the extensive empire. Communications were based on a 30,000-km network of paved roads, many of which still exist, along which relays of runners carried messages.

The imperial language, *quechua,* was imposed throughout: the sons of the royalty among the conquered peoples were taken to Cuzco to learn it along with other important elements of Inca culture. The Incas had no writing as we know it, but used a system of *quipu* or knotted pieces of string to record important dates and numbers, which were memorised by a special group of officials. The Inca ceremonial centers at Machu Picchu, Cuzco and elsewhere show their mastery of architecture, based on cutting and fitting large blocks of stone together without mortar.

Lost tribes

There are thought to have been anything between five and 50 million inhabitants throughout South America before the arrival of the Europeans. Over the past 500 years, these

1860s and 1870s. Small groups of people who continued to live similar lives to those of their ancestors thousands of years earlier managed to survive on the distant coasts of Patagonia and Tierra del Fuego.

The prevalent attitude towards them is shown in an extract from Charles Darwin's journal when he visited these coasts in HMS *Beagle* in 1832: "I could not have believed how wide was the difference between savage and civilised man: it is greater than that between a wild and domesticated animal ..." Such attitudes led to the hunting and extermination of the indigenous people of the far south even in this cen-

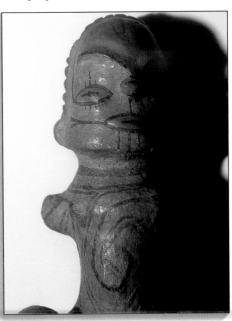

indigenous peoples have been incorporated into the dominant system or persecuted, and their own cultures looked down upon. In the 1530s, the great Inca empire was conquered by Francisco Pizarro with just 150 men (*see page 26*). In the south of the continent, the Mapuche people of Chile resisted the European influence the longest, living independently until the end of the last century. In Argentina, the indigenous peoples of the pampas were conquered in what was known as the "War of the desert" in the

tury, and a similar ignorance continues to threaten other survivors of the first peoples of South America from Ecuador to Brazil and Venezuela. It is only in the northeastern Amazonian regions that small tribes who have had no contact with the outside world continue to exist.

Elsewhere, the descendants of the Inca and other Andean highland tribes, the Mapuche of southern Chile, the Tairona and other groups in Colombia and Ecuador live today as part of the mixed European and Latin American civilization around them, and yet they also stand apart, with many of their beliefs and traditions still powerful beneath the surface. ❏

LEFT: Gold treasure from Bogotá Gold Museum.
ABOVE: Inca "Mamacona" or "chosen woman" figure.
ABOVE RIGHT: Marajó figurine, Brazilian Amazon.

LOST EMPIRES AND DISCOVERED TREASURE

What was life like in South America before the Europeans arrived? It's a mystery that continues to enthrall, and there are some intriguing clues

As no writing has been found from pre-Columbian South America, the artefacts left behind are likely to remain clues, giving us exciting glimpses into the lives of a host of very different communities that flourished and declined through various times and locations. The central Andes is by far the richest region for finding artefacts of the ancient past – partly because the dry desert conditions prevalent in the area are much more suitable for preserving ancient remains than the humid climate of the Amazon rainforest. But there is no doubt that the central Andes, especially the region that is now Peru, was a center for skilled activity of all kinds for centuries, producing numerous advanced communities long before the great Inca civilization arrived on the scene. Some ancient finds have echoes in the modern cultural practices of local communities, while others, like the mysterious people who built the megaliths of San Agustín, Colombia, seem to have disappeared without a trace.

MAKING SENSE OF THE PAST

Trying to remember all the names of the pre-Columbian groups can be a mind-boggling task. Most were named by archeologists after the locations where their remains were found, and grouped according to type, location and dating. Their complexity can be confusing, but the visitor with enough time to go to the excellent museums and archeological sites from Colombia to Chile will retain a picture of a fascinating era when civilizations waxed and waned, fought and conquered one another, and exchanged goods, skills and ideas.

▷ **GOLDEN YEARS**
Metallurgy flourished in South America long before the Incas, as this Chimu funerary mask shows (Lambayeque Valley, Peru).

△ **SAN AGUSTIN**
Little is known about the people who built 500 stone statues at this Colombian site (*see page 99*).

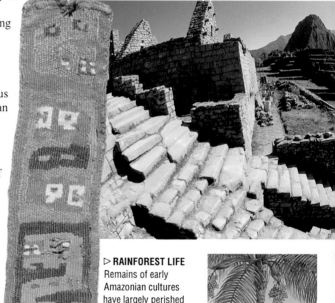

▷ **RAINFOREST LIFE**
Remains of early Amazonian cultures have largely perished in the humid climate.

◁ **MADE TO LAST**
This striking belt was woven by the Huari people of ancient Peru – 1,500 years ago.

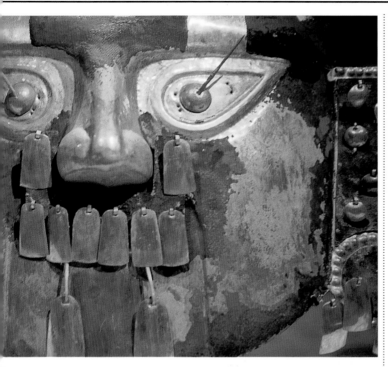

LIFE AND TIMES OF THE MOCHE

If the Incas were master architects and empire builders, the much earlier Moche culture must be one of the most artistic and intriguing in South America. The Moche settled near the modern city of Trujillo in northern Peru, and flourished for a few centuries before and after the time of Christ. What sets the Moche apart is the high quality and quantity of the artefacts they left behind; from adobe pyramids to finely-crafted gold jewelry. The recent discovery of the tomb of the "Lord of Sipán," pictured above, was one of the most important finds ever in the Andes (*see also page 166*), displaying Moche mastery of metallurgy. The vast collection of Moche ceramics found provide a remarkably accurate and detailed record of life 2,000 years ago, and some superb textiles have also been found.

◁ **MACHU PICCHU**
The most fabulous of all the Inca ceremonial centers, yet just one of many awe-inspiring Andean citadels in near-inaccessible locations.

▽ **GATEWAY OF THE SUN**
The pre-Inca site of Tiahuanaco, near Lake Titicaca (*see page 168*) in Bolivia, was built in beautiful and sophisticated masonry.

◁ **INCA HAT FROM CHILE**
In the late Inca period, vicuña wool was worn only by kings, as cloth was a symbol of wealth.

▷ **MAIZE WORSHIP**
This Moche maize effigy may have been a fertility charm, used to help ensure a good crop.

THE EUROPEAN CONQUEST

In the 16th century, most of South America quickly fell to Spain and Portugal,

except for the far south, which would remain unconquered for three centuries

At the end of the 15th century, Christopher Columbus explored the shores of Central and South America. Soon afterwards another Italian sailor, Amerigo Vespucci, was to give the new continent its name. Both these Italian explorers were in the pay of the Spanish crown, and before long, numerous Spaniards

were arriving. From their bases on the islands of Hispaniola, Puerto Rico and Cuba, they started to explore Central America and the South American mainland.

Gold was the lure that enticed most of them into the unknown territories of the great continent. *El Dorado* was the legendary paradise where, Midas-like, everything was made of gold. In 1531 Francisco Pizarro set out to find these fabled riches in the Inca empire, which then stretched from Quito in the north down through the areas now known as Peru, Bolivia and northern Chile. With only 150 followers, Pizarro managed to take control of the entire Inca empire in just two years. This was

achieved with ruthless determination aided by the fear that the Spaniards, mounted on horseback and using firearms, struck into the indigenous armies. Also, after years of refined centralization and uniformity, the Inca empire was severely weakened at the very moment that Francisco Pizarro began his conquest.

Downfall of the Incas

Before the Spaniards arrived, the Incas had expanded their empire from Cuzco, Peru into Quito, in modern Ecuador. The Inca Tupac-Yupanqui had founded the magnificent city of Tomebamba (now Cuenca) after subduing the southern Cañari people. His son, Huayna-Capac, married the daughter of the Duchicela king to consolidate their kingdoms.

Their son Atahuallpa was to become Huayna-Capac's favourite, but Atahuallpa's half-brother Huascar, descended from Inca lineage on both sides, was the legitimate heir. In 1527, Huascar ascended the Cuzco throne, dividing the empire for the first time, between Quito and Cuzco. Atahuallpa won the ensuing five-year civil war, killing his brother and establishing the new capital of Cajamarca in northern Peru. But the war had severely weakened both the infrastructure and the will of the Incas.

The Spanish arrived in Cajamarca in 1532. At a pre-arranged meeting, Atahuallpa and several thousand followers – many unarmed – entered the great square, where a Spanish priest called on him to embrace Christianity and accept the sovereignty of the Spanish king, Charles V. When Atahuallpa refused, Pizarro and his men ambushed the Incas. Pizarro was the only Spaniard wounded, when he seized Atahuallpa, while hundreds of Incas were killed.

Pizarro took Atahuallpa prisoner, demanding a room full of gold to pay his ransom. This was done, but the Inca was not freed. During his captivity, Atahuallpa learned to speak and write Spanish and to play chess. After nine months, the Spaniards accused him of treason, and garotted him. The Spaniards then marched on the Inca capital, Cuzco, and immediately used the Inca bureaucracy and administrative divisions for their own ends. By 1533 they were in command of the entire Inca empire.

The Spaniards founded the city of Lima in 1535. Lima grew and prospered, as did its religious zeal, prompting some to dub it the "Rome of South America". Churches and monasteries sprang up, each more ostentatious than the next. Nuns, bishops, priests and monks flocked to Lima, and with them, eventually, came the terror of the Holy Inquisition, which meted out its frightful tortures in Peru from 1570 to 1761.

Lima was the seat of the Spanish Empire in South America for several centuries. The jungle

Orinoco and Amazon river systems. This brought the Spanish and Portuguese crowns into conflict over who should be allowed ownership of the new territories. The dispute was settled at the Treaty of Tordesillas in 1494, which established that Portugal should have the right to all lands east of the mouth of the Amazon – which meant the whole of the Brazilian coastline. Pedro Alvares Cabral claimed Brazil for Portugal in 1500. For many years, its most important export was dyewood or Brazil wood, but European settlement was slow, as the Portuguese preferred to trade with their new colony rather than to settle it. Eventually, a system of

city of Machu Picchu was the last redoubt of Inca rule, which ended completely in 1536, when Manco-Capac was defeated and killed.

Further north, Gonzalo Jimenez de Quesada set out to explore New Granada (Colombia). He quickly subdued the Chibcha kingdoms, and in 1538 Santa Fé de Bogotá was founded.

The birth of Brazil

Europeans were soon busy exploring down the Atlantic seaboard of South America and the

LEFT: Indians buckling under the weight of colonial demands. **ABOVE:** the meeting of Pizarro and Atahuallpa at Cajamarca.

"captaincies" was set up, in which ownership of the land was granted by the Portuguese crown to individuals. Many of these people, such as Martim Afonso, brought in cattle and began to cultivate sugar, using enslaved Indians initially, and then black people shipped from Africa.

The new cities of the south

In the far south, explorers were still seeking a sea route from Europe to Asia. Between 1519 and 1522, Fernando Magellan's fleet rounded Cape Horn and sailed out into the Pacific Ocean, making them the first Europeans to land in Patagonia and Chile. Sailors like Antonio Pigafetta enhanced the mystery of the new lands to wide-eyed Europeans, with lurid descriptions of the strange beings encountered there: giants, men with heads under their arms, or with tails like pigs.

Another wave of Spaniards set out to explore the Rio de la Plata (River Plate) network. Pedro de Mendoza founded Buenos Aires in 1536, and Asunción de Paraguay the following year. But the settlers were soon driven out of Buenos Aires by the indigenous people. It was only in 1580 that colonists sailed down from Asunción and set up the fort on the south bank of the River Plate again, this time successfully.

On the Pacific Ocean side, Pedro de Valdivia

The Spanish had to make do with maintaining garrison towns on the coast, and making marauding slave runs into Indian territory.

In Argentina, the "frontier" was no more than 200 kms south of Buenos Aires until well into the 19th century.

A Spanish treasure trove

This first wave of conquest of South America lasted only two generations. From then until the beginning of the 19th century, the Spanish and Portuguese crowns sought to administer their vast empires. Economic activity was based on mining – first for gold, then silver, which

pushed south from Inca territory into Chile, and established the capital city of Santiago in 1541. The Incas had only exacted tribute as far south as the Bío Bío River, and Valdivia fared little better when he marched south of the river, meeting his match in the Araucanian warriors, for whom death in battle constituted a supreme honor. In 1554, they captured Valdivia, bound him to a tree, and beheaded him. Legend has it that the executioner ate Valdivia's heart.

The south (now Patagonia) belonged to the Araucanian (or Mapuche as they are known today), and other Indians well into the 19th century. They organized a cavalry force of 10,000 men and learned to use firearms and cannon.

THE HORRORS OF DISEASE

Diseases brought by Europeans wrought more devastation on the native peoples of South America than the weapons they brought. Indigenous populations, who had evolved over centuries without developing immunity to diseases like smallpox, cholera, syphilis, measles and even malaria, fell by 95 percent in some regions. Further waves of disease were brought with African slaves, and the ensuing reduction in the native population led to the importation of more African slaves, who had built up more resistance over the years.

by the middle of the 16th century became South America's most valuable export.

Agriculture was developed, with Spaniards being awarded large tracts of land and also "given" large numbers of local indigenous peoples to work it, in what was known as the *encomienda* system, a feudalistic method of securing plantation labor in exchange for a subsistence living. Taxation in the form of animals and vegetables was exacted from the indigenous people, and labor was unrewarded.

But the power in South America was firmly located in the growing towns and cities. It was here that Spanish authority was rooted, and here too that the Catholic church followed in the wake of the conquerors. Most of South America became a viceroyalty based on Lima and its port at Callao. From here, Spain attempted to impose a commercial monopoly on all its South American colonies. The inhabitants of the colonies were only permitted to sell their products to Spain, and could only purchase products from the mother country. A Council of the Indies was set up in Seville in southern Spain to administer the territories. The riches of South America were dispatched back to Europe in yearly fleets, which soon attracted the interest of English, Dutch and French pirates.

A new society

Through the 16th and 17th centuries, the Spaniards consolidated their rule. In each country there were a small number of Spanish-born administrators and clergy. Below them in rank were the *criollos*, people born in South America but claiming both parents as having Spanish blood. But the fastest growing sector of the colonial population were the *mestizos*, mixed race people, most of whom were born of a Spanish father and an indigenous mother due to the preponderance of male immigrants. One of the conquerors of Chile, Francisco de Aguirre, admitted to having at least 50 such children, and proudly affirmed that "the service rendered to God in engendering mestizos is greater than the sin incurred in so doing."

Many indigenous groups remained outside Spanish society, or were forced to work in slave-like conditions on the big estates. As

more labor was needed, so the trade in slaves from Africa grew. The slaves were brought mostly to the Caribbean coast of Venezuela and Colombia, and to the coast of Peru. But it was Brazil where African slaves made most impact on the rest of society. As the Brazilian sugar plantations grew in importance, so did the numbers of slaves shipped in from west Africa and Angola, rising to a million by the 18th century.

As the demand for sugar fell, the discovery of gold and diamonds in Minas Gerais led to a further boom in Brazil, and Rio de Janeiro became increasingly important as a port. In 1763 it was made the capital, and its importance increased

still further by the end of the century, with the growth of Brazil's new treasure crop, coffee.

As Brazil's economic strength grew, so relations with Portugal became more difficult. Brazilian merchants wanted to be free to trade with other countries, and local politicians wanted more control over their own affairs.

A similar situation grew up in the Spanish colonies. Most of the treasures shipped back to Spain had been used to finance its wars in Europe, but by the end of the 18th century, Spain had fallen behind both France and Great Britain as an industrial and colonial power. By the 19th century, European wars were to lead to the loss of its South American empire. ❑

LEFT: Pukara (fortress), the last Inca stronghold in Chile. **RIGHT:** Pedro de Valdivia, who was put to death by the Mapuche after invading their territory.

INDEPENDENCE

Spain's defeats on the battlefields of Europe led to the loss of all its South American
territories, but independence for the criollos brought neither peace nor democracy

When the Emporer Napoleon invaded Spain in 1808, the consequences were felt all over "Spanish America", as *criollos* took advantage of Spain's weakness to free themselves from the demands of the Spanish empire. In previous decades, republican ideas from the revolutions in North America

commanding a British naval squadron on the way home from South Africa, decided to capture Buenos Aires and open it up to British trade. He occupied the city for several months until the *porteños* (inhabitants of Buenos Aires), rose in rebellion and captured the whole enemy force. Reinforcements from Britain

and in France had been taken up enthusiastically by many South Americans, who wanted to be able to trade freely with other countries apart from Spain, and also to elect their own leaders.

Rebellions in the south

In the 18th century, Buenos Aires (the modern capital of **Argentina**) was a thriving smuggling center, allowing trade to enter South America without having to pass through Lima or Panama, as the Spanish Crown decreed. The city grew in importance with the 1776 creation of the Viceroyalty of La Plata and the relaxation of trade restrictions.

In 1806 an Englishman, Sir Home Popham,

were defeated by a popular militia. The victory gave *porteños* confidence in their ability to govern themselves.

The fortunes of Asunción, which is now the capital of **Paraguay**, were tied by the Rio de la Plata (River Plate) to those of Buenos Aires. When the Spanish colonial seat in Lima closed the port of Buenos Aires to ensure that trade (and taxation) would pass through Lima, Paraguay suffered as well. As the power of Buenos Aires grew, the leaders of Asunción began to resent their own growing insigni-ficance, refusing to go along with the Argentine declaration of independence in 1810. A military junta led by Fulgencio Yegros declared the of Paraguay independence on May 14, 1811.

Montevideo, modern capital of **Uruguay**, had also been in British hands for a brief period in 1807. Later, dictates from Spain and Buenos Aires aimed at limiting contraband and expelling small landholders from the great *estancias* caused growing resentment in the region. In 1811 revolutionary forces representing the interior and led by José Gervasio Artigas, a *criollo* army commander, rebelled against the Spanish authorities in Montevideo. One of the aims of the revolution was to redistribute wealth to the poor, including Indians and freed slaves.

With the assistance of Buenos Aires, the revolutionary forces managed to eject the Spanish authorities, but Artigas and a growing number of *orientales* did not want to substitute the old colonial power with the newer power of Buenos Aires. In 1815 he succeeded in ejecting the *porteños* and establishing his authority throughout the new country.

In 1816 the Portuguese invaded, fearing the spread of revolutionary ideas to Brazil. They defeated Artigas in 1820, with support from sections of the upper class who resented his confiscation of their lands. The country remained in Brazilian hands after Brazil's independence, in 1822. However, many *orientales* were becoming disillusioned with the Brazilian influence, and in 1825 a revolt, led by the legendary "Thirty-three Orientales" began against Brazil. Independence was finally declared on August 25, 1825.

Britain played a part in Uruguay's independence and in mediating a peace settlement. The River Plate was one of the most important trading channels to South America, and British trade interests did not want it to be controlled by Argentina alone, or disrupted by Brazil.

The wars of independence

The collapse of the Spanish monarchy when Napoleon's troops entered Madrid had dramatically shown *criollos* all over the continent that Spanish rule could be defeated.

By 1810, these political leaders had declared autonomous governments or juntas in many parts of Spanish South America. When Spain attempted to repress these movements, the real wars of independence broke out. In the south

LEFT: Early painting of Punta Arenas, Chile.
RIGHT: General Simón Bolívar, *El Libertador*.

these were led by the Spanish-born general José de San Martín. He managed to defeat Spanish forces in Argentina, and then in 1817 led his army across the Andes – a tremendous feat of organisation – to help the Chileans in their struggle. In 1811, **Chile** had opened its ports to neutral countries, in defiance of Spain's monopoly on trade. But forces loyal to Spain had regained control, and the Chilean insurgents had been forced into exile in neighboring Argentina. Many of them returned to Chile with General San Martín, and this time were successful in overthrowing Spanish rule.

In the northern part of South America, the

independence struggle was led by *El Libertador* – "The Liberator" – Simón Bolívar. The struggle began in his native Venezuela, where he successfully fought off the Spanish loyalists to become Dictator. He was very successful at first, winning six battles against royalists in 1813, but with the defeat of Napoleon in 1815 and the restoration of the Spanish monarchy in Europe, the fight to recover the colonies began in earnest. Bolívar was forced to retreat to Haiti and Jamaica: letters he wrote from exile were to become the fundamental ideology behind the independence struggle. Three years later, he was back on the mainland, leading a force of Venezuelans and British veterans from the

Napoleonic Wars. The Battle of Boyaca in northern Colombia on August 17, 1819, marked the end of royalist resistance there, and not long afterwards, Bolívar entered Santa Fé de Bogota in triumph.

Peru had been the centre of the Spanish empire in South America, and it proved the hardest country of all to liberate. Gradually San Martín's forces advanced from the south and Bolívar's from the north, and independence was declared in Lima in 1821, but parts of the country remained in Spanish control until 1826.

VENEZUELAN HERO

Simón Bolívar inspired even foreign romantics. The English poet Byron named a boat after him and planned to sail it to Venezuela.

last days at Santa Marta in Colombia. His verdict on his life's dreams was harsh: "America is ungovernable. He who serves the revolution plows the sea".

San Martín had a similar experience in Argentina, discovering that the new generation of politicians had no place for a troublesome general. Eventually he left his home in South America and lived out his last years in France.

It was only years later that these heroes of independence were honored: every country in

When General Antonio José de Sucre's victories in Peru helped Bolívar put an end to Spanish rule there, the provinces of "Upper Peru" were declared a new republic named in honor of the Liberator: **Bolivia**. Although they had nothing in common, these disorganised territories from the Amazon to the icy sierra were now forced to make their way as a nation.

The immediate years following independence were in many ways more difficult than the battles themselves. Bolívar dreamt that the different countries could stay united as **la Gran Colombia**, but within a decade **Ecuador** and **Venezuela** had seceded.

Disillusioned and dying, Bolívar spent his

South America now has statues, street names, and even currencies named after them.

Rise of the dictators

For several decades after Independence, there was virtual civil war in most of the emerging republics. The fight for control was usually between two groups: those from the interior who wanted some kind of loose federal political arrangement, and those from the cities who traded more with the outside world and wanted strong central control of the new nation. Those groups were usually identified with conservatives and liberals, allegiances which survive to this day. Often the struggle for power between these two factions was only settled by the emergence of a strong autocratic leader, which hindered the growth of democratic rule. By the mid-19th century, many South Americans found they had thrown off the tyranny of rule from Spain for a more brutal local variety.

Brazil: independence without war

Portugal, Brazil's imperial power, was also invaded by Napoleon's troops. The Portuguese Emperor Dom João fled and moved his entire court to Brazil in 1808. Brazil then became a dominion in its own right, until the Emperor returned to Portugal in 1821, leaving his son

Pedro's son took over the Brazilian throne, and outlawed the importation of slaves in 1850, but the practice continued in the country. Brazil was dominated by the large estate owners of the north, who employed huge numbers of slaves to grow sugar and other crops without much concern for efficiency or social progress. Dom Pedro II deliberately set out to encourage European immigrants to settle in the south of Brazil. This new population settled in Rio Grande do Sul and made São Paulo a new pole for development. There were increasing tensions between these two power groups, with the question of slavery being at the center of

Dom Pedro I in charge. When Pedro was recalled to Portugal in 1822, he rebelled, replacing the Portuguese insignia with the new national colours of yellow and green, and shouting, "Independence or death!" This in effect was Brazil's declaration of independence, celebrated each year on September 7th.

In the early 19th century, Brazilian society was made up of about a million people of European ancestry, the local indigenous groups, and some 2 million black slaves. In 1847, Dom

LEFT: the Llanero Lancers in Venezuela's wars of independence. **ABOVE:** many blacks freed from slavery were press-ganged into the Brazilian army.

the debate over what kind of country Brazil should be. Eventually in 1888 the Brazilian Parliament voted to abolish slavery, making Brazil the last country in the western hemisphere to do so. This move brought the conflict in Brazilian society out into the open, and the following year Pedro II was desposed and a constitutional republic created. As in many other countries of South America, the new parliamentary regime was weak compared to the real power that the military had, which was often used to impose their own solution to political problems.

The battles of independence were over, but the struggle for power in South America's new republics had only just begun. ❑

INTO THE 21ST CENTURY

The republics of South America have trod a rocky road to a tenuous stability,
and many have failed to prosper, despite being rich in natural assets

By the late 19th century, South America was completely free of Spanish rule, but power and influence was still in the hands of a privileged minority. The land was largely under control of the owners of huge estates, who were usually resistant to any change. The economies were dominated by exports, whether territory of Patagonia, finally subduing and largely destroying the indigenous cultures in the process. In Argentina, General Julio Roca's "Conquest of the Wilderness" in the 1880s opened up the pampas and Patagonia. Any native standing in his path was killed, the rest herded into reservations. The land was used to

of products like coffee in the case of Brazil and Colombia, wheat and beef from Argentina, or minerals such as copper from Chile and later, oil from Venezuela. Governments found it easier to tax these exports and buy imported goods than to encourage local industry. Britain took the lead in selling products to South America.

Despite this new kind of dependency, the independent South American countries quickly forged a strong sense of their own identity. Wars consolidated national boundaries, but could be extremely destructive to populations as well as burgeoning economies.

In the south, the governments of Argentina and Chile eventually occupied the whole of the

BUYING BRITISH

Britain did brisk trade with South America in the 19th century. In the late 1850s the British Consul in Argentina wrote the following about the *gauchos*, wild horsemen of the Argentinian pampa:

"Take his whole equipment, examine everything about him – and what is there not of hide that is not British? If his wife has a gown, ten to one it is from Manchester. The camp kettle in which he cooks his food, the common earthenware he eats from his knife, spoon, bits and the poncho which covers him – are all imported from England".

raise cattle for European markets, taking advantage of new methods of freezing meat.

By the end of the century, the ten republics of South America were firmly established. But the struggle for power in the relatively new nations had only just begun, and would overshadow the events of the following century, with the result that for much of the past 100 years, South America has found itself on the sidelines of world history. Its involvement in the great wars of the 20th century has been minimal – few South Americans fought in them, and the continent suffered no occupation or damage. But the ideological battles which divided Europe

South Americans. On the threshold of the 21st century it is nearly ten times that figure. In a relatively short time, South America has evolved into a continent where more than two-thirds of the population live in towns or cities. But with ownership of many national assets in foreign hands, profits were rarely invested in the country, and rural poverty was not alleviated, which further fuelled the trek to the cities.

The haves and have-nots

In the towns and cities, the 20th century saw a powerful growth of both the middle and working classes. **Argentina**'s booming beef industry

and the rest of the world for many years were reflected in the region. Its military rulers often brought in fascist ideas formulated in Spain or Italy, whilst guerrilla groups with Marxist ideologies sought to bring revolutionary change.

An urban society

These political developments were responses to the challenges and tensions within South American society. The population has grown rapidly: in 1900 there were around 40 million

---

LEFT: mine workers in Chile's northern desert.
ABOVE: the Peróns on the balcony of the Casa Rosada, Buenos Aires.

and conquest of more territory in Patagonia meant that more labor was required, and in the 1880s thousands of European immigrants flocked to the country, mainly poor peasants from Italy and Spain. It was the greatest influx of immigrants in relation to population patterns in world history. But the immigrants usually arrived penniless, and did not get to share in the country's boom wealth, as the great landowning families refused to break up their massive holdings and snapped up even more land by using false names. The immigrants were given small plots, but only to work for three to five years before moving on. Unlike North America, which was settled by millions of small landowners, Argentina remained the property of around 200 close-knit families referred to simply as "the oligarchy". The new immigrants remained in the urban areas, and the population of Buenos Aires grew from 750,000 in the early 1900s to more than two million in 1930.

As the economy expanded, the moneyed classes looked to Europe for their inspiration, and largely ignored the social inequalities and growing protest movements around them. The Great Depression of the 1930s ushered in a period of political instability and military rule characterised by the typical alliance of the

trade unions and organised labor. During his 15 years in power, Vargas built up a strong state and promoted Brazilian industry, in ways reminiscent of Mussolini in Italy.

After Vargas' fall, a long period of constitutional rule followed. Brazil's economy and population grew rapidly, a growth symbolised by the construction of Brasilia as the country's new capital in the late 1950s (*see page 239*). But as in the rest of South America, the growing numbers of landless people in the rural areas, added to increasingly militant political groups in the major towns and cities began to pose a threat to stability – or so it appeared

armed forces with conservative elements in society to try to halt political reforms or any of the new ideas finding political expression.

In **Brazil** the pattern was also one of economic instability leading to periods of military dictatorship. In the early part of the 20th century, most of the country's wealth came from the export of rubber and coffee. But Malaysia began to grow rubber too, and in 1930 the world price of coffee fell dramatically. With military backing, Getulio Vargas seized power from a weak civilian government. The so-called "father of the people" used a populist rhetoric to win the support of poor workers and peasants, and brought in legislation that encouraged

to the armed forces, who took over Brazil's government once more in 1964.

Foreign ownership

Many South American countries saw the wealth generated within their own borders trickle away overseas. **Bolivia** is arguably the worst example, with most of its silver going to Spain where it was used to finance European wars (*see page 173*), and the profits from its massive tin wealth staying in the hands of a few entrepreneurs and mostly being squandered abroad, leaving it today one of the world's poorest countries.

Another country which is still extremely poor, **Ecuador**, did brisk international trade in bananas, coffee, cocoa pods and Panama hats. The sole beneficiaries, however, were a few hundred *criollo* families and the foreign companies who controlled the industries. For decades Ecuador has been the world's largest exporter of bananas, but until the 1960s the entire industry was owned by the Boston-based United Fruit Company. Until the recent growth of the oil industry, bananas accounted for most of Ecuador's export earnings – and the fact that all the profits left the country is one reason why Ecuador has remained so poor for so long.

Colombia's wealth was also traditionally based on the export of bananas and coffee. But

oil was found in Lake Maracaibo. At that time, Venezuela was ruled by the dictator Juan Vincente Gomez, who had no scruples about siphoning off a large part of this new wealth, nor about rewarding his family and cronies with lavish gifts (including the archbishop who gave him special dispensation to eat meat on Good Friday). Little of the profits from the "black gold" found their way to the vast majority of Venezuelans, who moved in increasing numbers from the poor, backward countryside to the attractions of the capital city, Caracas.

The death of Gomez in 1935 led to riots and strikes until the typical combination of military

these industries were either owned by foreign companies like the United Fruit Company, or by a small number of national landowners who had control of vast plantations. As the population grew, poverty increased, as did social tensions, exploding in 1948. Years of violence and civil war followed (*see page 91*).

Neighbouring **Venezuela** suffered political turmoil in spite of the discovery of huge oil deposits, which did bring great wealth to the country – but not without a struggle. In 1917,

LEFT: Brazil's President Juscelino Kubitschek at the 1960 inauguration of Brasília. **ABOVE:** the bombing of La Moneda, Santiago, Chile, during the 1973 coup.

officers and conservative landowners took power. Eventually one strong man emerged – Colonel Pérez Jimenez, who brought in a series of populist measures, allowing labour organisation and investing some of the oil profits into public works and low cost housing. Once again though, this autocratic rule led to instability.

In 1958, after riots which caused the death of 600, Jimenez was overthrown. Elections heralded an unbroken period of parliamentary rule.

Territorial conflict

North America had one major civil war, but many of the republics of South America have been severely weakened by repeated territorial disputes. Some benefitted – in the 19th century, Chilean dictator Diego Portales won a war with a Peru/Bolivian Confederation (1836-39), taking Antofagasta, later claiming Patagonia, Tierra del Fuego and Magallanes, and founding Punta Arenas in 1847.

In the 1879 War of the Pacific, Peru and Bolivia declared war on Chile, which ended up taking over southern Peru, including the valuable nitrate and mineral mines, and Bolivia lost its only access to the sea. In 1903, Brazil annexed a vast stretch of Bolivia's Amazon basin, known to be rich in rubber trees.

Wars could be costly for the winners too.

Paraguay won much of the southern Chaco from Bolivia in the 1932 Chaco War. While Bolivia held on to its Chaco oil fields, no oil has ever been found in the Paraguayan Chaco lands. The desperately-fought war bled both countries dry economically and in manpower.

Tension still exists between Peru and Ecuador over a conflict which first emerged in 1942, when Peru took most of Ecuador's southern jungle region. Known as El Oro, this area is rich in precious metals and oil, and was where Ecuador's best coffee was grown. A three-month conflict in 1995 cost both sides hundreds of casualties and also had a very damaging effect on the Ecuadorian economy.

A turbulent decade

Ironically, it was the countries with the most stable political traditions and the biggest economic growth which suffered the most brutal military dictatorships in the 1970s. Uruguay had the longest democratic tradition and one of the world's first welfare states, but the 1950s and '60s saw economic downturn, social disruption and the rise of guerrillas. A military takeover in 1973 led to 12 years of dictatorship with widespread repression and torture (*see page 313*).

In the 19th century, Chile was the most stable nation in the region, expanding to become a major economic force. But there was still extensive foreign ownership and vast disparities between rich and poor. In 1970 the Socialist party was elected under Salvador Allende, but in 1973 the military wrested control under General Pinochet, once again with the backing of conservative forces (*see page 280*).

Pinochet remained in power for 17 years, not only reversing the political direction the country had been taking, but also bringing in the free market economic model which has since been adopted by practically all the other countries of South America. In many ways, this has meant their economies have come full circle: earnings once again mainly come from exports, in Chile's case from copper as before, with new products such as wine, soft fruit and salmon also being developed. Local markets have been opened up to all kinds of foreign goods, with the result that national firms have either gone out of business or have been bought up by larger and more efficient foreign concerns. This has led to a new economic stability, but with high levels of unemployment and a masking of the need to make difficult choices about the future.

The new challenges

On the threshold of the 21st century, the future will be bright if South America can learn to integrate as a region, fulfilling Bolívar's dream of unity. To do this, its governments need to do much more to narrow the huge gap between the rich and poor, to harmonise life in the cities and the countryside, and above all to do all they can to offer the enormous young population – almost 40 percent of the total – the chance to realise their full potential. ❑

LEFT: the modern face of South America: Alberto Fujimori, president of Peru.

The Drug Trade

A common sight in Bolivian street markets is huge sacks of coca leaves for sale. The local people buy them to make tea or to chew in order to stave off the effects of altitude, cold, or lack of nourishment (*see page 188*). In many highland and jungle areas of South America, indigenous groups use their knowledge of plants and essences to concoct drugs for use in ceremonies.

But in the past 30 years, with the spectacular growth of the export of refined drugs to the United States and Europe, drugs and drug-trafficking have become a huge problem for the region. Coca leaves are converted into the basic paste for cocaine in distant hideouts (chewing coca leaves does not have the same effect as taking the powdered drug, as massive amounts are needed to make cocaine).

In the 1970s, the fight for control of the production and distribution of cocaine for foreign markets led to increased violence. Hoodlums from Colombian cities such as Medellín and Cali made vast profits out of the shipments, and showed little mercy for rivals or anyone trying to maintain the rule of law. They formed "cartels" to keep prices up and competitors out, and soon drugs became Colombia's most valuable export.

Successive United States governments, aware that the problem was manifesting itself on the streets of their own cities, tried to harness attempts to control the trade. They insisted that South American governments carry out programs to "eradicate" the plantation of crops like coca; that police and armed forces co-operate with the Drug Enforcement Administration in tracking down the traffickers; and that South American governments be willing to extradite those convicted of trading in illegal drugs.

This led to a virtual civil war in Colombia at the end of the 1980s, as traffickers like Pablo Escobar took on the state in their efforts to avoid arrest. Escobar and his followers are believed to have blown up a passenger aeroplane with 200 people on board, and several hundred policemen among others were killed in their war against the state. Escobar was finally killed after escaping from jail, and the power of the Medellín and Cali drugs cartels was tamed. This did not mean the problem went away – new people took over, and the trafficking moved to other countries – Brazil, Ecuador,

RIGHT: coca leaves from the Andes, which can be used to produce cocaine.

and Mexico, which shares a long border with the principal client, the United States.

Throughout South America today, the drugs trade is still a huge if largely invisible presence. Drugs money has financed new banks, hotels, and buildings from expansive beach resorts in Chile or Uruguay to high-rise blocks in downtown Bogotá and Caracas. It is one of the chief reasons for the high levels of corruption in government and other officals – in Colombia for example, President Ernesto Samper, who was in power from 1994 to 1998, was never able to shake off allegations that his successful election campaign benefitted from several million dollars' worth of contributions from

the drugs bosses (*see page 92*). From poorly paid border guards and customs officials, to equally badly paid police and army recruits, to politicans and high-ranking officers, money from the illegal trade perverts the system.

A persistent complaint – and half justicifaction – often heard in South America is that drugs are not really their problem, as they are mostly consumed in the developed world. In Colombia for example, the guerrilla movements justify their involvement in the trade as a way of destroying capitalism. But this argument ignores the increasing consumption of crack, cocaine and other hard drugs by the youth in South America, and the distorting effect the trafficking has on economies and public morality. ❑

A LAND OF MANY FACES

The people of South America are as diverse as the countries many of them came from, yet they also share a distinctive Latin American heritage

Ever since Colombus landed in what is now the Bahamas and thought he had arrived in the East Indies, the indigenous peoples of the Americas have been lumped together and collectively termed Indians. Today, indigenous farmers in the Andes are described as *campesinos* – this term has been made official in Bolivia. The number of terms used to describe ethnicity in South America may daunt the visitor – it's an indication of not just the continent's racial diversity, but also of the importance of ancestry here.

Mestizo, or *mameluco* in Brazil, describes someone who is part indigenous, part white. *Mulatto* describes someone whose origins are African and European. In Brazil, *cafuso* describes someone of American Indian and African heritage.

All this complex ethnic terminology probably grew out of people's attempts to define their identity in a continent which has seen so much immigration in the past 500 years, and where national boundaries have only been defined in the last century or two and are often in dispute. This is a continent where people from the world's most diverse nations and cultures meet, mix and intermarry, and where the Japanese ancestry of the president of Peru or the Syrian descent of the president of Argentina raises few eyebrows. Yet the surface multiculturalism of South America hides a complex mesh of social and racial hierarchies.

The new arrivals

South America's ethnic make-up changed dramatically after the arrival of Europeans in the 16th century, who were predominantly Spanish and, in Brazil, Portuguese. They initially arrived as single men, intermarried with the indigenous women, and brought in black slaves from Africa. By 1888, when slavery was finally abolished in Brazil, immigration from Europe

PRECEDING PAGES: Quechua people at a wedding near Cuzco, Peru; Carajás boy, Amazon. **LEFT:** Quechua woman. **RIGHT:** teenage girls, Santiago, Chile.

was being actively encouraged, particularly to Brazil and Argentina. Most of the immigrants initially came from Spain and Italy, but there were also Germans, eastern Europeans, Syrians, Lebanese, Japanese and Chinese.

The people of the Andean countries – Peru, Colombia, Ecuador, Bolivia and Chile – are

predominately mestizo. These countries also have the highest "full-blood" Amerindian populations, partly because there were a lot of indigenous people living in this region at the time of the Conquest, and partly because of the large-scale destruction of the indigenous societies in the southern regions and lowlands.

People of African descent are concentrated in northern Brazil and parts of Colombia, Venezuela and the Guianas, places where their ancestors were taken as slaves. Argentina and Southern Brazil are predominantly caucasian, and Chile is roughly 20 per cent white.

The countries of Guyana, Suriname and French Guiana, on the north Caribbean coast, have a particularly interesting ethnic make-up, due to their histories as crop-producing outposts of three world empires – Dutch (Suriname), British (Guyana) and French (French Guiana). African slaves were brought in to work the plantations, and many then fled into the rainforest to form "Bush Negro" communities, retaining many of their African traditions. After the abolition of slavery, indentured labour was imported from other parts of the empires, leaving all of these countries with highly mixed populations made up of Asians,

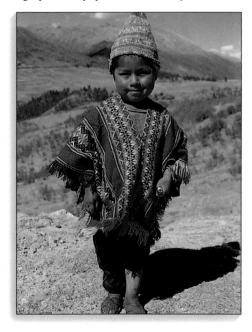

Amerindians, Africans, Portuguese mulattoes and Europeans.

New communities

The Bush Negroes are not the only group to have taken advantage of South America's formidable territory in order to pursue their lifestyle of choice. This continent has a number of distinct independent communities which often transcend national boundaries, such as the *gauchos* of Argentina (*see page 338*), and the fundamentally religious Mennonite groups (*see page 274*). Don't be surprised if you come across lederhosen on the Caribbean Coast, or Welsh hats in Patagonia – these are the legacy of groups of immigrants who might have felt restricted in their country of origin, or who just wanted to build a new life in a new country.

The continent's racial diversity is reflected in its languages. Although Spanish is by far the dominant language in South America today, and Portuguese is the official language of Brazil, many other languages are spoken.

Native American languages are frequently spoken in the Andean regions, and in Bolivia, Spanish, Quechua and Aymara are all official languages. In Peru, Spanish and, since 1975, Quechua, are both official languages. In Paraguay, Spanish is the official language, but most people speak Guaraní. The Guianas follow a colonial pattern, with English the main language of Guyana, Dutch the main language of Suriname, and French the language of French Guiana.

The racial hierarchy

In many areas the melting pot has been blended so completely that local people are unexpectedly homogeneous. In the cities of northern Chile, Bolivia and Peru, for example, pale European tourists are distinctive enough to turn heads, as do people with darker skin colouring, who will frequently hear themselves described as *moreno* or *negrita*.

In many South American countries, skin colour and racial origins have a distinct bearing on status. The palest people are frequently concentrated in smart professional establishments, behind the counters of smart department stores or in front of television cameras. In bars, restaurants and on long-distance buses you can often detect a striking colour difference between the faces that appear on the television screen and the faces watching it, with the few dark or black faces on screen usually relegated to servile roles.

Off the screen, indigenous people – particularly in the Andes region – are usually seen laboring in the fields or behind market stalls. Many indigenous people have steadfastly continued to practice their ancient customs and traditions, often in the face of strenuous opposition. The distinctive dress of Bolivian campesina women is believed to have developed as a response to the conquistadors' prohibition of tradtional dress. The death penalty was imposed in many cases for Indians who resisted conversion to Christianity, so it's not surprising that the countries of South America are overwhelmingly Catholic (except for Guyana, previously a British colony. Yet many communities have incorporated their ancient religious traditions into Catholicism, producing hybrid religions in some areas, like *Macumba* in Brazil (*see page 246*).

In the years following the Conquest many indigenous societies were forced to either adapt or be obliterated. The tribal societies in the low-lying Amazon regions were devastated by European disease and violence. Some of the

Lifestyles under threat

People who live in South America's urban regions may feel economically and socially under pressure to deny their Indian ancestry, but for many tribal peoples of the Amazon, their heritage and distinctive traditions are among the few resources they have left in their struggle for the survival of their communities. Many of these lifestyles are in fact constantly changing and adapting in response to their changing environment, which is particularly vulnerable to the encroachments of the technological age.

In some areas, tribal groups are benefitting

numerical reduction may be explained by the fact that Indian heritage persists in being seen as a stigma in most South American countries, to the extent that most people prefer to describe themselves as white rather than mestizo, particularly in urban areas. Take the typical response to a question frequently asked of tour guides by admiring tourists, enthralled by the history of the Inca or the Aymara:

"And are you descended from the Incas?"

"Oh, no! My grandparents were Spanish – in fact, my sister's baby is as white as you!"

LEFT: Peruvian boy in the Sierra.
ABOVE: young street vendors, Brazil.

BRAZILIAN HOLOCAUST

In 1639 the Spanish Jesuit Cristóbal de Acuña wrote that Amazon "Indian settlements are so close together that one is scarcely lost sight of before another comes into view." But this state of affairs was not to last – 17th-century officials in Brazil boasted that they killed 2 million Indians in the lower Amazon. Brazil's indigenous population was estimated at 2½ –6 million at the time of Conquest. Today it has fallen to less than 200,000 and the number of tribal groups probably fell by a third in the 20th century alone. Many rainforest tribes are still vulnerable to modern diseases.

from an increased tourist interest, which brings in some income while encouraging the continuity and development of their way of life. Some such schemes are criticised as creating tribal theme parks, but there is reason to believe the alternatives for the tribes concerned could indeed be oblivion.

Some indigenous groups, like the Mapuche of southern Chile, have found it necessary to take political action to ensure their survival. But in a few cases, ethnic and social unrest have been left to foment, spawning guerilla movements, notably in Peru, where the Sendero Luminoso ("Shining Path") terrorised locals

and visitors for years, and where another guerrilla group, Tupac Amaru, seized worldwide headlines with their seige of the Japanese Embassy in Lima in December 1996.

Social hierarchies

The middle classes are becoming more influential, but in many South American countries, old social hierarchies refuse to shift. Numerous revolutions and government coups have failed to dislodge the influence of the handful of old family names that still wield formidable influence. These social hierarchies often originally derived their power from the old feudalistic *encomienda* system, whereby families of

Spanish conquistador origin would control huge estates, worked by indigenous serfs who would provide labor in return for being allowed to work small plots of land for their own use. This system was still officially condoned in Ecuador until 1971.

Women's changing roles

South America has an increasing number of independent businesswomen, but their status is often questionable in this predominately Catholic continent, where children, children and more children are the focus of every family. In some countries, jobs advertised on television are divided into separate sections for *chicos* (boys) and *chicas* (girls). Women traveling alone may sometimes feel ignored by staff in public places – not out of deliberate rudeness, more likely because a man is expected to return and speak for them! A woman staying in a hotel alone may encounter raised eyebrows, propositions, or even late evening demands from hotel staff to change rooms.

These attitudes seem more pronounced the further up the price scale you go, especially in institutions used to catering for business*men*. Just as was the case in Europe and America, it takes quite a few pioneers to break stereotypes which have accumulated over generations.

There may be more independent businesswomen, but the respectably employed woman is nothing new. South America has a long-established class of women who regularly and visibly combine motherhood with a full day's work, out in the fields surrounded by their children, or managing a busy restaurant or café while feeding and entertaining a noisy brood.

THE YANOMAMI

The Yanomami people of northern Brazil and Venezuela were undiscovered until the 1970s, when the world began to encroach on their Roraima rainforest home. Latter-day gold miners have moved in and, in 1993, 20 Yanomami were massacred by *garimpeiros* (miners). The Yanomami have managed to publicize their plight, but attempts by the rest of the world to do something about it have not been so successful, notably since the disastrous Amazon rainforest fires that broke out during the droughts of early 1998 and destroyed an area of forest the size of Belgium.

Young people

At all levels of society, it seems, children are the focus of South American life. Families are large, contraception is often frowned upon, and women tend to start producing children at a lower age than in Europe and North America.

Some visitors might be alarmed at the incessant noise of children's exuberant shouts, which will often continue late into the evening – these playful noises are not tolerated or endured but indulged and encouraged, with the adults often joining in! The best thing to do for everyone's peace of mind is to shrug your shoulders, join in, and put off any quiet-time activities you

publicise and alleviate the situation, but for many children of poor families in South America, life can be a very hard slog indeed.

Music and dance is an outlet for all levels of society on this exuberant continent. Youth is celebrated and indulged, not by prolonging it with plastic surgery, but more through the feelings of youth, recaptured throughout life at fiestas and in the dance clubs, where anyone can dress up in tight Lycra and get away with it. Youth brings romance, often rapidly followed by procreation and more children. But there is nothing perfunctory about this eternal cycle. Try to count the number of times you

 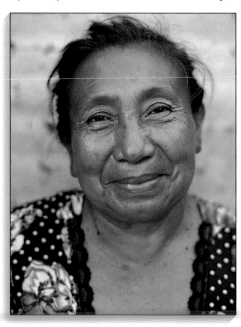

planned until the next day's *siesta*. Or invest in a good pair of earplugs.

The importance of children in South America makes the plight of the street children, orphaned and abandoned to scavenger lifestyles on the streets of big cities like Rio de Janeiro, seem all the more shocking. This is another case of social status coming into play, with the children forced to carry the burden of their parents' social disgrace. People from inside and outside South America have worked hard to

LEFT: Chieftain and his wife, western lowlands, Ecuador. **ABOVE:** Venezuelan farmer.
ABOVE RIGHT: Goajira woman, Venezuela.

hear the words "*mi corazon*" ("my heart") in popular songs. Latin American men may have a reputation for "machismo", but it's probably just a front to disguise the very obvious passion for romance that pervades this emotionally-charged part of the world.

Fun, pleasure and romance are of the highest priority in South America, and can transcend the boundaries of religion, race, politics and social standing. Everyone, whatever their background, is expected to indulge in the lighter side of life at least occasionally. Music, dance, a determination to enjoy life whatever the burden – the diverse people of South America are clearly linked with a common bond. ❑

THE IRRESISTIBLE LURE OF THE UNKNOWN

From gold-crazy conquistadors to modern eco-adventurers, South America has attracted a long line of explorers, in pursuit of elusive dreams

The earliest Spanish and Portuguese explorers were primarily concerned with charting the length and breadth of the newly discovered continent. In 1520, the great ocean navigator Fernando Magellan rounded the globe, giving his name to the stormy straits he passed at the southern tip of present-day Chile. In the same era, conquistadors Gonzalo Pizarro and Francisco de Orellana led arduous expeditions into the Amazon jungle in search of the mythical city of gold, El Dorado. They never found much gold but, in 1541, Orellana's expedition sailed down the world's mightiest river to the sea, becoming the first Europeans to cross South America.

△ **SURVIVAL RATIONS**
Humboldt and Bonpland were reduced to a diet of ground cacao beans and Amazon River water when damp and insects destroyed their supplies.

SCIENTIFIC EXPLORATION

In the 18th century the Age of Enlightenment in Europe sparked off a new, scientific interest in the little-known South American wildlife.

One of the foremost European explorers was Alexander von Humboldt, a Berlin-born student of botany, chemistry, astronomy and mineralogy. With his companion, French botanist Aime Bonpland, Humboldt set off on an expedition from Venezuela to Ecuador in 1799, charting the link between the Orinoco and Amazon rivers. He assembled meticulous lists of plants and animals, which led to the publication of *Essays on the Geography of Plants*, pioneering studies into the relationship between a region's geography and its flora and fauna.

▷ **MARINE IGUANAS**
Whilst on the Galápagos Islands, Charles Darwin observed these unique reptiles, which have a breathing system that has adapted them to life in the ocean.

△ **CHARLES DARWIN**
The originator of the theory of evolution was inspired by studies made during an expedition to the Galápagos Islands in 1835.

THE ORIGINAL INDIANA JONES

In 1906, a British army officer, Colonel Percy H Fawcett, came to South America, contracted by the Bolivian and Brazilian governments to help demarcate their jungle borders.

Fawcett's own plan, however, was to locate the fabled continent of Atlantis. He arrived armed with an 18th-century Portuguese document, and a stone idol thought to be of Brazilian origin and identified by psychics as having come from Atlantis.

On Fawcett's second expedition in 1925, he was accompanied by his son Jack and a man called Raleigh Rimell. The three men all vanished, the predators swallowed up by their prey. But the story did not end there. Subsequent tales of Fawcett's quest attracted more explorers over the years, many of whom sent back mysterious reports of white men living with jungle Indians; none, however, succeeded in finding him.

Fawcett's mystery and fame still lives on today, and he is credited as being the real-life inspiration behind the great Hollywood hero, Indiana Jones.

▷ FALKLANDS FOUNDER

As well as having the Bougainvillaea plant named after him, the 18th-century French navigator, mathematician and soldier Comte Louis Antoine de Bougainville also first colonized the Falkland Islands for France. He then made his name by becoming the first Frenchman to successfully circumnavigate the globe.

△ AMAZON CRUISE

Despite the harsh realities met on arrival, expeditions were often well-funded and publicized, to considerable popular enthusiasm.

▽ GREEN HELL

Early explorers endured long, mosquito-ridden journeys, with little food, and fear of attack by fierce beasts, and even cannibals.

MUSIC AND DANCE

South America pulsates to the beat of many rhythms as, through music and dance,

people express their joys, their struggles and often their longing for home

A bus journey in South America can be a whole new experience; a bumpy ride from somewhere you can't remember to somewhere you can't pronounce. Your driver will probably make numerous unscheduled stops to pick up passengers, call over a friend or jump out on an errand, and may also want to demonstrate his DJ skills to his "captive" audience. As your bus pitches and thunders down perilous mountain trails or bleak, dusty stretches, local musical delights blare at deafening volume from crackling speakers. For the driver, savouring the delights of his playlist, staying on the road is not always top priority.

Music is considered a staple in the Latin American diet, being as important as food itself, feeding and replenishing the soul. Popular Latin music is laden not just with passion, sentiment, happiness and anguish, but with history and nostalgia. Just as early musical expression symbolized resistance for slaves and fuelled struggles for independence in the 17th and 18th centuries, music and dance is revered by the underdogs of modern Latin American society. It is a tonic to counteract the harsh socio-economic realities of everyday life.

Dancing for everyone

Dancing serves as a pressure valve, a reprieve from life's chaos or a celebration that tomorrow it's Friday and you feel lucky. Throughout Latin America dance is viewed as a fundamental right that may be expressed freely and openly at any hour or occasion of the day. It offers a refreshing change from attitudes in many nothern hemisphere countries, where dance seems so often to belong exclusively to youth and beauty, and has subsequently been exiled to the nightclubs.

To understand the evolution of musical and dance forms on the continent is to attempt to fathom the tremendous demographic upheaval that took place over 500 years. The richness

and diversity of Latin music is indicative of the many colonizing and colonized forces present on the continent over the centuries. Africa, native South America, Europe and the United States all had a hand in the shaping of this magical land and its music.

Music grew from a brutal and loveless rela-

tionship, out of enslaved Amerindians and Africans, early European settlers and colonial powerbrokers. Often oceans away from their homelands, these early inhabitants all had their music and dances. They were a way of remembering home and who you were in an uncertain landscape. Thrown together in an ethnic melting pot, many traditions were either discarded or bonded together. It makes for an enthralling tale of survival of the fittest, trium-phant underdogs, resistance and compromise.

Out of this struggle was born regional and national musical traditions which, in a sense, represent different colonial experiences and development. So there are historical reasons for

---

LEFT: the exuberant display that is *Carnaval*, Brazil.
RIGHT: traditional dancing in Trujillo, Peru.

the tango belonging to Argentina, the samba to Brazil and the cumbia to Colombia.

A spicy mix

Arguably the most international of all Latin American rhythms is what we now call **salsa**. The term itself is really nothing more than a marketing ploy adopted by the United States music industry in the late 1960s, which assumed that people could not cope with the many different types of music Latin America had to offer. Son, mambo, guaracha and many other styles were lumped together so that they could be easily packaged for consumption.

rhythms of regular pulses provided by the *clave* (two sticks that beat at a 2–3 or 3–2 tempo) and the *campana* (cowbell), and accents that are off-beat (piano, bass and brass). This is all useful to know if you want to blame your dance partner for messing up when they are clearly the better dancer.

If salsa means sauce then the musical ingredients in these complex arrangements need a master chef to work. As music is food for the soul to Latin Americans, culinary references in the lyrics are compulsory. *Azucar!* (sugar) is salsa legend, Celia Cruz's trademark exclamation, while other musicians will call out for salt,

Salsa means "sauce" and the name was inspired by many musicians who would scream "Salsa!" at a pulsating audience to excite them even further. This artificial grouping of many different styles means that most discussions about the origin of salsa become as hot and spicy as the dancing that the music inspires. Most unbiased opinion however follows the view that today's salsa is really a jazzed-up version of **son**, whose origins date back to Eastern Cuba in the 1880's.

Son intermingled African rhythms with Spanish verse forms, and its early means of expression were drums, maracas, Cuban tres guitar and claves or sticks tapping out the beat. The beat is syncopated and loaded with poly-

pepper, and other seasonings as an invitation for a particular instrument or singer to join in. This seems perfectly natural, so long as the chops cut the mustard.

Modern son and salsa, predominant in Colombia, Venezuela and Central America, have been enhanced by the addition of the piano, bass and heavy brass sections. Cuban **charanga** replaces the brass with violins and flutes, but the structure is similar. In Cuba the accent remains heavily on improvisation, and the force of this and fluctuations in the salsa rhythm has caught out even the most expert musicians. Whilst jamming with some Cubans even the great Dizzy Gillespie couldn't keep up, famously crying out in bafflement "Where's the beat?"

The accompanying dance may look easy but it is as intricate and erratic as the music, fluctuating between regular and counter movements. Salsa is electrifying, sensual and dynamic, yet it can be cheeky and passionate at the same time. Don't be discouraged by the stylish, fast footwork, for much of the rhythm is contained within set steps. You will get as much of a kick out of observing the rhythmic exchange between the couples spinning and strutting their stuff or caught in a swaying embrace as from actually taking part.

foreign intervention this century as well as being a vehicle to address social problems.

Its infectious rhythm adheres to a frenetic, repetitive "thump, thump, thump" beat present in disco and rock music. An ensemble of guitar, *guira* (scraper), tambour and *marimba* (African piano) or accordion traditionally plays the merengue. The beat is crisp, accelerated and at times chaotic, with one beat suddenly dropped and another picked up. Merengue is less intense than salsa and it starts with a bang and adrenaline rush, making you feel instantly giddy and producing a strong urge to jump about in a silly fashion or run around the room.

A crisp, frothy beat

Merengue came to South America via the Dominican Republic, in the Caribbean. It comes, as you might expect, from the French "meringue", meaning "whipped egg whites and sugar". Both the dessert and the dance have a frothy, exciting mix. From its origins in the formalized 18th-century dances of the French court, merengue acquired African influences as it settled in the Dominican Republic. It provided the beat for many protest marches against

LEFT: belting out rythms in a Caracas nightspot, Venezuela. **ABOVE:** strumming up a storm in Porlamar, Isla Margarita, Venezuela.

The lyrics adopt a tongue-in-cheek tone, heavy with double meaning and conveying either a social critique or commentary on everyday life. Native Dominican superstars Juan Luis Guerra and Wilfredo Vargas command great respect among their audience for their musical creativity and brazen addressing of the country's social and political problems in their lyrics.

The dance that compliments merengue is easily picked up compared to salsa. The basic version consists of bending one knee then the other forward and then back in clockwork alternate movements whilst not lifting your heels off the ground. Couples mirror each other, as in salsa, and when dancing close together, the woman places her right foot in between the man's feet. The couples resemble palm trees swaying in the breeze as they move to the beat.

Recent adaptations have seen merengue embracing North American crazes such as rap, hiphop and techno music. This has proven highly popular among the youth in Dominican and Caribbean barrios in the United States, who see hiphop merengue as a Latin expression of the "brotherhood" practiced by their African-American counterparts. The new sound was first introduced by a group of young people of Dominican descent calling themselves *Proyecto Uno*. The adaptability of the rhythm

initial disdain on the immodest hips and swift foot movements of a dance whose sexual connotations could only arouse dismay and moral approbation. Indeed, it was to be a long time before tango was considered sufficiently refined to be acceptable in higher social circles. In fact it wasn't until tango caused a sensation in the steamy dancehalls of pre-First World War France that it gained international acceptance.

Today, tourists ensure the survival of tango in the steamy cafés and clubs of Argentina. But its appeal has become global – it owes its popularity, at least in part, to Al Pacino's dance scene in the film *The Scent of a Woman*.

and the facility of the dance has given it the upper hand over salsa in many Latin communities in the US and in Andean South America.

A dance for lovelorn men

The **tango** is closely associated with Argentina (*see page 330*). To many the most sensual and erotic of all South American dances, its origins lie in the Buenos Aires slums of a century ago. There, lovelorn male migrants, bereft of female company, would re-enact the intimacy of man and woman. Hence, the tango was a dance of men. One male would play the part of the female coquette whilst the other represented the rough wooer. The upper classes looked with

Samba-mania

If the tango is Argentinian, the samba belongs to Brazil. **Samba** comes from an African word, *semba*, meaning "a type of belly dance". It originated in Africa as a reel dance and is first recorded in the 1875 festivals in Bahia in northeast Brazil. Samba today takes many forms. Ballroom, carnaval, pagode (a slower São Paulo version) are a few. It is universally popular and has influenced the **bossa nova** musical form, the first recording of which was made by Elizabeth Cardosa in the 1950s.

The samba danced at *Carnaval* differs from one city to the next. Its proper name is *samba enredo* – first introduced in the 1930s, this is the form of samba most of us would associate with phenomenal footwork and bum-shaking. Samba dancers are reminiscent of leaves shaking violently in the wind as they are driven along by the feverish beat of the *bateria* (rhythm section) of drums and percussion.

Brazil's biggest show

It was the Portuguese who brought the practice of *Carnaval* to Brazil at the end of the 17th century as a festivity celebrated by pelting each other with flour and water bombs (*see page 236*). The music and dance is essentially African in origin. *Carnaval* is undoubtedly one of the biggest displays of modern Brazilian popular culture, blending festivity with show; art with folklore as everyone takes to the streets in extravagant and colorful costume.

The excitement escalates from the Christmas period and Lemanjá New Year celebrations. In the run-up period, an eerie hysteria hangs heavily in the air like the tension before a monsoon. The observer is washed along by a wave of infectious anticipation and then buffeted by relentless musical elements for four days and nights as this tropical storm sweeps over the country. It is a test of stamina that leaves you feeling numb, exhausted and giddy whether you participate or are kept awake by it.

Carnival in Rio is distinct from the rest of the country with its purpose-built Sambadrome stadium and world-famous samba schools of up to 4,000 participants each, who jealously compete for the title of champion. The din filling the Sambadrome comes from the samba percussion *baterias* and sounds like torrential rain beating down on a tin roof. Scantily clad women shake violently as if possessed and a chorus of several hundred voices chant responses to the samba caller.

The rest of the country prefers a giant street party. In recent years the Bahia carnival, which is held in the colorful northeastern city of Salvador, has grown in popularity. Held as a massive street party, *trio electricos* – floats which transport deafening speakers pumping out 100,000 watts of samba, axé and frevo music – lead the processions through the winding cobbled streets. The air dances and heads undulate. The smell of *vatapá* – a maize and shrimp

dumpling dish – forms a haze, served by mountainous Baiana women swathed in traditional white dresses.

Home to Brazil's acclaimed writer Jorge Amado and international musical exports Olodum, with their army of drummers who have played with Michael Jackson and Latin music superstars Daniela Mercury and Caetano Veloso, Bahia is the bastion of Africanism in Brazil. It is also home to the Santeria religion known as **Candomblé** and the African martial arts dance **capoeira**. Bahia is considered the center of musical innovation in Brazil, and draws heavily on its African roots. Many dance

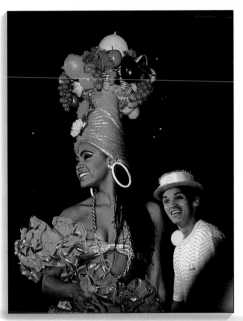

crazes originate in the northeast before being eagerly snapped up by the rest of the country.

The plaintive panpipes

A world away from the samba drums and salsa tambours is the haunting, plaintive sound of Andean panpipe music – **peña**, played in such countries as Ecuador, Bolivia and Peru. Drums, rattles, flutes, panpipes and the famous *charango* (a miniature guitar made from an armadillo shell) characterize it. Peña is a mixture of pre-Columbian and Spanish instrumentation, which traditionally involves no lyrical accompaniment – but this has changed recently. The music is now accompanied by

LEFT: tango, the passionate dance.
RIGHT: a fruity night out in Rio.

ballads sung most often in Quechua, Aymara and Spanish. These plaintive yet raucous songs record the daily lives, romances and ribald interludes of rural Amerindian communities.

It is music to dance to. Andean music is a foot-stomping version of a barn dance. It is very moving. It shakes the soul and makes the air jump. The sound can be frenetic, accelerating from a ballad to a musical duo reminiscent of that classic country piece *Duelling Banjos*. The pitch becomes feverish and your feet seem to move of their own accord. This kind of indigenous and folk music attests to the survival of the ordinary, compromised history of local pop-

ulations. Music is, in a sense, the last place to hide what is left of yourself.

Songs of struggle

Traditional music has been used by dictatorial powers as propaganda – nevertheless, it has also been a useful source of social revolution and protest. The **Nueva Cancion** (New Song) movement which emerged in Chile the 1960s and '70s put music at the forefront of the struggle in Latin America. One of the leading lights of *Nueva Cancion* was the musician and poet Violeta Parra, who received little recognition in her own country, Chile, until after her death

PANPIPES OF THE ANDES

The panpipe goes back at least 2,000 years. Ecuadorian panpipes were named *rondador* after the nightwatchmen in colonial Ecuador who played the instrument on their rounds. A typical *rondador* is made of varying lengths and widths of cane or bamboo tied together in one long row; the different lengths and diameters produce distinct tones. The *zampoña* is the panpipe typical of Peru and Bolivia. The *zampoña* is tuned differently from the *rondador* and usually has two rows of pipes lashed together, producing a deeper, breathy sound.

by suicide in 1967. *Nueva Cancion* was to voice the struggle and suffering of those Chileans who were persecuted during the dictatorship of the 1970s and '80s. Cuba's equivalent, *Nueva Trova*, produced Sylvio Rodríguez and Pablo Milanes, two of Latin America's most respected musicians. Milanes has only recently returned to Chile after vowing never to appear there when the brutal dictator Augusto Pinochet was in power.

General Pinochet was aware of the danger that *Nueva Cancion* posed to his regime when he imprisoned Chile's greatest prize, singer Victor Jara, in the notorious football stadium in Santiago. The inspirational Jara sang to his fellow activists, and for his crime Pinochet had his hands smashed, his tongue cut off and then had him murdered.

Another important Chilean dance style is **la cueca**. It began as a pantomime; a game of coy evasion and rebuttal by women and playful conquest by men. The woman holds a white handkerchief. It was a dance of remarkable restraint. There was no physical contact between the pair until the point of the *vacunao* when the man claims the woman with a pelvic movement, gentle kick or swat.

What is more moving about the cueca, however, is that it was employed by women to protest the mass disappearances of their sons and husbands under Pinochet's regime during the 1970s and '80s. It became a dance of anger and grief. The women would dance alone, their partners lost, disappeared. Their plight was brought to world attention when the British artist Sting paid tribute to them in his song *They Dance Alone*.

Dances of the countryside

On a more cheerful note, the giddy **cumbia** is a popular coastal dance from Colombia. It consists of a rousing, regular beat with a steady "molasses" bass line and brassy horns.

Urban myth has it that the movements to the cumbia reflect gender-based rural activities. The man makes a sweeping movement with his hand that mimics the machete cutting a path through the bush. The woman, with one hand, raises her petticoats, and with the other hand, holds a candle. This purportedly alludes to her guiding the man through the wilderness.

There is a close relation between the cumbia and **vallenato** (*see page 103*); both come from the coastal regions of Colombia. Traveling vallenato musicians would move from one small town to another. They were gossips. They shamelessly drafted local scandal and intrigue into their songs. The lyrics were built piece by piece from the feckless lives of isolated communities. Crowds would gather and eagerly devour the news brought by these musicians. This was before the era of telephone and the gossip was better. It was juicier.

In recent years vallenato has enjoyed a surge in popularity. Maybe the phone isn't what it used to be. Carlos Vives spirited this revival with his modern sound. He appeared in a Colombian television soap opera as a wide-eyed *campesino* called upon to defeat Lucifer in a singing contest. The fate of a village lies in his hands. At first things don't look good for Vives. You worry about the village and his dubious wardrobe. Still, Vives and his accordion manage to deal a fatal blow to Lucifer by striking an original chord, securing the future of the village and the vallenato.

As is so often the case in South America, music conquers all. ❑

LEFT: dancing the *cumbia*, Colombia. RIGHT: singer Violeta Parra, often described as the "mother" of Chile's *Nueva Cancion* movement.

FURTHER STEPS

Major music retailers stock Latin music. The *Tumi Latin American Music Sampler* (Tumi music label) is a good introduction, featuring panpipes, vallenato, cumbia, forro, salsa, merengue and son. The more adventurous may wish to attend dance classes specializing in salsa, samba or merengue. Informal classes offering tuition for beginners are best. They are great fun but, being little advertised, may be hard to locate. Your best bet is to inquire at a Latin American restaurant or bar, contact University Hispanic departments, or check out the Internet. Don't confuse Latin ballroom with any of these options.

ARTS AND CRAFTS

Visitors to South America will find art all around them – indigenous crafts,
pre-Columbian treasures, colonial baroque art and powerful modern paintings

For nearly five centuries, Latin Americans saw themselves through the eyes of others. In 1492 Spain conquered a continent it had not known to exist; within a few short years it had overwhelmed the population who already lived there – the 30 million or so indigenous peoples of Latin America – and made them "disappear". Those 20 percent or so who were not killed or assimilated were pushed into the background, seen as "barbarians" and savages.

The Indian populations of South America and the black African communities imported as slaves were rarely painted after the Flemish artist Theodore de Bry produced his famous engravings of the Conquest. When they did appear it was usually as curiosities, exotic figures in the landscapes of European travellers documenting this New World after Spain finally lost its South American empire in the early 19th century – artists like Jean-Baptiste Debret in Brazil, or Camilo Fernández in Colombia (his watercolors can be seen in Bogota at the Biblioteca Nacional).

Occasionally you can catch glimpses of the work of anonymous Indian artists – in the paintings of the Cuzco school in Peru, for example, with its black Madonnas and curious Indian faces painted in the background or carved into the frames. Yet the arts of the Indian and the black population did survive, in what we now call craftwork or folk arts – papier-mâché figures, painted gourds, fine weaving and so on. In a way, contemporary crafts represent a continuous line from that past, although at the same time they have changed beyond recognition from their original models.

A new conciousness

It was not until the mid-19th century that Latin American painters began to see their own world as worthy of attention. José Correia de Lima painted Brazil's black people for the first time (Museu de Belas Artas, São Paulo), while in Peru, Pancho Fierro recorded the Indian and mestizo people on Lima's streets (Museo de Arte de Lima). In the Museo Nacional de Artes Plasticas in Montevideo, Uruguay, the paintings of Juan Manuel Blanes record the inhabitants of the pampas, the open grasslands where

LEFT: modern art captures an age-old scene, Peru.
ABOVE RIGHT: making *shigras* (sacks), Ecuador.

ECHOES OF THE PAST

Many contemporary crafts and traditions of the Andes have clearly evolved from pre-Columbian times. By studying local culture and artisans, modern archaeologists have been able to advance their understanding of ancient artefacts. The people of northern Peru still regularly use ceramic pots surprisingly similar to their ancient Moche precursors. Similarly, the back-strap loom, which is attached to the weaver's back so that she can adjust the tension by moving her body, is still in use in modern Peru, yet much earlier models are depicted in 2,000-year-old ceramic.

the gauchos lived. Pedro Figari, painting much later, created delicate and evocative images of a life of poverty in a similar world.

Change was coming – and it exploded upon South America at the beginning of the 20th century. After a century of political independence, the ties of external domination were still strong. Any bid to find real freedom meant turning the artistic gaze inward and rediscovering both the reality and the traditions that were authentically Latin America's own.

Ironically, the new cultural nationalists were often artists who, as their contemporaries so often did, first traveled to Europe in search of

berated around the whole continent, influencing university students, who began to demand an art and an education that reflected their own reality.

The *Semana de Arte Moderna*, a famous exhibition which took place in São Paulo in 1922, announced the new movement in music, literature and all the arts. Most representative of its extraordinary innovations was the work of painter Tarsila do Amaral. Her famous painting *Central Railway of Brazil* marries bright colors and geometric forms set in a primitive landscape, like much of Amaral's work, and is on display in the Museo de Arte. Contem-

culture. Many became involved in the new modernist movements there and brought the avant garde back to Latin America, where it came face to face with a different and dramatic reality. Latin America's modern art movements were born out of that encounter.

The past rediscovered

The 1910-1920 period was a time of political and social upheaval – and of nationalism above all. Every country of Latin America began to rediscover – unearth almost – its past; Hiram Bingham's "rediscovery" of Machu Picchu in Peru in 1911 was a signpost to what was to come. In 1910 the Mexican Revolution rever-

poráneo of the University of São Paulo. Amaral, with contemporaries such as Anita Malfatti, represented one face of the new movement; beside them Emiliode Cavalcanti and Cándido Portinari used the mediums of etching, woodcutting and engraving to portray the experience of the ordinary people of Brazil.

European influences

Joaquín Torres-García, like his contemporary Barradas, returned from Europe and the United States to his native Uruguay in 1932, and began to generate his own version of the geometric three-dimensional designs learned from the Constructivists. The exciting and inventive

MADI group, founded in Buenos Aires in 1945, developed that work in entirely new directions.

The extraordinary purity of Armando Reverón clearly owes its origins to Manet and the post-impressionists, searching as it does for the perfect expression of light and color that led him finally to the blinding whites of his last canvases. Reverón's claim was to have captured the essential atmosphere of his own coastal town in Venezuela – an achievement far removed from the innovative and daring new directions for which his country earned an international reputation. For in the capital, Caracas, the architect Carlos Raul Villanueva

dimensions in the museums and streets of Rio, where much of their work may still be found. In Chile, Roberto Matta drew on European surrealism to create a universe of mysterious gardens and landscapes full of color and menace.

The Indigenista movement

Yet even the most non-representational kind of painting in Latin America has wrestled with the past, the "invisible" South America. The powerful Indigenista movement that began in the late 1920s in Peru, Ecuador and Bolivia sought out the Indian communities in all its artistic expressions – in music, literature and in paint-

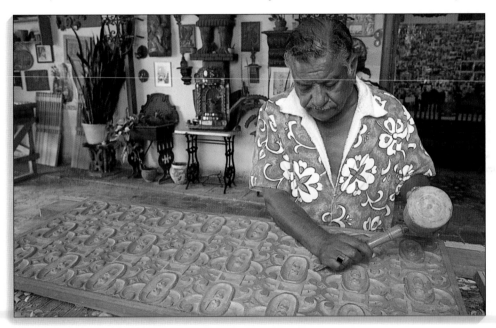

was building a new university and inviting a younger generation of exciting new artists to participate in the design of new and very modern spaces (see page 69). This invitation was eagerly accepted by artists like Alejandro Otero, Jesús Rafael Soto and Carlos Cruz Diez, whose disturbing optical games with light, movement and geometric form can be seen in their settings in Caracas Central University.

The "neo-concrete" artists of Brazil – Lygia Pape, Lygia Clark and Helio Oiticica among others – explored space and color in several

LEFT: masks, Terra Nova, along the Amazon near Manaus, Brazil. **ABOVE:** woodcarving in action, Peru.

ing. José Sabogal was the doyen of *indigenismo* in the visual arts, influencing a whole generation in Bolivia and Ecuador. But for some he was too close to an exaggerated socialist realism that owed much to the Mexican muralists.

A newer generation of artists took that brute realism in new directions – particularly the controversial artist Oswaldo Guayasamín, who moved towards a kind of primitive abstraction, his paint piled on the canvas as if the physical gesture of painting itself conveyed the emotions it contained. His enormous popularity and commercial success have invited the accusation that he paints to pander to the metropolitan world's vision of the south.

Satires on complacency

Colombian artist Fernando Botero's bitterly satirical portraits of a plump and complacent Latin American bourgeoisie have brought him both success and the enmity of some of his subjects. This variety of individual expression has its counterpoint in movements whose object is to create art that is collective in its nature.

The radicalization of Chilean political life between 1968 and 1973 produced a mural art reflecting a movement in the streets. This movement was founded by the group Brigada Ramona Parra, named after a young art student who was killed in a demonstration. Else-

where, that impulse took art into the realms of sculpture and performance – art as a kind of public statement, ranging from Chilean Eugenio Dittborn's poignant "airmail paintings", mailed to exhibitions around the world, to Argentine Antonio Berni's provocative and highly political collages.

A meeting of art and crafts

In another direction, art left the studio to reconnect with a completely different, popular tradition – colourful, naïve, passionate. It had its representatives in Brazil, and in Chile in the work of Luis Herrera Guevara.

It was here that art met "craft". In the aftermath of the Chilean military coup of 1973, for example, groups of women began to make *arpillerías* – patchworks – that employed traditional skills to make powerful symbolic statements about freedom, pain and the search for the "disappeared". Of course, these crafts had evolved and changed from their origins in pre-Columbian America or in Africa, yet they remained the property of the poorest sections of South American society.

They often produced useful items – beautifully woven *ruanas* (capes) in Ecuador, sweaters of llama or alpaca wool in Peru, woolen ponchos, hats and gloves in the Andes. They are functional as well as beautiful. The growth of tourism has often contributed to the resurgence of some of these traditional domestic crafts – in the Ecuadorean community of Otavalo, for example (*see page 202*). But it has almost certainly changed them too.

Hand-made clay sculptures with enormous hands and feet can be bought everywhere in Peru – but their faces are those of the highland peoples. The beautifully painted scenes inside bamboo stalks or hollowed-out nuts are survivals of authentic skills as well as attractive mementos for sale to tourists.

In the greatest markets of the continent, like Huancayo in Peru, plastic items and tacky electronic goods cohabit on blankets on the street with delicate paperlace cutouts or fine ceramics. This coexistence of dramatically different levels of life and methods of production is the the contradictory reality of South America. ❑

CHECK YOUR SOUVENIRS

It's not difficult to find good reproductions of the featherwork of Paracas or the fine beaten gold of the Inca highlands. But it's illegal to take authentic historical artefacts out of most South American countries. So many have already been hoarded in Europe and North America that visitors are strongly discouraged from continuing the depletion of the historical past – and there are stiff penalties for those who are caught. It's also illegal – as well as irresponsible – to export certain materials such as the feathers of protected bird species, which are sometimes found in handicrafts at local markets.

ABOVE: *Maternity*, woodcarving by R.P. Athyde, Ceará Museum, Fortaleza, Brazil. **RIGHT:** tapestries in an Otavalo market, Ecuador.

ARCHITECTURE

South American cities have been at the forefront of modern architectural

movements, and there are also much older architectural wonders to be seen

We do not have the names of those who built the extraordinary Inca cities – Cuzco and Machu Picchu – or the magnificent ceremonial structure of Sacsahuayman in Peru. Pablo Neruda, the great Chilean poet, called them only "John Stonesplitter and John Woodheaver". But whoever they were, their constructions were built to last forever. In Cuzco, the Spanish colonialists built their houses on the walls of the Inca city, for example.

There are still remains of older ancient cities like Chan Chan on the coastal plain. Elsewhere, the ancient indigenous peoples of what are now Argentina, Chile and Brazil, did not leave monumental signs of their passing. Mostly they were hunters, gatherers or fishers without imperial ambitions. But Cuzco was built at what the Incas saw as the centre of the world, and to symbolize this, it is divided into four districts representing each corner of the empire, surrounding a central square.

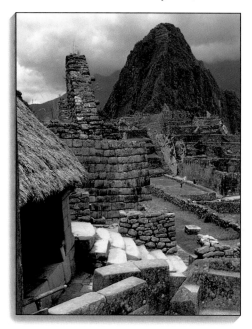

The Spanish influence

When the Spanish conquered native America, they brought their own values, their own religion and their own forms of artistic expression. Where they could, as in Mexico, they destroyed the buildings they found and used the stones to make their own cathedrals. Where they could not move the stones, as in Cuzco, they built their own cities on Inca foundations. But they were able to preserve the structure of the cities, since Spain built its cities on a grid system around a central square. For in a real sense, Spain's was an urban culture and, apart from the great plantation houses, rural building was left to the communities who lived there, relying on their skill in using local materials.

For more than 300 years, Latin America's building styles originated in Spain – at first, the highly decorative *plateresque* style; later with echoes of European baroque, where elaborate decorated surfaces and cascades of gold reflected the confidence of a colonial order. Compared with the first imperial buildings in Mexico, Quito's churches were austere in their façades; yet inside, they could be exuberant – sometimes blue and red washes were added to the endless swirling gold; sometimes they were influenced by the imported *mudejar* (moorish) styles, with wooden beams, carved closed balconies and geometrical patterns.

Despite the codes of austerity that were

MASTERS OF MASONRY

Stone was considered sacred, or *huaca*, to the Incas. Hundreds of sites display the outstanding masonry skills of the Incas, as well as the artistry of individual stones, like the famous 12-angled stone at Cuzco, or *Inti-huatana* at Machu Picchu, the "hitching post of the sun". The Incas were also expert at earthquake-proofing their buildings. The colonial church of Santo Domingo was built on top of Qorincancha, the Inca Temple of the Sun, at Cuzco. Over the centuries the Inca foundations proved much more resistant to earthquakes than the Spanish construction.

imposed by the Spanish imperial centre in Madrid, Latin America did adapt these received styles, particularly in the late 17th- and 18th-century baroque edifices.

The Native American influence

Indigenous craftsmen in Bolivia left their mark on Sucre Cathedral and the churches of San Lorenzo in Potosí or San Francisco in La Paz, and in Peru in the carved soft lava stone used in Arequipa. Bright colors, animals and plants and occasional dark-skinned faces carved into the stone are testimony to their presence, for example in the façade of the old Jesuit University in

expression are the statues of the Prophets at Congonhas do Campo (*see page 242*).

Looking to Europe

Landscape and geography affected construction too. New Granada (as the Andean republics were called under Spanish rule) lay across an earthquake zone, to which many of Lima's buildings have fallen victim. The Torre Tagle Palace (now the Ministry of Foreign Affairs) is one of the few colonial buildings to have survived, as well as some of the smaller colonial buildings of the old city.

Once freed from Spain, the leaders of a

Cuzco's central square. And in Brazil, where the imported Portuguese style encountered no local architecture to stand in its way, the reality of the tropics found its way into the baroque façades of Pernambuco or the extraordinary San Francisco da Penitencia churches of Recife and Bahia. The most outstanding expression of this "tropicalized" baroque is the work of the crippled sculptor-architect Aleijadinho on churches and other buildings throughout Ouro Preto. His most enduring and idiosyncratic

LEFT: Machu Picchu, Peru: a miracle of architectural achievement on an Andean mountain top.
ABOVE: famous 12-angled Inca stone in Cuzco.

newly independent continent turned their attention to other parts of Europe. The 19th century produced an imitative grandeur, mimicking the wide avenues and grand palaces of France and London and their new enthusiasm for neo-classical styles. La Moneda, the famous presidential palace in Santiago that was destroyed by bombing during the 1973 military coup against Salvador Allende, was a typical example.

In Buenos Aires, growing to dominance in the latter half of the 19th century, its newly wealthy bourgeoisie used architecture to emphasise their European roots, producing their own versions of the Champs Elysées – usually called La Alameda. In Lima this change was exemplified by the demolition of the old city walls to make way for the new avenues.

Outside the planned, structured heart of Latin American cities, buildings tend to be somewhat improvised and transient. By the late 19th century the spaces between the grand houses and tenements had themselves become living places for a poor immigrant population. In the 20th century these areas would swell, spreading like mushrooms (*callampa*, the name for a shanty town in some South American countries, means mushroom) around and through the burgeoning metropolises. The hillside *favelas* of Rio (*see page 237*) are extreme examples.

planners, and Brazil's 1930 revolution, which was led by young military officers promising to modernize and industrialize at every level, provided the opportunity. The architect Gregorio Warchavchik set out the new ideas: architecture would be functional and geometric, celebrating the materials and structures of a new urban and industrial world.

The Ministry of Education and Health in Rio was the landmark of the new movement. Completed in 1937 by a team that included Lucio Costa and Oscar Niemeyer, it was the center of a completely urban utopia. Not just buildings, but whole cities would be built like efficient

Beacons of the technological age

The past 60 years have brought Latin America – and in particular Brazil and Venezuela – to the very centre of innovation in architecture. The architects responsible for the modernist revolution in Brazil had traveled to Europe and brought back new and experimental ideas. They seized on the ideas of the great Swiss architect Le Corbusier and the Dutch architect Mies van der Rohe in particular as they imagined great modern cities. The continent would be catapulted into the 21st century by gilding its new urban spaces with the most daring "machines for living". Le Corbusier's lecture tour of Argentina and Brazil galvanized local urban

machines with clean lines, open and flexible spaces set in planned landscapes like those designed by the Brazilian architect and landscape gardener Roberto Burle Marx. The high blocks along Rio's Copacabana beach are one such example; the recreational complex at the suburb of Pampulha another. The church of São Francisco de Assis at Pampulha, decorated by Portinari, symbolized the marriage of plastic and the constructive arts.

The triumph of the idea was Brasilia (*see page 239*), the most ambitious of several new cities purpose-built in the late 1950s which illustrate the meeting of architecture and sculpture. Oscar Niemeyer, the principal architect, imagined a city that would in turn create a way of living. In just ten years the Brazilian movement transformed architecture everywhere, as the 1943 "Brazil Builds" exhibition at New York's Museum of Modern Art, testified.

Modern icons

Less well known abroad, but equally dramatic in its significance, was the movement led by Carlos Raul Villanueva in Venezuela, and in particular, Caracas. Villanueva's first major projects – the El Silencio (Silence) and El Paraiso (Paradise) workers' housing complexes built in the 1940s – symbolised a utopian and

sense, Villanueva created more than buildings – this was a landscape where natural lines and plants and trees were symbolically represented in concrete and metal.

In Argentina, where the neo-classical forms persisted longer than elsewhere, the Teatro Colón (*see page 328*) expressed both the high point and the ending of the movement. The next generation of architects were as responsive as their colleagues elsewhere to the modern movement as the country began its process of industrialization. Clean sharp lines and open space characterized the work of new architects like Amancio Williams, whose house in Mar

optimistic modernism. As in Brazil, the mass housing projects represented the promise of an organized and smooth transition to urban growth; the concrete and glass that were its chief materials were not indigenous but they were cheap and readily available. Like the Brazilians, Villanueva saw architecture as a meeting point between spatial and visual arts. The new Central University, the construction of which began in the early 1950s, expressed the confidence of a newly oil-rich country. In a

LEFT: colonial buildings, Quito, Ecuador. **ABOVE LEFT:** statue honoring the workers who built Brasília. **ABOVE RIGHT:** Casa Natal, Bolívar's birthplace, Venezuela.

del Plata for his brother, the composer Alberto, was entirely functional and without artistic pretensions. In Chile the long, low buildings of Emilio Duhart and Alberto Piwonka reflected an adaptation of the same ideas to the earthquake-prone Santiago valley.

In the 1980s and 1990s, architectural innovation has taken place largely in the commercial sphere. Banks and major multinationals have replaced the state as the major clients for a new experimental work. As a consequence, for the moment at least, architecture and urban planning has become largely dissociated from the sense of social responsibility with which an earlier generation approached its work. ❑

THE GREAT OUTDOORS

Not all outdoor activities in South America center on the rainforest – increasingly sophisticated leisure facilities are available, from sand-skiing to paragliding

South America is a paradise for outdoor enthusiasts. Down the spine of the continent is the Andes, the longest continuous range of mountains in the world. This lofty landscape has snow-capped peaks for mountaineers, trekking, horseback riding, mountain biking on remote trails through isolated villages, and world class kayaking and river rafting.

Within the Amazon basin to the east lies thousands of miles of virgin rainforest best explored by dug-out canoe. Coastal beaches offer excellent surf and the northern Pacific and Caribbean reefs are great scuba diving destinations. Adrenaline sports such as snowboarding, paragliding, and bungee jumping are on the increase. But there is little regulation of the adventure travel business, so care needs to be taken in finding a reputable company.

National Parks

Nahuel Haupi, the first national park in South America, was created in Argentina in 1903. Since then nearly 200 parks have been established throughout the continent, protecting beautiful wilderness. Access to parks is becoming easier with improved transportation and infrastructure. In the more developed countries, notably Chile and Argentina, the parks have established trail systems with visitor centers.

Cusco, Peru is the Mecca for outdoor adventure. The most popular excursion is the Inca trail trek to Machu Picchu. Cusco's surrounding mountains are also perfect for mountain biking. There is a popular ride to the Inca terracing and salt ponds at Moray. Instead of the traditional bus tour, the Sacred Valley can now be experienced by rafting the Urubamba River, on horseback, or paragliding from the cliffs.

Further south, the spectacular alpine and coastal wilderness of Southern Chile brings in visitors from October through April. The town of Pucón is a good base for hikes, climbs, river rafting, mountain biking and horseback riding

into the nearby national parks of Huerquehue and Villarrica. Even further south is spectacular Torres del Paine National Park (*see page 298*).

Mountaineering

The high peaks of the Andes attract high-caliber international climbers every year. Acclimatiza-

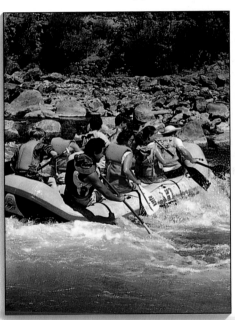

tion, proper equipment and preparation are paramount. The highest of these peaks is Aconcagua (6,962 meters/22,841 ft) in Argentina. In northern Peru, from June to September, the small town of Huaraz is filled with climbers organizing expeditions to the many glaciated peaks in the Cordillera Blanca, the highest being Huascaràn at 6,768 meters (22,200 ft). Snowboarders sometimes precariously descend its slopes. Ecuador's volcanoes can offer the novice a taste of high-altitude mountaineering.

Skiing

The world's highest ski run is at 5,420 meters (17,782 ft) in La Paz, Bolivia, on the slopes of

LEFT: Argentina: a climber contemplates Mt. Fitzroy.
RIGHT: tackling the Urubamba River, Peru.

Chacaltaya (*see page 180*). It was developed in the 1930's and is still accessed by the oldest ski lift in South America – horror stories abound regarding its safety. More sophisticated ski areas have been developed in Chile and Argentina, with the huge ski area of Las Leñas in Argentina considered the most prestigious. The resorts near Santiago such as Valle Nevado and Portillo also have many challenging slopes. The best time to go is June to October.

Cycling

Every year a few serious cyclists pedal the length of the Andes to the southern tip of the

canyons" in Southern Peru, said to be twice as deep as the Grand Canyon. Condors soar above, a volcano smokes in the distance and walls tower hundreds of meters on either side. The Bío Bío River in central Chile has a temperate climate, excellent white water, spectacular gorges and waterfalls and Mapuche settlements, making it one of the most exciting rivers in the Andes to run.

Paragliding

In Río de Janeiro, Brazil, you can paraglide tandem over Atlantic rainforest, soaring above the skyscrapers of Río and landing at Pepino beach,

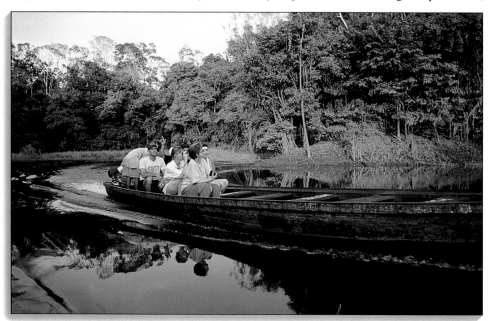

continent, Argentinian Tierra del Fuego. Most recommend taking detours off the Pan-American Highway, for example up into Cajamarca or the Cordillera Blanca in northern Peru, for the best views and to avoid traffic. For the more lighthearted cyclist there are one-day cycle tours to coast down the flanks of the active volcano Cotopaxi, or pedal from the mountains of Baños to the jungle town of Puyo in Ecuador.

Rafting and kayaking

Beginners can descend the fun and safe class III rapids of the Upper Napo River, near Tena, Ecuador. More experienced rafters can run the Colca River floes down the "Everest of river

São Conrado. Paragliders are often seen flying off the coastal cliffs of Miraflores in Lima, Peru. The craze has also hit Merida in Venezuela and Tucumán in Argentina. You can also have a go at ballooning in Río from the Autodromo de Jacarepaguá, a half-hour ride ascending to 1,500 meters (4,921 ft).

Beach and watersports

Crazy *buggeiros* (buggy drivers) will take you out on their buggies along the beaches and sand dunes of Río de Janeiro. The noise may disturb people trying to relax on the beach, but others love the wild spins in the dunes and dodging incoming tides. Some of the most popular areas are the Natal Beaches of Río Grande do Norte. The massive sand dunes in the desert of Huacachina, near Ica in Southern Peru offer a different kind of dune-fun. All you need is a board (cheap to rent) for sliding down the sand and to be prepared to walk to the top of the dunes.

Surfing

The Humboldt Current brings constant surf to the west coast of South America. Various towns along the Pacific coast such as Montañita, Ecuador and Huanchaco, northern Peru, have become hip places for foreign surfers to hang out. Puerto Chicama, set in the arid coastal

marine life. Morrocoy National Park is also a popular center for snorkeling and scuba diving off Venezuela's coastline.

Jungle trips

Dug-out canoe trips along small tributary rivers in the Amazon basin are far more exciting than floats along the wide Amazon River where the banks are too far off to see any wildlife. Adventure trips into the Cuyabeno Nature Reserve in Ecuador, Manu National Park in southern Peru, and from Rurrenabaque, Bolivia offer real jungle experiences, with piranha fishing and hiking through swampy forests. ❏

desert of northern Peru, has become famous for its long left point break.

Snorkeling and diving

You can snorkel with hammerhead sharks, rays, starfish, seals, and penguins at the Galápagos Islands, Ecuador. Scuba diving is also possible. Along the Caribbean coast, palm-fringed beaches offer the perfect start for snorkeling and scuba diving. The small coral islands of Los Roques, off the coast of Venezuela, are teeming with

LEFT: birdwatching along the Ariau River, Amazonas state, Brazil. **ABOVE:** a party of trekkers pitch camp in an Andean valley.

Caribbean Sea

South America

0 500 km
0 500 miles

N

Barranquilla Maracaibo Caracas
Cartagena Isla de Margarita
TRINIDAD AND TOBAGO
PANAMÁ Monteria Barquisimeto Valencia Puerto la Cruz
Trinidad
ATLANTIC
Panamá Cucuta San Cristóbal El Tigre Ciudad Guayana
LLANOS Georgetown
Medellín Bucaramanga VENEZUELA Paramaribo
OCEAN
Puerto Ayacucho GUYANA Cayenne
Bogotá GUIANA HIGHLANDS SURINAM French Guiana (France)
Cali COLOMBIA Boa Vista
Esmeraldas Pasto Macapá
Equator
ECUADOR Quito Bragança
Chimborazo 6310 AMAZON Manaus Belém São Luís
Cuenca Santarém Parnaiba
Guayaquil Iquitos BASIN Marabá Imperatriz Teresina Fortaleza
Loja Mossoró
Piura Cruzeiro do Sul Araguaína Picos João Natal
Chiclayo Cajamarca Pôrto Velho Pessoa Caruaru
Trujillo Huascarán 6768 Rio Branco Ji-Paraná BRAZIL Petrolina Recife
Chimbote Pucallpa Ariquemes Feira de Santana Maceió
Huánuco PERU Guajará-Mirim Aracaju
Callao Huancayo Riberalta PLANALTO Bom Jesus da Lapa Salvador
Lima Ayacucho Trinidad Cuiabá BRASILEIRO Ilhéus
Ica Cuzco Cáceres Goiânia Brasília Montes Claros
Juliaca BOLIVIA La Paz Corumbá Uberlândia Belo Horizonte Governador Valadares
Arequipa ALTIPLANO Cochabamba Pantanal Campo Grande Vitória
Tacna Oruro Santa Cruz GRAN São José do Rio Prêto Campos
Arica Sucre CHACO Londrina Rio de Janeiro
Iquique Tarija PARAGUAY Foz do Iguaçu São Paulo
Calama PUNA Asunción Curitiba
Antofagasta Salta Florianópolis
CHILE Tucumán Resistencia Passo Fundo
Copiapó La Rioja Santiago del Estero Santa Maria Porto Alegre
La Serena San Juan Córdoba Salto
Aconcagua 6960 Mendoza Santa Fé URUGUAY
Valparaíso Rosario Punta del Este
Santiago San Luis Buenos Aires Montevideo
Talca San Rafael PAMPAS
Concepcíon ARGENTINA Mar de Plata
Temuco San Carlos de Bariloche Bahia Blanca
Osorno
Puerto Montt
Isla Grande de Chiloé Trelew
PACIFIC ATLANTIC
OCEAN OCEAN
Perito Moreno PATAGONIA
El Calafate
Puerto Natales Río Gallegos Falkland Islands (UK)
Punta Arenas Isla Grande de Tierra del Fuego
Ushuaia South Georgia Island (UK)
Cabo de Hornos

Galápagos
Equator

AMAZON Rio Amazonas
Río Amazonas
ANDES
ATACAMA

ANTARCTICA

PLACES

A detailed guide to the whole of South America, with major sites cross-referenced by numbers to the maps

First-time visitors may be daunted at the range of sights and new experiences on offer in this diverse region. On a short visit it's best to confine yourself to a limited geographical area, or to certain types of experience, and there are many to choose from: rain-forest expeditions, archeological tours, adventure sports, tropical beach life, subantarctic forays, music and nightlife, and much more.

To help you plan your South American itinerary, we have divided the subcontinent into four sections, devoting a chapter to each country. We start at the north coast: Colombia, Venezuela, Guyana, Suri-nam and French Guiana, countrieswhich run from west to east. Colombia and Venezuela have an abundance of tropical white-sand beaches as well as large modern cities. All of these countries have densely-forested interiors which harbor a plethora of exotic species and are home to some of the world's most traditional communities.

Next, we come to the countries of the Andean Highlands, Peru and Bolivia, linked by enormous Lake Titicaca, and Ecuador. In this region – also in Colombia – are found the treasures of fascinating ancient civilizations, as well as the distinctive living cultures of the Andean people. These countries are also known for their natural diversity, with mountains, tropical lowlands and desert. Ecuador in particular is a mecca for wildlife enthusiasts, who flock to the famous Galápagos Islands, 970 kms (600 miles) off its coast.

From the Andes we move west to Brazil, which sprawls over an area nearly half the size of all South America and almost as large as the United States. Everything in Brazil seems to be on a large scale – its massive Amazon rainforest in the north, the huge and vibrant cities of the east coast, its passion for football, sensual music and dance culture, and of course its world-famous carnival.

Finally we head south, to the Southern Cone, where long, thin Chile lines the west coast from tropical to subantarctic latitudes. The Atlantic coast is covered by the relatively small Uruguay and huge Argentina, which shares the Lake District, Patagonia and the island of Tierra del Fuego with Chile. Landlocked Paraguay, directly north of Argentina, is also bordered by Bolivia and Brazil. The Southern Cone countries are characterised by large urban centers, wide open spaces, sheep and cattle ranching and a pioneering tradition.

The tiny Chilean islands of Juan Fernandez lie 670 km (415 miles) west of Valparaiso, and 3,790 km (2,355 miles) west of the Chilean coast lies Easter Island, one of the most isolated inhabited islands in the world, and a colony of Chile since 1888. Five hundred kilometers (300 miles) east of Argentinian Patagonia lie the chilly Falkland Islands, Great Britain's most far-flung colony. ❑

PRECEDING PAGES: Moreno Glacier, Glacier National Park, Argentina; the Amazon rainforest; the colonial city of Potosí, Bolivia.

THE NORTH COAST

Great adventures start here – on the balmy Caribbean Coast,
or in the remotest reaches of the rainforest

Hot palm-fringed beaches, languid lifestyles and fast nightlife characterize South America's northern Caribbean Coast, but just inside the coastal belt are miles of tropical rainforest, and mountain ranges high enough to provide some cool respite in these equatorial zones. Both Colombia and Venezuela attracted gold-seekers in colonial times, and later fortunes were made from Venezuela's oil, or "black gold", while in Colombia it was drugs that made fortunes – and unfortunate headlines. Today, gold and diamond hunters are causing controversy in Venezuela's rainforest.

The people who live in the highland regions are mostly *mestizos* – mixed European and Amerindians – while on the coast, African heritage bears testimony to the slavery of colonial times. In Guyana, Surinam and French Guiana, fascinating communities of African heritage have settled in the interior, living in the traditional manner of their ancestors. There are also Amerindian communities in these regions and too in Venezuela, some of whom were unknown to the rest of the world until the 1960s.

Colombia, in the northwest, is notorious for its guerrilla networks and urban violence, but most of the country is safe for visitors, and it is becoming an increasingly popular destination among tourists for its friendly people, exciting dance culture and breathtaking scenery. Colombia has some remarkable historical sites, including the ancient ruins of San Agustín (*see page 99*), the Spanish fortress city of Cartagena (*see page 103*), and the finest gold museum on the continent, which is in the capital city, Bogotá (*see page 94*).

Venezuela is an oil-rich country with beautiful beach resorts, many of which surround the paradise island of Margarita (*see page 120*). Venezuela is also a naturalist's dream, with some magnificent wildlife and dramatic scenery. The landscape of the central regions around Mérida and Trujillo (*see page 116*) is alpine and picturesque, with many outdoor sports on offer in the hills. The remote, Guayana Highlands (*see page 121*), where the world's highest waterfall, Angel Falls (*see page 122*) cascades, are characterised by enormous sheer rock formations, golden savannah and dense jungle.

East of Venezuela lie three smaller and less well-known countries – Guyana (*see page 127*), Surinam (*see page 130*) and French Guiana (*see page 132*). These sparsely-populated lands mainly attract visitors who want to explore their extensive rainforest hinterlands, inhabited by people who lead very distinctive and traditional lives. All five continents are represented in the populations of these countries, due to their histories as plantation outposts for three different world empires. ❑

PRECEDING PAGES: young boy in a colorful Caribbean restaurant.
LEFT: a perfect morning on a perfect Venezuelan beach.

COLOMBIA

Map on page 90

Despite its initial notoriety as the land of El Dorado and latterly the drugs capital of the world, this is still a beautiful, friendly country of enormous natural diversity and historical treasures

Colombia has gained a fearsome reputation as the world's foremost producer of cocaine and for relentless violence and civil unrest. This, however, tells only part of the story of a country where myth and modernity mingle to produce a diversity of culture which can be matched by few other countries. This is where the myth of El Dorado and the lure of untold riches caught the imagination of the Spanish conquistadors. Miners still pursue this dream, in search of emeralds as well as gold. Modern and outward-looking on the surface, the architectural and social legacy of Spanish colonial rule is here for all to see, as well as the remains of some of the great pre-Colombian civilisations.

Geographically Colombia is the fourth largest country in South America and is unique in having both a Pacific and Atlantic coast. In the south lies the forbidding Amazon jungle. Three *cordilleras* (mountain ranges) stretch north from the southern border with Ecuador to meet the lowland plains of the Caribbean. Most of the country's 36 million inhabitants live in the central region which incorporates the capital, Santa Fé de Bogotá, set high amid the mist and rain of the eastern cordillera, and the two modern cities of Medellín and Cali. In between the cordilleras lie the valleys of the Cauca and Magdalena rivers, the most fertile agricultural areas. Eastern Colombia is made up of vast, largely uninhabited grasslands known as *Los Llanos*, stretching down to the Orinoco basin. The northern Sierra Nevada of Santa Marta is the highest coastal mountain range in the world. On a clear day you can stand on a Caribbean beach and see snow-capped mountains.

PRECEDING PAGES: Bogotá by night. **LEFT:** Bogotá Cathedral, Plaza Bolívar. **BELOW:** Puerto del Reloj, Cartagena.

While Bogotá is undoubtedly the cultural centre of the country, each region has developed a distinct identity which is reflected in almost every strand of life. Musical styles range from the traditional string-based forms of the Andes to the accordion-led *vallenato* and *cumbia* of the Caribbean coast. One of the country's most popular figures is the Nobel Prize-winning writer Gabriel García Márquez with his particular brand of "magical realism". Other writers such as Alvaro Mutis are less well known but have helped place Colombian literature firmly on the map.

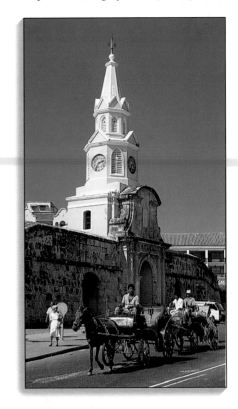

Football is by far the most popular sport, and the country has produced several world class cyclists.

Colombia's exports include coffee, oil, emeralds, cut flowers, bananas, coal and small quantities of gold. The population is predominantly mestizo, although there are sizeable Afro Caribbean populations on the Caribbean and Pacific coasts and around Cali, and more than 50 indigenous groups.

The turbulent past

Colombia has a turbulent political history. The 19th century was marked by 50 insurrections, eight civil

Colombia

0 — 100 km
0 — 100 miles

Isla de
San Andrés ★

Caribbean Sea

Aruba

Curaçao

Bonaire

PANAMA

Istmo
del
Darién

*Golfo
de
Panamá*

PACIFIC

OCEAN

Península
de la Guajira

Riohacha

Maicao

Puerto
López

P.N.
Macuira

Manaure

Península
de Paraguaná

Punta
Fijo

Puerto
Cardón

Golfo
de
Venezuela

Punta
Cardón

Chepo

La Palma

Yaviza

Bahía Solano

Quibdó

⑮ Santa Marta

⑲ Barranquilla

⑰

Cartagena

Islas del Rosario

⑱

P.N. Tairona

La Ciudad
Perdida

Ciénaga

Fonseca

5775▲
C. Colón

P.N.
Sierra
Nevada

⑯

Valledupar

Fundación

Aracataca

Plato

Magangué

Mompós

El Banco

⑳

Sincelejo

Montería

Golfo de
Darién

Planeta Rica

Turbo

Caucasia

Nechi

③

Parque
Nacional
Paramillo

P.N. Los
Katíos

Santa Fé
de Antioquía

Yarumal

Medellín

②

Bello

Barrancabermeja

Puerto
Berrío

Manaure

Puerto Fijo

Maracaibo

Altagracia

Cabimas

Cd. Ojeda

Villa del
Rosario

Machiques

Lago de
Maracaibo

Lagunillas

P.N.
Ciénagas
de Catatumbo

El Vigía

Ejido

Mérida

500▲
Bolívar

P.N.
Sierra Nevada

Trujillo

Valera

Apartadero

Barinas

Ciudad
Nutrias

VENEZUELA

Coro

Chichiriviche

Tucacas

Morón

San Felipe

Carora

Acarigua

San Carlos

San Juan

Guanare

El Amparo

Pto. Cabello

Valencia

Barquisimeto

El Baúl

P.N. Archipiélago
Los Roques

Islas Los Roques

Caracas

Maracay

Calabozo

Parque
Nacional
Aguaro-
Guariquito

Cazorla

LLANOS

Aguachica

Ocaña

Cúcuta

⑬

San Cristóbal

San Antonio

Pamplona

⑪ **Bucaramanga**

Málaga

⑭

P.N. El Cocuy

Barichara

Socorro

San Gil

Duitama

⑤ Honda

Villa de
Leyva

Chiquinquirá

⑫ Tunja

Sogamoso

Zipaquirá

Yopal

Paz de Aripora

Arauca

Elorza

San Antonio

San Fernando
de Apure

P.N.
Cinaruco-
Capanaparo

Puerto
Carreño

Puerto Ayacucho

Samariapo

Puerto
Inírida

San Fernando
de Atabapo

San Carlos
de Río Negro

Bogotá

①

Girardot

Villavicencio

La Poyata

Puerto López

El Porvenir

Granada

COLOMBIA

Miraflores

Mitú

San José
del Guaviare

Parque
Nacional
El Tuparro

Manizales

Nevado del Ruiz
5400▲

Cartago

⑤

Pereira

⑥

Armenia

Ibagué

Espinal

4560▲
Nevado

P.N. Las
Hermosas

Palmira

⑦ **Cali**

Buenaventura

⑧

P.N.
Los Farallones
de Cali

P.N.
Muchique

Silvia

⑨

Popayán

P.N. Puracé

4670▲

San Agustín

Pitalito

⑩

Florencia

San Vicente
del Caguán

Neiva

P.N. Cord.
5750▲

Tierradentro
Pan de Azúcar
Pilimbalá

Parque Nacional
de los Picachos

Parque
Nacional
Tinigua

Parque
Nacional
Serranía
de la Macarena

Río Meta

Río Casanare

Río Apure

Río Arauca

Río Guaviare

Río Inírida

Río Vichada

Río Tomo

Río Uvá

Río Guaviare

Río Orinoco

Tumaco

San
Lorenzo

Túquerres

Ipiales

Tulcán

Otavalo

Pasto

Mocoa

Puerto Asís

P.N.
La Paya

Tarapoca
Reserva
Cuyabeno

Río Caquetá

Parque
Nacional
Chiribiquete

Río Apaporis

Río Vaupés

Río Uaupés

Equator

Ibarra

Quito

Cotopaxi
35▲ 5897

Latacunga

Baeza

Coca

Nuevo
Rocafuerte

Parque Nacional
Yasuni

Pantoja

Río Napo

Río Putumayo

Chimborazo
6310▲

Ambato

P.N.
Llanganates

Puyo

Riobamba

ECUADOR

P.N.
Sangay

Guayaquil

Cuenca

Gualaquiza

Loja

P.N.
Podocarpus

Zumba

Intuto

Río Tigre

Río Pastaza

Río Morona

Puerto
América

Río Marañón

Nauta

Río Yavarí

Iquitos

M a y a n a s

Tarapaca

Río Içá

Leticia

P.N.
Amacayacu

Río Amazonas

Parque
Nacional
Cahuinari

Río Japurá

Río Jutaí

B R A Z I L

wars and several constitutions. The most violent civil war, the War of the Thousand Days, began in 1899, but the ensuing bloodshed and loss of 130,000 lives wrought few changes. The government remained in the hands of a criollo minority who paid scant attention to the mestizos, mulattos, blacks and Indians who formed the bulk of the population.

Meanwhile, the United States took advantage of Colombia's chaos to foment a secessionist movement in Panama, then a Colombian state. Soon afterwards, work began on the Panama canal. Before receiving the Nobel Peace Prize, President Theodore Roosevelt boasted: "I took the Canal Zone and let Congress debate." The Colombian government grudgingly accepted the loss in 1921.

The United Fruit Company of the United States created huge banana plantations along the coast, paying starvation wages and, in 1928, ending a long-running strike by using the Colombian Army to machine-gun unionists. As the banana boom died, coffee became the new hope for the economy, but the pattern of large plantations repeated itself. Small fluctuations in the world price would devastate whole areas of the countryside.

Map on page 90

By the end of the 1980s, Medellín drugs cartel boss Pablo Escobar had an estimated wealth of $3 billion, making him the 14th richest man in the world, according to Forbes magazine.

Unprecedented brutality

In 1948, Jorge Eliecer Gaitan, a popular Liberal politician pushing for real political change, was gunned down in the streets of Bogotá. A spontaneous explosion of frustrations known as *La Violencia* (the violence) ensued, bringing angry crowds to the streets of the capital. Civil war in the countryside followed (the *Bogotazo*), with fighting between peasants, police and soldiers reaching unprecedented levels of brutality. At least 300,000 people lost their lives. By 1953, armed peasant groups were beginning to develop a clear revolutionary philosophy. The Liberals and Conservatives quickly united in fear of a communist advance. In 1957, they agreed to share power for the next 16 years. Once again, the same politicians were back in power, ensuring that nothing would really change. Meanwhile, the various peasant armies in the countryside dragged on their battle with the armed forces, a fight that continues to this day, giving Colombia the dubious honor of having the oldest guerrilla forces in the continent.

BELOW: the *Bogotazo*, 1948.

Sporadic efforts to bring peace and greater democracy failed in the early 1980s, when the M-19 guerrilla group took over the Palace of Justice, central Bogotá. In the ensuing battle, more than 100 people lost their lives, including 11 judges of the Supreme Court.

Drug economy

The presidency of Virgilio Barco opened the way for full competition in democratic elections but the government now had a battle against a new force – the Medellín drug cartel headed by Pablo Escobar, that controlled 80 percent of the world traffic in cocaine. The evil trade undoubtedly helped the economy.

Escobar died in a hail of bullets in 1993, putting more business in the hands of the Cali barons. Over the next two years the authorities had a number of successes, not least when the treasurer of the Cali cartel gave himself up to the US Drug Enforcement Administration. Among the damaging claims he made was that President Samper's 1994 election campaign was funded by $6 million of drugs money. Samper's term of office was dogged by these accusations. He managed to survive an investigation unscathed, though two of his top ministers were imprisoned. Relations with the US were irreparably damaged. The country suffered a recession and unemployment rose, while left-wing guerrillas, right-wing paramilitaries and the security forces fought on, ignoring pleas from ordinary Colombians for a peace settlement.

Andres Pastrana won the presidency in 1998, promising economic regeneration and peace. The success of his Conservative Party campaign, which was backed by author Gabriel García Márquez, was seen by some as a bid for change after 12 years of Liberal Party rule. Despite Colombia's image of chaos – and the occasional sign that goes up on highways telling people not to dump corpses – most visitors are unaffected by the violence, which usually occurs in remote jungle and mountain areas. Nobody who visits this friendly and fascinating country fails to be impressed by its creative energy and quixotic beauty.

Bogotá, capital and intellectual hub

Shrouded by clouds in the midst of the northern Andes, the city of **Bogotá ❶** grew 20-fold in the second half of the 20th century. Layers of history peel away like the rings of an onion: outlying slums give way to towering skyscrapers of polished steel and glass; grand government palaces tower over quaint English mansions. The centre is colonial Spanish with flower-covered courtyards and vice-royal monuments of stone and weathered brass.

This highland city, 2,642 meters (8,670 ft) above sea level, is often viewed with incomprehension by people of the Colombian coast, who see its inhabitants as cold and aloof. Reflecting a popular view, Gabriel García Márquez once described Bogotá as "a gloomy city where on ghostly nights the coaches of the viceroys still rattled through the cobbled streets".

The image has never worried *Bogoteños*, who see themselves as intellectual, cultured and cosmopolitan. Anything and everything can be found in Bogotá's chaotic avenues: opulent restaurants, teams of homeless kids, vendors selling emeralds, peasants in ponchos, endless traffic jams and walls covered with graffiti. Above all, it is the intellectual hub of Colombia, a place where – despite a complete lack of government aid to the arts – you can find dozens of theaters, vibrant university life, classic museums, streets full of bookshops and avant-garde art galleries, all in a creative tumult that has had Bogotá dubbed "the Athens of South America".

Orientation

Bogotá's **El Dorado airport** is impressively efficient, with the world's second-largest landing field. Miles of glasshouses surround the airport, growing some of Colombia's lesser-known exports – flowers.

The best view of the city is from the top of **Cerro de Montserrate**, which can be reached by a funicular railway and cable car. Every Sunday, *Bogoteños* stroll to the summit, where an amusement park is set up alongside a statue of *El Señor Caido* (the fallen

BELOW: traditional dance in a Bogotá nightclub.

Christ). Below, the city is arranged in a warped grid, with numbered *calles* running east-west and *carreras* running north-south. On the way down, at the foot of the hill, call in at the **Quinta de Bolívar**, a magnificent colonial mansion with expansive lawns and gardens, once the home of Simón Bolívar. It is now a museum (open Tues-Sun), full of paintings depicting the life of *El Libertador*, as well as many of his personal effects.

Map
on page
90

The city center

In 1538, three conquistadors met at what is now the heart of the old city, the **Plaza de Bolívar**, to found a town in the fertile lands of the Muisca Indians. Despite killing the Indians and later each other with surprising rapidity, the outpost grew, and became capital of Gran Colombia. The Plaza has a statue of the Liberator at its center, naturally. To the south, the **Capitolio Nacional**, where Congress sits, looks like a classic Greek temple. Beyond is the **Palacio Presidencial**, sacked in 1948 during the *Bogotazo* uprising. Every day at 5pm there is a changing of the guards, whose uniforms were modeled on pre-First World War Prussian outfits, complete with shiny silver spikes on their helmets.

On the western side of the plaza is the **cathedral**, which was begun in 1565, destroyed by an earthquake two centuries later and only completed after Colombia's independence. Alongside are the **Capillo del Sagrario** and the sumptuous **Teatro Colón**, the city's principal theatre, which can only be visited during performances. The **Palacio de Justicia**, at the north of the square, was taken by guerrillas in 1985, and left with a gaping hole in its side from the ensuing fire fight with the army. It remained unoccupied for several years before being demolished, but has now been rebuilt and is due to open again soon.

Painted interior, Puracé National Park, near Popayán (see page 99.)

BELOW: hotel interior, Villa de Avila, near Bogotá.

A Golden Heritage

Protected like Fort Knox, the Museo del Oro (Gold Museum) in the heart of Bogotá is unsurpassed. Its breathtaking collection of bracelets, earrings, masks, statues and rings runs to more than 29,000 pieces from a dozen pre-Columbian cultures, all revealing a mastery of technique that leaves modern jewelers astounded.

The Gold Museum in Lima is a pale collection of tinsel in comparison to its counterpart in Bogotá. This is largely due to the impatience of the gold-crazed Spanish conquistadors, who were too busy plundering the Inca empire to the south to search deep below the surface of the earth for the occasional piece of jewelry from long-forgotten cultures. Thus the great art of the Incas and other Peruvian cultures, easily robbed by the Spaniards, was melted down into gold bars to be shipped back to the royal coffers, while the jewelry of the Colombian cultures was left to be discovered by the archaeologists of later years and also, sadly, by the

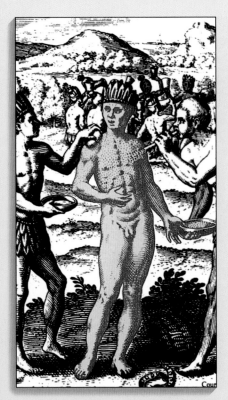

ever-present *guaqueros* or grave robbers who have scoured the countryside for generations.

The metal-working tradition of the Americas developed from the middle of the second millennium BC up to the 16th century. The gold technology of ancient Colombia is considered remarkable, embracing all the known gold working techniques then available in the New World. Its diversity is extraordinary: each of the cultures, isolated by the country's wild and inhospitable geography, developed its own peculiar style.

Hammering was the most primitive technique for making gold objects, although great skill is required to manage the metal. Some cultures in Colombia developed smelting, using combinations of alloys to strengthen the gold. Joining techniques were perfected to connect sheets of gold into more complex figures, and it is probable that the technique of lost-wax casting – using molds of wax models which dissolve on contact with the alloy – was first developed in Colombia.

Pre-Columbian people used gold for decoration and religious rites, recognizing the value of a metal that did not tarnish. Clear guidelines were laid down as to who could and could not wear the metal, while in some areas it was also used as an item for trading.

Run by the government-owned Banco de la República, the Museo del Oro is in the center of Bogotá at the Parque de Santander (open Tues–Sun). On the first level there is an excellent model of La Ciudad Perdida, the ancient lost city of the Taironas (*see page 102*).

One of the museum's prize possessions is a tiny boat created by the Muisca people, showing the ritual of throwing gold into Lake Guatavita as an offering to the gods, while the chief gilded himself with gold, giving rise to the first myth of "El Dorado."

The climax of any visit is the huge strongroom on the top floor. Only 20 people at a time are allowed to enter the room, which is in complete darkness – until the lights are turned up to reveal more than 12,000 pieces, almost blinding in their brilliance. Piped Indian music transports visitors to the mysterious golden world, the reality of which can now only be imagined. ❑

LEFT: Muisca Indians turn their king into "El Dorado," the Gilded One.

The colonial quarter

A short stroll from the Plaza de Bolívar takes you to Bogotá's colonial quarter, **La Candelaria**. Single-story whitewashed buildings seem to creep up a hillside, their red tile roofs and decaying cupolas stretching out to the city center.

Like all of South America's colonial cities, Bogotá has a wealth of religious art. **Iglesia de Santa Clara** (Calle 9, Carrera 8), built during the 17th century, has a sumptuous interior with works by the most famous of Bogotá's painters at the time, Gregorio Vasquez de Arce y Ceballos. On a less sublime note, history records that the church became notorious for the kidnapping of several novices – on one occasion Vasquez himself was implicated and imprisoned.

Heading back into the modern city, wander along Avenida 19 to see the amazing range of books on display. Colombia is South America's largest exporter of the printed word. Nearby, on Calle 18A/Carrera 1 is the campus of the **University of the Andes**, one of the continent's most respected centers of learning.

To get a taste of the flourishing emerald business, head for the corner of Avenida Jimenez and Carrera 7. Colombia controls 60 percent of the world's production of these precious gems, and fortified shops sell them to travelers with a few thousand dollars to spare. Emeralds are graded by their brilliance, color and purity, and every shop has special lights and filters to detect fakes.

Bogotá's most famous and unmissable museum is the **Museo del Oro** (*see page 94*). The **Museo Nacional** (open Tues-Sun; entrance fee), housed in the Panopticon building, was designed as a prison by Englishman Thomas Reed, in the early 19th century, and was built so that each of the 200 cells could be observed from a single vantage point. It was used as a prison until 1946, and has been lovingly restored. Each corridor displays a different episode from Colombian history. The lower level is devoted to art.

Cathedral of salt

Traveling along a highway two hours north of Bogotá, through lush countryside once ruled by the Muisca, a morning excursion can be made to the **Cathedral of Zipaquira**, carved out of solid salt (open Tues-Sun; entrance fee). The salt mines had been worked for centuries by the local Indians when the Spanish took them over. By the 1920s, such a large cavern had been dug that the Banco de la República decided to build a cathedral inside. Carefully cut from a mountainside above the small town of Zipaquira, a tunnel leads into a sulfur-laden darkness. Finally an altar appears silhouetted in the distance: the cathedral is 23 meters (75 ft) high and has held more than 10,000 people at one time, but the walls are black, giving the unsettling sensation of walking through space. Despite the lack of color, they are 75 percent pure salt – as can be affirmed by a quick taste – and mining is still going on elsewhere in the mountain. Colombians will proudly tell you that the mountain could keep the world supplied with salt for more than 100 years.

The other side of Medellín

Four hundred kilometers (249 miles) northwest of Bogotá is **Medellín ❷**, Colombia's second largest city and the capital of Antioquia province. In past

Map on page 90

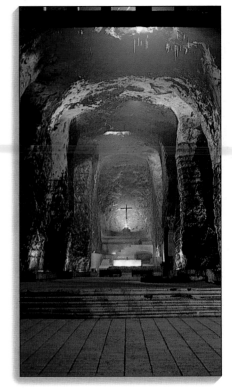

BELOW: altar of the Salt Cathedral, Zipaquira.

TIP

Medellín's annual
flower festival in
mid-August is one of
the most colorful
events in Colombia.

years the city has done its best to shed its infamous image as murder capital of the world and the home of the country's main drug cartel. This has largely been dismantled and much of the associated violence has disappeared. The city is sometimes known as the "city of eternal spring" due to its pleasant climate. Residents have a reputation for being passionate about most things including business, food and enjoying themselves. One of the best ways to see the city is on the metro, much of which runs above street level. Don't expect too much in the way of colonial architecture – Medellín is above all a modern city – however, the red brick cathedral on **Parque Bolívar** is interesting. There is a permanent exhibition of the work of Colombia's best known sculptor and artist, Fernando Botero, in the **Parque San Antonio** (Calle 46 and Carrera 46).

Bananas and coffee

For a more relaxed pace, head northwest on the road towards Turbo to **Santa Fé de Antioquia**. Set among rolling hills, Santa Fé is a beautifully preserved colonial town. Two-storey houses with brightly painted balconies line the streets. At weekends people travel in from the countryside, often on *chivas* – open sided buses covered in gaudy paintings, some by renowned local artists. From Santa Fé the road continues northwards to the port of **Turbo ❸** in the banana-growing region of **Urabá**. Unless you are going to **Los Katíos National Park** this area is best avoided. In recent years the region has seen some of the country's worst violence and human rights abuses. A few travellers pass through the region heading overland to Panamá – this is definitely not recommended.

South of Medellín lies the main coffee-growing region, the *zona cafetera*. Coffee remains Colombia's biggest export and almost all the hillsides around

BELOW: coming
home from market,
San Agustín.

Map on page 90

here are dotted with small coffee farms. **Manizales** ❹, some 270 km (168 miles) south of Medellín, is regarded as the capital of the coffee-growing zone. It is a modern city, founded in the mid-19th century when Antioquian farmers migrated south in the search for new agricultural land. The city suffered several fires and earthquakes in the early 20th century, but its huge cathedral survived. Its streets are built on steep hills – strolling can be tiring. From Manizales you can gain access to **Los Nevados National Park** via the village of **La Enea**. This is a trekker's paradise, often enjoyed by students from the University of Tolima. The park's highest peak is the **Nevado del Ruiz volcano**, which exploded in 1985, wiping out the town of Armero on the other side of the cordillera.

From Manizales the road to Bogotá passes through **Honda** ❺, a picturesque colonial town and weekend resort on the Rio Magdalena. Directly south of Honda is **Ibagué** ❻, a rapidly expanding industrial, but still pleasant city.

Salsa city

Going west from Ibagué the main road ascends steeply to cross the central cordillera. The pass can be freezing cold and for much of the year it is shrouded in mist. The Pan-American Highway then heads south and descends into the fertile valley of the Rio Cauca where sugar, rice and cotton are grown, providing important sources of income for **Cali** ❼, Colombia's third largest city.

Cali was founded in 1536 but remained relatively small until the early 20th century when, with the arrival of the railway and the growth of the sugar industry, the city expanded at an unprecedented rate. Today it is the most important commercial centre in southeast Colombia, and this is reflected in the modern architecture and high-rise office buildings around the city center. There are

Cali is famous for its nightlife, in particular its salsa scene. The city's annual festival takes place between Christmas and New Year, with bullfighting, beauty contests and impromptu salsa parties.

BELOW LEFT: mysterious statue in the Magdalena Valley. **BELOW RIGHT:** the muddy streets of San Agustín.

Fruit and vegetable market, Popayán.

several interesting colonial churches such as **San Francisco** (Carrera 6, Calle 10) and **La Merced** (Carrera 4, Calle 7), as well as **La Ermita**, a gothic-style church built in the 1930s, the star of numerous postcards of the city. A short walk north from the center is the church of **San Antonio**, built in the mid-18th century on a hill, the **Colina de San Antonio**, with good city views. In the main square, **Parque Caicedo**, tall, arching palm trees can provide shade from the heat and humidity that smothers the city during the day. At night, fanned by cooling winds, the city comes alive and its numerous dance clubs can be heard from miles away. On Friday nights these joints are really jumping – if you have the stamina, head for the suburb of **Juanchito** where people dance till dawn.

For a more relaxing pace, visit one of several haciendas north of the city. One of the most interesting is **El Paraíso**, a beautifully preserved colonial mansion where the writer Jorge Isaccs wrote *Maria*, a highly regarded work of romantic realism. The house and its garden has been turned into a museum (closed Mon; entrance fee). Nearby is the hacienda of **Piedechinche** with a sugar refinery and sugar museum (closed Mon; entrance fee). The haciendas can be visited on a tour with a Cali travel agent, or take a bus to Amaime on the road between Buga and Palmira and from there walk or hitch a lift.

Traveling northwest from Cali for 120 km (75 miles) takes you to the Pacific coast port of **Buenaventura** ❽. The town looks fairly ramshackle, but some of the country's best salsa musicians were born here, so there is usually something going on at night. From here, launches run up the coast to the fishing villages of **Juanchaco** and **Ladrilleros**, which have dark sandy beaches.

A few hours south of Cali by road is the city of **Popayán** ❾, founded in 1536 following a brutal campaign to exterminate the local Pubenza Indians.

BELOW: Cali: drug money is often laundered through construction projects.

The town prospered in colonial times due to its location on the road between Lima, Quito and Cartagena. In 1983 its Holy Week processions ground to a halt when a massive earthquake struck the region, reducing most of the city's oldest buildings to rubble. Almost all have been painstakingly restored. One of the most successful restorations is the white cathedral on the main square, the **Parque Caldas**. Behind the altar, there is an impressive statue of the Madonna. Other churches worth visiting include **La Encarnación** (Calle 5, Carrera 5), **San Agustín** (Calle 7, Carrera 6) and **Santo Domingo** (Carrera 5, Calle 4). Popayán's Holy Week processions are famous throughout the Catholic world.

Silvia, a small village in the hills north of Popayán, is home to the culturally distinctive Guambiano Indians, who come to sell their goods at the market on Tuesdays. Just northeast of Popayán, near **San Andrés de Pisimbalá,** is the important archaeological site of **Tierradentro**. The site is made up of a number of prehispanic burial chambers, some of which have motifs and figures carved onto the walls, and stone statues. Little is known about the culture that built the tombs, but the statues are believed to have been carved at a later date, probably around the same time as those further east at San Agustín.

Some of Colombia's richest and most aristocratic families lived in Popayán, and the city proudly proclaims to have produced 11 Colombian presidents.

Natural beauty and ancient wonders

From Popayán a poor road goes east to **Puracé National Park**, an outstandingly beautiful spot with volcanoes, lakes, waterfalls and thermal springs, and many species of wildlife including bears, condors and tapirs. The park's altitude, from 2,500 to 4,800 meters (8,202 to 15,748 ft), accounts for the natural diversity. There are tourist facilities at **Pilimbalá**, at the northern end of the park.

Southeast of Popoyán is the small village of **San Agustín ⓾**, famous for its ancient stone statues, mysterious remnants of a lost culture from one of the most important archaeological sites in South America. Layers of red-tiled roofs lead past a white church tower to the surrounding hills, covered with banana trees. The mountains beyond are a rich green because it rains every day for nine months of the year in a light, erratic drizzle; but even if the rain stops, the humidity can be stifling and the white streets blinding. The few cars in the village are old and clapped-out. Transport is mostly by horse: on every corner, cowboys in ponchos, wide-brimmed hats and leather boots stand by their trusty steeds. A handful have sold out to motorbikes, but the conversion has not affected their swaggering.

BELOW: selling lottery tickets, Cali.

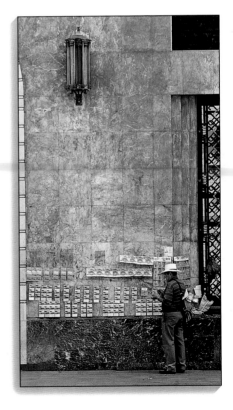

Baffling figures

The statues of San Agustín have continued to baffle archaeologists. Around 500 figures have been found in the surrounding Magdalena Valley: some resemble masked monsters, others eagles, jaguars or frogs. Nobody knows who carved the statues or for what reason. Even today, investigators can only date the civilization from between the 6th and 12th centuries AD. Some experts argue that it was earlier, others that it grew later and was suppressed by the Incas, since this was the northernmost point of their empire.

Some of the statues are arranged neatly in archaeological parks near the village. Within walking distance are the **Bosque de los Estatuas**, with more than 35 figures, and the **Alto de los Idolos**, where the largest statue is seven meters (23 ft) high. Nearby are four *mesitas*, ancient burial sites with mounds, statues and funeral temples. Most exciting to visit are the statues deeper in the countryside. Many can be reached only on horseback as the paths are difficult and often knee-deep in mud, though the landscape is spectacular.

TIP

Every August a festival of kites takes place in Tunja's main square, and in December there is a festival of lights.

Cradle of liberty

North from Bogotá the rugged eastern cordillera runs for just under 1,000 km (620 miles) to the modern industrial city of **Bucaramanga** ⓫ also known for a local delicacy – the *hormiga culona*, an edible species of ant. Before the Spanish arrived much of this area was populated by the Muisca Indians. There is little evidence left of their culture but the wild, mountainous landscape is arguably the most dramatic in Colombia.

North of Bogotá the first major city you encounter is **Tunja** ⓬. The Spanish founded the city in 1539, but there was a settlement here long before that. A monument and bridge commemorates the Battle of Boyacá, the decisive battle in the independence struggle, which was fought just south of the city. For a short time after independence, Tunja was the capital of Nuevo Granada. Simón Bolívar referred to it as his "cradle and workshop of liberty". The capital shifted south when a number of important families moved to Bogotá. A measure of Tunja's importance during colonial times lies in the number of churches that were built – anyone interested in religious art should visit. The cathedral contains several paintings by Gregorio Vasquez. Also worth visiting are, between Calles 19 and 20, the churches of **Santo Domingo** (Carrera 9), with its ornate

BELOW: villages in the Nariño region, southwestern Colombia.

wooden interior, and **Santa Clara** (Carrera 7), with its 16th-century convent.

Tunja is a good base to explore the small villages and towns scattered around the Boyacá highlands. One of the most popular is **Villa de Leyva** which, with cobbled streets lined by low, whitewashed, tile-roofed houses, has become a national monument. The main focus of the town is the wide central square with a museum dedicated to the work of well-known painter and sculptor Luis Alberto Acuña (open Wed-Sun). The town is deeply rooted in national history. Antonio Nariño, an intellectual and statesman who led the call for independence at the end of the 18th century, lived and translated Thomas Jefferson's *Declaration of the Rights of Man* at a house on Carrera 9, Calle 10.

There are several other buildings worthy of note, including the **Carmelite monastery** and its church opposite in the Plazuela del Carmen. But what makes this town special is its unhurried atmosphere, particularly during the week. From Villa de Leyva buses and collectivos leave for nearby towns like **Ráquira**, known for its pottery, and **Chiquinquirá**, where pilgrims from all over Colombia converge to visit a painting of the Virgin by Alonso de Narváez, supposedly Colombia's oldest painting. From Chiquinquirá the lawless emerald mining towns of **Muzo** and **Coscues** can be reached, although the journey, on an unpaved road, can be arduous in the rainy season.

From Tunja a twisting road goes northeast for 460 km (286 miles) to the Venezuelan border at **Cúcuta** ⓭. The scenery along the route is spectacular and passes through several whitewashed towns such as **Málaga** ⓮ before arriving at **Pamplona**, which has one of the oldest universities in Latin America. The main road from Tunja goes north to **Santander**, a province filled with old colonial towns, most notable of which are **San Gil**, **Barichara** and **Socorro**, from

Map on page 90

Cowboy in flowers, Medellín flower festival.

BELOW: pueblo Paisa, near Medellín, Colombia.

where the comuneros led the first revolt against the Spanish in 1781. This event is remembered in the town's **Casa de Cultura** (open daily; entrance fee), housed in a colonial mansion on the Calle Real beside the brick cathedral.

The Caribbean coast

Arriving from Bogotá in Colombia's Caribbean coast is like stepping into a completely different world. It is as if there were two separate countries: one cool and remote, the other tropical and sensual.

A gateway to the coast and many attractions of the north is **Santa Marta** , capital of Magdalena province. One of the most pleasant cities in Colombia, it was founded by the Spaniards in 1525, but there are few colonial relics in the popular modern resort town. Visitors come here to loll in the sun along **El Rodadero Beach**, considered the best in Colombia; to stroll up and down the tourist promenade while being bombarded with *salsa*; or simply sit in a pavement bar and enjoy the view across the bay to the rocky island of **El Morro**.

Santa Marta is a convenient jumping-off point to **Tairona National Park**, ideal for those seeking isolation. This stretch of untouched jungle, once the territory of the Tairona Indians, is at the foot of the **Sierra Nevada de Santa Marta**, a pyramid-shaped mountain that drops sheer into the Caribbean Sea. Further east is the **Santuario de Flora y Fauna Los Flamencos**, a nature reserve which, as the name suggests, is full of pink flamingos.

Santa Marta is also the place to reach **La Ciudad Perdida**, the Lost City of the Taironas that was only found in 1975. Larger than Machu Picchu in Peru, the discovery is considered one of the most important of the 20th century in South America, confirming that the Taironas were not just accomplished craftsmen but

BELOW:
Caribbean sunset.

Map on page 90

built one of the largest cities on the continent, with wide boulevards and road links. The city was discovered by *guaqueros* (grave robbers) in the tropical jungle of the Sierra Nevada. Calling it *El Infierno Verde* (the green hell), they fought over the finds until the government stepped in. Today it can be reached in 20 minutes by helicopter or three days on foot. In the absence of any written records, archaeologists can only guess when the city was built – probably the 13th century – and what disaster led the inhabitants to disappear without trace.

García Márquez country

The first image many foreigners have of South America comes from the Caribbean coast of Colombia, thanks to the works of author Gabriel García Márquez. His writings have preserved the life and history of the region, and today the small town of **Aracataca** where he was born and raised – and which he fictionalized as the town Macondo in his 1967 novel *One Hundred Years of Solitude* – can be easily visited for a glimpse of coastal life. Buses leave several times an hour from the Santa Marta terminal. Aracataca has a plaza with a statue of Bolívar, an old church tower, several shabby billiard halls and a couple of empty restaurants. Tucked away in a back street is a modest building with the sign "GGM Museum". In a garden full of chickens is the house where Márquez was born in 1928 – wooden, whitewashed and without a stick of furniture.

A few hours south of Aracataca is the city of **Valledupar ⓰**. Founded in the mid-16th century, there is little evidence of its colonial past apart from the main square, where people sit around a giant mango tree to shelter from the searing midday heat. Every year this space becomes the focus of the country's attention during the festival of the "Legend of the Vallenato". For five days at the end of April Colombia's top accordion players battle it out in Valledupar to be crowned King of the Vallenato, a popular style of music which originated here. The festivities are fuelled by rum and large quantities of *aguardiente* (literally "burning water").

Cartagena, Spain's New World fortress

Of the many colonial jewels in South America, **Cartagena de Indias ⓱** is perhaps both the most romantic and least known. Placed on the tropical Caribbean coast, saturated by heat, music and feverish dreams, this fortress city of the Spaniards is a living museum. Just walking its streets recalls the days of bloodthirsty pirates, galleons full of bullion, and swordfights beneath the palm trees. Founded in 1533 by the first of Spain's scurvy-ridden conquistadors, the town quickly blossomed to become the main colonial port on the Caribbean and the gateway to the whole South American empire. But as the wealth plundered from Indians piled up in galleons to be taken to Cadiz, the city became a target of every pirate and desperado cruising the Caribbean seas.

During the 16th century, Cartagena was besieged no less than five times by buccaneers and cutthroats. The Spanish decided to create fortifications so powerful that the port would be impregnable. Stone ramparts and battlements were constructed over many decades, the like of which had never been seen in the

Sir Francis Drake sacked Cartagena in 1586 and extorted a 10 million peso ransom from the inhabitants. This was shipped back to England for Queen Elizabeth, along with the bodies of several crocodiles, blasted from nearby swamps with cannons and stuffed with straw.

BELOW: taking a break, Caribbean coast.

Americas. The pirate attacks continued, but never with the same success – Cartagena was even able to survive several sieges by the English and the French.

Exploring the old city of Cartagena

Arriving from the airport, a highway passes along Marbella beach towards **Las Murallas**, the stone ramparts that still surround the old city. Many small forts, where cannons and other defensive weapons were placed to ward off sea attacks, remain intact. The colonial section of Cartagena is only a small part of the metropolis, but it contains enough relics to warrant several days' exploration.

Facing the **Plaza de Bolívar** is the **Palacio de la Inquisición**, one of Cartagena's finest buildings. Its museum recalls the fearful proceedings of the Holy Inquisition, during which 12 people suffered a public *auto-da-fé* – burning alive in the plaza. When Cartagena declared its independence, this palace was one of the first places that the angry crowd came to sack. However, the building is currently undergoing major refurbishment which could take some time, and only parts of it are open to the public.

Farmer stitching a saddle blanket, Antioquia province.

BELOW: fortress at San Fernando, Cartagena.

Adjoining the Plaza Bolívar is the fort-like **cathedral**. Three blocks south is the **Plaza de la Aduana**, once used as a parade ground for troops, and now based around a statue of Christopher Columbus. Call in at the **Museo de Arte Moderno** in the former Royal Customs House, then take a stroll under the **Puerto del Reloj**, which once linked the inner walled town to the poorer Getsemaní district by a drawbridge over a moat. Following the city wall closely around to the south, you will run into the **Iglesia y Convento de San Pedro Claver**, named after a Spanish monk who spent his whole life looking after the African slaves. Nicknamed the "Slave of the Slaves", St Peter Claver (1580-

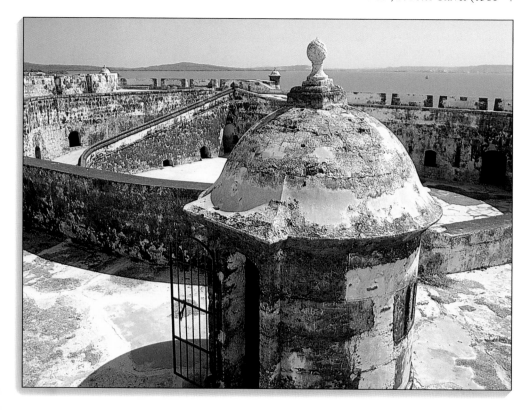

1654) was the first person to be canonized in the New World. Today the monastery is a haven of solitude and peace, with arched stone patios built around a garden of flowers and foundations.

There are dozens of other colonial houses, churches and monuments worth visiting in Cartagena. Drop in at the colonial **Casa de la Candelaria** – once a noble's mansion, now a restaurant – then stroll around the city walls to **Las Bovedas**, built two centuries ago as dungeons, with walls 15 meters (50 ft) thick. Today they are home to tourist shops and a bar.

Map on page 90

Barriers of stone

To keep their gold extra secure, the Spanish built even more extraordinary fortifications in key points. Looming over the city from the San Lorenzo Hill is the impregnable **Castillo de San Felipe de Barajas**, a complicated system of batteries, tunnels and hiding places engineered from massive chunks of stone. The tunnels, which can be visited, were constructed so that any sound would echo and warn guards of approaching soldiers. The view over the old city from the castle is one of the best in Cartagena. Located at the entrance to Cartagena Bay is the **Fuerte de San Fernando**, a fort which can only be visited by water. A huge chain was hung between it and another outpost across the bay to prevent surprise attacks. Many films have been shot in its well-preserved interior. On top of a large hill behind the city is the **Convento de la Popa**. The Augustinians built a wooden chapel at the summit in 1607, soon replaced by a monastery with an image of the patroness of Cartagena, La Virgen de la Candelaria.

Near the Puerto del Reloj is the city's dock area, **La Muelle de los Pegasos**, where you can sit at a juice stall and watch the port life go by. La Muelle is the departure point for tourist boats to the idyllic **Islas del Rosario** ⑱, just a couple of hours away. For a cheap seafood dinner, stroll up **Avenida Venezuela** and call in at the *ostrerias*, small booths selling delicious shrimp and oyster cocktails. For more sophisticated nightlife, head for **Bocagrande**, a resort suburb several minutes out of town by taxi. The food and dancing is the best Cartagena can offer.

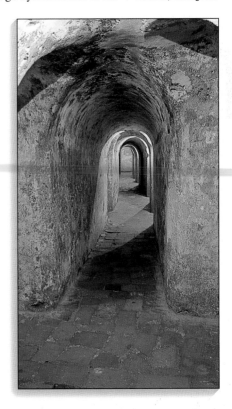

BELOW: Spanish tunnel inside the San Fernando fortress, Cartagena.

Around Cartagena

Heading northeast along the coast is the large port city of **Barranquilla** ⑲, famous for its magnificent carnival, held in February. **Mompós**, 240 km (149 miles) south of Cartagena on an island in the Rio Magadalena, was declared a World Heritage Site by UNESCO in 1995. In the 18th century the Rio Magdalena changed course, isolating Mompós, which had flourished in the Spanish era as the river provided the most important line of communication between the interior and the north coast. The city now has some of the finest examples of colonial architecture in Colombia. Of particular note is the yellow church of **Santa Barbara**, with a Moorish octagonal tower. The **Casa de Cultura** (open daily; closed 12-2pm; entrance fee) is beside the church of **San Agustín**, where crowds gather during the town's impressive Holy Week processions. Buses and launches depart here for the hot, dusty and decaying town of **El Banco** ⑳. ❏

VENEZUELA

*A Caribbean country yet with some fabulous natural treasures
in its interior, Venezuela has a great deal to offer
both beachcombers and adventurers*

Map
on pages
110–11

Nearly 3,000 km of Caribbean shoreline and adjacent islands provide Venezuela with tantalizing warm-water beaches, excellent sailing and underwater delights, plus some of the world's best bill and bonefishing. Inland attractions range from the snow-capped Andes to vast plains with sprawling cattle ranches, from quaint villages to modern metropolitan areas with non-stop nightlife. Venezuela has immense natural beauty, with virgin tropical rainforests inhabited by indigenous tribes, the Guayana Region rich in gold and diamonds and famed Gran Sabana, a paradise for bird-watchers and fishing.

As one of the world's largest oil-producing countries, petroleum has been the single most influential element in Venezuela's recent history. During six decades of boom, beginning in the 1920s, there was so much money flowing in that monthly shopping trips to Miami, premium Scotch whisky and French champagne became the norm even for general office workers. With the seemingly bottomless pot of "black gold," agriculture was virtually abandoned as people left the farms to get a piece of the pie in the principal urban centers near the coast. Development of national industry waned as imports soared with easy cash, and no one took note of growing government corruption and lack of investment in the basic structure of the country.

When petroleum prices began to tumble in the early 1980s, no one wanted to believe it was anything but a temporary situation. But, with the infamous "Black Friday," 18 February 1983, hard reality hit. The value of the national currency, which for years was frozen at Bs.4.3:US$1, was slashed to Bs.7.5:US$1 and exchange controls were imposed. The party was over.

The real crisis was not felt until Carlos Andrés Pérez returned for a second presidential term in 1989, riding on the popularity from his first time in office in 1974-79. His tough economic measures led to two bloody military coup attempts that year, with government forces turning back disorganized rebels. Pérez survived, but on 20 May, 1993, he was indicted by the Supreme Court on charges of corruption for alleged misuse of secret funds. The Senate voted to remove him from office and he was convicted in 1996.

Rafael Caldera, president in 1969-74, was re-elected in 1994. Faced with mounting foreign debt, the failure of 17 financial institutions representing nearly half the total of the nation's deposits, massive capital flight, and the public's lack of confidence, the value of the bolívar was slashed and exchange controls simultaneously imposed from June 1994 to April 1996. The devaluation of the currency hit Venezuelans hard, and made the country a bargain destination for tourists.

Talk rather than action followed promised spending cuts, and the country's huge public debt continued to

PRECEDING PAGES:
La Llovizna,
Guayana Highlands.
LEFT: Parque Central, Caracas.
BELOW: taking it
easy in Ciudad
Bolívar.

mount. The mid-1990s failure of banking institutions holding 55 percent of the deposits of the population exacerbated the situation. Since then, plummeting real earnings and high unemployment have placed 80 percent of Venezuelans below the poverty level, contributing to rising crime. Robberies directed against the "haves" have turned them into prisoners of their privilege, living behind guarded doors. Meanwhile, violence among the poor in the barrios of Caracas is on the increase.

Venezuela has been on the difficult road to recovery ever since: rebuilding national industry, working to stimulate agriculture, dealing with inflation surpassing 100 percent for the first time in history in 1996, learning how to be competitive with the elimination of price controls and shift to a free market economy, while adapting to the impossibility of the government continuing to be the paternalistic provider. Still, optimism remains high, and everyone from individuals to state governments seems to be working to make it happen through personal initiative. Happily for visitors, this is never more evident than in the area of tourism, where its potential as an alternative to dependency on the profits of petroleum is finally being recognized.

Caracas: city of fortune

The first view of the country for most visitors is El Litoral – the central coast, location of **Simón Bolívar International Airport** and adjacent **National Airports**. Venezuela's capital city, **Caracas ❶** is 27 km (43 miles) away across the coastal mountain range. There are some hotels around the waterfront between **Macuto** and **Caraballeda**, some 30-45 minutes to the east, but this area is more of an entry and departure point than a destination.

The mountains of **El Avila National Park** form a dramatic backdrop for Caracas, called home by some four million inhabitants. The first view is a shock – hillsides surrounding the airport access road and slopes ringing the metropolis are blanketed with thousands of haphazardly constructed *ranchos* (shacks), inhabited largely by illegal immigrants and poor people who came from rural areas seeking their fortune, but quickly found that without papers or marketable skills, formal jobs were not available. The central valley and upscale residential areas of the east and south show another side: modern, dynamic, affluent.

Centro is the traditional heart of the city and **Plaza Bolívar** is the core of its historic zone, with treasures including the 19th-century **Capitolio**; the 17th-century **cathedral** and adjacent **Museo Sacro**. **Casa Natal** was the birthplace of South America's "liberator," Simón Bolívar. Next door, the **Museo Bolívariano**, has mostly military-related memorabilia associated with him. **Concejo Municipal** was the birthplace of Venezuela's call for independence (visit the fascinating **Museo Criollo** inside, which has a display of miniatures created by Raúl Santana depicting every aspect of *criollo* life at the turn of the century, along with paintings by the impressionist Emilio Boggio).

Casa Amarilla, formerly a jail and a presidential residence, now houses the Foreign Ministry. Facing the northwest corner of the plaza is the **Gobernación**, seat of government of the Distrito Federal, which has a gallery on the ground floor. The **Iglesia de San Francisco,** dating back to 1575, has walls lined with gorgeous gilded altars and is connected to the **Palacio de las Letras**, the academies of history, language, and science. All of these buildings are within a block or two of the plaza. Several blocks north of the cathedral is the striking twin-tower pink and gray **Panteón Nacional**, resting place for over 130 of the nation's greatest heroes.

Though it will require a taxi ride if you are on foot, a visit to the excellent colonial art museum **Quinta de Anauco,** in San Bernardino, is well worth the effort. Surrounded by gardens cultivated with plants of the period, this elegant colonial home, which was built in 1797, has been restored and adorned with outstanding colonial art and furnishings.

Inhabitants of Caracas are known as caraqueños.

BELOW: hats and hammocks, Ciudad Bolívar.

Financial hub

Interspersed with colonial gems in Centro are sleek glass-faced skyscrapers, harboring the nation's financial, business and political movers and shakers. Shoppers here can delight in the nine-story gold center **La Francia,** facing the Plaza Bolívar, or small shops for shoes, clothing and jewelry stretching east from the plaza to the **La Hoyada** metro station.

Chuao has one of the city's largest shopping centers, housed in an attractive mall, **Centro Ciudad Comercial Tamanaco** (CCCT), filled with top-of-the-line shops, restaurants, nightclubs, travel agencies, Viasa's office with advanced luggage check-in service, a supermarket, and a four-star hotel. Facing it is the distinctive **Cubo Negro** (black cube) office building, one of the many examples of attention-grabbing contemporary architecture in the city, with a dramatic hanging kinetic sculpture by Venezuelan artist Jesús Soto.

Traffic and parking are perennial headaches in Caracas but the fast, clean, economical subway system, the metro de Caracas, takes you across the city in minutes. Though a slower option, there is also a non-stop flow of dirt-cheap buses that go everywhere. Taxis are numerous and inexpensive, but few drivers speak English, so have your destination written in Spanish if you can.

A few minutes east from Centro (the northeast exit from the **Capitolio** metro station is closest to the plaza, diagonal from the Capitol), get off at the **Bellas Artes** stop and one block south is **Parque Central**. This massive urban renewal project has 56-story twin towers, seven 44-story apartments the outstanding **Museo de Arte Contemporáneo de Caracas Sofía Imber**, with sculpture garden and restaurant. There is also a fabulous hands-on museum for children, **Museo de los Niños,** and the **Museo Teclado,** a keyboard museum with

Map on pages 110–11

TIP

The best way to get around Caracas is by the metro (subway). To save money, buy ida y vuelta (round trip tickets for one destination), multi abono (10 rides of any distance for a discounted rate), or integrado (metro plus metrobus).

BELOW LEFT: old and new in Caracas.
BELOW RIGHT: Los Caobos Park, Caracas.

Colonial façade, Coro.

weekly concerts. Nearby is the spectacular **Teatro Teresa Carreño** and the **Teatro Rajatabla**, home of a popular alternative theater group. Other attractions are the **Museo de Ciencias Naturales** and **Museo de Bellas Artes**, with international contemporary art. The **Galería de Arte Nacional,** showing Venezuelan artists, is approached on weekends through lines of local artisans' stands. Behind them is the sprawling **Los Caobos Park** and in the background the **Ibrahim bin Abdulazis al Ibrahim Mosque**, the largest in South America.

Continue on the metro to **Plaza Venezuela,** then walk east to **Chacaíto** along the kilometer-plus "gran avenida" of **Sábana Grande.** This wide pedestrian boulevard is lined with shops, cafés and chess tables, where office workers often spend their lunch hour. It is delightful by day, but at night hookers and transvestites take over and the adjacent hotels are primarily rented by the hour.

A little further east, exit the metro at **Parque del Este** to explore the 81-hectare (200-acre) park by Brazilian landscape architect Roberto Burle Marx, with planetarium, mini-zoo and artificial lake. The **Museo de Transporte** facing its east side is connected by walkway over the busy freeway.

Among the city's other parks, two blocks south of **Plaza Venezuela**, with a giant central fountain, is the **Jardín Botánico** which has extensive gardens, an arboretum of some 100,000 trees and sculptures by national artists. Or take the No. 2 spur of the metro from Capitolio to the **Zoológico** stop to visit the 486-hectare (1,200-acre) "no cages" **Caricuao Zoo.** The greatest concentrations of upscale restaurants are found in the commercial zone of **Las Mercedes** in the shopping center of the same name. **La Candelaria**, just east of Centro, is an eminently Spanish sector famous for its dozens of traditional restaurants and *tascas*, bars which feature many hearty *tapas* appetizers.

West of Caracas

Colonia Tovar, about an hour away by car, is a village high in the mountains that was founded in 1843 by Germans from the Black Forest, who transplanted their architecture, language, cultural practices, farming tradition and cuisine. On weekends, *caraqueños* jam the narrow streets lined with produce and crafts stands. It has numerous cozy hotels and a yearly international chamber music festival in March or April. **Maracay ❷**, 90 minutes west of Caracas via free-way, is the entry point for **Henry Pittier National Park**, Venezuela's oldest protected environmental zone (since 1937), renowned among bird-watchers for over 500 species seen here, and by non-birders for its winding scenic routes sur-rounded by bamboo groves, cloud forests, and mammoth vine-draped trees.

Entry via **El Limón** leads to the beautiful palm-lined arc of **Bahía de Cata**. A short distance before the park is **Ocumare de la Costa**, with various lodging options. Continuing past **Cata**, the beach of **Cuyagua** is a favorite for surfers. Follow the route via Las Delicias to reach the picturesque colonial village of **Choroní** and the coast at the fishing village of **Puerto Colombia,** with many *posadas* (guest houses), a few kilometers on. The broad, palm-shaded swimming beach is about one kilometer to the east. Local fishermen offer boat transfers to the popular beaches of **Chuao** and **Cepe** from Puerto Colombia.

From **Valencia ❸**, Venezuela's manufacturing capital, take the road north for a 20-minute mountain drive to the coast, passing **Las Trincheras hot springs**. From there, turning east takes you to **Puerto Cabello**, Venezuela's most impor-tant port. Here, a beautiful waterfront colonial zone faces **Castillo Libertador**, an impressive fort built in 1732. **Fortín Solano**, the last colonial fortification erected in Venezuela, completed in 1770, stands on a hill in the background.

Turning west at the coast brings you in 40 minutes to **Tucacas**, the first entrance to **Morrocoy National Park** – alternatively, continue to another entrance via **Chichiriviche**, with the bonus there of a drive through **Cuare Wildlife Refuge** where the flashiest inhabi-tants are scarlet ibis and a flock of some 20,000 flamingos. The park is also popular for its white sand, palm-fringed islands and keys. Boat shuttles are available from Tucacas and Chichiriviche.

The westbound coastal highway traverses desert plains to reach **Coro ❹**, which was declared a World Heritage City by UNESCO for its concentration of outstanding colonial structures, including an excep-tional **Diocesan Museum**. A side trip north to the windswept **Paraguaná Peninsula** takes you past the towering sand dunes of **Los Médanos de Coro National Park** to **Adícora**, a windsurfer's paradise. Fans of colonial architecture can admire houses which demonstrate the Dutch influence of the nearby islands of **Curaçao** and **Aruba**.

Source of the black gold

Arriving at the country's westernmost state, Zulia, one encounters **Lake Maracaibo**, the largest lake in South America (and one of the world's most valuable, with the greatest portion of Venezuela's enormous oil reserves and some 40 percent of the country's gas reserves). Cross the **Rafael Urdaneta Bridge**, the

BELOW: Guajiro woman at market north of Maracaibo.

Map on pages 110–11

longest pre-stressed concrete span in the world, to reach the state capital, **Maracaibo ❺**, Venezuela's second-largest city. Maracaibo is the center for the nation's oil industry with a core of upscale residential areas and multinational company offices. It is also where one sees thousands of Guajiro and Paraujano Indians, the women proudly wearing traditional long flowing dresses.

Near the seven-block-long park **Paseo Ciencias** is the **colonial cathedral** and the **Casa de Capitulación.** The **Basílica de Nuestra Señora de la Chiquinquirá** honors Zulia's beloved patron saint nicknamed "La Chinita". **Calle Carabobo** is a street of colorful "Maracaibo-style" houses, now mainly shops and restaurants, and a huge handsome former municipal market has been restored and converted into the **Centro de Arte de Maracaibo Lia Bermúdez**.

A cheap shuttle boat service runs from El Moján to the colonial fort and extensive beach of **San Carlos Island**. At nearby **Sinamaica Lagoon** boat excursions with indigenous guides visit communities of Paraujano Indians who live in houses built on stilts in the lagoon.

Where the Andes begin

The Andean states of **Táchira** and in particular **Mérida** and **Trujillo** are the most picturesque in the country. Though accessible by air, this area should be visited by car to appreciate the stunning landscapes of glacier-fed lakes bordered by colorful flowers. There are quaint villages with traditional architecture, and wayside restaurants where you can savor trout or smoked cheese on a wheat flour *arepa* washed down with warm, spiked *ponche andino* or *calentado*.

Taking the Transandean Highway from the coast through **Barquisimeto ❻**, with side trips to the weavers' colony in **Tintorero** and to **Quibor**, known for

TIP

For a fast route to Táchira, take Highway 6 along the west side of Lake Maracaibo, following signs out of town indicating Machiques.

BELOW: drilling on Lake Maracaibo.

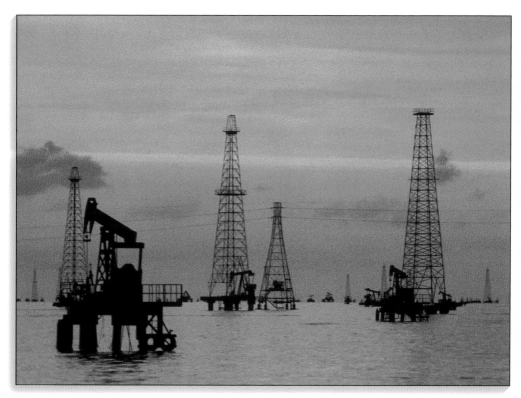

its ceramics and ancient indigenous heritage, you will enter the area from Guanare ❼, in the heart of the central farmlands. Here, you can visit the impressive **Templo Votivo Nacional de la Virgin de Coromoto**, inaugurated in 1996 by the Pope and dedicated to Venezuela's patron saint.

Map on pages 110–11

Alternatively, go via **Boconó**, driving through coffee plantations, or approach from **Barinas** via **Santo Domingo**. Because of their isolation (roads here were not surfaced until the mid-1950s), the Church became the center of social as well as religious life for the *andinos*, and this is still evident. Visitors are likely to encounter some sort of religious or folkloric celebration during their stay.

El Aguila Pass crowns the highest paved road in the country at 4,007 meters (13,146 ft). The surrounding *páramo* (moor) is dominated by the *frailejón*, with fuzzy silver-green leaves and bright yellow flowers atop a tall stem (peak blooming time: October). Near **Apartaderos ❽**, is the **Observatorio Astronómico Nacional del Llano del Hato**, with four giant telescopes and public viewing.

East of the highway from **Santo Domingo** lies **Sierra Nevada National Park**. Principal entrances to its many hiking trails are at **Laguna Mucubají**, the largest of Mérida's 200-plus glacial lakes, most full of trout, and **Mucuy Alto**.

A rather touristy but nonetheless interesting stop, about 20 minutes north of Mérida city, is **Los Aleros**, the reproduction of an entire Andean village as it would have looked before the highway came through. Along with traditional construction and period artifacts, demonstrators carry out daily chores and live music of the era and even a wedding are performed daily. Park creator Alexi Montilla followed up with the all-encompassing **Alexi's Venezuela de Antier**, between Mérida and the restored colonial village of **Jají**.

Views of Venezuela's snow-capped peaks, the highest of which is Bolívar, at

BELOW: national observatory near Apartados, Mérida state.

5,007 metres (16,427 ft), can be enjoyed in the year-round spring-like weather of the city of **Mérida** . Posadas around **Plaza Las Heroinas** (by the cable car station) are the gathering places for those wishing to do mountain activities like trekking, climbing and paragliding, with equipment rental, guides and *Toyoteros* – drivers of four-wheel-drive vehicles who take visitors to the remote mountain villages of Los Pueblos del Sur, or to entry points for excursions.

Mérida has the world's highest (4,765 metres/15,633 ft) and longest (12.5 km/ 8 miles) cable car – as of publication date, only open to the third station. The city has 43 parks and plazas, including **Los Chorros de Milla**, with mini zoo, pretty gardens, and its namesake cascade; and **El Acuario,** which has an aquarium and vignettes with life-size figures showing life in the Andes of the past. The new **Museo de Ciencia y Tecnología** is also worth a visit, as is the massive, eclectically-styled cathedral on the **Plaza Bolívar**.

No state more fully epitomizes the unique character of Venezuela's vast *llanos* (central plains) than **Apure**. Huge *hatos* (cattle ranches) covering thousands of hectares, the *llaneros* who work them, moriche palms, the traditional *joropo* music and dance, and an incredible abundance of wildlife are its trademarks. Some *hatos* can be reached by road, via the state capital of **San Fernando de Apure** from the east, or **Ciudad Nutrias** from the west; others are accessible only by private plane, boat, or four-wheel drive.

The Eastern Gold Coast

The marine paradise of **Los Roques Archipelago National Park** is only 35 minutes away by air, though both day-trips and overnight stays are very expensive. Along with excellent diving and beautiful (but shadeless) beaches,

Roadside basket shop in the Andes

BELOW: Plaza Bolívar, Mérida.

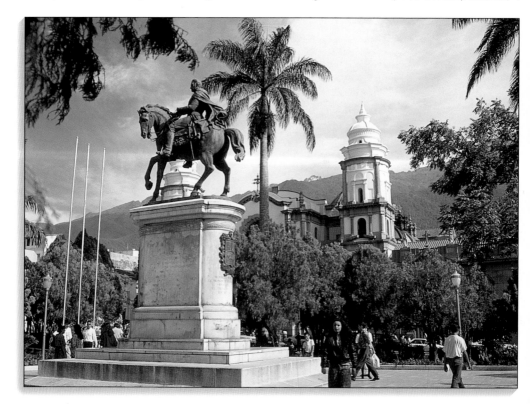

Los Roques offers unparalleled gamefishing. From Caracas to the "Route of the Sun," between Puerto La Cruz and Cumaná, follow the eastern coastal highway – avoid this route during Carnival, Holy Week and *puentes* (long weekends), as traffic comes to a standstill for hours. While most people head directly to Barcelona and Puerto La Cruz, other great beaches en route include the outer banks of the **Laguna de Unare** (enter via Boca de Uchire) and **Puerto Píritu**.

Barcelona, Anzoátegui state's capital, has a well-preserved historic zone with such attractions as the **Museo de Tradiciones**, along narrow streets bordered by vintage architecture. At the other extreme, beaches along a narrow neck of land lead to the mammoth **El Morro Tourist Complex**. Some 12 km (7½ miles) east along the coast lies **Puerto La Cruz ⑪** – action never stops along its beachfront boulevard, **Paseo Colón** (but leave swimming to island beaches, since the water here is contaminated). **Pozuelos Bay**, dotted with luxury yachts and traditional fishing boats, and the dramatic rocky islands of **Mochima National Park**, forms the seaward backdrop for the boulevard. A shuttle service is offered by a boatmen's union from the eastern end of the beach to the island beaches, with the best snorkeling and diving spots.

Continuing eastward along the coastal highway, you can stop off at beaches like **Playa Colorada** and **Arapito** on the way to **Cumaná ⑫**, Venezuela's oldest continental city (founded in 1521). A ferry crosses from Cumaná to the **Araya Peninsula ⑬**, landing near ruins of a colonial fort and pretty beach. Further east, try the fabulous beach of **Playa Medina** near the Río Caribe.

To the south, near **Caripe ⑭**, is the **Cueva del Guácharo** (officially Monumento Natural Alejandro Humboldt), the country's largest and most perfect cave, named for the *guácharos* (night-flying oil birds) which call it home.

Map on pages 110–11

TIP

The dry season (mid-November to the end of April) is the time to visit Los Llanos, when wildlife is concentrated around shrinking watering holes – for the rest of the year, rain is incessant and many places are inundated (or closed), with fauna widely dispersed.

BELOW: Caribbean islands of Los Roques Archipelago National Park.

La Asunción church,
Isla Margarita.

Margarita and the Pearl Islands

Isla Margarita, less than an hour by air from Maiquetía or two to four hours by ferry from Puerto La Cruz, is the main attraction of the three-island Pearl group which constitutes Nueva Esparta state. Water temperature varies from 73°F to 86° F around the island's numerous white sand beaches. Sporting activities include watersports, fishing and horseback riding. The island is beginning to rival Hawaii as a windsurfing hotspot – **El Yaque Beach** ⓑ is considered one of the world's top beaches for the sport. With numerous historical sites, a rich tradition of crafts, shopping (the island has more than 2,000 duty-free shops), lodging ranging from intimate posadas to luxury resorts, a multitude of restaurants and a lively nightlife, it is little wonder that Isla Margarita has become a prime tourist destination.

Spanish settlement of the Pearl Islands in 1500 was the first in all South America. The colonizers were attracted by the discovery of the first pearls found in the New World in the rich oyster beds surrounding the island of **Cubagua**. However, greed leading to over-harvesting, a devastating storm leveling the stone buildings, and pirates who took whatever the storm had not destroyed, brought an end to the settlement barely four decades later.

Ruins of the site (along with pristine beaches) on this nearly uninhabited island can be visited on day tours from **Porlamar** ⓰, Margarita's largest city. Most of the island's hotels and duty-free shops, plus numerous restaurants, night clubs and casinos are concentrated in downtown Porlamar. The city also has a ferry service to **Coche Island**, which is just beginning to develop its great tourism potential, with excellent windsurfing and several small resort hotels.

The majority of accommodation on Margarita is near the most popular

BELOW: Playa El
Agua, Margarita.

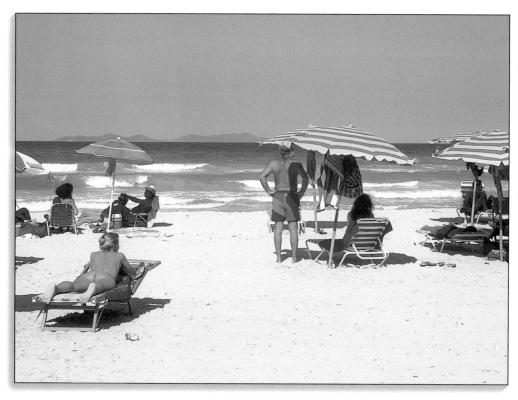

beaches. North of Porlamar, **Playa Guacuco** ⑰ has some tourist facilities. Further up the coast, Playa **El Agua** ⑱ is the most popular (a beautiful beach, but with a treacherous undertow). The beaches continue to **Manzanillo** ⑲, the islands's most northerly point, and down to the west.

The capital city **La Asunción** ⑳ is smaller and more peaceful than Porlamar. Sights in this historical town include the 16th-century colonial cathedral (one of the oldest churches in Venezuela), the **Museo de Nueva Cádiz**, which depicts the history of the town of the same name, destroyed by an earthquake in 1541, and the colonial fort **Castillo de Santa Rosa**. Ten kilometers (six miles) northeast, **Pampatar** ㉑ also has some interesting colonial buildings including a pretty colonial church and fortress.

The town of **Juangriego** ㉒, famed for its sunsets, offers a tranquil beach and nearby communities known for handicrafts. Pottery is made at **La Vecinidad** and **El Cercado**; basketry is the craft at **Pedrogonzález**; hammocks can be purchased at **Tacarigua**, and straw hats at **San Juan**. Within the town of **Tacuantar** is the artisan village **Taller de Arte Así con las Manos – Tierra, Agua y Fuego**. Contrasting with the bustling eastern half is the island's rugged, scarcely-populated **Macanao Peninsula** to the west. **La Restinga Lagoon National Park** lies along the narrow link between the two sections. Boatmen can take you through channels among mangrove swamps en route to the spectacular beach along the outer banks of the lagoon.

The Guayana Region: the last frontier

Venezuela's vast southern sector (encompassing Delta Amacuro, Bolívar, and Amazonas states) is known as the Guayana Region, named for its base, the Guayana Shield, composed of pre-Cambrian rock, among the oldest on the continent at 1.2 to 2.5 billion years. The most unique features in Bolívar and Amazonas are *tepuys*, mesas of ancient stone soaring majestically above the floor of the savannah or jungle. The most famous of these are **Roraima**, subject of Sir Arthur Conan Doyle's *Lost World* novella and **Auyantepui**, from which Angel Falls drops.

Except for a few kilometers of roads near the state capitals of **Delta Amacuro** (Tucupita) and **Puerto Ayacucho** (Amazonas), travel is almost exclusively by boat (though bush pilots can land by various Indian missions). Difficult access has been the greatest factor in maintaining the mystery, natural state, and allure of the region for adventure travelers.

The tourism potential in the huge delta of the **Orinoco River**, making up most of Delta Amacuro state, has only recently been exploited. Now some half a dozen rustic tourist camps operate here, with emphasis on observation of fauna and visits to the Warao Indians, principal inhabitants of this unique ecosystem. Warao means "the boat people," a name that relates to their only means of transport. Warao crafts, particularly basketry and open-work hammocks of moriche palm fibers, are highly prized.

Bolívar, Venezuela's largest, and one of the most richly endowed states, has huge reserves of gold, diamonds, iron, bauxite, hardwoods and water power

Map on pages 110–11

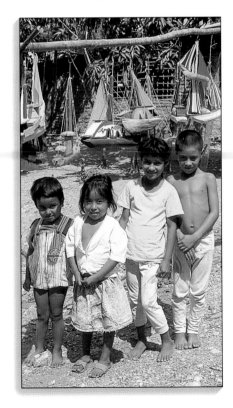

BELOW: roadside stalls on the "Route of the Sun," east of Caracas.

Obelisk marking the meeting place of three countries: Venezuela, Guyana and Brazil, on top of Roraima Tepuy.

BELOW: water-logged plant life on Roraima Tepuy.

from its great rivers. **Ciudad Guayana** ㉓, on the northern border, was created in 1961, as headquarters for development of Venezuela's heavy industry. Mammoth steel, iron, and aluminum plants use electricity generated at **Guri Dam**, one of the most powerful hydroelectric plants in the world, an hour to the southwest, with extremely interesting free tours. Tourist attractions include **Cachamay Falls** and **Park**, **Llovizna Park** and ruins of the colonial **Caroní Mission Church**. About an hour away are the 17th- and 18th-century forts known as **Los Castillos de Guayana La Vieja,** overlooking the Orinoco.

An hour west of Ciudad Guayana by freeway is **Ciudad Bolívar** ㉔, the state's capital, and an eminently historic city. Founded in 1764 on the banks of the Orinoco, it became a patriot stronghold, Simón Bolívar's base of operations, and capital of the Third Republic, 1817–21. It was also a gold center, and a thriving hub for goods going by river from the plains to the north coast.

The opening of the highway joining San Fernando de Apure with the central coast spelled the demise of the river trade and its commercial importance. But evidence of the city's prosperous past can be seen in the impressive architecture of the historic buildings, including the colonial **cathedral**, the **Museo Correo del Orinoco**, the **Museo Etnográfico de Guayana**, the **Casa del Congreso de Angostura**, and the **Museo Manuel Piar**. Other worthwhile stops are the **Museo de Arte Moderno Jesús Soto** (honoring the city's – and one of the nation's – most famous modern artists) and the **Quinta de San Isidro** (where Bolívar often stayed, now a museum). The **Angostura Bridge** can be observed from the river banks, the only span across the 2,140-km (1,330-mile) length of the Orinoco (all other crossings are by ferry). The rest of the state is mostly accessible only by small planes, with vast unexplored areas and a population of widely-scattered indigenous groups and miners.

The paved road, completed in 1991, linking Ciudad Guayana with **Santa Elena de Uairén**, by the frontier with Brazil, permits even city cars to traverse the length of Canaima National Park and famous Gran Sabana: along the highway, observe gently rolling hills of this vast savannah dotted with moriche palms; settlements of Pemón Indians with typical thatch-roofed, mud-walled dwellings; and stately tepuys in the distance (including the famed **Roraima**, the highest in the Guayana Region). There are numerous impressive falls along the roadside, including **Kama Merú** and **Quebrada de Jaspe**, with river bed and stair-step falls of semi-precious reddish-orange jasper! The mission of **Kavanayén** and the spectacular falls of **Chinak-Merú** can be visited by four-wheel-drive.

Canaima ㉕, one of the first areas in Venezuela to be developed for adventure travel, and a principal tourist destination, is in the northwest corner of the three million hectare Canaima National Park. The park is only accessible by air, and visitors can take day tours from Maiquetía, Porlamar or Ciudad Bolívar, or stay over at one of the lodges there. Canaima's principal draw is its proximity to **Angel Falls**, named after the American bush pilot Jimmy Angel, who is credited for "discovering" them in 1935. The falls are the world's longest, at 979 metres, of which 807 metres are free fall, and cascade over the edge of **Auyantepui**, the park's largest tepuy, which covers 700 sq. km (435 sq. miles). Weather permitting, visitors may get a look at the falls from the air. Excursions of several days' duration are offered from Canaima in the rainy season, from May to November.

A tenuous wilderness

Flying over Amazonas, with a vista as far as you can see of virgin tropical forest, interrupted only by the snaking black lines of rivers or occasional clearings centered with dwellings of an Indian community, engraves a lasting impression of the vastness of the state and the magnificence and diversity of nature it embraces. Though it covers an area larger than Portugal, Holland, and Denmark put together, Amazonas state only has about 45,000 inhabitants, most of whom belong to indigenous groups.

Paved roads extend only some 100 km (62 miles) from the capital, **Puerto Ayacucho ㉖**, in its northwestern extreme. The rapids of the Orinoco River near that city long prevented extensive penetration. The construction of various tourist camps, near the capital as well as deep in the interior, has allowed visitors to savor this extraordinary territory. Independent travelers can reach Puerto Ayacucho by car (or even bus) from Caracas via Caicara del Orinoco in about 10 hours, passing through landscapes dominated by enormous rounded stone formations called *laja*, and Panare and Guahibo communities. Do not miss Puerto Ayacucho's outstanding **Ethnological Museum**. Near the capital are the giant petroglyphs of **Tobogán de la Selva**, and the Piaroa and Guahibo Indian settlements. More distant (and costly) excursions by boat or charter plane include trips to **Autana**, the sacred mountain of the Piaroa, and visits to the Yanomami Indians, who are struggling to maintain their traditional rainforest lifestyle (*see page 48*). ❏

Prehistoric-looking outline formed by Caroní River, near Angel Falls.

BELOW: Angel Falls.

GUYANA

This lush, exotic and richly-forested former British colony is geographically larger than Britain, but has a tiny population

Map on page 128

Guyana means "Land of Many Waters" in a local Amerindian language. Life in this country on the northeast shoulder of South America is indeed dominated by its mighty rivers – the Essequibo, Demerara and Berbice. They act as highways into the rainforests, mountains and savannahs of the interior, regions which are, in turn, dissected by a network of lesser tributaries and creeks. Initially colonised by the Dutch in the 17th century, the territories which make up present-day Guyana came under British rule in 1814, and remained so until independence in 1966. It is populated mainly by the descendents of African slaves and indentured Indian workers, together with smaller numbers of Chinese and Portuguese, brought to work the sugar, coffee and cotton plantations of the coast. Amerindians, the original inhabitants, number just five percent.

Because of her colonial history, modern Guyana is South America's only English-speaking country, and is Caribbean in culture and outlook. However, unlike her Caribbean neighbours, Guyana has no palm-fringed powdery sand or limpid waters. Instead, the narrow coastal belt consists mainly of reclaimed swamps, marshland and deltas of the great rivers, rich in alluvial soil and intensively cultivated. These areas, and small towns such as **New Amsterdam ❶** and **Charity ❷**, are protected from the sea by a system of dams and dikes (a practice initiated by the Dutch). Ninety percent of the population, a mere 750,000 in a country larger than Britain, live on this coastal belt.

Georgetown ❸, the capital, lies below sea level on the east bank of the Demerara River. The city is laid out in a grid with wide streets lined with colonial buildings constructed of tropical hardwoods. The skyline is dominated by **St George's Anglican Cathedral**, said to be the world's largest wooden building; and the tower crowning the immense, covered Stabroek Market where the full pageant of Guyana's ethnic mix barters goods of every conceivable desciption, from manioc flour to gold. The **Georgetown Cricket Club** where test matches are played, and the pan-yards where steel bands prepare for the annual carnival, speak loudest of Guyana's Caribbean identity. Georgetown also has comfortable modern hotels and a lively nightlife. However, it is to explore the interior that the great majority of visitors travel to Guyana.

Towering forest and fabulous falls

Kaieteur Falls, the world's highest single-drop waterfall, is at the top of most visitors' lists. It is feasible to journey overland to the falls by driving to **Linden ❹**, the bauxite mining town, then continuing along a track through the rainforest to join the Potaro River for four days' struggle by boat against the current. It is

PRECEDING PAGES: Rupununi River, Guyana. **LEFT:** close to the edge, Kaieteur Falls, Guyana. **BELOW:** Bartica, Guyana.

Turtle petroglyph.

also just possible, at certain times of year, to journey to **Kangaruma ⑤**, near Kaieteur. The easier option is to fly by light aircraft from Georgetown. For about an hour and a half passengers gaze down at a disc filled to the horizon in every direction with forest, interrupted by glinting hairs of water. Occasionally they might identify tiny riverside settlements where solitary gold panners and diamond prospectors sieve for their fortunes.

Abruptly, the forest rises about 300 meters (1,000 ft) at the point where two folds of the earth's crust overlap. The Potaro River flows calmly through the forest, spills over and plunges down, uninterrupted for 226 meters (741 ft) of its 250-meter (822-ft) fall. Airborne tourists are usually treated to a full-frontal vista of the entire falls, before sweeping low over the foaming white cauldron and dropping down on a strip of jungle cleared for a runway. A mile-long forest trail leads to the falls, as the gathering roar seems to come from every direction, including below the ground. The viewing promontory is just yards from the falls. Thousands of gallons of black water flow over the lip every second, seemingly in slow motion, turning copper, yellow and finally a foaming white frenzy.

If this doesn't give you your fill of falls, you can fly for 30 minutes on to **Orinduik Falls**. Here the Ireng River thunders over a series of steps and terraces on a fold of rock which marks Guyana's border with Brazil. Although Orinduik does not offer the full, elemental drama of Kaieteur, the location is stunningly beautiful with views over the rolling, grass-covered Pakaraimae Hills.

Rainforest idyll

A stay at at rainforest lodge is another feature of Guyana's fledgling tourist industry. The most comfortable and genuine of these is **Timberhead**, reached from Georgetown by whooshing up the wide, aptly brown sugar-coloured Demerara River, then chugging up the oozing Kamuni Creek, its waters blackened by decomposing vegetation. The banks are overhung with undergrowth supported by aerial roots. Enormous Blue Morpho butterflies flitter about in abundance. Parrots and toucans flash in the foliage, and troupes of monkeys can be heard crashing through the branches overhead. There are jaguars, pumas, tiger cats and bush pigs in the forest, though sightings are rare.

Further south, along the upper reaches of the Rupununi River, the landscape changes dramatically into savannah grassland bordered by a ridge of mountains pricking the horizon. Here *vaqueros* (cowboys) ride across the plains, barefoot in the stirrup, rounding up their cattle.

A flight over the rainforest to the airstrip at **Lethem** ❻ near the Brazilian border takes you to the heart of this region. A trip across the savannahs by open-backed jeep reaches **Dadanawa Ranch**. From here, visitors ride horses into the mountain foothills, where streams refresh the scenery. Nights can be spent under the stars, after meals of beef roasted on open fires. The area is a bird-watchers and naturalists' dream. The most dedicated book into the Rock View Eco-Tourism Resort at **Annai** ❼, where the savannah meets the Pakaraima Mountains. Harpy eagles and giant otters are among the trophy sightings.

As you fly over Guyana's endless rainforest, it's easy to believe that there are forest-dwellers who have never had contact with the outside world. As recently as the 1960s, contact was made for the first time with the Wai-Wai, a tribe living as hunter-gathers between the Essequibo and Amazon watersheds. To minimise the impact on their culture, very few expeditions into their territory are permitted, and every potential participant is interviewed.   ❏

Map on page 128

Jungle lodges are rustic but with basic comforts.

BELOW:
Orinduik Falls.

Map on page 128

SURINAM

This little-known former Dutch colony has a fascinating cultural mix in its sleepy coastal towns and in its swathes of rainforest

The 1667 Peace of Breda treaty granted New York to Britain and Surinam to The Netherlands. In the intervening centuries the two places have become, respectively, perhaps the most renowned city on Earth, and one of the world's most obscure countries. The irony is not lost among Surinamese, for many of whom it is self-evident that the Dutch got the better deal.

Surinam is the former Dutch Guiana, sandwiched between Guyana (formerly British Guiana) and Guayane, or French Guiana, which remains officially a department of France. The Surinam coast was first settled by English and Dutch merchants in 1613, followed by Jews from Holland, Italy and Brazil. Slaves were shipped from West Africa to work the plantations, mainly of sugar and cotton. Imports of slaves were banned in 1818, and slavery itself abolished in 1863. During this period, Indians, Pakistanis, Chinese and Javanese from Dutch Indonesia arrived as indentured labourers. Add to these the indigenous Amerindians, the Africans, the Brazilian Jews and the Europeans, and the result is one of the most extraordinary ethnic cocktails in the world.

Surinam gained independence from Holland in 1975. Since then, relations between the two countries have rollercoastered, reaching a low point in 1982 when military dictator Colonel Desi Bouterse, who had seized power two years earlier, had 15 opposition leaders executed. Economic aid was terminated and diplomatic relations severed, not to be restored for five years, when democratic elections were held again. Meanwhile, huge numbers of Surinamese emigrated to The Netherlands, leaving a depleted population which today numbers little more than 400,000. The official language is Dutch, while Sranan Tongo, an English-based Creole, is widely used as a lingua franca.

Surinam's sleepy capital

As in the other Guyanas, roughly 90 percent of the people live in towns strung along the loamy mud flats of the coast. The capital, **Paramaribo** ❽, is a small, quiet city of faded and peeling colonial wooden buildings arranged in a grid pattern, on the west bank of the Surinam River. It is hard to comprehend the violence and upheavals of the 1980s as you wander the sleepy squares graced by statues of Simón Bolívar and Mahatma Gandhi. (Home-grown Surinamese heroes and potentates are thin on the ground.)

Surinam is remarkably free of racial tension. The synagogue stands fraternally next to the mosque. Down the road, the wooden **Saint Peter and Paul Cathedral** is undergoing resoration. The **museum**, in the old Dutch **Fort Zeelandia** is a modest affair. The **central market** is more lively; the aroma of spices brought from India and sold by sari-draped

BELOW: Islamic mosque, central Paramaribo.

women, mingles with the smells of fresh shrimps sold by African fishermen.

A popular day trip from Paramaribo is to cross the Surinam River by ferry to the Dutch fort of **Nieuw Amsterdam**, and drive eastwards along the coast, through the old Jewish settlement of **Jodensavanne** ❾ and the bauxite-mining town of **Moengo**. The road ends at **Albina** ❿, a thriving little frontier town on the Marowijne, the river border with Guyane. Another road, westwards, passes through the village of **Totness** ⓫, curious only for its name, which dates back to a Scottish settlement that has long since dispersed. The only other town on the road is **Wageningen**, the rice-growing centre, before **Nieuw Nickerie** ⓬, the border town with Guyana at the mouth of the Corantijn.

Into the forest

Like its neighbors, the majority of Surinam's territory is covered by dense, virgin rainforest, cut through by great, black rivers. In "Operation Grasshopper," a government-sponsored scheme, a few short airstrips deep in the darkest interior have been hacked out of the forest. Near three of these, the Movement for Eco-Tourism in Surinam (METS – owned by Surinam Airways), have built simple lodges where visitors can experience life in the rainforest.

Fish market, Paramaribo.

BELOW: Surinam River.

Two of them are on islands in the **Gran Rio**, in the heart of Saramaccan country. The Saramaccans are a tribe of so-called "Bush Negroes," the descendents of African slaves who escaped as rebellions swept through the newly established plantations on Surinam's coast. They speak a hybrid language of West African dialects, smattered with English, Dutch and Portuguese words learnt on the plantations. Many of their practices – their drum-playing, dancing and animist religious beliefs – can be traced directly to West Africa. Other means of forest survival were learnt from indigenous Amerindians. For example, they cultivate manioc on small slash-and-burn clearings, and build tightly huddled villages roofed with strips of plaited palm.

A typical visit to this area begins with a light aircraft flight to **Kayana Airstrip**, and transfer in a motorised dug-out canoe up to **Awarradam Lodge** at some impassable rapids. Here, the air is heavy and moist. The double wolf-whistles of Screaming Piha and a cacophony of croaks, caws and the occasional growl of a howler monkey, float over the canopy. Sightings of larger creatures are rare – unless you count the peccary (bush pig), shot or trapped in the forest, which the lodge's Bush Negro staff roast on open fires. However, the Black Caiman, an Amazonian crocodile up to 6 feet (2 meters) long, is common. They are often seen lazing by the bank during the all-day canoe trip to **Kavalu Island**, facing the Bush Negro village of **Asidonopo**. Outsiders are usually welcomed by the village chief or "Kapiteni" and introduced to villagers who sing as they spin cotton or grate manioc, while mischievous naked children follow.

Palumeu, the third lodge, is next to an Amerindian village deeper into the interior on the Tapanahony River, a tributary of the Marowijne. Palameu is the most stunningly located of all the lodges, on a broad hillside clearing with sweeping river views, but the people are shyer and interaction can be awkward. ❏

Map on page 128

FRENCH GUIANA

Formerly home to a notorious penal colony, this heavily forested and naturally diverse département of France is today the launch site for Europe's Ariane rockets

To the east of Surinam lies the small French colony of French Guiana, almost a fifth of the size of France with more than 300 km (190 miles) of coastline. Eighty percent of the inhabitants live in the coastal regions, as beyond the coast lies a dense carpet of Amazon rainforest.

Ancient petroglyphs near the village of Kaw bear testimony to thousands of years of human habitation in the area, but as in neighboring countries, European colonization, from the early 17th century, dramatically changed the ethnographic make-up of the region. The territory was tenuously held by the French in the face of short-lived appropriations by the British, Dutch and Brazilian Portuguese. African slaves were brought in to work the plantations, to be replaced when slavery was abolished by indentured laborers from other parts of the French Empire, notably Indo-China. After a minor gold rush in the 1850s the territory became best known as a brutal penal colony, immortalised in the novel *Papillon* by Henri Charrière, and in the famous film of the same name. The Jewish army officer Alfred Dreyfus, whose imprisonment for treason in the 1890s caused a political storm, was held at the notorious Devil's Island.

French Guiana became an overseas *département* of France in 1946. In the 1960s a satellite and space exploration center was established at Kourou, which

BELOW:
Devil's Island.

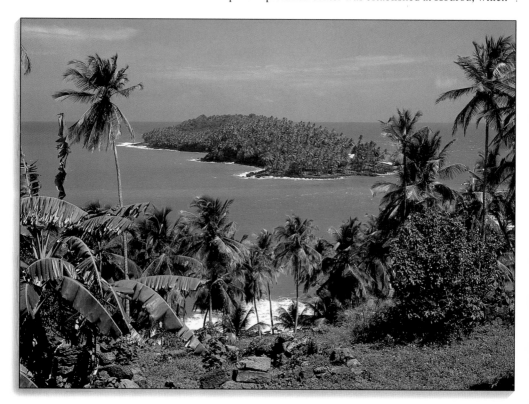

brought jobs and urban development, but the rest of the country has suffered unemployment and economic stagnation. The population is highly racially-mixed, with input from Africa, Europe, native South America, China and Vietnam. There are many Amerindian groups living in the rainforest areas, and also communities of "Noir Marrons", or Bush Negros, descendents of African slaves, who live in a traditional African manner with Amerindian influences along the banks of the River Maroni.

Cayenne ⓭, French Guiana's capital, has some interesting colonial buildings, but is considered a relatively expensive town. The **Musée Départemental** has a mix of historical and archeological artefacts including some exhibits on the penal colonies. There is a vegetable and flower market, and a fish market on Wednesdays, Fridays and Saturdays.

The town of **Kourou** ⓮, 55 km (34 miles) northeast of Cayenne, revolves around the **French Guiana Space Center**. There is a **Space Museum** (Mon-Fri and Sat afternoons; entrance fee), from where rocket launches can be witnessed. The modern part of town, known locally as the "white city" due to the preponderance of families from mainland France, is very different from the more traditional old village at the mouth of the Kourou River. Boats are available from here to the three **Îles du Salut** ⓯, which lie 15 km (nine miles) to the north. The famous **Île du Diable** (Devil's Island) is inaccessible due to hazardous landing conditions, but accommodation is available on the Île Royale.

The Transportation Camp at **St Laurent du Maroni** ⓰, 250 km (150 miles) north east of Cayenne, was the largest prison in the territory, and can be visited. The town also has a rum distillery (open Mon-Fri, mornings; free), and dugout canoes can be hired for trips on the Maroni River. About 40 km (25 miles) north of St Laurent, at the mouth of the Maroni and Mana rivers, is **Les Hattes Beach**, which is a breeding site for leatherback turtles. The laying season is from April to July and hatching takes place from July to September. The turtles have no shell but a dark blue leathery skin, and measure up to 170 cms (67 ins) long when fully grown. Nearby is the Amerindian village of **Awala Yalimapo**.

The interior of French Guiana has much to interest naturalists and adventure seekers. Roughly 60 km (40 miles) south of Cayenne are the **Kaw Marshes**, an area of forest and mangrove swamps rich in birdlife and inhabited by the rare black caiman. Houseboat accommodation is available in the village of **Kaw** ⓱. At **Montsinéry**, 43 km (27 miles) southwest of Cayenne, a botanical hiking trail leads to the **Annamite Penal Colony**, where deported Indo-Chinese were detained. Other hiking trails lead to waterfalls and wildlife-infested creeks. The interior can also be explored by *pirogue*, or dugout canoe.

South of Cayenne, the village of **Cacao** is inhabited by a Hmong community of Laotian descent. Visitors can sample traditional Hmong cuisine, and Hmong handicrafts can be purchased. There are inland jungle expeditions centered around the gold-mining village of **Saül** ⓲, and in the west, the town of **Maripasoula** ⓳, home to Bush Negro communities, is a popular expedition destination. ❑

Painted "maluana" disk of the Wayana people.

BELOW: children in the Place Leopoldo, Cayenne.

ANDEAN HIGHLANDS

The ancient heart of the subcontinent, these high-altitude countries continue to fascinate, both for their imperial past and for the rich cultural heritage they proudly maintain

Clustered around some of the most inhospitable territory in South America are the countries of the Andean highlands: Peru, Bolivia and Ecuador. The area was home to some of the world's most extraordinary civilizations for thousands of years before being finally united by the Inca empire in the 14th century. Although the Incas were the most famous rulers of South America, they had a relatively brief moment of glory before the Spanish conquistadors crushed them into submission (*see page 26*). The colonists subsequently kept themselves distant from their subjects and to this day the old Inca lands are dual societies: one indian, impoverished and traditional; the other *mestizo* or white, looking to Europe or the United States for cultural inspiration.

Nowhere is this more so than in the Inca heartland of Peru. The capital, Lima (*see page 146*), lies on the barren coast facing the sea, while the ancient capital of Cuzco (*see page 152*), regarded by the Incas as the navel of the world, remains in the mountains, nursing its shattered past. From these two cultural poles Peru's many wonders can be reached: the ancient Inca Trail leads from Cuzco to Machu Picchu (*see page 158*), arguably South America's most spectacular ancient city. In the south are the baffling Nazca lines (*see page 150*); in the north the ancient adobe city of Chan Chan (*see pages 164-5*). The world's deepest canyons are near the colonial city of Arequipa (*see page 159*). Peru's Amazon region (*see page 161*), is unforgettable, despite being opened up to settlement at breakneck speed.

Across from Lake Titicaca (*see page 170*) is the land-locked mountain country of Bolivia. The most ethnically native American and the poorest of South America's republics, this is a land of ancient traditions and colonial relics. Carved from the bleak *altiplano* or "high plain," La Paz is the highest capital city in the world (*see page 177*). In the shadow of spectacular peaks, the nearby Yungas (*see page 182*) is a sub-tropical region of banana, coffee and coca leaf. Back in the windswept heights is the town of Potosí (*see page 190*), once the Spanish empire's main source of silver and still a mining town.

To the north of Peru is the Republic of Ecuador. This compact country can be explored in short trips from the mountain capital Quito (*see page 201*), a colonial gem now placed on the World Heritage list. Nearby is the town of Otavalo (*see page 202*), famous for a remarkable weaving tradition which is attracting new wealth, while around the capital are mountains and nature reserves (*see page 205*). A short jump east lands you in the steamy Oriente jungle (*see page 209*). In the west lie the Pacific beaches of Ecuador's coast (*see page 212*), 600 miles beyond which are the country's pride and joy: the marvelous wildlife-rich Galápagos Islands (*page 214*). ❑

PRECEDING PAGES: pre-Columbian gold mask; Peruvian llamas.
LEFT: traditional weaver, near Cuzco.

PERU

Map on page 144

The birthplace of ancient empires, Peru has towering mountains, steaming rainforests and parched deserts. It's the ultimate destination for culture seekers, adventurers and eco-tourists

N o other country in South America, possibly in the whole world, has such an astonishing archeological heritage as Peru. Most tourists come to see the monumental citadel of Machu Picchu – the other big archeological attraction is the mysterious desert lines of Nazca, which can only be viewed from the air. This is a country literally packed with archeological wonders – the fabulous remains of Inca and pre-Inca civilizations housed in numerous museums, as well as countless pyramids and ruined cities, many still unexcavated. Then there are the treasures of the colonial period which gild the magnificent cities of Cuzco and Arequipa. Lima, the capital, once the center of the Spanish empire in South America, is an exciting city that moves at a frenetic pace. Many of its colonial buildings fell victim to earthquakes and urban planning, but it still has some beautiful architecture and an enormous range of museums.

Peru is an exceptional country even for those who don't have an interest in history or archeology. Arid desert in the south and the splendid Pacific coastline with beaches that attract surfers from around the world give way abruptly to the snowy heights of the Andes mountain range that edges along the country's coastal belt. Beyond the Andes lies the Amazon basin, a rainforest area teeming with exotic plants, insects, birds and animals.

Tourism is rapidly developing as this is a country that recognises the importance of protecting its rich natural and historical heritage. But poverty is still widespread, from the poor indigenous communities eking out a living in the barren Andean plains to the people who inhabit Peru's volatile coastline, which is frequently hit by drought, earthquakes, and in the late 1990s, by the floods brought by El Niño, which causes upheavals every couple of decades in this area.

Peru is a developing country, but lingering poverty together with the residue of unresolved social and political conflict and guerrilla activity has left a legacy of lawlessness in some areas, and visitors should check the situation with their country's embassy before they go. Most areas of tourist interest are quite safe, although there have been reports of mugging in and around Cuzco and Lima – personal effects should not be flaunted. Take care, but don't let such reports spoil your trip – thousands of tourists enjoy the wonders of Peru without encountering any trouble at all.

Peru after independence

José de San Martín proclaimed Peru's independence in Lima on July 28, 1821, although most of the country was still held by the Spanish crown. Simón Bolívar finished the job of freeing the country and, in 1826, the last Spanish troops surrendered. The first years of independence saw few real changes in the

PRECEDING PAGES: the Colca Canyon.
LEFT: portal of Lima Cathedral.
BELOW: Quechua girl.

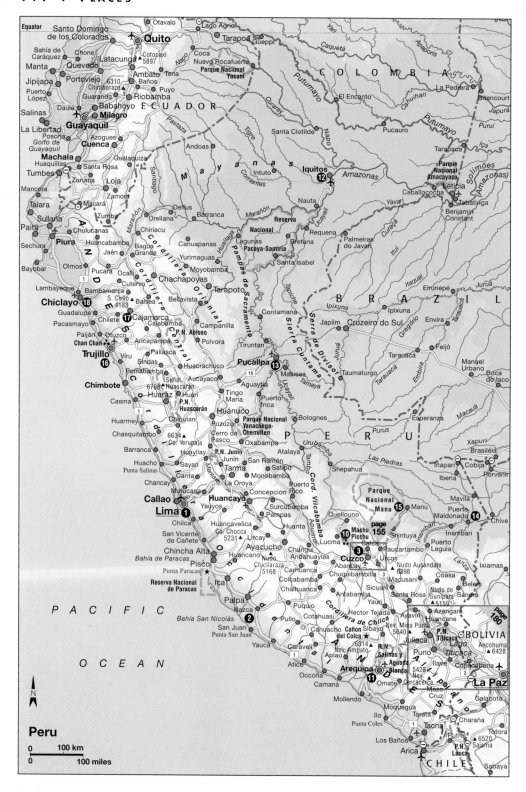

Peru

0   100 km
0   100 miles

way that Peruvians lived. But midway through the century, military man Mariscal Ramón Castilla took over the presidency, and under his rule modernization shook the country. Basic services such as water and street lights were installed in Lima and a rail line – the first on the continent – linked the capital with the nearby port of Callao. Castilla abolished slavery and directed approval of the 1860 national constitution. But setbacks were incurred in the bloody War of the Pacific, which lasted from 1879 to 1883. Despite these tumultuous changes, life in the 19th century continued much as in the 17th for the bulk of the population: the Indians living in the highlands. The two worlds of Peru, the "Indian" and the "European", were drifting further apart.

Map on page 144

Colonial door knocker.

A divided nation

Of all the nations of South America, Peru saw the most important clash between the native and European cultures – a clash that has continued to modern times, proving fertile ground for terrorism in the highlands, an energetic chaos in Lima and an amazing creativity. Peru has been run by a number of military strongmen. Most intriguing among them was the left-wing military dictator General Juan Velasco Alvarado, who undertook a flawed agrarian reform program, temporarily turned over the biggest newspaper – *El Comercio* – to a peasant group and renamed all of Lima's streets after national heroes. An example is Avenida Wilson, named after the US president, which the dictator relabeled Garcilaso de la Vega after the mestizo who chronicled the Spanish conquest of Peru.

Sprinkled amongst these dictators have been 30 elected presidents, all of them conservatives until the 1985 election of left-of-center Alan García Pérez. The charismatic García drew popular support from the poor and non-urban dwellers who cheered his decision not to pay the foreign debt incurred by past governments. But the US cutoff in development aid, the unwillingness of businesses to invest in the country and political maneuvering by the far left and far right sent the nation of nearly 20 million into an economic crisis in late 1988 after two years of growth. Prices of food and gasoline doubled overnight on more than one occasion, the currency devalued rapidly, and people spent days in passport lines before heading to Venezuela or the United States in search of jobs.

BELOW: macaw, Peruvian Amazon.

The political division and social upheaval accompanying García's presidency opened the way for an independent candidate, Alberto Fujimori, to take over as president. Having attracted controversy for temporarily dissolving Congress after he took power, Fujimori got the economy sufficiently under control to win a second term in 1995. He also succeeded in weakening the guerrilla group *Sendero Luminoso* (Shining Path), whose activities in the mountains had severely affected tourism in the 1980s. After waging a savage campaign against the guerrillas, government forces captured their leader, Abimael Guzmán, in 1992. Since then many other guerrilla leaders have defected, and the terrorist situation is largely under control, although there have been sporadic incidents, most notably the Japanese Embassy siege of 17 December 1996, when 13 members of the Movimiento

Revolucionario Tupac Amaru took nearly 500 guests celebrating the Japanese Emperor's birthday hostage. One hostage died during the seige, which was ended when Peru's special command stormed the embassy on 22 April, 1997.

Lima: capital of the New World

Spanish conquistador Francisco Pizarro considered the site where he founded **Lima** ❶ on January 18, 1535, inhospitable: rain seldom fell, earthquakes were common and winter was a time of gray skies and dreary wet fog. But his soldiers saw it as the best place for a quick sea escape in the event of an Indian uprising. Little did they suspect this open plain would become the political and military capital of the New World, seeing the reigns of 40 viceroys before the "City of Kings" was declared capital of an independent Peru in 1821.

The **Plaza Mayor** (formerly the Plaza de Armas) is where for centuries the power of the new colony was concentrated, and it remains one of the city's most active and attractive squares. At its center are rose gardens, a stone fountain and park benches that draw young couples looking for a place to chat, countless shoeshine boys and families in their Sunday best posing for photos. A favorite photo is one with the **Palacio de Gobierno** in the background. The foundation of this building is the same that Pizarro built, but its façade was changed in the early 1900s. When President Alan García Pérez took power in 1985, he eliminated the Prussian-style helmets and elaborate uniforms the president's military guard had worn for years, calling them too showy. You can see their more modern garb every day at 12 noon during the ceremonial changing of the guards, but visits have to be pre-arranged in the Oficina de Turismo of the Municipalidad. The best spot for viewing the ceremony is the wide front balcony of the **Palacio Municipal**. The original structure used as a city hall burned down in 1923, but its neoclassical replacement is impressive, with marble stairways, gilt mirrors and crystal chandeliers. Don't leave without seeing the library. This small room with massive leather chairs, huge wooden tables and a smell of old books offers a calming respite from the traffic outside. Its circular stairway was hand-carved from a single piece of Nicaraguan cedar.

Across the square, the **Archbishop's Palace** has one of the most beautiful wooden mudejar style balconies in the city. Take a peek in the archbishop's patio before heading next door to the **cathedral**, which contains Pizarro's remains. A block away is the **Museo Banco Central de Reserva**, with a small but impressive pre-Columbian collection (open Tues-Fri; weekends 10am–1pm). Nearby is the splendid **Palacio de Torre Tagle**, constructed in 1735, now used as the Foreign Ministry. A few blocks to the northeast is the jewel of Lima's old churches, **San Francisco monastery.** Lovingly repaired after every earthquake that damaged it in the past four centuries, this cloister features fine mosaic tiles from Seville, frescoes discovered when an earthquake demolished portions of an outer wall, and an impressive collection of religious art. Most fascinating are its catacombs, which served as Lima's cemetery through the colonial period.

Saints and sinners

Behind the Palacio de Gobierno is **Estación Desamparados** (railway station), the city's first iron building. Brought in pieces by boat from England and rebuilt here in 1908, it was formerly the depot for all trains out of the capital, but is no longer in operation. Also behind the president's office is the bridge that leads to **Rimac Ⓐ**, one of Lima's oldest neighborhoods, named after the river that flows

Maps
Area 144
City 146

BELOW: changing of the guard, Plaza Mayor, Lima.

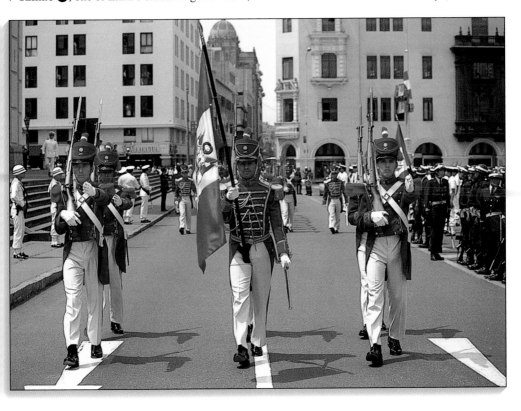

along its edge. A working-class *barrio*, where women in doorways chat with their neighbors while children play soccer in the streets, it once was the city's top spot for promenading. Then, the stars were the *tapadas* (*see below*) – seductive women whose skirts shamelessly showed their tiny feet, whose necklines were scandalously low and whose heads and shoulders were covered by a veil that bared only one eye. In the afternoons, they were most likely to be found on the **Alameda de los Descalzos**, courting and flirting but never lifting their Moorish-style veils to reveal their identities. This promenade, built in 1611, is lined with Italian marble statues representing the months of the year and bordered by lawns and flowers. It leads to the **Convento de los Descalzos**, or Monastery of the Shoeless, whose friars wore only sandals on their feet.

Lima was home to two of South America's most famous saints: Rosa de Lima and Martín de Porres. Rosa, who died of tuberculosis at age 31, had a fervent following during her short lifetime and was credited with curing thousands, performing innumerable miracles and even saving the city from pirate attacks. For Martín de Porres, fame came after his death. He lived in the **Santo Domingo** monastery in Jirón Camaná, but was barred from becoming a priest because he was black. His duties in the monastery included working as the janitor, and statues and paintings of the saint usually show him with a broom in hand. Both saints are buried in Santo Domingo, which is open to visitors.

Lima's religious devotion may have been proportional to the terror inflicted by the Holy Inquisition. Chills will run up your spine when you descend into the depths of the **Museo de la Inquisición** in Plaza Bolívar (open Mon-Fri; Sat 9am-12 noon; free). Gruesome tortures were inflicted to obtain "confessions" of heresy, Judaism and witchcraft. The "guilty" had their property confiscated

BELOW: the scandalous *tapadas*, or "covered ones".

THE SCANDALOUS TAPADAS

If the 17th century was Lima's religious period, the 18th century was its romantic era when poetry, promenading and pomp were the mainstay. It was during this time that the tapadas appeared, the shockingly sensual upper class mestizo women. It wasn't long before a rivalry arose between these flirtatious tapadas and the more reserved Europeans. While the Spanish females cinched their skirts to show their tiny waistlines and fluttered fans before the eyes of admirers, the mestizos narrowed their skirts to emphasize their ample hips and bared their arms. But they always kept their faces veiled – with the exception of one eye. French feminist Flora Tristan, visiting her father's homeland, described the tapada's Moorish costume as a "skirt... so tight that it allows just enough room to put one foot in front of the other and to take very little steps.

This costume so alters a woman – even her voice since her mouth is covered – that unless she is very tall or very short, lame, hunchbacked or otherwise conspicuous, she is impossible to recognize. I am sure it needs little imagination to appreciate the consequences of this time-honored practice which is sanctioned or at least tolerated by law." Those "consequences" ranged from men unknowingly flirting with their own wives to infidelity.

and were marched off to the Plaza de Armas (now Plaza Mayor) to await their fate, which ranged from public flogging to burning at the stake.

Map on page 146

Lima's most active square is **Plaza San Martín**, linked to the Plaza Mayor by the pedestrian walkway **Jirón de la Unión**, once the most fashionable shopping district in the Peruvian capital. Plaza San Martín is where most of the money changing houses are located (alongside the Gran Bolívar Hotel). A few hundred meters south of the plaza, the **Museo de Arte ❸** has an extensive collection of pre-Columbian and colonial relics (open Tue-Sun; admission fee).

Outside the city center

Some of the most interesting museums, shops and beaches are located in Lima's suburbs, accessible by bus or taxicab from downtown. Just south of the city center, on Av. Javier Prado Este, is the excellent **Museo de la Nación ❹** (open daily; small fee), with artefacts from prehistoric times to the present, attractively displayed (Spanish only). The **Museo de Oro ❺** (Gold Museum) is further south, in the suburb of Monterrico (open daily; entrance fee). It has a striking collection of pre-Columbian gold, silver and other artefacts.

Craftsman with gold jewelry.

Southwest of the center, in the suburb of Pueblo Libre, is the **Museo Arqueológico Rafael Larco Herrera ❻** (open Mon–Sat; Sun 9am to 1pm; entrance fee). Primarily a pottery museum, it has a fascinating collection, with a separate annex housing Moche erotica and warehouses open to the public which display an astonishing number of artefacts from the prolific Moche potters – a virtual photo-gallery of Moche life. Also in Pueblo Libre is the **Museo Nacional de Antropología y Arqueología ❼** (open Tue-Sat; small fee), with informative pre-Columbian displays and some colonial paintings. In the suburb of San Isidro, brilliant red bougainvillea grow beside the pre-Inca burial site of **Huallamarca**. It has a small museum with mummies and artefacts.

BELOW: elaborate colonial façade.

In the suburb of **Miraflores ❽**, stomping ground of the children of Peru's wealthy families, you can people-watch at outdoor cafés, shop or enjoy good meals and music. The pretensions of the Miraflores youths – the *Mirafloriños* – are described with precision in the novels of Mario Vargas Llosa. Miraflores is the best place for theaters, trendy boutiques and nightclubs. Nearby is **Barranco ❾**, the romantic bohemian neighborhood made immortal in Peruvian waltz and still home to the city's best artists, poets and jazz bars. Here you'll find the lover's lane, **Puente de los Suspiros**, or Bridge of the Sighs, lined by fragrant jasmine trees and hyacinth bushes. It heads down to a lookout point over the Pacific Ocean, and to a steep stairway to the beach. Strolling here at sunset you may hear Peruvian flute music or Argentine tangos wafting from windows.

The most important archeological site near Lima is **Pachacámac**, 31 km (19 miles) south of the city, and accessible by bus or tour from the city center. Rising to prominence in about AD 700, this pre-Inca shrine was later used as an Inca temple for adoration of the sun god, and it is believed that the Inca Huayna Capac once had a residence here. Francisco Pizarro used the buildings for a residence of his own.

The mysterious Nazca lines

Until the 1930s, **Nazca** ❷ was like any other small Peruvian town, with no claim to fame except that you had to cross one of the world's driest deserts to reach it from Lima. But that desert has since drawn thousands to this tiny, sun-bleached colonial town, which was devastated by an earthquake in 1996. The *pampa*, or plain, north of the city, has become one of the greatest scientific mysteries in the Americas. The Nazca lines are a series of drawings of animals, geometric figures and birds ranging up to 300 meters (1,000 ft) in size, scratched on to the arid crust of the desert and preserved for about 2,000 years, owing to a complete lack of rain and unique winds that clean – but have not erased – the pampa. The huge figures that the lines form can only be seen from the air.

In 1939, North American scientist Paul Kosok, flying over the dry coast in a small plane, noticed the lines that were previously believed to be part of a pre-Inca irrigation system. A specialist in irrigation, he quickly concluded that this had nothing to do with water systems. By chance, the day of the flight coincided with the summer solstice and, on a second flight, Kosok discovered that the line of the sunset ran tandem to the direction of one of the bird drawings. He dubbed the Nazca pampa "the biggest astronomy book in the world". But it was a young German mathematician who became the expert on the lines and put Nazca on the map. Maria Reiche was 35 when she met Kosok, and he encouraged her to study the pampa. She dedicated the next half century to the task.

Unraveling the mysteries

Reiche, who died in 1998 at the age of 95, devoted her life to studying the lines, which she measured, cleaned, analyzed and charted daily from the air and from

BELOW: aerial view of hummingbird design, Nazca lines.

a 15-meter (49 feet) high platform she built. She developed the most widely accepted theories on the hundreds of drawings that cover a 50-km (31 miles) belt
between Nazca and Palpa, describing them as an "astronomical calendar."

"This work was done so that the gods could see it and, from above, help the
ancient Peruvians with their farming, fishing and all their other activities," said
Reiche. For example, she speculated that the drawing of the monkey was the
Nazca symbol for the Big Dipper, the constellation representing rain. When
rain was overdue – a common occurrence in this plain where it only rains the
equivalent of about half an hour every two years – the monkey was sketched so
that the gods, looking down, would be reminded that the earth was parched.

Reiche also shed light on how the Nazca people could have made the huge
sketches with such symmetry. She determined that they used a basic unit of
measurement, probably the distance from their elbows to their forefingers, and
based all calculations upon this. As for symmetry, Reiche believed they used
ropes tied to stakes to form circles and arcs that they cut with straight lines.

There are, of course, those who do not accept Reiche's theories, denying that
the Nazca people would have drawn something they themselves could not see.
Because the drawings are only visible from the air, the International Explorers
Club set out in 1975 to prove a theory that the Nazcas had aircraft. They made
a hot air balloon, the *Condor I*, out of cloth and reed, and flew it for 60 seconds,
reaching an altitude of 100 meters (328 feet). But the flight proved little.

Pre-Columbian mummy, Chauchilla cemetery, Nazca.

Extra-terrestrial runways

The most damaging theory about the Nazca lines came seven years earlier,
when Erik Von Daniken published *Chariots of the Gods*, in which he proposed
that the pampa was part of an extra-terrestrial landing
strip – an idea that Reiche discarded impatiently. Von
Daniken's book drew thousands of visitors to the
lines, but newcomers in search of the drawings set
out across the pampa on motorcycles, four-wheel-
drive vehicles and even horses, leaving unerasable
marks of their visits. Now it is illegal to drive or even
walk on the pampa: Reiche used the profits from her
book, *Mystery on the Desert*, to pay four guards to
keep a constant watch on the plain.

There is a metal ladder at the side of the Pan American highway if you want to view the pampa from
ground level, although there is not much to see from
so low. The best way to capture the impact of the lines
is to fly over them. AeroCondor offers flights from
Lima, Ica and the small airport in Nazca, and flights
can be booked at the Alegria, Montecarlo, Nazca and
Turistas hotels. Flights last up to 45 minutes and can
be bumpy – skip breakfast unless you have an iron
stomach. Lunch and a stop at the **archeological museum** in downtown Nazca is included in the day-long
Lima package. Aeroica in Nazca also has 45-minute
flights over the lines. If you want to make the flight
more economical, some of the pilots at the Nazca
airstrip may be open to offers.

From the ground, the Nazca pampa is hot, dry and
dusty, but from the air it is a puzzle that will thrill you
as you try to decipher the lines and figures.

BELOW: detail from
an ancient Paracas
textile.

Map on page 144

Ceramic bull on a rooftop for good luck, Cuzco.

Cuzco: capital of the Inca Empire

The people who sell goods in Cuzco's market speak Spanish with tourists and Quechua with one another. The buildings behind them are colonial style, built on Inca foundations. The elaborately carved façades on the city's many churches have detailed scenes of angels, saints and biblical characters – but their facial features are Indian. **Cuzco ❸** stands as a living testimony to the fact that the Inca civilization – one of the world's most sophisticated – could not be erased.

Of course, the Cuzco of today is dramatically different from the awesome city that Francisco Pizarro and his conquistadors found when they reached the capital of the Inca Empire, home to that kingdom's noblemen, priests and their servants. Five hundred years ago, an estimated 15,000 people lived in the city, which was linked to the rest of the empire by way of the *chasquis* – the long-distance runners who carried news and messages from the four corners of Tawantinsuyo to its capital. It is now a fairly modern Andean community with a population of about 140,000 and daily rail, plane and bus service to Lima.

When the Spanish headed here after executing Atahuallpa in Cajamarca, they entered the fertile valley where Cuzco is located to find a lush, green countryside filled with fields of corn and golden and purple patches where *kiwicha* and *quinua* – varieties of amaranth, a high protein grain – were planted. Corn was perhaps the most valuable crop in the kingdom. It was used for bartering and as a food staple that appeared in everything from main dishes to the alcoholic *chicha*, prepared by young women who chewed the corn, then spat it into jars where it fermented with their saliva. The amaranth, a grain high in protein that grows well despite extremes in temperature and moisture, nearly fell victim to the Spaniards' attempt to "civilize" the Indians. The conquistadors called it the

BELOW: hilltop view of Cuzco.

"subversive grain", as it made the Indians healthy, and thus harder to enslave. Pressured by the Spanish, the Vatican outlawed its cultivation and consumption. But now, four centuries later, *kiwicha* and *quinua* once again flourish in the Sacred Valley, used in everything from soup to cookies.

In pre-Columbian times, anyone entering Cuzco was greeted with the phrase, "*Ama sua, ama quella, ama lulla*" – "Don't lie, don't steal, don't be lazy," summing up what was important in this cooperative society. Laziness, in fact, was a capital offense punishable by death. Everyone in an Incan community except for royalty and priests was required to work on projects such as roads, irrigation ditches and aqueducts owing to a philosophy that if all participated, all would take care of the finished product. When the Spanish took control of this country those cooperative projects – known as *mingas* – were replaced by forced labor. But they were not completely replaced; today there are still *mingas* in the Peruvian highlands. Women begin preparing a community meal on *minga* day while the townspeople, regardless of age, set to work.

At its peak, Cuzco was a city with sophisticated water systems, paved streets and no poverty. But its leaders were not all wise and competent. One Inca chief, Urco, perpetrated such atrocities that his name was erased from Incan history and his mention forbidden. Another hung his enemies along the roadsides in the empire's cities. Yet another had the entire population of a nearby city executed for the rape of a virgin selected to dedicate her life to the sun cult. But these excesses fail to overshadow the magnificence of a civilization whose architecture could not be destroyed and whose feats could not be matched.

Walking into the past

The most startling and curious characteristic of Cuzco at first glance is its architecture. Huge walls of intricately fit stone pay testimony to the civilization that 500 years ago controlled much of the South American subcontinent. The Spaniards' attempts to destroy every trace of the "pagan" Inca civilization proved too ambitious a task, and the Europeans ended up erecting their own buildings on the indestructible Incan foundations, often using the same huge rocks that had been cut by the Incas. The cathedral in Cuzco is made in part from stones hauled from Sacsayhuamán, the Inca fortress outside the city.

To explore this intriguing city, the **cathedral** is a perfect place to start (open to visitors Mon-Sat). It is located on the **Plaza de Armas** which, in Incan times, was known as Huancaypata and in addition to being the exact center of the empire was the spot where the most important religious and military ceremonies were held. Although the most spectacular view of the cathedral comes after dark when its lights turn the plaza into a breathtaking sight, its interior can only be seen during the day – and you won't want to miss it. Built on what was once the palace of Inca Viracocha, the cathedral mixes Spanish Renaissance architecture with the stone-working skills of the Incas, and took a century to build. Its María Angola bell in the north tower can be heard up to 40 km (25 miles) away. Made of a ton of gold, silver and bronze, the bell,

Map on page 144

TIP

An excellent value US$10 ticket allows entry to many highlights of Cuzco and the Sacred Valley, including the cathedral, the Regional History Museum, Coricancha, Sacsayhuamán, Qenko, and Pisac.

BELOW: Andean market.

which is more than 300 years old, is reportedly the largest on the continent.

El Triunfo church (open to visitors Mon-Sat), to the right of the cathedral, was built in honor of a Spanish victory over the Indians, who unsuccessfully tried to burn the thatched roof chapel that originally stood on the site. On the other side of the cathedral is the church of **Jesús María** (irregular opening hours). At only 250 years old, it is one of Cuzco's "newer" structures. In a city with so many churches, it is an honor to be dubbed the "most beautiful" and that is exactly the title that belongs to **La Compañía de Jesús** (open Mon–Fri), sitting on what was once the palace of Inca Huayna Capac on the main plaza. Construction of the church, with its intricate interior, finely carved balconies and altars covered in gold leaf, took nearly 100 years to complete.

The street to the side of the church leads to what was the most important place of worship in the Inca Empire. The **Santo Domingo Church** (open daily), was once the **Templo del Qorincancha** – the Temple of the Sun – the most magnificent complex in Cuzco. Its walls were covered in gold, and windows were constructed so the sun would cast a near-blinding reflection of golden light off the precious metals inside. Spanish chronicles describe the astonishment of the Europeans when they saw Qoricancha's patio filled with life-sized gold and silver statues of llamas, trees, flowers and delicately hand-crafted butterflies.

Coaxing a llama.

Virgins of the sun

Yet another Christian enclave formerly used as an Inca holy place is the **Santa Catalina Convent** (open Mon–Sat), which centuries ago housed a different group of cloistered women – the Chosen Women, or virgins who dedicated their lives to the sun god. Now a colonial-style building occupied by Roman

Maps on pages 144, 155

Catholic nuns, this was home to 3,000 women who were trained to serve their heavenly husband, the sun, or attend to the pleasure of his earthly son, the Inca.

The mingling of indigenous and Spanish cultures resulted in the dark religious painting style touched with brushings of gold known as the School of Cuzco. In these paintings you will see archangels dressed as Spaniards and carrying European guns, surrounded by cherubs with Indian facial features. School of Cuzco paintings of the Last Supper show Christ and his Indian-looking apostles dining on roast guinea pig or Peruvian cheese. Scenes of the crucifixion depict Christ hung on a cross decorated with Indian symbols. There is a fine collection of this art, which flourished from the 16th through 18th centuries, at the **Museum of Religious Art** (open Mon–Sat) on Calle Palacio heading downhill from the Plaza de Armas. This building, where the palace of Inca Roca once stood, has Moorish features and complicated carvings on its doors and balconies. Outside is the **Twelve Angled Stone**, a masonry masterpiece of Inca architects, proving that no stone was too irregular to be fitted without mortar.

The valley of ruins

The best known of these ruins is the megalithic fortress of **Sacsayhuamán** ❹, a bold example of Inca architectural skills. Constructed from massive stones – including one that weighs 125 tons – this military complex overlooking the city of Cuzco has a double wall in zigzag shape. It also marks the birthplace of the river that runs under Cuzco, channeled through stone conduits honed by the ancient Incas, invisibly supplying the city with water. Archeologists estimate that tens of thousands of workers labored on this massive structure for more than seven decades, hauling the immense stone blocks that make up its double out-

TIP

If you decide to take the short hike to Sacsayhuamán, keep in mind that it is uphill from the city. Alternatively, take a minibus tour, or hire a cab to take you up and wait for you. This is one of the area's most spectacular spots to take photos at dawn.

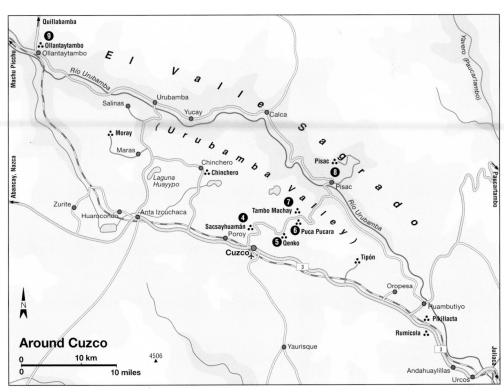

Around Cuzco

0   10 km
0   10 miles

The massive stone ramparts of Sacsay-huamán fortress.

BELOW: Sacsay-huamán, near Cuzco.

side walls and erecting the near–indestructible buildings that made the complex one of the most wondrous in all the empire. Inti Raymi, the Inca feast of the winter solstice, is celebrated every year on June 24 at Sacsayhuamán, with a procession, ceremony and much merrymaking.

Less than 7 km (4 miles) from Sacsayhuamán is **Qenko** ❺, an Inca shrine with architectural features that include a 5-meter (18-ft) high stone block that *cuzqueños* claim looks like a puma. Its name means labyrinth, and this ceremonial center – dedicated to the worship of the mother earth – includes water canals cut into solid rock and a subterranean room. Further along the road to Pisac is a smaller fortress, **Puca Pucara** ❻, believed to have guarded the road and the Sacred Valley of the Incas. It has hillside terraces, stairways, tunnels and towers. To the north is **Tambo Machay** ❼, sacred bathing place of the Inca rulers and their royal women. A hydraulic engineering marvel, its aqueduct system still feeds water into a series of showers.

From there you head down some 400 meters (1,500 ft) into the valley on the curvy road leading to **Pisac** ❽, a friendly village known for its fishing, Sunday market and the ruins above the town. To reach the ruins, climb past the mountainside terraces (local children will serve as guides for a small fee). It's a high-altitude hike that may leave you winded and your heart pounding. The stones in Pisac's buildings are smaller than those at Sacsayhuamán, but the precision with which they are cut and fit will amaze you, as will the lovely view. If you plan to do a full circuit of the valley, continue to the great fortress of **Ollantaytambo** ❾, 72 km (45 miles) from Cuzco. This elegant and intricate granite complex has temples, baths and impressive military installations.

Back in Cuzco, bargains are on offer from street artisans, but their sales techniques can sometimes be a little too persistent. In the evenings the sound of highland music can be heard, wafting out of restaurants all over the city. One of the finest floor shows is at **El Truco**, where the *pisco sours* pack a punch and the musicians and dancers are first rate. Eating a plate of *anticuchos* – a shish kebab of beef heart – and watching the performers in their traditional clothing, singing in Quechua and playing reed flutes, makes you forget temporarily that the Incas lost their showdown with the Spanish.

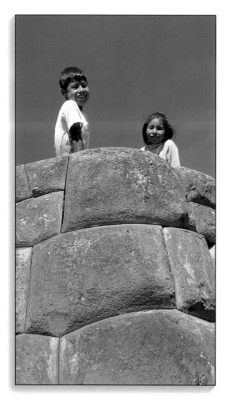

The Andes

At 7,200 km (4,500 miles), the Andes, the longest mountain chain in the world, forms the backbone of South America. The range stretches from Colombia down to southern Chile and Argentina, and is made up of dozens of parallel mountain ranges known as *cordilleras*. In Peru, these ranges cluster together, providing trekkers with easy access to some of the world's highest peaks outside the Himalayas.

Except for the most rugged and remote areas, the Peruvian Andes are not altogether untouched wilderness. Every single piece of arable land is farmed by local campesinos.

The formidable Peruvian *sierra*, or mountainous region, was conquered by the Incas, whose terraced system of agriculture enabled large areas of steep yet fertile land to be cultivated. This ancient system is still employed in some areas, and countless remains of ancient terracing give an insight into the productivity achieved by this civilization. Passing through these remote, yet populated areas is a bit like stepping back into the past. One- or two-room huts constructed of crude adobe bricks and topped with *ichu* grass have changed little in design since Inca times. There is no electricity, and fresh running water is drawn from a nearby stream. Small courtyards house chickens and *cuy*, or guinea pig, considered a delicacy in the sierra. Corn and other grains can often be seen drying in the midday sun.

Map on page 155

Cuzco means "navel" in Quechua, because the Incas considered the city the center or source of their universe.

The Inca Trail

Of all the popular treks in South America, the three- to five-day hike along the Inca Trail to Machu Picchu is the best known. The adventure from Cuzco begins with a four-hour overcrowded train ride along the Urubamba River, known by the Incas as the **Sacred Valley**. At Km 88 the train pauses briefly, allowing hikers to disembark. Trail permits costing around US$15, which includes entrance to Machu Picchu, can be bought here.

The first 12 km (7 miles) meander through easy terrain of dusty scrub rushes, low-lying hills, and a few hut dwellings. Then comes the **Warmiwañusqa Pass**, beyond which lies a wealth of Inca ruins. Struggling to the top of this 4,000-meter (13,000-ft) pass is no small challenge. The hiker soon identifies with its name, which translates as "Dead Woman's Pass." From here Inca history begins to unfold. The small guard post of **Runkuraqay**, often shrouded in mist, is the first reward of the Inca Trail. Further along, the more elaborately-constructed ruins of **Sayajmarka** ("dominant town") perch on top of a narrow cliff. The fine stonework for which the Incas are famous is apparent. An incredible "paved

BELOW: craft stall and assistant, Chinchero.

TREKKING IN THE ANDES

One of the best places for trekking information is the South American Explorer's Club in Lima. Membership fee is US$40. Their office at Avenida Portugal 146, Breña, keeps reports on trails, maps and books. Another good place for trekking advice is the Casa de Guías in Huaraz (Parque Ginebra 28G. Tel: 72-1811, fax: 72-2306). Bring a down jacket and some warm clothes for chilly nights at 4,000 meters (13,100 ft) and above. A tent and a good sleeping bag are essential. To be certain of good quality equipment, it's best to bring your own, but it can be hired in the major trekking centers. Check the quality of what you hire, since items are often the worse for wear.

Before setting off, spend a couple of days getting used to the thin, high-altitude air around Cuzco and Huaraz, or you will quickly become exhausted. Stock up on food for the duration – you won't be able to buy anything on the way. A gas or kerosene burner for cooking is essential: there is no wood for fires at higher altitudes, and using up scarce reserves at lower levels only adds to the serious problem of soil erosion that plagues the area. And of course no litter whatsoever should be left behind. A guide who knows the area well can be invaluable – ask around, as competence varies!

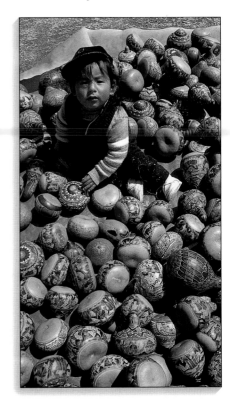

Machu Picchu

The mystery of Machu Picchu did not start in 1911 when Hiram Bingham stumbled on the snake-infested mountaintop citadel hidden by a vast tangle of vines and trees. This site on the steep summit overlooking the raging Urubamba River was always a mystery – because only a chosen few in the Inca Empire were allowed to glimpse it. To call it a "lost city" is misleading; it was more like a sanctuary.

Machu Picchu means "Old Peak," and the higher Huayna Picchu (Young Peak), stands vigil over it. The site is accessible on the four-hour bus and train service from Cuzco or by hiking the Inca Trail (*see page 157*). The area is semi-tropical, at 900 meters (3,000 ft) lower than Cuzco.

Machu Picchu was home to priests, high functionaries, craftsmen and servants and, most importantly, the *mamacunas*, or virgins chosen to dedicate their lives to the sun god. It was a city of streets, aqueducts where

crystal clear waters still run, of liturgical fountains and walkways. Even after Bingham's discovery, the city remained inaccessible until the 1940s, when an archeological expedition working at the site discovered the Inca Trail cutting through the valley.

The fate of this city's inhabitants remains unknown. Spanish chronicles of the Cuzco area make no mention of it. Theories of its demise range from epidemics to suggestions that the occupants were ostracized and forgotten in the bloody political disunity sweeping the empire before its fall.

Excavations have only added to the mystery. The skeletons of 173 people were found, 150 of whom were women. No gold objects were discovered. At the tomb of the high priestess, as Bingham called it, the remains of a woman and a small dog were found with some ceramic objects, two brooches and woolen clothing. The woman had suffered from syphilis.

Today's visitors enter the ruins near the Hotel Turistas, but the only entrance to the city in ancient times was the narrow doorway at the southwest section of the citadel. The city's cultivated land was farmed on narrow terraces on the steep slopes of the mountaintop, and the thousands of steps connecting them have survived for centuries.

The city is divided into sections: the cemetery, jails, small dwellings and temples. The Temple of the Three Windows allows sunlight to pass through its windows to the Sacred Plaza. Climbing higher is the astronomical observatory and *Intiwatana*, the curiously-shaped stone block believed to have been a solar clock or, as some claim, "the hitching post to the sun," where the sun's rays cast shadows used in planning seasonal activities and religious ceremonies.

Some of the buildings in Machu Picchu were two stories high, originally topped with sharply-peaked straw roofs. What amazes architects today is the precision with which building stones were cut and assembled.

A steep and perilous path rises from the site to the top of Huayna Picchu. At the skirt of Huayna Picchu is the construction known as the Temple of the Moon, and from the summit there is an extraordinary view of the ruins and the Urubamba valley. ❑

LEFT: Machu Picchu.

highway" snakes along the valley below, masterfully constructed by a people the Spaniards did not consider civilized.

Puyapatamarka ("cloud-level town") is fascinating for its circular walls and finely engineered aqueduct system, which still provides spring water to the ancient baths. Below, another surprise awaits. Along the road to **Wiñay Wayna**, huge steps like a stone stairway almost half a mile in length lead down into dense jungle. This stretch of the trail was only discovered in 1984. Before then, a modern footpath served to reach the same ruins. Tenaciously clinging to a steep hillside, the last set of ruins is also the most stunning. Wiñay Wayna presents an astonishing picture when first seen from a distance. That something so complex could be constructed in a ravine so vertical is beyond comprehension.

An hour away lies the jewel in the crown – **Machu Picchu ❿**. In order to see it at sunrise, most trekkers stay at the rather precarious camp just beyond Wiñay Wayna, where rainy nights are filled with the howls of campers who hired leaky tents in Cuzco. The high pass of **Intipunku**, the Sun Gate, provides the first glimpse of the fabled city. Arriving as the Incas did centuries ago, the trekker begins the final descent into Machu Picchu, sharing a path with history.

Arequipa: the "white city"

Although **Arequipa ⓫** was far from Lima and isolated between desert and mountains when the country was young, it was on the route linking the silver mines of Bolivia to the coast. For that reason, the oasis at the foot of the Misti volcano grew to be the Peruvian town with the largest Spanish population and the strongest European traditions. Today, with buildings of white volcanic stone lending it the name "white city," it remains Peru's second most important city.

Arequipa's **Plaza de Armas** is one of Peru's most beautiful. One full side is occupied by the massive **cathedral** (open daily), which was rebuilt twice in the early 19th century after it was destroyed by fire and earthquake. Its clock is the city's unofficial timepiece. Make sure you see the cathedral's organ, brought from Belgium, and its elaborately carved wooden pulpit, the work of French artist Rigot in 1879. Two-story arcades grace the other three sides of the plaza, with palm trees, old gas lamps and a fountain amidst an English garden.

The city is full of dignified patricians' homes built in the 18th century and which have for the most part, withstood its frequent earth tremors. The one-story colonial structures are replete with massive carved wooden doors, grilled French windows and high-ceilinged rooms around spacious patios. The best for visiting are **Casa Ricketts**, built as a seminary in 1738 and now used as a bank, the 200-year-old **Casa de la Moneda** or former mint, and the **Casa Moral**, named after the venerable mulberry tree on its patio.

No visit would be complete without a stop at **La Compañía** church. The sacristy's ceiling is covered with miniature paintings and carvings of crimson and gold. The view from the steeple is fabulous, especially at sunset when the light casts a rose glow to the city's white *sillar* rock buildings.

The most astonishing stop in Arequipa is the **Santa**

BELOW: the Inca Trail.

Map on page 144

Convent of Santa Catalina, Arequipa.

Catalina Convent, opened in 1970 after 400 years as a cloister for nuns. Despite the fact that its doors were closed all that time, there was little heed paid to the nuns' vows of poverty and silence. During its heyday, this convent's sleeping cells were furnished with English carpets, silk curtains, cambric and lace sheets and tapestry-covered stools. As for silence, Flora Tristan, visiting in 1832, said the nuns – daughters of aristocrats – were nearly as good at talking as they were at spending huge sums of money. Each had her own servant and dined with porcelain plates, damask tableclothes and silver cutlery.

When the convent opened its doors again, its anecdotes and scandals were resurrected. But don't believe it when they tell you the story of Sister Dominga, the 16-year-old who entered the convent when her betrothed left her for a rich widow, then staged her own death to escape. This beautiful young woman really did place the body of a deceased Indian woman in her convent bed one night then set the room on fire, but the whole thing occurred at another cloister in Arequipa – **Santa Rosa**. The Mother Superior refused to believe rumors that the young nun was really alive and living outside the cloister until Dominga sent her a message demanding return of the dowry she had paid to enter the convent.

Independent spirits

Arequipeñas are a proud lot and a century ago they started a movement to secede from Peru. Even today Lima residents heading south to the "White City" jokingly ask one another if they've remembered to bring along passports.

BELOW: Plaza de Armas, Arequipa.

Outside Arequipa, set in beautiful countryside, is **Sabandía** and a flour mill that was restored, stone by stone, in 1973. Three hours away and drawing nearly as much tourist attention as the city itself is the **Colca Canyon**, deeper than the

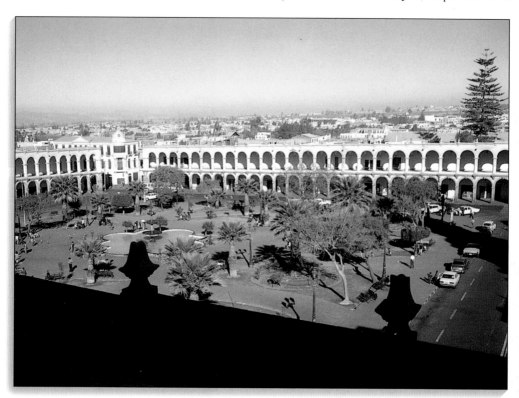

Grand Canyon in the United States. From the Colca River at its base to the mountains above, the chasm reaches depths of 3,400 meters (11,000 ft). Colca and the slightly deeper Cotahuasi Canyon, also near Arequipa, are believed to be the world's deepest. A series of canyon trips, usually starting with a bus ride from Arequipa then a switch to *burros* (donkeys) or trekking, allows you to explore this rift full of small towns. As an added treat, at the Cruz del Cóndor viewpoint you may even see a condor, soaring on the warm thermal currents.

To unwind in Arequipa after a hard day's sightseeing, do what the locals do and head to a *picantería* for a cold Arequipeña beer and some spicy stuffed peppers, rabbit or marinated pork. Your beer will be accompanied by a dish of *cancha* – salty fried corn for munching.

Map on page 144

Condor over Colca Canyon.

The Peruvian Amazon

Three-fifths of Peru is jungle – the Amazon. Despite the encroachment of modern life, this is where adventures can still happen and the exotic reigns. Here the "roads" are rivers and the vehicles are colored motorboats and canoes. It is the home of witch doctors and folk medical experts, who say that its unique fauna might contain anything from new contraceptives to a cure for cancer.

The Amazon is the one place the Incas never managed to penetrate. When the Spanish conquistadors arrived, they heard wild tales of a golden city hidden in the heart of the jungle. In their search for El Dorado, they found nothing but disease and hostile tribes, although the legend lives on.

The Spanish explorer Francisco de Orellana is credited with discovering the Amazon River. He named it after the fierce female warriors in Greek legend when he erroneously took the long-haired Yagua men, who confronted him wearing fiber skirts, for women. A later Spanish expedition was fictionalized in the 1973 Werner Herzog film *Aguirre, the Wrath of God*. Klaus Kinski starred as the demonic conquistador Aguirre, who killed for pleasure during his 1560 trek along the Amazon River to what is now Venezuela.

In later years, the search for gold was replaced by missionaries' quest to "convert the savages" by teaching them to take up farming, adopt a sedentary lifestyle and send their children to mission schools. The indigenous people did not succumb easily, and from the late 1600s to the mid-1700s they managed to keep the jungle free of a European invasion, thanks to an uprising led by Jesuit-educated Quechua Juan Santos, who united warring tribes to expel the Europeans. The missionaries eventually returned, and today, the Catholic presence in the rainforest has received strong competition from Protestant evangelists.

BELOW: Colca Canyon.

The rubber barons

The colonization of the Amazon was consolidated at the end of the 1800s with the rubber boom. The period was one of overnight wealth for European and US rubber barons and overnight enslavement for the people of the rainforest.

The best-known of the rubber barons was Carlos Fitzgerald – the *Fitzcarraldo* of Herzog's 1982 film of the same name – the son of an English immigrant and a Peruvian woman. Accused of spying for Chile during the 1879 war with Peru, Fitzcarraldo fled to the Amazon where he made a great fortune in rubber and became obsessed with a plan to travel from the Ucayali River (which flows into the Amazon) through the Madre de Dios River by steamship. Although only an 13-km (8-mile) isthmus separated the two, it was widely believed impossible to cross from one to the other. Although Fitzcarraldo's quest failed, steamships later made the trip, effectively linking the Atlantic and Pacific oceans – with thousands of Indians hauling the ships across the isthmus.

Fitzcarraldo and other rubber barons had no cause to miss Europe; they imported every luxury that struck their fancy. Their women were dressed in the latest Paris fashions, the men drank imported wines, and European theater and opera stars regularly performed in the midst of one of the world's densest jungles. But the opulence ended in 1920 when rubber grown in Asia and Africa began to compete on the world market.

Boom towns and exotic wildlife

Peru's most important rubber boom city – and the largest city in the Peruvian Amazon – is **Iquitos** ⓬. The old days of wealth are still evident in the houses covered with Portuguese tiles and, on the **Plaza de Armas**, in the ramshackle two-story metal house designed by Gustave Eiffel for the Paris Exhibition of 1889 and transported to Iquitos piece by piece by rubber magnate Jules Toth. On the waterfront is the colorful **Belén** port, where the houses float on rafts. From here, irregular riverboat services run to Leticia in Colombia and onwards to Manaus in Brazil, preserving a taste of the days when air travel was unknown and the only way to reach Iquitos was through weeks of journeying overland and

BELOW: local riverboats carry both passengers and cargo.

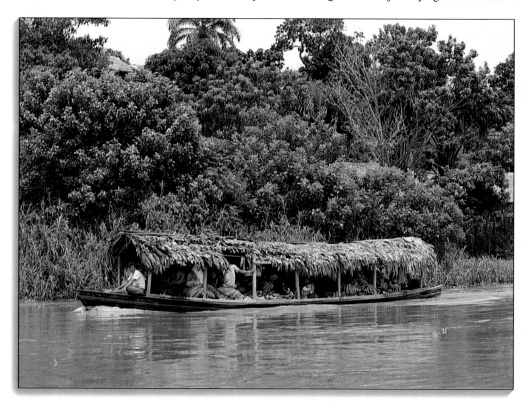

upriver. Although it is a bustling city of 400,000 one only has to go a short distance from Iquitos on the Amazon, Yanamono or Manatí Rivers to be in virgin jungle. On the way are the rustic wood and palm houses on stilts inhabited by the *ribereños* – mestizos who live on the river and speak a lilting Spanish reminiscent of Brazilian Portuguese. Exotic birds fly in and out of vine covered trees, attracting birders from around the globe, while brilliantly colored butterflies, tapirs, monkeys, peccaries and pink river dolphins fascinate visitors.

Tourists generally stay in lodges in the jungle, the oldest and most recommended being the three **Explorama** complexes, ranging from the ultra modern Explorama Inn with electricity 24 hours a day and private bathrooms in every cabin to the primitive Explornapo camp, where kerosene lamps, night walks and mosquito netting tents add to the mystique.

The people in this part of the Amazon live isolated lives, except when they head off in their dugout canoes or hitch a ride on the "river buses" – boats which cruise up and down the river collecting passengers and their cargoes of bananas, yucca, corn, dried fish and chickens headed for Iquitos.

Another important Amazon city is **Pucallpa** ⓭, a frontier lumber town and the last navigable port for ocean-going vessels on the Amazon. It is 9 kilometers (6 miles) from **Lake Yarinacocha**, a 22-km (14-mile) body of water luring tourists fascinated by its spectacular sunrises and sunsets, its fishing and the undisturbed Shipibo Indian villages along its banks. Its forests are full of cedar, pine, mahogany and bamboo and serve as home to nearly a thousand bird species, endless varieties of butterflies and exotic mammals – including sloths. Local boats called *pekepekes* after the chugging sound made by their small motors are available for hire for day trips to some of the isolated villages or to

Map on page 144

BELOW LEFT: Amazon indians still use blowdarts to shoot their prey. **BELOW RIGHT:** young puma, a rare sight.

San Pedro cactus, Chiclayo.

see the Shipibos and buy their hand-painted pottery and textiles. Further south is **Puerto Maldonado** , just a few hours by river from one of the world's most important wildlife reserves and capital of the least populated, least developed and least explored province – or department – in Peru. The **Manu National Park**, covering more than 13,000 sq km (5,000 sq miles), has everything from ocelots and jaguars to alligators and otters.

More than 500 bird species have been identified by its research station. A trip to **Manu** ⓫ is usually accompanied by camping on the banks of the Madre de Dios, or the River of Serpents as the Indians call it. Closer to Puerto Maldonado is the smaller **Tambopata Wildlife Reserve** with bird, dragonfly and butterfly species, including some that have only recently been identified.

Peru's historical north

Trujillo ⓰, the "travelers' resting place" along the Spaniards' route between Lima and Quito, is a graceful coastal city. Founded in 1535 and named after Francisco Pizarro's birthplace in Spain, it soon became worthy of the title the "Lordliest City", and even today its well-preserved wooden balconies – designed so upper class women could look out but their jealous husbands' rivals could not look in – and ornate window grills pay testimony to the colonial days.

More recently, the city is famous for being the first in Peru to declare independence from Spain, while in 1932 APRA (Alianza Popular Revolucionaria Americana) crowds were turned on by the army.

The best place to start exploring Trujillo is the **Plaza de Armas**, bounded by city hall, the bishop's palace and the newly-renovated cathedral with its marble pillars and gilt hand-carved wooden altars. The colonial building next to the cathedral is now the **Hotel Libertadores**. Off the main square, colonial mansions abound. **Casa de la Emancipación** is typical of the houses built in the 16th and 17th centuries and contains much of its original furniture. Although earthquakes have taken their toll, there are other mansions worth seeing, including **Casa de Mayorazgo**, **Casa Urquiaga** and **Casa Bracamonte**. Or stop by the **Casa Ganoza Chopitea**, now an art gallery (open Mon–Sat), and the **Palacio Iturregui** (open 8–11am; free), which houses the Club Central, with its permanent exhibition of ceramics (open 11am–6pm; entrance fee).

BELOW: girl at a fiesta, Trujillo.

Land reform in the 1970s turned most of the sugar *haciendas* outside the city into cooperatives, but the opulence of the past is still evident. The most impressive are **Casa Grande** and **Hacienda Cartavio**, which produce sugar for Cartavio Rum.

Trujillo's pre-Hispanic past is on display at the University of Trujillo **Archeological Museum** (irregular hours). The **Cassinelli Museum** (open Mon–Sat; entrance fee) has an intriguing collection of pottery and unusual artefacts in a former service station north of Av. España, an elliptical street where a wall once stood to protect the city from pirate attacks.

An ancient adobe city

On the fringe of Trujillo are the ruins of **Chan Chan**, which was one of the world's largest adobe cities at the time it was discovered by the Spanish. Made up of seven citadels spread over 20 sq km (8 sq miles) and enclosed by a massive adobe wall, Chan Chan was home to the Chimu people, who fished and farmed, worshiped the moon and left no written records. On the city walls are carvings of fish, sea birds, fishnets and moons. The Chimus had such a sophisticated irrigation and aqueduct system that they were able to turn the arid wasteland around them into fertile fields of grains, fruits and vegetables. It wasn't until the Spanish sabotaged those water conduits, forcing the Chimus to leave the protection of the city, that they were able to conquer them.

Three hours' drive north of Trujillo is the tiny town of **Lambayeque** and the remarkable **Brüning Museum** (open daily), which has Peru's finest publicly-owned gold collection as well as the fabulous finds from the **Sipán** archeological dig (*see page 167*). Visitors can see the digs and view the contents of the tomb of the Lord of Sipán. Nearby is the new excavation at the **Túcume pyramids** – a project originally directed by Norwegian Thor Heyerdahl. A steep stairway at Túcume takes you to a lookout point over the pyramids.

Map on page 144

Where the last Inca leader met his fate

Historically, the most important northern city is **Cajamarca** ⑰. Now a cattle and dairy area where some of Peru's best cheese is made, this is the city where the Incas and Spaniards had their final confrontation. According to Spanish chronicles, the Inca Atahuallpa (*see page 26*) was taken prisoner after offending the Europeans by accepting a proferred Bible then, after touching, smelling and listening to it, tossing it to the ground as useless. To pay the ransom demanded by the conquistadors for his release, people from all over the Inca

BELOW: the "House of the Grandson" near Huaraz.

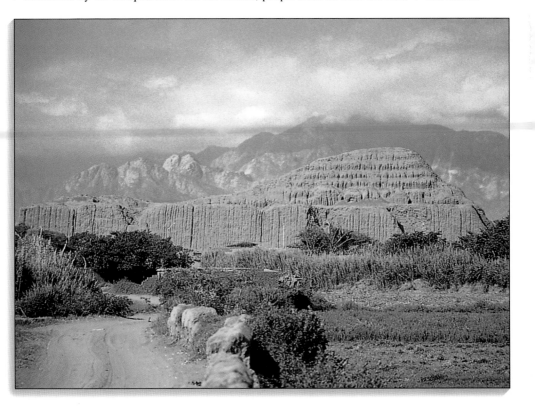

empire brought gold and silver, filling the **Rescue Room**, a block from the Plaza de Armas, twice over with silver and once with gold. But the effort was futile and the Spaniards garrotted the last Inca on the main square.

That square, now the **Plaza de Armas**, is the hub of this slow-paced city of 120,000 and is ringed by colonial buildings and two churches. Opened in 1776, the **cathedral**'s carved wood altars are covered in gold leaf and its façade is of intricately carved volcanic rock. But conspicuously absent are its bell towers, which were left unfinished to protest Spain's tax on churches. The church of **San Francisco**, older and more ornate, has the city's **Religious Art Museum** and eerie catacombs. Also on the plaza is **Salas Restaurant**, described by one *Cajamarquino* as the "city's nerve center". Not only is it *the* place to catch up on the latest news and gossip, but it has the city's best home cooking.

Digging for the Past

In 1996 the largest tomb excavated in the Americas was unearthed in the Lambayeque Valley in northern Peru. It was 15 meters (50 ft) deep and contained the remains of a high priest or prince, aged 25–30, wearing a spectacular gold mask with emerald eyes. In the tomb with him were many brilliant artefacts including gold and copper, gold gloves and 7.5 sq meters (80 sq ft) of gilded cotton cloth. There were also the skeletons of 24 women, possibly sacrificed at his death. The whole burial complex is made up of 14 tombs, the second largest of which contained 500 kg (110 pounds) of gold, and it dates back to 900–1000 AD. It is just another find in a dazzling history of archeological discoveries.

Only a few years before this discovery, archeologists in northern Peru followed a bloody trail of thievery to the intact tomb of a Moche warrior-lord, the

Gold figure, Vicus culture, Brüning Museum.

BELOW: the ancient adobe citadel of Chan Chan.

richest documented burial chamber ever uncovered in the Americas. Walter Alva is the Peruvian archeologist in charge of the Sipán dig, financed in part by the National Geographic Society. Alva was pulled into the project when local police called him in February of 1987 to say they had confiscated some pre-Columbian treasures headed for the black market. As director of the Brüning Museum in Lambayeque, Alva was accustomed to the constant trafficking of archeological artefacts. But he had no idea of the immense value of what the police would show him – copper masks, a gold face mask with silver and lapis lazuli eyes, detailed larger-than-lifesize peanuts of solid gold and various ornaments and ceramics. The Moche lord was buried within a wooden coffin – the first time such a burial box has been discovered.

Many of the items taken from the dig were sent to Germany for examination, along with the remains of the Sipán lord, to undergo sophisticated forensic tests before returning to be put on display at the Brüning Museum. The continuing excavation at Sipán promises to provide crucial new evidence about the life of the Moche, a sophisticated pre-Columbian civilization that left no written word but whose extensive ceramics have been used to unravel some of the secrets of their society. Guided tours of the area are available from the nearby city of **Chiclayo** ⑬ and are highly recommended.

One of the most intriguing projects in the area was set up under the direction of the Norwegian explorer Thor Heyerdahl. His archeological dig at **Túcume**, not far from Sipán, brings together a team of European and Peruvian archeologists funded by Heyerdahl's Kon-Tiki Museum. Túcume is a plain with 27 arid hills which are actually pyramids covered by centuries of dust and dirt, and can also be explored with the help of guided tours from Chiclayo. ❑

Map on page 144

Although Peru has strengthened its laws on the sale of archeological artefacts, large quantities are still smuggled out of the country. Ancient ruins are also plundered by squatters in search of materials to construct their own dwellings.

BELOW: totora reed boats, Huanchaco.

A REMARKABLE CRAFT

In 1948, a Norwegian expedition led by Thor Heyerdahl embarked on a voyage which would take them from Callao in Peru to French Polynesia in a balsa raft, the *Kon-Tiki*. Heyerdahl's intention was to prove that American indians could have colonised the Pacific Islands on balsa rafts, and his expedition launched a whole area of scientific investigation. If his original theory has since been discredited, interest in the sea-going craft of the pre-Columbian South Americans and Pacific Islanders has only increased. Many modern adventurers have their rafts built by Bolivians from the Lake Titicaca region, who are considered the best balsa raft craftsmen in the world.

When the Spanish first reached the Americas they recorded the indian craft in detail, which ranged from the totora reed bundle rafts used today by the fishermen of Huanchaco, Peru, to huge cargo-carrying rafts. Chronicler Augustín de Zárate described rafts that could carry 50 men and three horses. In the 17th century, European navigators began to understand the "guara," or centerboard, a navigation instrument used by the indians. Visitors to Peru can witness the ancient craft in action around Lake Titicaca, or at Huanchaco, near Trujillo, where fishermen build and sail distinctive canoes made from bundles of totora reed.

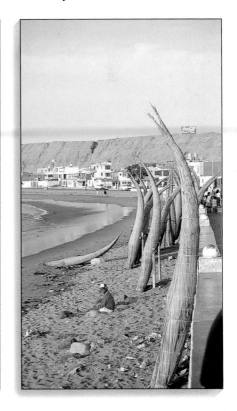

LAKE TITICACA: PERU'S LEGENDARY WATERWAY

Surrounded by snow-capped Andean peaks, this lofty expanse of clear, fresh water has fired the imagination for generations

▷ **REED BOATS**
People of the Lake Titicaca region have been building tortora reed boats since time immemorial to sail the vast expanses of the lake.

Linking Peru and Bolivia, the world's highest navigable lake is a large, remarkably clear blue body of water covering more than 8,000 sq. km (3,000 sq. miles) with more than 30 islands. The lake may look inviting, but bathers beware – at 4,000 meters (13,000 ft) above sea level, its waters are freezing all year round. Lake Titicaca is full of history, ancient legends, sacred sites and living history, as age-old traditions are continued and developed on and around its waters.

BIRTHPLACE OF THE INCAS

The Isla del Sol, in the middle of the lake, is at the center of the Inca creation myths as recorded by 16th-century Spanish chroniclers. One myth tells of the emergence of four sisters and four brothers from a stone door on the island, two of whom were the Incas Manco Capac and Mama Ocllo (or Huaca). Another legend relates that the sun was born on a sacred rock on the island. Ruined Inca temples and sacred sites can be visited on the Isla del Sol and the nearby Isla de Luna (pictured above). Inca history holds that when the Spanish reached Cuzco in Peru, the Incas took the 1,800-kg (2-ton) gold chain of Inca Huascar from Qoricancha, and hurled it into the lake. Some years ago the late French oceanographer Jacques Cousteau spent eight weeks exploring the lake with a mini-submarine. He found no gold but he did discover a 50-cm (20-inch) tri-colored frog that apparently never surfaces. In 1996 the oldest known temple in South America was found near the lake, occupied between 1500 and 1000 BC, nearly 2,500 years before the Incas. Its discovery adds to the historical fascination of this remarkable region.

△ **GATHERING REEDS**
Although the last full-blood Uros died in 1959, modern Uros islanders still use reeds to build homes, boats, islands and even for food.

◁ **TAQUILE TRADITIONS**
The colorful textile designs of Isla Taquile are not just for decoration but can denote social or marital status. Some are reserved for special times of the year.

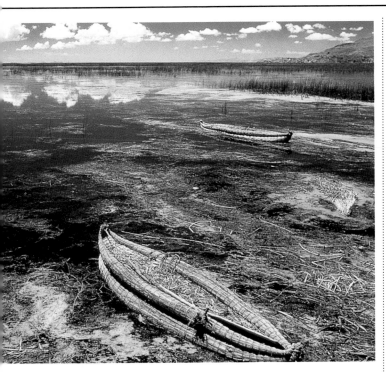

THE WEAVERS OF ISLA TAQUILE

On the Peruvian side of the lake is Isla Taquile – the island of weavers. Under the Spanish it was a haçienda, and later it became a prison, but the Taquile people have managed to regain owner-ship. Since 1970 they have been running their own tourism operations to ensure their old traditions are not lost.

There are no hotels, but islanders open their homes to overnight guests, and there are small eating establishments special-izing in lake trout.

Poverty has bred a cooperative lifestyle, which has won the islanders their reputation for hospitality. Textiles can be purchased from the weaving coopera-tives, most knitted from finely spun sheep's wool dyed bright red and blue, though the colors and weaves can reveal age, social position and marital status. More textiles can be purchased at Amantaní, a peaceful island with temples and a throne of carved stone on one shore.

◁ **FRESH FISH**
Lake Titicaca has waves, and can get very choppy! Trout from the lake can be tasted at restaurants in Copacabana and elsewhere.

▽ **UROS ISLANDERS**
The reed Uros Islands have become a popular tourist attraction. Islanders make small model boats out of reeds to sell to tourists.

◁ **FIESTA OF THE VIRGIN**
The quiet Bolivian town of Copacabana, beside the lake, bursts into life at fiesta time.

▷ **TIAHUANACO**
This mysterious pre-Inca site has advanced stonework that is over 2,000 years old.

BOLIVIA

Landlocked and isolated, Bolivia is one of South America's most unlikely treasures, attracting the most intrepid visitors for its rich cultural heritage and literally breathtaking mountain scenery

Map on page 174

Geographically, Bolivia takes you from the heights of the *Altiplano*, the Andean plateau which elevates northeastern Bolivia, down to the balmy valleys of the Yungas and east to the fertile lowlands of the *Oriente*. Linking these physically dissimilar territories are, in the north, hair-raising zigzag roads which cling to near-vertical cliffs. Further south, the plateau shelves off a little more gently, in the area known as the *Valles*.

Bolivia is also noted for its material highs and lows, particularly the vast gulf between rich and poor. The poverty is obvious – just look around on the streets of La Paz, behind the cheerful smiles of the traders and colorfully dressed *campesinos* (indigenous farmers), or drive past families toiling in the fields early in the morning. Bolivia's wealth is not so obvious, but is hinted at in certain genteel cafés in La Paz. Much of it, like the riches of the silver and tin mines, was concentrated in the hands of a few, and spirited away to Europe. Much of the country's physical wealth was taken by neighbouring countries in a succession of disastrous wars. Today, Bolivia is the subcontinent's poorest nation, with about two-thirds of its population, many of whom are subsistence farmers, living in poverty. The country also has a high mortality rate.

There is wealth though in Bolivia, a sizeable part of it generated in the coca fields of the Oriente and turned into cash on the streets of American cities – some say there is a "trickledown" effect in the coca-growing areas. But it's not just drug profits that are evident on the upwardly mobile streets of Santa Cruz, which has seen an unprecedented boom recently. Bolivia's fertile eastern plains have undergone new agricultural development, encouraged by government initiative, giving rise to an increasingly prosperous middle class with attitudes more conducive to widespread and lasting economic security than the hierarchical stagnation of yesteryear.

PRECEDING PAGES: musicians, La Paz. **LEFT:** La Paz seen from the rim of the altiplano. **BELOW:** Aymara man playing the *zampoña*.

The lust for silver

In 1544 an Indian named Diego Huallpa discovered silver in the Cerro Rico of Potosí, and from that moment, the country's fate was sealed. For the next two centuries, everything in Bolivia was geared towards extracting this vein of precious metal, the greatest ever discovered. Towns were founded for the sole purpose of supplying Potosí with goods traded from other parts of the empire or to transfer silver back to Europe. Nothing mattered to the Spanish except the ore and its transportation from the freezing wilderness, least of all the fate of the local Indians. As in Peru, the magnificent Inca systems of terracing and irrigation fell into disrepair. Christianity was imposed, although the conversion was at best superficial. More obvious was the imposition of a new form of dress for Indian women. Layered dresses, unusual hats and plaited hair typify the most common tourist view of the Bolivian people today – this appearance actually came about by Spanish decree in the 18th century. Even the way women parted their hair was ordered by the Viceroy of Toledo. The Indian populations were theoretically free subjects of the Spanish crown, but in reality, they were forced to pay massive tributes, lived at the beck and call of brutal overlords, and were regularly dragged from their agricultural communities to work in the mines of Potosí. Indians died by the thousands in the harsh and brutal conditions while colonial Potosí grew to match any city in the Old World.

Two-thirds of the Bolivian population are of indian origin, the highest proportion of any country in South America.

The amount of silver that was taken from Potosí is staggering: 16 million kg (16,000 tons) arrived in Seville between 1545 and 1660, three and a half times the entire European reserves of the day. The wealth was squandered on Spain's futile religious wars, or wasted by the extravagance of its nobles and clergymen, almost all of it ending up in the coffers of Flemish, German or English bankers.

The creation of Bolivia in 1825 (*see page 32*) launched the country into an apparently endless series of military governments, mostly bloodless reshufflings in the palaces of La Paz, with wealth and control being kept in the hands of a small number of families of Spanish descent. Meanwhile, Bolivia proceeded to lose large chunks of its territory in wars with its neighbors.

The only good news seemed to be the discovery of rich veins of tin in Oruro and Potosí, by a prospector named Simón Patiño. But Patiño amassed a personal fortune from this new boom, becoming one of the ten richest people on earth by the early 1900s. While Patiño lived in luxury, he kept miners on starvation wages, in dreadful conditions, and he quashed industrial disputes by organizing massacres as he vacationed in Switzerland with the crown heads of Europe.

Moves for change

A period of intense self-reflection followed the 1930s Chaco War, creating a growing movement for change, culminating in the new Movimiento Nacionalista Radical (MNR) behind Victor Paz Estenssoro. Winning the elections of 1951, the party was blocked from office by a military coup and Paz Estenssoro was forced into exile in Buenos Aires. But the miners began an armed revolt and after heavy fighting defeated the military. Paz Estenssoro returned to La Paz and the MNR began to put its reforms into action. In the following years Bolivia saw the nationalization of tin mines, the granting of votes to indians and extensive land reform. Unfortunately, the mines were still dependent on foreign capital and land given to indians was in plots too small to be quickly productive. The economy began sliding and the MNR was ousted in another military coup.

Dictator followed dictator with monotonous regularity. The 1970s were dominated by General Hugo Banzer Suárez, who led a right-wing coalition before

Map on page 174

Stone cross on Chacaltaya, with Huayna Potosí in the background.

BELOW: colorful cemetery near La Paz.

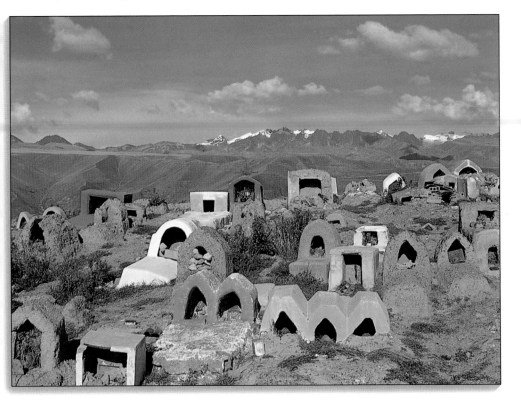

finally bowing to the democratic will in 1978. The country's most infamous dictator came to power in 1980 in a coup which cost hundreds of lives: General Luis García Meza sent his tanks into La Paz, rounded up and shot left-wing leaders, and bombed mining camps in Oruro. He ran an extraordinarily corrupt regime, inviting ex-Nazi Klaus Barbie to help organize his security forces and selling off national assets to line his own pockets. Finally García Meza was driven from power and in 1982 democracy was restored under Dr Hernan Siles Zuazo, who is unfortunately best remembered for leading Bolivia into one of the world's highest inflation rates, hitting a mind-boggling 35,000 percent a year.

Tin price collapse

In 1985, with the economy on the verge of collapse and cocaine the major export, the now octogenarian Paz Estenssoro returned as president. Reversing his radical stance of 35 years before, Paz Estenssoro embraced the conservative policies recommended by the International Monetary Fund and embarked on a dramatic austerity plan. With the collapse of tin prices, he sacked 20,000 miners from the state-run company COMIBOL, using the military to head off their union protests. Inflation ground to a halt, at the price of massive unemployment.

Inconclusive results in the 1989 elections led to a congressional vote to elect the President, and the center-left Jaime Paz Zamora came to power under an alliance with right-wing ex-dictator Hugo Banzer Suárez. Unless a candidate receives at least 50 percent of the popular vote in Bolivian general elections, the result is decided by congress. Unemployment boosted cocaine manufacture as people looked for new sources of income, and in the early 1990s the US embarked on Operation Support Justice, an anti-narcotics programme in Bolivia,

BELOW: woodcut of Potosí from 1555, the earliest known drawing of a New World mining enterprise.

Map on page 174

tied to $78 million in aid. But high-profile raids on illegal laboratories led to few arrests and the Americans were shortly asked to leave. Such programs have often provoked violent demonstrations by angry campesinos. Many defend their traditional right to grow coca for uses other than drug production. Others, desperately poor, defend the chance to grow a crop which is more durable than rice or potatoes and which can be many times more lucrative.

The 1993 elections brought the MNR's Gonzalo Sánchez de Lozada to power, but opposition to his programme of aggressive economic and social reform brought about social unrest. In March 1997, Bolivia negotiated an agreement with Mercosur, the Southern Cone trade organisation. Ex-dictator Hugo Banzer Suárez won only 22 percent of the vote in the close-run 1997 elections, and formed a coalition to take power. Banzer's government has pledged to end drug production and trafficking by the end of his term in 2002.

Bolivia is still South America's poorest country, with a per capita GDP of $1,100. Although there is some scope for optimism, the country still has a long way to go before it can begin to solve its economic inequalities and to improve the dismal statistics of unemployment and child deaths from malnutrition.

La Paz: the highest capital

If you're going to fly to Bolivia's unofficial capital, **La Paz** ❶, try to get a window seat. The views are extraordinary as the aeroplane sweeps across Bolivia's highest mountain ranges to dive into the city, which sits in a natural canyon. The one disadvantage is that some travelers arriving in the airport, at an altitude of almost 3,600 meters (12,000 ft), are struck by the vague nausea of *soroche*, or altitude sickness. A day or two of taking it easy is a certain cure.

In such a magnificent setting, La Paz at first seems an ugly blur of orange brick and gray corrugated iron roof. But on much closer inspection, it is one of South America's most unusual and lively cities.

The streets of La Paz, made of slippery bricks, are steep and tiring in the thin mountain air. They meet at the **Plaza San Francisco** with its huge stone church containing a statue of Jesus with a blue fluorescent halo. The snowcapped **Mount Illimani**, at more than 6,000 meters (19,000 ft) in height, dominates the skyline from most parts of La Paz. The modern city center has a collection of shabby skyscrapers and streets clogged with traffic.

The city's traditional center is the **Plaza Murillo**, where the Italianate **Presidential Palace** is located – often referred to as the *Palacio Quemado* (Burnt Palace), twice gutted by inflamatory crowds since it was first built in the 1850s. Nearby is the modern **cathedral**. The surrounding streets are the most atmospheric in the city: **Calle Jaén** is still cobbled and without traffic, lined by preserved colonial buildings. Another atmospheric area is behind the church and monastery of San Francisco near the upper end of Av. Mariscal Santa Cruz. Dating from 1549, the carvings are rich and ingenious.

The café of the **Club de La Paz**, on the corners of Avenidas Camacho and Colón, is a cultural landmark. This antique wooden retreat has seen innumerable

Elegant colonial streetlight in La Paz.

BELOW: Bolivian girl.

A Night at the Peña

After a long day of sightseeing, the best place to head for is the local *peña*, or folk nightclub. Here, you can sit and enjoy the haunting music of the altiplano while sipping a cold beer, glass of wine or potent *pisco sour*, made from grape brandy.

Starting off at around 10pm, peñas are usually relaxed, informal bars which offer set musical programs. Up to a dozen groups can play on a single night, giving an idea of the range and variety of Andean music; while the rhythms of the altiplano are related, every region has its own unique sound. A group from Potosí is quite different to one from the shores of Lake Titicaca, and different again to one from Cuzco in Peru. The musicians are often accomplished mimics and the show generally includes a few comic turns, which can be quite hilarious, even if you don't understand the language.

In La Paz, one of the best peñas to head for is the Naira at Sagárnaga 161, a dark and intimate venue with a fine repertory of musicians. Other well-known penãs are in the restaurants Los Escudos on M. Santa Cruz and La Casa del Corregidor on Murrillo 1040.

The basic instruments used are the single-reed flutes known as *quenas*, *zampoñas* (deep wooden pipes), drums and rattles. The famous *charango* is a miniature guitar made from an armadillo's shell, with 15 strings that the player strums and plucks to create a penetrating, tiny sound. Along with the Andean harp, the charango is an unusual example of the local culture mixing successfully with the Spanish. Stringed instruments were one of the few cultural innovations that the Andean Indians were glad to accept from Europe. The effect of these instruments is mesmerizing. Andean music evokes the loneliness and austerity of the bleak and harsh altiplano.

The music is traditionally played without vocal accompaniment, but in recent decades ballads – called *waynos* – have been added, sung mostly in the Quechua or Aymará tongues, or in a mixture of native languages and Spanish. They often deal with the daily lives of campesinos in the fields:

Do you want me to tell you
Where I'm from?
I'm from behind that hill,
Amid the carnations,
Among the lilies
My sling is of Castilian fabric,
And my lassoo of merino wool:
Very long-lasting,
Very strong.

Others are much more progressive:
The priest of Andahuaylas
Keeps telling me to get married.
Maybe he knows, maybe not,
Where I went last night.

As an expression of indian culture, the music has often had a mixed reception from the country's rulers. On radio, it must compete with modern pop, as well as salsa and samba. At its worst, it has "crossed over", producing Western songs on Andean instruments – even *Rock Around the Clock* on panpipes. But as indian cultures are increasingly gaining acceptance, the presence of altiplano tunes is definitely growing. ❑

LEFT: zampoña player, La Paz.

business and political deals, and was probably where many of Bolivia's coups were hatched. It was a favorite hangout of Klaus Barbie before he was arrested in the early 1980s and returned to France for trial as a Nazi war criminal.

Witches and markets

The real attaction of La Paz is the street life. Narrow alleyways stretching up the hillside behind the Plaza San Francisco are generally packed with brightly-dressed Bolivian campesinas selling blankets, nuts, herbs and – for the *gringos* – woolen jumpers with llama motifs. Near here is the famous **Mercado de Hechicería**, or Witchcraft Market, where elderly ladies sell magic charms for every possible occasion. You can pick up a small bottle full of colored pieces of wood and oil which, depending on its contents, will give good luck with love, money or health. A somewhat macabre market specialty is the dried llama fetus, traditionally buried in the foundations of a new building to bring good fortune to the occupants. Also available at many markets are plaster figures of the Indian household god Ekeko, a red-nosed grinning character who is believed to bring prosperity. During the Alacitas Fair, at the end of January, you can buy toy houses, sheep or tiny airline tickets for this Bolivian version of Santa Claus – and he will grant you a real one before the year ends.

When visiting these markets, food turns out to be one of La Paz's most unexpected attractions. Street vendors sell papaya milkshakes, spiced chicken and rice, fried trout caught in Lake Titicaca or pieces of heart with hot nut sauces skewered on a wire. The markets near Plaza San Francisco have a particularly good range of delicacies, served by ladies grown large on their own cooking. Take a seat at one of the booths for tea and goat cheese in the early afternoon –

Map on page 174

Bolivian folk musi-cians have penned many unforgettable tunes, including El Condor Pasa, *which became a huge hit for Simon and Garfunkel in the 1970s, and more recently, the* lambada.

BELOW: *Cholas* (indigenous women of the city) selling vegetables.

the perfect vantage point to watch Bolivian life go by. Later on, a potent *chicha* (fermented maize drink) might be more appropriate, or the excellent local beer.

La Paz has an unusual collection of museums, such as the **Museo Murillo** on Calle Jaén, in an old mansion owned by one of the country's greatest heroes, Pedro Domingo Murillo, who led an unsuccessful revolt against the Spanish in 1909 and was hanged for his efforts. There is a good collection of colonial furniture and a room devoted to medicine and magic. In the same street, the **Museo de Litoral** has artifacts from the War of the Pacific, which deprived Bolivia of its only access to the sea. A defiant emblem over the cashier reads: "Bolivia Has Not Lost and Will Never Lose Its Right to the Pacific". The **Museo Nacional de Arte**, in the 18th-century baroque palace of the Count of Arana, near the cathedral at Calle Socabaya 432, has colonial and local paintings, and the **Museo Nacional de Etnografía y Folklore**, in the palace of the Marquis of Villaverde, Calle Ingavi 915, has good cultural exhibits from Ayoreo and Chipaya indians.

Beyond the city

La Paz is the perfect base for exploring the Bolivian highlands. The easiest excursion is to the so-called **Valle de la Luna** (Valley of the Moon) **Ⓐ**. Only 11 km (7 miles) away from downtown La Paz in distance, but light years away in appearance, this is a bizarrely eroded hillside full of pinnacles and miniature canyons. Known technically as "badlands", its desert formations are constantly shifting and can be explored for hours.

Chacaltaya Ⓑ, an hour and a half by bus from the city center, is the world's highest developed ski area. The ski slopes, at between 5,200 and 5,420 meters (17,000 and 17,782 ft) above sea level, are definitely only for those acclimatized to the altitude. For those less interested in snow sports or who tire at such dizzy heights, the peak still provides some spectacular views of the Andes.

Most visitors to La Paz use the opportunity to visit the Bolivian side of nearby **Lake Titicaca** (*see page 168*) the great high-altitude expanse of water shared with Peru. One easy excursion is to the small village of **Copacabana** Ⓒ, famous for its miracle-working Dark Virgin of the Lake, the patron saint of Bolivia. An image of the Virgin was taken to Rio de Janeiro in the 19th century and the village found itself giving its name to a (today more well-known) Brazilian beach. The Bolivian Copacabana is a quiet and relaxing place, where visitors can stroll along the lakeside or loll in one of the many fish restaurants. But it comes alive during its regular fiestas, when the Virgin is paraded through the streets, copious amount of alcohol is consumed and any new buses and trucks are solemnly blessed with beer poured over their bonnets.

For those with a day to spare, take a boat trip to the **Isla del Sol** (Island of the Sun) Ⓓ. This lush and idyllic spot contains a sacred rock at its northwestern end, where the Incas believed that their founding parents, Manco Capac and Mama Ocllo, emerged from the waters of Lake Titicaca at the call of the sun god.

Glimpses of an ancient civilization

The splendid ruins of **Tiahuanaco** Ⓔ (*see page 22*), on the southern tip of Lake Titicaca, are easily accessible from La Paz. With less than one-sixth of the site excavated, this site is fast becoming one of the most important in South America. Tiahuanaco boasts a magnificently carved Gate of the Sun, Acapana Pyramid and chambers cut from stone with faces staring from the walls. For those whose appetites have been whetted by a visit to the ruins, many of the

Map on page 180

BELOW: baptismal goods for sale, Copacabana.

finds are now housed in La Paz, in the **Museo Nacional de Arqueología** (on the corner of Federico Zuazo and Tiwanaku streets).

Down to the valley

Sweeping down from the Andean heights near La Paz to Bolivia's steaming Amazon basin is the lush, sub-tropical region known as the **Yungas**. The combination of a warm climate with magnificent mountain views has made the zone a favorite for short visits from the capital and for the growing number of trekkers now flocking to Bolivia.

The Yungas – the name simply means "Valleys" – is in a completely different climatic zone to the Bolivian capital, less than 100 km (60 miles) away on the bleak, barren *altiplano*. The drive to La Paz is one of the most spectacular in South America, going over a high-altitude mountain pass to dive into fertile valleys with drifting tropical mists, ancient Inca terraces and abundant fruit.

At 1,500 meters (5,000 ft) above sea level, the small town of **Coroico ❷** is the zone's main commercial center. Coroico itself is little more than a tidy main square surrounded by a few cheap restaurants and hotels. But there are plenty of tranquil walks in the dripping green countryside near the town, beyond the plantations growing coffee, coca and bananas. The gentle strolls provide spectacular views of snow-capped mountain ranges on the horizon leading to jungle-covered valleys, as well as to several rivers for swimming. The best views of the Cordillera Real are from the little church above the town, at the top of Cerro Uchumachi. Also worth a visit is the **Mothers of Clarissa Convent**, where Bolivian nuns make peanut butter, biscuits and quite drinkable local wine.

The nearby towns of **Sorata** and **Chulumani ❸** are equally relaxing places

BELOW: llama traffic, Yungas.

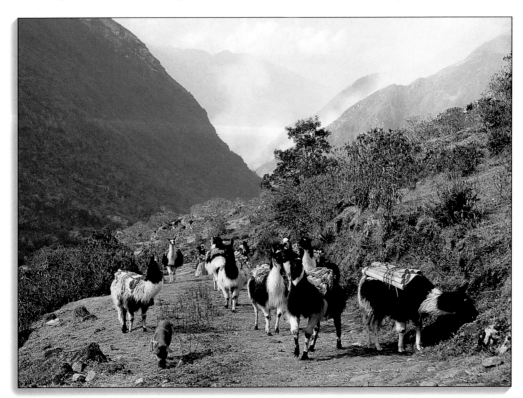

to visit, both villages with small guesthouses and walks. The roads to both places are magnificent and Sorata in particular is said to have the most beautiful setting in Bolivia. A day hike from Sorata leads to the bat-filled **San Pedro cave**. Less adventurous spirits will be content with strolls through the flower-filled valleys that locals insist was the original site of the Garden of Eden.

Map on page 174

Bolivia's "Inca Trail"

Coroico is enjoying a new popularity as a starting point and a goal for two popular treks, neither of which need any special experience to tackle. The most popular walk begins at **La Cumbre**, the highest point of the road from La Paz to the Yungas. It takes about four days, following an ancient Inca road that is in better repair than the path to Machu Picchu in Peru, though it lacks any sites as magnificent as the Inca ruins along the way.

Starting in the freezing and treeless heights, this path quickly descends into the more lush and habitable Yungas. Most walkers advance slowly at first, gasping in the thin mountain air and rhythmically plodding over the chilly pass. At this altitude, there are no signs of human habitation. But further into the valleys, small villages begin to appear, which are often inhabited by numerous yelping dogs but few people. In one village, enterprising campesinos have used parts of the fuselage from a grief-stricken airplane to make a bridge over a stream and a set of chicken coops. More villagers can be seen walking along the path at lower altitudes, usually Bolivian women weighted down with sacks of potatoes or sticks. Finally the Inca path gives way to rough, landslide-prone Bolivian roads, where passing trucks head to the town of Coroico.

BELOW: devil dancer in the *Diablada* parade, Oruro Fiesta.

The Gold-Diggers' Trail

Another trek begins where the last left off, in Coroico. Taking a road back into the mountains, the trail runs further down into the **Beni jungle** along the so-called "Gold-Diggers' Trail". It follows the **Tipuani Valley**, a region first fossicked by the Incas. They exhausted all the surface gold, which was used for ornamental purposes in their temples and art. Today thousands of Bolivians have tossed in their old lives in cities to try their luck in the jungle, and are now digging tunnels in the hope of instant wealth.

The trail once again follows an ancient Inca road, this time mossy and crumbling, through jungle-clad mountains and dramatic gorges. It passes many small mining communities that can only be reached on foot, like the village of **Fatima**, put together from bamboo and corrugated iron only a few years ago.

But the primitive jungle setting sits incongruously with signs of sudden wealth: makeshift bars have new refrigerators, with crowds of men already drunk on beer at 9am. Residents come panting down the mountainside after trips to the capital carrying portable cassette decks and non-stick frying pans.

Other settlements, such as **Llipi**, have up to 600 people living with the overpowering smell of rotting garbage and stale urine. Its main street has 15 bars, six pool halls and three brothels, where miners relax with considerable gusto. The path ends at the hot and dusty town of **Guanay ❹**, a rather unsalubrious Amazon outpost. From there buses can be taken back to Coroico and La Paz.

Heading south: Bolivia's most famous fiesta

The town of **Oruro ❺**, 230 km (143 miles) south of La Paz, originally came to prominence as a mining town, but its mines are now redundant. Its mining past is remembered in the **Museo Etnográfico Minero.** Other places to visit include the **Casa de la Cultura**, a former residence of tin baron Simón Patiño, **Museo Antropológico** (ethnic history), the **Museo Mineralógico** (minerals).

But Oruro is best known today for its annual fiesta, **La Diablada**, the most famous in Bolivia, held eight days before Ash Wednesday. The celebrations begin the night before. At dawn on the big day, eager spectators take their places early, huddling against the cold mountain winds. Soon the street vendors are out in force, selling cans of beer. Older people turn up their noses at tinned drinks, preferring a more potent breakfast of *chicha*, the local maize beer. By 10am the crowd is ready for the Devil Dance.

Satan and Lucifer lead a procession of hundreds of dancing devils in fantastic outfits, leaping and pirouetting along the steep roads. Other dancers are dressed as pumas, monkeys or insects. The lead is soon taken by China Supay, the Devil's wife, who tries to seduce the Archangel Michael with her wiles.

Some dancers dress as the Incas, in headdresses shaped like the condor, while others appear as black slaves brought over by the Spaniards, clanking through the streets in chains. Bolivian girls in pink and black mini-skirts bounce along the steep streets, dancing with men dressed as giant white bears. The procession ends up at a football stadium, where dancers perform two masques. The first is

BELOW: preparing for the procession at the Festival of Jesus, La Paz.

a reenactment of the Spanish Conquest, performed, naturally enough, as a tragedy. In the second, the Archangel Michael defeats the forces of evil with his flaming sword, taking on the devils and the Seven Deadly Sins. The result is announced by the Virgen del Socavón, the patroness of miners, and the dancers enter a chapel to chant a hymn in Quechua.

Despite the Christian gloss over the proceedings, the Diablada is a pagan ceremony of thanks to Pachamama, "Earth Mother," to commemorate the struggle between the forces of good and evil. The conquering Spaniards were only able to convert the indians superficially, changing a few names of deities to fit the formulae of the church. The *diablada* survived and grew during colonial times as an expression of the indians' frustration. The Europeans sat on their elegant balconies and looked on, while the subjected peoples were allowed their annual dose of freedom – an act of rebellion that became a safety valve.

Central city

Bolivia's third largest city, **Cochabamba ❻**, 160 km (100 miles) east of Oruro, lies in a fertile area known as Bolivia's granary, at an altitude of 2,400 meters (9,200 ft). This city is an intriguing mix of old, entrenched tradition and burgeoning new energy. The heart of traditional Cochabamba revolves around the **Plaza 14 de Septiembre**, with its typical mélange of elegant and imposing edifices, street vendors, busy office workers and the more elevated personages, defiantly braving the cloying weather in wool and tweed. Notable buildings include the **cathedral** and the colonial churches of **Santo Domingo** and **San Francisco**. In the evening, trendy bars and pizza restaurants around **Avenida España** fill with young people with disposable income. Out in the wealthy

Map on page 174

Llama fetuses and other fetishes are sold in street markets all over Bolivia.

BELOW: yet another bus breakdown.

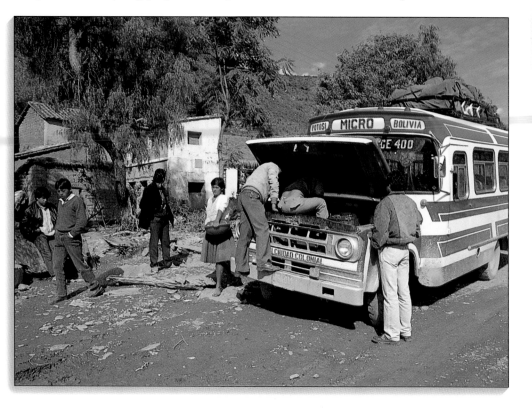

northern suburbs there are some unexpectedly snazzy office buildings, restaurants and shopping malls, a world away from the gently decaying city center.

The name Cochabamba is derived from the Quechua "Khocha Pampa", which means "a plain full of small lakes."

Tin baron Simón Patiño left his mark on Cochabamba in the form of the **Palacio de Portales**, built between 1915 and 1925 – all the furniture was imported from Europe. The **Museo Arqueológico** has an excellent selection of pre-Columbian artefacts dating back to 15,000 BC.

Just south of the city center, perched on a hill, the **Heroínas de la Coronilla** monument commemorates the women independence fighters who defended Cochabamba from Spanish forces in 1812. East of the city center, at the end of Avenida de las Heroínas, a statue of Christ stands atop the **Cerro San Pedro**.

There are a number of Inca ruins in the vicinity of Cochabamba, and though none rival Machu Picchu or Tiahuanaco, they are worth visiting. **Inkallajta**, described as the "frontier post of the Inca Empire", is an extensive site located on a turn-off from the old Cochabamba–Santa Cruz road. If you don't have your own transport, you may well have difficulty finding someone to take you there, however there are some guided tours available. **Inka Rakay,** 27 km (17 miles) west of Cochabamba, is better known for the wonderful views of the Cochabamba Valley than for the ruins themselves.

Along the Rio Mamoré

BELOW LEFT: open-air transport.
BELOW RIGHT: campesinas in their distinctive dress.

Puerto Villaroel ❼ is the departure point for boats heading north to Guayaramerín on the Rio Mamoré. It's a cosy little village where everyone seems to know everyone else, and from **Ivirgazama** (last opportunity for river trippers to purchase mosquito nets and hammocks) the road becomes a dirt track. **Trinidad ❽**, in the heart of the Bolivian Amazon, is the capital of Beni

Province, with airport connections to Cochabamba and La Paz. The **Laguna Suárez**, 5 km (3 miles) away, is a popular wildlife-spotting and rest spot. Wildlife can also be seen at **Chuchini**, 17 km (11 miles) from Trinidad. Chuchini has an archaeological museum displaying remnants of the ancient Beni culture. The 300-km (200-mile) trip along the Rio Mamoré to **Guayaramerín ❾** takes three or four days. This bustling frontier town at the northern tip of the country is split in two by the river. The Brazilian side is known as Guajará-Mirim. The Bolivian side is an incongruous mix of dusty backstreets and brash duty-free shops selling perfume, jeans and flashy electronic goods.

Riberalta ❿, three hours away by bus, is a very pleasant, slow-paced and friendly little town, with a cluster of low-key eating establishments grouped around the main plaza, ideally placed for perusing the town's social circuit. Towards dusk, motorbikes begin to trundle around the square, none of them exceeding 32 km (20 mph). By mid-evening, most of the town's youngsters plus a few motorbiking grandpops and even whole families complete with gurgling babies in the saddle are in gentle two-wheeled orbit. Long conversations are held from bike to bike, while romances fizz into life and fizzle out again.

It is possible to travel between Riberalta and **Rurrenabaque ⓫** by boat along the Rio Beni, but you'll probably have a long wait for a boat. Boat traffic suffered due to the construction of a road link, however the road is unsurfaced and can be a very sticky experience, especially during the rainy season – be warned! Rurrenabaque is a very pretty small town which is currently enjoying a tourist boom due to its lush rainforest location, which makes it an ideal centre for jungle expeditions and boat trips on the Beni and Tuichi Rivers. The town has some good restaurants and abundant low-budget accommodation.

Map on page 174

BELOW: barges on the Rio Mamoré, Trinidad.

GENTLY DOWN THE STREAM

Taking a river boat trip is one of the best ways to sample real Bolivian life. But be warned – if bucket toilets and tummy troubles give you nightmares, this is definitely not the trip for you! Barges chug up and down Bolivia's Rio Mamoré from Puerto Villaroel to Guayaramerin on the Bolivia-Brazil border, delivering fuel and fruit. Bookings are informal – ask around in the village of Puerto Villaroel and people will tell you if a boat is due to leave. If you're in luck, it will have room for passengers. The most important things to bring with you are a mosquito net and a hammock – beds may be in short supply. It's also a good idea to bring food and water, as supplies of these may be limited too. There may be occasional trading trips to jungle villages along the river bank, but passengers are not always taken along.

Don't expect any cruise-style entertainment either – you have to find your own way to fill the days. This is not as difficult as it might initially seem – you can catch up on your reading, chat to the crew and polish up your Spanish or Quechua as well as doing a bit of bird-watching or dolphin-spotting. At dusk, if the weather is clear, find a comfortable spot on deck, lie back and prepare yourself for a truly star-studded evening's entertainment!

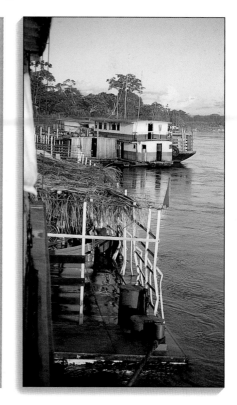

Coca Leaves

To the outside world, the small green coca leaf is best known as the raw material for the drug cocaine. But in the highlands of Peru, Bolivia and Ecuador, it has been part of traditional Indian culture for more than 4,000 years. Coca leaves are on sale in any mountain town market. Ask at a café for *maté de coca*, and you will receive a hot and refreshing drink of coca tea, said to be the best cure for *soroche*.

Some three million South Americans chew coca regularly, adding a little bicarbonate of soda to get the saliva going. It gives energy and dulls the senses against cold. Miners chew up to 1 lb (2.2 kg) a day.

Coca is used at every stage of life. Before giving birth, a woman chews the leaves to hasten labor and ease the pain. Relatives celebrate the birth by chewing the leaf together. When a young man wants to marry a girl, he offers her father coca. When somebody dies, *maté de coca* is drunk at the wake and a small pile of leaves is placed in the coffin.

Local *yatiris* (soothsayers) use coca to tell the future, after scattering the leaves over a woolen blanket and reciting a prayer.

Coca was first cultivated in the Andes around 2,000 BC. Three millennia later, the Incas turned its production into a monopoly, one more way to control subject populations. Its use was restricted to royalty, priests, doctors and the empire's messenger runners, known to travel up to 250 km (150 miles) a day aided by chewing the leaves.

By the arrival of the first Europeans, the Incas had relaxed their monopoly on coca and its use had spread beyond their empire. Italian explorer Amerigo Vespucci, arriving in the Caribbean in 1499, noted with distaste that the islanders "each had their cheeks bulging with a certain green herb which they chewed like cattle." But within months of Pizarro's arrival at Cuzco in 1533, he found some of his own men secretly chewing coca.

The Catholic church first tried to ban coca chewing, denouncing it as "the delusion of the devil." They quickly changed their tune when it was found that Indians needed it to survive the brutal conditions in colonial mines and plantations. To keep the captive labor force under control, the church then went into the coca business itself.

Coca was almost unheard of in Europe and the United States until the mid-1800s, when Parisian chemist Angelo Mariani marketed a wine made from the leaf. Immensely popular, this *Vin Mariani* quickly inspired several American soft drink companies to produce drinks based on coca.

At the same time, cocaine was first being developed. It was quickly taken up by such luminaries as Sigmund Freud, who called it a "magical substance." Sir Arthur Conan Doyle wrote of his fictional character Sherlock Holmes regularly partaking of cocaine. But moves were already afoot to ban the drug.

Scientists who have studied coca agree that there are no dangers in chewing the leaf, nor is it addictive, but because of its association with cocaine, coca leaves are strictly banned in most countries. Taking home so much as a strip of coca leaf chewing gum or a coca teabag could get you into trouble. ❑

LEFT: bags of coca leaves, commonly seen at Bolivian markets.

The Oriente and Bolivia's official capital

The city of **Sucre** , 600 km (370 miles) southeast of La Paz, is Bolivia's official capital, although much of the government business is based in the big city on the altiplano. Sucre is a small, elegant city of important historical significance. Notable buildings around the Plaza 25 de Mayo include the Casa de la Libertad where Bolivia's declaration of independence was signed, and the cathedral, with nearby Museo de la Catedral. The city has many interesting religious buildings, including the churches of San Miguel, San Francisco and Merced and the Convento de San Felipe Neri. The Franciscan monastery of La Recoleta and its Museo are on top of the Cerro Dalence to the southeast of Sucre, and afford excellent views of the city. There is also a Museo de la Historia Natural and the very interesting Museo Textil Etnográfico (San Alberto 413), which displays Andean textiles traditionally woven from llama and alpaca wool. Five kilometers south of the city, the **Castillo de la Glorieta** was built in a mixture of European styles by the Argandoña family.

Traditional textiles can be purchased at the typically Andean village of **Tarabuco**, 65 km (40 miles) east of Sucre, which is renowned for its weaving. South of Sucre is the Cordillera de los Frailes mountain range, with trekking, rock paintings and hot springs. Dinosaur bones have been found at **Cal Orko**, 7 km (four and a half miles) from Sucre. Guided tours are available from Sucre to see the bones. Che Guevara memorial tours are also available in Sucre, visiting some of the locations the revolutionary passed through on his final journey, including the small village of **La Higuera**, where he was killed.

Five hundred kilometers (300 miles) east of Cochabamba is **Santa Cruz** , Bolivia's boomtown. Its first, shortlived boom, came from rubber in the late 19th century. The current growth spurt was encouraged by a government-led "March to the East" from the 1950s and has been powered by petroleum and tropical lowland crops like soybeans, sugar, rice, cotton, and last but not least, cocaine. Santa Cruz is not a popular tourist destination, though it does have some interesting museums and an interesting ethnic mix due to the numbers of people who swarmed to the city to take advantage of its economic success. There is a sizeable Japanese community and a strong Andean cultural presence, with *peñas*; the city also has an abundance of nightclubs and karaoke bars. Santa Cruz is linked by rail to Brazil and Argentina, but this mode of travel has been described as an endurance test.

City of silver

Perched at 4,000 meters (13,000 ft) above sea level in the shadow of a cursed mountain, **Potosí** , in the south west of Bolivia, 550 km (340 miles) southeast of La Paz, is the highest city of its size in the world. It was built in this inhospitable location by Spanish conquistadors for just one purpose: silver mining. Today the Andean city is only a shadow of its former glory, when – during the 1600s – Potosí was as large as London and many times more opulent. But anyone visiting Bolivia should make the journey to Potosí. Not only is it one of the least-touched colonial cities on the continent, Potosí has become, for many,

Map on page 174

In 1967 the hero of the Cuban revolution, Che Guevara, was hunted down and killed in eastern Bolivia, where he was trying to incite the campesinos to rise in revolution.

BELOW: entrance to the Casa de Moneda, Spain's New World mint, Potosí.

a symbol of Latin America's fate. It proves a rule of thumb: the richest regions in colonial times are the poorest today.

"As rich as a Potosí"

Appropriately, **El Cerro Rico** (Rich Hill), is always visible from the city's streets. The Incas had known that there was silver in the bare red mountain but did nothing to exploit it. The Spaniards, however, were quick to begin mining, soon discovering that the hill held the largest silver deposit the world had ever seen. A frontier city was quickly created on the bleak mountainside, with conquistadors and missionaries flocking from Spain to win a slice of the fantastic wealth. Local Indians were press-ganged to work in the mines, dying by the thousands in horrific conditions.

Even today, people in Spain use the phrase "as rich as a Potosí" when they try to describe an unimaginable fortune. The city's churches were built with silver altars and the lavish feasts of Spanish nobles glittered with the precious metal. Even the horses were said to be shod with silver in Potosí. When the silver gave out, and the Spaniards left, the city survived on tin mining. Now tin is almost worthless, and Potosí has become a fascinating relic.

Testimony to the former riches are the scattered crumbling villas, stone carved doorways and forgotten abbeys of the city. Ancient houses teeter from both sides to nearly meet in the middle of narrow, winding streets. Potosí is still crowded with masterpieces of colonial architecture and artworks blending the styles of medieval Europe and pre-Conquest Indian.

BELOW: Tarabuco festival.

Potosí's most impressive building, considered one of the finest examples of Spanish civil construction in Latin America, is the **Casa Real de Moneda**. First built in 1542 and reconstructed in 1759, it was used as a mint by the colonizers. Now a museum, it has rooms full of religious art, collections of colonial coins and the original wooden minting machines once worked by negro slaves. Guided tours take up to three hours to work through the many exhibits, which contain anything from altars removed from collapsed churches to relics of Bolivia's foreign wars. One of the prize displays is a pair of iron strong boxes used to transport silver from the New World to Spain, using no less than 15 locks to secure them, while a huge gallery makes a valiant, but still incomplete attempt to provide portraits of the country's many presidents. Wear plenty of warm clothes, as the museum is like a refrigerator inside.

Many of Potosí's churches are crumbling into disrepair – in fact, some are dangerously close to collapse. A stroll through the city will take you past **San Francisco**, **La Compañia** and **San Lorenzo**, as well as the **cathedral** and **Cabildo** in the main plaza. Wandering through the town, look out for famous old mansions such as the **Casa de las Tres Portadas** on Calle Bolivar 19–21 and the **Crystal Palace** at Calle Sucre 148–156.

A city drained of its wealth

Potosí is much more than a collection of ruined colonial buildings. Many of the Andean Indians in the area live in a way that has changed little over the centuries. The **town market** is a fascinating place to explore, full of round women selling produce and butchers carrying whole animal carcasses over their shoulders – usually covered in flies and with the beast's hairy tail still dangling from the meat. But there are few signs of the city's past wealth. The poorest parts of the city, closer to the Rich Hill, were traditionally occupied by miners and their

Map on page 174

TIP

At more than 4,200 meters (13,780 ft) above sea level, it's a good idea to acclimatize to Potosí's altitude with a day or two of relaxation around the city before you expose your lungs to the exertion of a trip down the mines.

BELOW:
Cerro Rico, Potosí.

Miners' shrine to El Tío, Potosí.

families. A monument to the Bolivian miner has been set up in one of the squares. The mining unions of Potosí and Oruro, once the most powerful force in Bolivian politics, were all but destroyed with the collapse of tin prices in the 1980s. There are few mines in operation these days, and unemployment stalks the streets. The wealth of Potosí proved a curse that is still with the Indians today. The city which helped finance the economic development of Europe in centuries gone by has slid deeper into Third World oblivion.

Realm of the Devil

Deep in the heart of Potosí's "Rich Hill", dust-covered miners were laughing with the Devil. Chewing coca leaves in a candlelit recess full of putrid air, they paid their respects to a small horned statue, the perceived owner of the silver beneath the ground. The miners visit El Tío – "the Old Fellow" – every day to leave a drink or burn a cigarette for luck.

"El Tío has always liked tobacco," joked one of the miners, "but these days he only accepts filter tips."

The image of the Devil in the Incarnación mine was made 300 years ago by Indian slaves press-ganged by the Spanish to dig silver in Potosí. Conditions in the mines have changed little since those days. With the collapse of the tin market in 1985, the state mines of Cerro Rico were closed, but since then Bolivian miners have been re-opening old shafts to find the silver that the conquistadors left behind. The digging is being carried out in such a primitive and dangerous fashion that many miners accept their work as a kind of death sentence.

BELOW: mining in 18th-century conditions, Potosí.

Every day at dawn, the miners gather outside the Incarnación mine on El Cerro Rico. The mountain that once held the world's greatest silver deposit is now a giant slag heap, an unnaturally symmetrical peak riddled with more than 5,000 shafts.

Inside Incarnación Mine

Incarnación is only one of the several private mines still operating, to which guides from the city will bring visitors for a small fee. Most people bring a few packets of cigarettes to share with the miners as they spend the first hour of their day sitting in the cold sun, chatting and chewing coca leaves, which have been in use long before the Incas to ward off hunger and fatigue. Visiting a mine is absolutely not for asthma sufferers. Claustrophobia sufferers won't like it much either – you need to crouch just to enter the mouth of the tunnels, while the miners' antique carbide lamps barely dent the darkness.

Ancient wooden shaft supports often sag in the middle. Stalactites hang from the rough walls of the tunnel near its mouth, but as the mine descends into the mountain, polar cold shifts to sub-tropical heat. Many of the shafts can only be passed on hands and knees. The air becomes thick and stale. Workers from the last shift become visible down cracks, stripped to the waist and hacking away with picks.

There are no power tools and no engineers in mines such as Incarnación. Blasting is done with dynamite bought in the supply store in Potosí, and the miners simply withdraw around a corner as the charge

Map on page 174

goes off. Each worker keeps the ore he finds himself. Miners on the lowest levels must climb long ladders to the surface with sacks of rocks on their backs.

The real enemy here is silicosis, caused by fine dust gathering in the miners' lungs. Within a few years of entering the pit, many feel a heavy weight on their chests. A few years later, they die coughing blood. Little wonder that Indian tradition holds the metals of Potosí to be the property of the Devil, or that the miners give El Tío his daily cigarette for luck.

Group tours lasting four to five hours are organized by recognized guides. Put on your old clothes and take a handkerchief to keep out the dust. A helmet and lamp will be provided. The tour costs around $5 and a donation to the miners' cooperative is appreciated.

Lake district with a difference

In the west, near the frontier with Chile, is one of Bolivia's most popular tourist destinations. The **Salar de Uyuni** is said to be the largest salt lake in the world, at 10,500 sq. km (4,054 sq. miles). More desert than lake, it's an eerie sight, lying 3,653 meters (11,985 ft) above sea level – bring warm clothes, as temperatures can plummet at this altitude. There is accommodation available in the town of **Uyuni** ⑮, including the Hotel Playa Blanca, which is built out of salt! Tours of the area can also be arranged from Potosí or Sucre. Most tours include the option of visiting **Laguna Colorada**, a bright red lake patronised by pink flamingoes 346 km (215 miles) southwest of Uyuni and **Laguna Verde**, a chilly aquamarine lake at 5,000 meters (16,400 ft) above sea level. Other attractions in the area close to the Chilean border include geysers at Sol de Mañana and hot springs at Aguas Termales Chalviri. ❑

BELOW: salt mining, Uyuni salt basin.

ECUADOR

Despite being one of the smallest South American countries, Ecuador has plenty of attractions: smoldering volcanoes, rainforest reserves, indian markets and, of course, the Galápagos Islands

Map
on page
198

Ecuador is one of the easiest and most rewarding countries to explore in South America. It is a peaceful enclave in the Andes without the social turbulence and sporadic violence of neighboring Peru and Columbia. Small (just 283,500 sq. km) but geographically varied, Ecuador's incredible natural diversity has made it the focus of worldwide biological research. The country has more species of plants (25,000) and birds (over 1,500) than the United States, which is 34 times larger. Sadly, these precious ecosystems are being degraded by a rate of deforestation higher than any nation in South America (280,000 hectares per annum), but INEFAN, the Ecuadorian National Park Service, with the help of national and international conservation organizations, currently protects 17 percent of the total land mass in national parks and ecological reserves. For a developing nation with a per capita GDP (Gross Domestic Product) of US $1,534, these conservation efforts are admirable.

Outdoor activities are Ecuador's biggest tourist draw. Within a day's drive or flight from the capital city of Quito you can experience virgin Amazon jungle, snow-capped peaks, tropical sandy beaches and Darwin's Galápagos Islands. Outfitters are set up for mountaineering, trekking, jungle canoe trips, mountain biking, rafting, parapenting, scuba diving and horseback riding.

PRECEDING PAGES:
Zumbagua market.
LEFT: Mount Sangay
eruption.
BELOW: reveler in
the Mamá Negra
parade, Latacunga.

Eight active volcanoes periodically erupt, spewing columns of ash and melt glaciers into mud flows that destroy Sierran villages. When the Andes are uplifted along geologic faults from the coastal plain, powerful earthquakes can shake the hillsides. A costly earthquake in 1987 broke the trans-Andean oil pipeline in several places, crippling the national economy for six months. Landslides are common during the rainy season, closing roads. Floods due to El Niño in 1982–83 and 1997–98 virtually paralyzed coastal communities.

But Ecuadorians have a tremendous capacity to bounce back and rebuild their country. The tradition of the *minga* (an obligatory community work project), inherited from the Incas, continues to draw citizens together to overcome nature's challenges.

A nation in movement

Although the country is traditionally divided into four regions – Sierra, Coast, Oriente and Galápagos – these regions blend at the margins to form a rich mosaic. Perhaps most telling of Ecuador's identity is the flow of goods and people between regions. Trucks filled with *plátanos* (green bananas) daily climb the cloud forests of the western slope of the Sierra to stock Quito's cool open air markets, while sacks filled with endemic varieties of potatoes are transported down to hot and humid barrios of Guayaquil. The Oriente pumps vital oil exports through a pipeline which

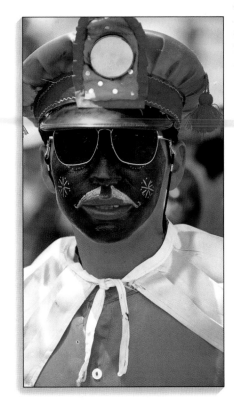

crosses the Andes to tankers docked at the port city of Esmeraldas. It is not uncommon to see a colorfully dressed highland *Otavaleño* on the coast selling woven goods, as well as a coastal *moreno* (Afro-Ecuadorian) on a bus on the Pan-American highway offering traditional homemade *cocada* (coconut candy).

The majority of Ecuadorians are Catholics but there is a growing number of Protestants (now estimated at more than 10 percent), due to missionary efforts which began after freedom of religion was guaranteed in 1945. Pre-colonial indigenous religions are rarely practiced in their pure forms except in isolated pockets in the Oriente, but elements are incorporated into modern Christianity.

Pre-Inca civilizations

In the 10th century AD, the Caras – forefathers of the modern Otavaleños (*see page 202*) – settled in the Quito area. They built an observatory to mark the solstices, and identified the equator as "the path of the sun." They were animists who worshiped the sun, and believed the moon was inhabited by humans. Their

The important Inca sun god Inti is often subtly portrayed in religious colonial art, and in return the Catholic celebration for Saint Peter is associated with the Inti Raymi festival (Winter Solstice).

economy was based on weaving, and the law required women to spin wool whenever possible, even when walking mountain trails.

Their successors were the Duchicela dynasty which established the powerful Kingdom of Quitu, which was eventually conquered by the Inca Tupac-Yupanqui. Ecuador soon played an important part in the collapse of the Inca Empire (*see page 26*), with the execution of the Inca Atahuallpa by Francisco Pizarro. While Pizarro plundered, his lieutenant Sebastian de Benalcázar battled northwards to the city of Quito. Arriving in late 1534, he found the city in ruins: Rumiñahui, Atahuallpa's general, had destroyed and evacuated it rather than lose it intact to the Spaniards. Benalcázar refounded Quito on December 6, 1534. Rumiñahui was captured, tortured and executed the following month.

Ecuador was initially administered by the Spanish as a province of the Vice-Royalty of Peru, and was the site of the first cultivation of wheat and bananas in South America. Colonial administration was based on the *encomienda* system, which was preserved after independence in the form of huge estates or *latifundis* owned by a tiny percentage of Ecuador's wealthiest criollo families. Land reforms were not enacted until 1964, freeing the Indians from compulsory agricultural labor. Often, however, it was unproductive land which was redistributed, and many *haciendas* (ranches) remained intact, governments being reluctant to attack the wealthiest and most powerful class, the landowners.

The injustices of Spanish rule prompted several violent uprisings. The first of these was the Alcabalas Revolution of 1592–93, when the populace, with the active support of the lower clergy, rebelled against increased taxes on food and fabrics. The reprisals were brutal.

The first president of Ecuador, a Venezuelan called Flores, arranged with his

Map on page 198

BELOW: Spanish engraving of conquistadors on the march.

successor, Rocafuerte, to alternate occupancy of the presidency, but then broke the deal, retained control of the army, and bribed Rocafuerte into exile. Finally ousted in 1845, he organized a Spanish invasion of Ecuador which was only averted by Great Britain's intervention. National development since then has been sporadic and almost incidental. Two of the best-remembered presidents, Moreno and Alfaro, were both assassinated by their opponents – one shot, the other slain by an incensed mob.

Stumbling through the 20th century

Girl from Esperanza.

Twentieth-century Ecuador experienced mainly military rule, the last period of which was from 1972–79. In 1978, the army drew up a new constitution under which an election was successfully held the following year. Ecuador became the first Latin American country to return to democracy after the military era which engulfed most of South America throughout the 1970s, and national politics have been stable since then.

Leon Febres Cordero, a Conservative elected in 1984, was kidnapped by troops loyal to a high-ranking general who was in jail for attempting two coups. Febres secured his release after 11 hours by granting the general an amnesty

Elections in 1988 brought to power President Rodrigo Borja Cevallos, a Social Democrat from Quito. During his presidency inflation fell, the foreign debt was serviced regularly and foreign investors continued to be attracted. These trends continued under his successor, Sixto Duran Ballen, of the Christian Social Party, who introduced an unpopular privatisation program.

Many people were surprised that Abdala Bucaram, "El Loco" (the Crazy One), was elected in 1996. The corrupt Bucaram was ousted in February, 1997,

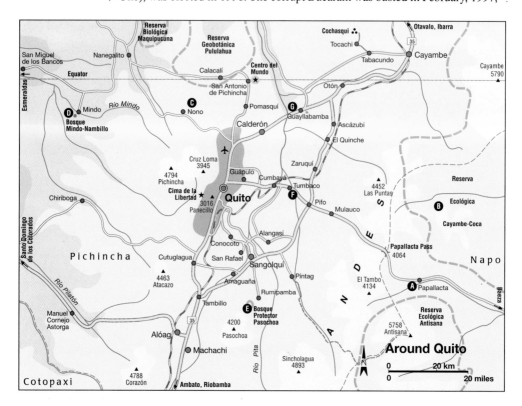

Around Quito

after thousands of citizens, dressed in black, marched through the streets of Quito and Guayaquil demanding his impeachment. The highly respected military was present, but force was unnecessary to maintain order as a new president, Fabián Alarcón, was democratically installed by the congress.

Map on page 198

Quito: Ecuador's expanding capital

Modern **Quito ❶** spreads further north and south into the intra-Andean valley each year, gobbling up rural farms. Most visitors stay in the **Mariscal** neighborhood, north of **Parque El Ejido**, where old Quito meets new, as the city's old colonial center is more pleasant to explore than the polluted modern sprawl.

Hotels, restaurants and stores bulging with handicrafts line **Avenida Amazonas** and nearby streets. **La Casa de la Cultura**, just off Parque El Ejido, is Ecuador's most comprehensive museum, with collections of pre-Columbian treasures and ornate gold, along with republican, colonial and modern art. Rivaling these collections is the smaller and more informal **Guayasamin Museum** in the Bellavista neighborhood. Oswaldo Guayasamin, Ecuador's most renowned painter (*see page 63*), displays his own bold portraits of indigenous people as well as his personal collection of exquisite pre-Columbian artefacts.

Back down the hill, among fast food joints, shopping malls and cellphones, is evidence of the Ecuadorian middle-class fascination with American culture. Quito has a wide selection of international restaurants, and for nightlife there is usually the latest US blockbuster movie, folkloric ballet shows, or even the choice to try out salsa dancing at an upbeat bar.

Further north, 24 km (15 miles) out of Quito, the **Centro del Mundo** (middle of the world) monument marks the equator. The obelisk houses a museum

BELOW: Quito's modern district.

The Otavaleños

O tavalo is a modern miracle of economic achievement which grew out of colonial oppression. Forced to become weavers by the Spanish, about half of Ecuador's Otavaleño people are today involved in weaving, which has made them the most prosperous indigenous group in Ecuador, possibly in all of South America.

Otavalo lies betwen Quito and the Colombian border. There are expatriate commuities in Colombia, Brazil and Spain. They export their finely manufactured textiles to the United States, Canada and Europe, while the bulk of their business remains in South America.

The modern Otavaleños are descended from the Cara tribe, which expanded from Colombia to the Ecuadorian sierra about 1,000 years ago. The Caras established trade links with neighboring tribes, and bartered cotton and blankets, along with dogs and salt, in exchange for *achiote* (a plant from which dyes are extracted), parrots and

monkeys. The arrival of the Incas in the late 1400s marked the beginning of 500 years of colonization, imposed labor and beliefs. After 17 years of fighting, the Inca Huayna Capac took Caranqui and massacred thousands of Caras. Large numbers of Caras were transported to Peru, while loyal Inca subjects were settled on Cara territory. The Incas introduced coca and llamas, an excellent source of wool, but they were too short-lived to seriously influence Otavaleño culture.

Under the Spanish, the *encomienda* system was established in Otavalo, putting Spanish settlers in control of an area and its indigenous inhabitants. The first weaving *obraje* (workshop) was set up in the 1550s with 500 workers, some as young as nine years old. Modern tools were introduced and within 50 years the Otavalo *obraje* was the most productive in Ecuador. Otavaleños labored 14 hours a day manufacturing cloth, woolen blankets and rope for export. In 1648 an *obraje* in Peguche was closed, because the number of suicides among workers had grown to alarming proportions.

The Otavaleños were forced to learn Quechua to facilitate their conversion to Christianity, although their Catholicism today incorporates ancestral beliefs.

Land reforms enacted in Ecuador in 1964 abolished the *wasipungo* system, based on enforced indigenous labor. The first store selling woven products opened in Otavalo in 1966, and within a dozen years there were 75. Weaving has decentralized from the savage *obrajes* and is now a cottage industry. Over the years, the ingenuity of the Otavalo weavers has brought them worldwide fame.

Every Saturday morning, the usually quiet streets of Otavalo teem with the life. By 9am Market Square, known as Poncho Plaza, is a feast of colors and textures: rolls of cloth, thick blankets, tapestry wall hangings, chunky sweaters, long patterned belts or *fajas,* and *cintas*, tapes the women use to bind their long hair. Most Otavaleño textiles are made of sheep wool, though some alpaca sweaters can be found. The mechanization of the modern textile industry, potentially disastrous for the Otavaleños, has been compensated by tourism and an emphasis on quality goods produced naturally. ❑

LEFT: an Otavaleña displaying her wares.

with displays of the different ethnic cultures of Ecuador, and is definitely worth a visit. Here you can straddle the equator with feet planted in both hemispheres!

Map on page 198

Old Quito: a walking tour

Old Quito displays Spanish colonial architecture at its finest. Walls of brilliant whitewash, deep blue railings and green tile rooftops dazzle the eye, reminiscent of a period when the city was a peaceful provincial capital dedicated to the creation of artistic beauty. Earthquakes in 1587, 1768 and 1859 caused severe damage to many churches, which nevertheless number an astonishing 87. In 1978, UNESCO declared Old Quito a World Heritage site.

The Spanish past blends with modern cultural migration as members of Ecuador's many ethnic groups make Quito their home. Life on colorful **Calle Cuenca** contrasts with the city's relative affluence. Fleshy black women sell tropical fruits, while an indigenous newspaperwoman with a baby at her breast cries " Comercio, hoy!" in a nasal refrain. Above it all stands the church of **San Francisco**, the first major religious construction in the continent and the spiritual heart of the city. Begun a few days after Spanish settlement in 1534, it took 70 years to complete. The creaking wooden floor contrasts with the spectacular baroque carvings of the main altar and the statue of **Our Lady of Quito**, a fine example of the "Quito school of art". This style blends Spanish and Moorish techniques with the indigenous imagination, and grew out of an institution started by pioneer wheat farmer Friar Joedco Ricke.

From San Francisco, it is a short walk through the clothes market on Calle Cuenca to **La Merced**, which contains paintings depicting scenes from Quito's past: Sucre riding gloriously into battle, volcanoes erupting, and suspiciously

Statue of the Virgin, Panecillo, Quito.

BELOW: the Plaza de la Independencia, Quito.

Corn on the cob sculpture, Quito.

BELOW: interior of the lavish church of La Compañía.

docile indigenous people being converted. Two blocks away is the **Plaza de la Independencia**, where the heroes of 1809 are immortalized. Today, *Quiteños* sun themselves, read the morning newspapers, and put the swarming shoeshine boys to work. The **Palacio de Gobierno** (Presidential Palace) has traditional guards and a mural by Guayasamin depicting Orellana's descent of the Amazon.

The adjacent **cathedral**, finished in 1706, is where Ecuador's illustrious lie, including Sucre. Among its collection of paintings is the *Descent From The Cross* by Caspicara, perhaps colonial Ecuador's best indigenous artist. A mere 25 years ago, Ecuador's poverty was such that these showpiece buildings, symbolic cornerstones of church and state, went unpainted.

One block south of the church of **San Augustín**, where the first declaration of independence was signed, is the pedestrian thoroughfare **Calle Eugenio Espejo**. Nearby is the magnificent **La Compañía**, built by the Jesuits between 1605 and 1768. Containing an estimated seven tons of gold, it is Ecuador's most ornate church. The remains of the *Quiteño* saint Mariana de Jesus lie beneath the solid gold main altar, and there is a bizarre collection of colonial art: one painting graphically depicts the grades of punishment reserved for sinners in Hell, with the most unpleasant fate reserved for adulterers and fornicators.

From 1828 until his death in Colombia two years later, Sucre lived a block from here: his house is now a museum, affording a rare glimpse of period aristocratic home life. A statue of Sucre occupies the Plaza of Santo Domingo, opposite the church of the same name, which is best seen at night when its domes are floodlit. Inside is an altar to St Judas, patron saint of "desperate causes," where satisfied worshipers have posted "thank you" notices.

The best-preserved colonial street is **Calle Ronda**, south of the Plaza Santa

TAKING THE TRAIN

Rail travel began in Ecuador in 1910, when the line between Quito and Guayaquil opened, reducing to two days a former nine-day trek along a mule path which was impassable for half the year due to rain. The train rattles along the "Avenue of the Volcanoes" from Quito as far as Riobamba, before descending a series of marvelously engineered switchbacks, which allow breathtaking views of the western Andean slope.

Fields of potatoes and corn give way to tropical lowlands. The northern line starts in Ibarra, a sleepy, provincial mountain town, and ends in the lively port city of San Lorenzo in the north west.

The train descends from rugged, dry scrubland to fields of sugar cane and coffee, papaya and bananas, and through dense rainforest. Unfortunately the 1997–8 El Niño weather system brought landslides and floods, which wrought havoc with some railway lines, and at the time of writing the Ibarra to San Lorenzo train had ceased to run, but the service may resume at a later date.

The Quito–Riobamba train now only runs on Saturdays, and the Riobamba–Guayaquil section has resumed a sporadic service after the landslides of early 1998 put it out of operation.

Domingo, which is entered down a ramp at the motley open-air market on Avenida 24 de Mayo. A quiet, narrow, cobbled lane, it is lined with 16th-century houses with overhanging balconies and heavy grilled doors. This brings you to the **Bridge of the Black Vultures**, where you can climb to the Virgin of Quito at the summit of **El Panecillo** ("little bread loaf"), with sweeping views of the valley and, on a clear day, the peaks of **Pichincha** and **Cayambe**.

Map on page 200

The **Sierra** is actually two mountain ranges (Western and Eastern Cordilleras) divided by a series of north-south trending central valleys. The major highland cities are spaced along the Pan-American Highway in these valleys, 2,000-3,000 meters (6,500–9,800 ft) above sea-level, and are blessed with temperate climates. This region, a beautiful patchwork quilt of fields, is very productive due to rich volcanic soils and little variation in air temperatures. The flat lowland plains are intensely farmed by modern agricultural methods, especially for the booming flower export industry. In the past few years, hundreds of automated greenhouses have been constructed to feed the world demand for roses and carnations during the northern latitude winters.

TIP

Take a taxi to the summit of El Panecillo – and don't go alone – as unfortunately numerous thieves are at work on the way up.

The steep hillsides above the valley floor are owned by Quichua indigenous cooperatives, working small parcels of land, which tractors could never till, with hand tools. Their crops of potatoes, carrots, beans, wheat and corn supply 75 percent of Ecuador's needs. Above are the cold, windswept *páramos* (alpine grasslands), home to grazing horses, cattle and sheep. Still higher, the craggy and glaciated volcanic peaks that dominate the skyline are home to some of the few remaining Andean condors and intrepid mountaineers.

Excursions near Quito

The main road to the Oriente climbs to the continental divide at the headwaters of the Amazon basin. The village of **Papallacta ⓐ** is located below the pass. Here you will find tastefully constructed thermal spring pools surrounded by lush cloudforest. The area is also known for some of the country's best fresh trout, introduced from North American stock. Quiteños escape here on the weekends for walks or horseback rides in the nearby **Cayambe-Coca Ecological Reserve ⓑ**.

BELOW: bargaining for a cow.

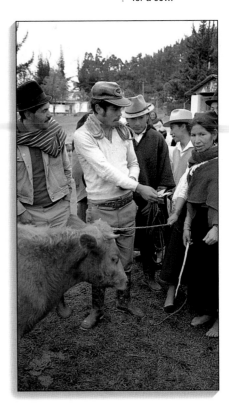

Towards the coast, less than two hours by bus from Quito, are the rural villages of **Nono ⓒ**, **Tandayapa** and **Mindo ⓓ**, which are becoming favorite birding spots. Private reserves and lodges have been set up to cater for visitors keen on exploring the western slope forests. **The Bosque Protector Pasochoa ⓔ** is a pleasant nature reserve southeast of Quito. Some of the last intra-Andean cloudforest is protected here on the slopes of the ancient volcano. Native trees and plants thrive on the rich volcanic soil and are home to 120 species of birds. A half-day hike on Ilaló, near the valley suburb of **Tumbaco ⓕ**, is worth the climb for the views of northern Ecuador's main peaks.

North of Quito

The Pan-American highway heading north first passes through the agricultural town of **Guayllabamba ⓖ**, several hundred meters lower and much warmer than

In 1917, a local weaver started to copy the famous Scottish tweed. Its commercial success led to the international recognition of the weaving skills of the Otavaleños.

Quito, which hosts crops of avocado and chirimoya (custard apple). Restaurants are full at the weekends with Quiteños who stop off for the town's specialty of *locro*, a hearty cheese and potato soup with optional avocado and pork skin. The new **Quito zoo** here houses the Galapagos tortoise, jaguar, several species of monkeys, and the Andean spectacle bear.

Further north, before reaching **Otavalo** ❷ (*see page 202*), you pass near the town of **Cayambe** ❸. This area is historically known for cheese-making, but the flower industry has surpassed cheese factories in economic importance. These large plantations can be toured, and a dozen roses costs about US$1. Cayambe is also the jumping-off place for excursions to the climber's refuge on the flanks of **Nevado Cayambe** (5,790 meters/18,996 ft), the wood-working indigenous community of **Oyacachi**, and the Inca ruins of **Quitoloma**.

The oldest hacienda in Ecuador, **Guachala**, built in 1580, is just outside Cayambe on the equator. In earlier times it was a textile factory producing Scottish-style tweeds. Several other important haciendas open to visitors are scattered around the Otavalo area, including **Cusin** and **Pisanqui**, offering a glimpse into the wealth and privilege enjoyed by large estate owners in the recent past.

About 5 km (3 miles) from Otavalo is an ecologically constructed mountain lodge, **Casa Mojanda**, with spectacular views from its adobe cottages of the nearby volcano, **Cotacachi** (4,944 meters/16,220 ft). Beneath the volcano lies **Laguna Cuicocha**, a collapsed *caldera* (crater) filled with an azure lake.

In the villages near Otavalo the cottage crafts industry is flourishing. **Cotacachi** is most famous for its leather work, **Peguche** and **Agato** for their weaving and **Iluman** for its double-sided ponchos and felt hats. To the north, **Ibarra** is a pleasant colonial town with many inexpensive restaurants and hotels,

BELOW: one of the Lagunas de Mojanda, near Tabacunda.

known locally as "La Ciuidad Blanca" (The White City) for its whitewashed walls and red-roofed colonial buildings. For a challenging but rewarding excursion, climb **Cerro Imbabura** (4,609 meters/15,121 ft), just south of town, with views of surrounding villages. This peak was once glaciated and indians harvested ice from the slopes. Twentieth-century climatic change has melted away the glaciers. A few hours west by bus, the subtropical **Chota Valley** is the only place in the Sierra that is populated by Afro-Ecuadorians.

On the new road to San Lorenzo is the **Cerro Golondrinas Cloudforest Reserve**. A four-day trek descends from the *páramo* through pristine submontane cloudforest and farmland. Visitors will see the positive effects of the conservation efforts in the area, such as the orchid farms, tree nurseries and reforestation projects. At the Colombian border is **Tulcán ❹**, the provincial capital of Carchi, best known for cypress trees in the graveyard which are elaborately carved to resemble animals, houses and geometric figures. At **El Angel Ecological Reserve**, nearby, you can see the giant frailejon plants, members of the daisy family, standing out of the *páramo* vegetation up to two meters tall.

South from Quito

Heading south from Quito takes you along the "Avenue of the Volcanoes," with excellent views of all the major peaks. Several haciendas have been converted into first class hotels, notably **La Cienega**, steeped in 400 years of history. From **Lasso** a dirt road heads up into **Cotopaxi National Park**, which encompasses the peaks of Cotopaxi, Rumiñahui and Sincholagua. Cotopaxi is one of the world's highest active volcanoes and attracts thousands of climbers to its 5,897-meter (19,347-ft) summit every year. At its base, **Laguna Limpio Pungo** harbors Andean gulls, Andean lapwings and the Andean fox. It is one of the best locations to observe *páramo* vegetation and recent volcanic features.

Just off the Pan-American highway on Thursdays at dawn, the quiet village of **Saquisilí** comes alive with Ecuador's largest indigenous market. People from outlying communities fill the streets and plazas with their local produce. A little further south is **Latacunga ❺**, destroyed three times by mud flows from Cotopaxi in the 18th and 19th centuries. In September the streets are filled with processions, dances and fireworks in honor of the black-faced Virgin Mary, an event known as **La Fiesta de la Mama Negra**.

To the west is the indigenous village of **Zumbahua** which hosts a colorful vegetable market on Saturdays. An hour's drive away is the starting point for walks to the deep blue volcanic lake of Quilotoa. This very Indian area is one of the few places where llamas are still employed as pack animals.

The capital of the Tungurahua Province, **Ambato**, was leveled by an earthquake in 1949 and rebuilt with concrete buildings that lend a drab feeling to the city. This is an important industrial and fruit-growing area. Between Baños and Ambato lies the resilient Quichua community of **Salasaca**, whose tapestries are sold throughout the country. Tourism remains a small industry in the immediate area, primarily because the Salasacas ship most of their handiwork out to the

Map on page 198

Tafi *nougat shop, Baños.*

BELOW: Baños thermal baths, possibly the best hot soak in the country.

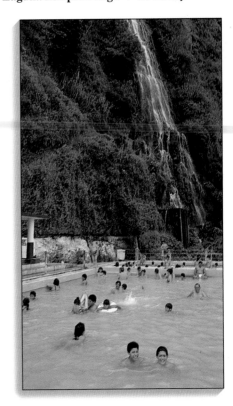

Saturday Otavalo market. The small outdoor market is open at weekends, and it is possible to see artists at work in their homes.

Hot springs and erupting volcanoes

Baños is perhaps the most popular tourist destination for Ecuadorians and foreigners alike. It is named after the thermal springs in town and is graced with a semitropical climate. There are numerous walks in the hills, a zoo, restaurants offering Ecuadorian and foreign cuisine, and lively nightlife. Ecuadorians come from all over the country to visit the **Basilica** which houses a statue of **Nuestra Señora de Agua Santa** (Our Lady of the Holy Water). Paintings hang on the wall depicting the miracles accredited to her. Baños is also a great place to shop for local handicrafts and sample tropical juices. Rafting, climbing the nearby active volcano **Tungurahua** (5,020 meters/16,470 ft), jungle trips, horseback riding and mountain biking can all be organized locally.

Further south, **Riobamba** ❻ sits on the flanks of **Chimborazo**, the highest mountain in Ecuador (6,310 meters/20,702 ft) and starting point for rail trips to the coast which pass through the town of **Alausí** ❼. Before the Inca period Puruhua people lived in the region, but during Inca rule they were moved away and people from northern Peru were ordered to move here. Today the region is dominated by different indigenous groups and the variety of hats and traditional dress reflects these strong cultures.

To the west of Riobamba is the expansive and remote **Sangay National Park**, home to the mountain tapir and Andean spectacle bear, and the daily erupting volcano **Sangay** (5,230 meters/17,159 ft). On the edge of the park is part of an old Inca highway that once ran from Quito to Cusco in Peru. Visitors can hike

Girl from Imbabura.

BELOW: Riobamba, beneath Mount Chimborazo.

Map on page 198

along the trail from **Achupallas** as far as the Inca ruins of **Ingapirca**, built in the 15th century to control the Cañari Indians the living in the area.

The Pan-American highway continues south to **Cuenca** ❼, the third largest city in Ecuador and formally the Inca town of Tomebamba. Most of the Inca stonework was destroyed by the Spanish and replaced by colonial architecture and cobbled streets. Today, patios, plazas, whitewashed buildings and red-tiled roofs make Cuenca probably the most attractive Ecuadorian city to visit.

Nearby **Cajas National Park**, with Inca ruins and more than 200 lakes, is a popular retreat for fishermen and hikers. Since Cuenca draws its drinking water from Cajas it is well protected from environmental impacts. South of Cuenca live the indigenous people of **Saraguro** ❾, who have strong cultural pride. Their town has become a center of the new indigenous political movement called *Pachacutek* (New Country). Here, men dress formally with short black trousers and women wear decorative shawls closed with a *tupus* (fastening pin). The sleepy town of **Loja** is the gateway to the southern Oriente and the Peruvian border. Quinine, the anti-malaria drug, was first exploited from the forests above the city in the 18th century, which led to their destruction.

Further down the valley, the village of **Vilcabamba** ❿ was made famous by the discovery in the 1960s of a large percentage of locals over 100 years old. Visiting foreign doctors have suggested that a mild and stable climate, low stress, simple and healthy diets, and physical labor on small farms create this anomaly. Foreigners have since settled in the region, seeking longevity. Several ecologically and health-minded hostels have sprung up as a result.

In February, when apples, pears and peaches are ripe, young people come to Ambato from as far away as the coast for several days of parades and all-night dancing on the streets at Ecuador's largest festival, the Fiesta of Fruit and Flowers.

Also in the vicinity is **Podocarpus National Park**, with a highland entrance at **Cajanuma** and rainforest entrance at **Bombascara**. Trails access the park and overnight camping is possible. An active environmental movement in Loja has kept multinational mining companies from moving in and causing deforestation and river poisoning. A spectacular mountain road goes to the quiet town of Macará on the Peruvian border. This route to Peru is safer and more beautiful than the coastal border crossing at Huaquillas.

BELOW: laden down in Cuenca.

The Oriente and the Amazon

The Ecuadorian **Oriente** is the upper Amazon basin east of the Andes, and is nowadays known as "the province of the future". It is a place of endless virgin rainforest cut by fast-flowing rivers and inhabited by jaguars, ocelots, anacondas, monkeys, tapirs, fish-eating bats, piranhas and more than 450 species of birds. Travel in this region is easier than in neighboring countries, as distances are shorter and transportation quite straightfoward.

The indigenous inhabitants of the Oriente include the Siona, Cofan, Quechua, Quijo and Huaorani tribes in the basins of the Napo, Aguarico and Pastazo rivers to the north; and the Shuars, Ashuars and Saraguros in the south. Colonization and oil development has affected the lifestyles of the tribes, and many traditions have died, such as those of the Shuar, who until the 20th century would shrink the heads of dead enemies. Before the 20th century, the ratio of Shuar men to women was estimated at one to two, due to

Shrunken head of a Jívaro (former name of Shuar people).

constant warring. Some of the Huaoranis, however, retain their ancient culture deep in the jungles bordering Peru near the **Rio Napo**. They hunt with spears, blowpipes and poison darts, keep harpie eagles as pets and watch-dogs, and make fire by rubbing sticks together.

Several missionaries, including the Bishop of Coca, have been killed for attempting to encroach upon their culture. Such disturbances of indigenous life date from 1541, when Francisco de Orellana's expedition departed Quito and stumbled upon the headwaters of the Rio Napo. Towns such as Archidona and **Macas ⑩** were soon established as bases for conquest and for conversion. Many were subsequently abandoned due to repeated attacks from the indigenous people, but the gold prospectors, the Franciscans and the Jesuits, driven by fierce faith in their gods, gradually pushed back the frontiers.

Oil and tourist booms

The loss of most of the Oriente to Peru following the border war in 1941 stirred the government's attention, which was rewarded in 1967 with the discovery of huge oil deposits near **Lago Agrio ⑫**. The face of the region has changed drastically since then, with towns constructed overnight to provide services for the booming oil industry, which quickly became Ecuador's main money-spinner.

This influx of people has sent wildlife deeper into the forests. In areas on the edge of the Amazon Basin, there is little fauna apart from birds and insects left. For those who are short of time, tours can be organised into the rainforest from the small town of **Misahuallí**. These trips can give a good understanding of how people living in the Oriente have adjusted to these outside influences.

The Napo flows on from Misahuallí to **Coca ⑬**, passing stilt houses with

BELOW: motoring along the Río Napo.

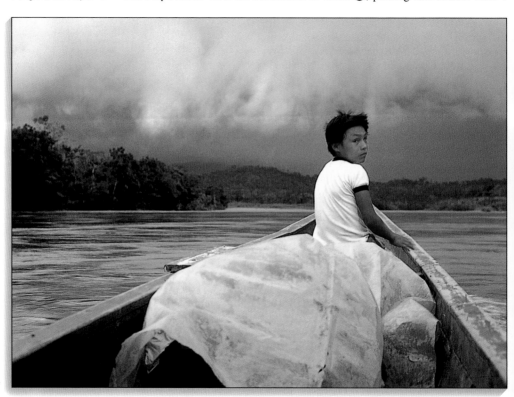

exotic menageries set in rambling banana patches. Farmers load fruit into their dugout canoes until they barely float and then paddle precariously off to market. The oil town of Coca itself has a seedy feel, reminiscent of the frontier towns of the great Wild West. Signs of oil development in the area cannot be ignored. Not too far from Coca however, pure rainforest abounds.

Map on page 198

The Río Napo here is ever-widening, bordered on either side by a forest canopy, thickest at the height of approximately 30 meters (100 ft), beneath which grows, in damp dimness, an astonishing assortment of ferns and wild lemon trees with tiny edible ants living inside the stems. Above the canopy, the giant kapok tree stands out, the tallest Amazonian species, which can reach up to 60 meters (200 ft) high and 40 meters (130 ft) around the base of the trunk. Local people on the move seek shelter at night in the hollows between its roots. Its branches are cluttered with bromeliads, strangler vines and belladona.

The Spanish chronicler Cieza de Léon visited the largely ruined Cuenca in 1547 and found fully-stocked warehouses, barracks and houses formerly occupied by "more than two hundred virgins, who were very beautiful, dedicated to the service of the sun."

Hidden in the forest, just off the River Napo, three hours downriver from Coca, is Sacha Lodge. An elevated boardwalk heads through the forest, arriving at a piranha-infested lagoon in front of the lodge. Resident naturalists and indigenous guides venture into the forest with visitors on nature walks, canoe floats or up into the 40-meter (130-ft) high observation tower to experience forest life high up in the canopy and maybe spot a sloth lazing atop his tree.

The rewards of a very early morning boat ride to the edge of **Yasuni National Park** may be the sight of flocks of macaws and parrots descending onto the cliff by the river to feed on the minerals in the soil. Yasuni is a national reserve created to protect and monitor the incredible bio-diversity of this unique rainforest area. The Tiputini River, a tributary of the Napo River, leads to the Tiputini Research Station, where researchers and eco-tourists wake to find groups of monkeys at their cabin window, exotic birds, and always the unnerving chance of a jaguar wandering through their camp.

BELOW: feeding monkeys in a jungle resort.

Coastal Ecuador

The tropical lowland west of the Andes has – along with its inhabitants, who comprise half the nation – been characterized as savage and uncivilized by mountain-dwellers, a place to be exploited. It is the traditional source of Ecuador's wealth, based on bananas, coffee and cocoa. In late 1997 and early 1998, the effects of the El Niño weather phenomenon caused serious floods throughout the coastal areas, washing hundreds of houses away, ruining crops and causing extensive infrastructure damage.

Coastal Ecuador begins in the north with **San Lorenzo** ⑭ and its neighboring villages, collections of wooden stilt houses suspended in steamy, timeless isolation amidst twisting mangrove channels. A new road now connects San Lorenzo to Ibarra in the Sierra, providing more reliable links with the outside world than the railway. It remains a ramshackle tropical town with a Caribbean feel, pulsating with the beat of Colombian salsa. At **La Tola**, on the edge of the San Lorenzo Archipelago, the coast road begins, a dusty track through mainly uninhabited swamps bursting with vegetation.

Esmeraldas ⑮, strung along the shore of the river

of the same name, exemplifies urban coastal culture. This city is loud and vibrant late into the night. Among a population chiefly *mestizo* and black, mountain *campesinos* in bowler hats sell fruit from stalls, Andean panpipes interrupt Caribbean dance music and techno rhythms, Chinese restaurants serve sweet-and-sour, and a shopping arcade is christened "Che Guevara".

Southwest of Esmeraldas are some of Ecuador's finest and most peaceful beaches. The road passes through **Atacames**, a small resort town, and on through **Sua**, a beautifully situated, lively fishing village, finally ending at **Muisne ⑯**, with beaches as remote as they are alluring.

The main road south follows the languid river through cattle farms and plantations of bananas, palm oil and rubber, rising 500 meters (1,600 ft) to **Santo Domingo de los Colorados ⑰**. The Colorados, or Zatchila people, who inhabit the region, paint black stripes on their faces and wear their hair dyed red with *achiote* (a plant dye) and cut in a bowl shape. Today they live mainly in areas to the south of town, and while retaining their curative knowledge of natural medicine, they dress traditionally only for special occasions.

Perhaps the most scenic of the lowland routes runs from Santo Domingo to **Manta ⑱**, the calmest and prettiest coastal city. On **Tarqui beach**, local fishermen unload their catch of shark, dorado, eel and the odd tortoise, which are cleaned and sold on the sand amidst an aerial frenzy of seagulls and vultures. The **Municipal Museum** houses relics of the ancient Mantans, who worshiped a fertility cult, and tore the hearts from sacrificial victims of war.

Manta is the gateway to the nearby Panama hat villages (*see page 213*). Fine wickerwork furniture and sisal hammocks are also manufactured here. South of Manta is **Machalilla National Park**, one of the most threatened dry tropical

BELOW: crushed ice vendor, Esmeraldas.

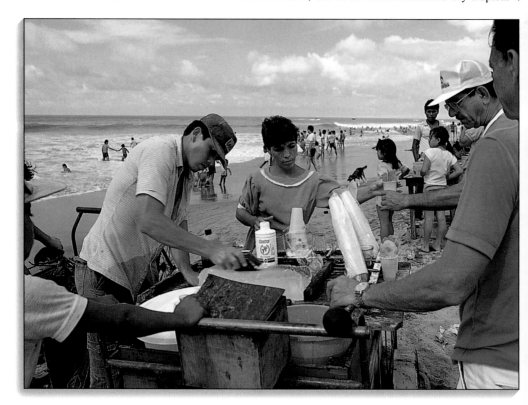

forests in the world. Now with national protection status, it is hoped that this unique forest with its bottle-shaped trees, the skyline dotted with kapok trees and more than 200 species of birds, will survive. The park entrance is just north of **Puerto Lopez ⑲**, a small fishing town. From here the road runs south past Alandaluz Ecological Center, a successful eco-cultural tourist complex with organic gardens, dry compost toilets and a recycling water system.

South of the the central coast, all roads lead to **Guayaquil ⑳**, Ecuador's largest and liveliest city, with approximately two and a half million inhabitants. The Spanish quickly established their regional shipbuilding industry here: enormous 250-ton sailing vessels transported goods from Europe to Lima via Mexico and Panama, and returned laden with gold and silver. New technology and ideas have always come first to Guayaquil: just as it had public streetcars and gas lighting before Quito, so it was the first city to realize independence in 1821, and has been the bastion of progressive liberal thought in modern Ecuador. The city has suffered countless burnings, by pirates on plundering raids during the 17th and 18th centuries, and more recently in 1896 and 1906, when damage was on such a scale that the entire city was rebuilt from scratch. A pleasant walk goes along the riverfront **Malecón Simón Bolívar** past **La Rotonda**, commemorating Bolívar's meeting with San Martín; up to **Las Peñas**, the only extant colonial district, and scenic **Cerro El Carmen**.

Shrunken heads from the Oriente, pre-Inca ceramics, colonial religious paintings and a changing modern art exhibition fill the **Municipal Museum**. The **Parque del Centenario**, where gymnasts and comedians routinely perform, divides Avenida 9 de Octubre, the city's commercial heart. To escape the frenzy, grab a moment of tranquility in **Parque Bolívar**.

Panama hat maker.

Map
on page
198

BELOW: Panama hats for sale.

ECUADOR'S MOST FAMOUS HAT

Montecristi is the center of production of the Panama hat, a cottage industry which has protected the heads of such notables as Teddy Roosevelt and King Edward VII. The hats are woven from the reed *Carludovica palmata*, cultivated locally and brought on horseback to craftsmen's homes. A top-quality or *superfino* specimen can change hands for up to US $1,000, and should be able to hold water when held upside down. It should also fold up to fit into a top pocket without creasing. Weaving should ideally be done at night or in dull conditions, and the process can take up to three months.

The hats have always been produced in Ecuador, but were shipped worldwide from Panama, hence the misnomer. Made since pre-Columbian times, they caught on among the conquistadors, who were impressed by the headgear of the people of Manabí Province. Soldiers fighting in the Spanish-American War of 1898, wore the hats, and the export market to the US subsequently took off. They caught on in Europe following the 19th century World Exposition in Paris, as many of Renoir's paintings illustrate. The hats were a big hit with US Prohibition gansters, and the market peaked in 1946. Since then demand has fallen, and some say that the production of superfinos will not survive much longer.

TIP

The Galápagos Islands
are a national park,
and all non-Ecuadorian
visitors must pay an
entrance fee of US $80
(discounts are
available for students
with ID and children
under 12.)

BELOW: cruising
around the
Galápagos.

The Galápagos Islands

The first sighting by Europeans of the Galápagos Islands was in 1535, though it is possible that the ancient Mantans, Incas and even Polynesians visited the islands, which lie 1,000 km (600 miles) off the Pacific coast of Ecuador. From their European discovery until their incorporation into Ecuador in 1832, the islands served as a refuge for European and American pirates, whalers and sealers, where they re-stocked supplies of firewood, water and giant tortoises for meat, which could remain alive for a year in ships' holds.

Just as the islands were undergoing permanent settlement, the *Beagle* dropped anchor in **San Cristóbal Bay ㉑** and the 26-year-old naturalist Charles Darwin strode ashore. Previous scientific expeditions had been mounted, but with Darwin's visit, the enormous biological and geological significance of the Galápagos islands was recognized. Although he stayed for only five weeks in 1835, Darwin made many of the observations upon which he based his theories of evolution and the mutability of species. He noticed 13 types of finch, each with a different beak designed to collect its particular food.

The islands' romantic appeal was tarnished over the next century, when a penal colony was established on the island of **Floreana**. Conditions were harsh; administrators gratuitously cruel. The original colonists, some 80 soldiers whose crimes of insurrection had been pardoned, fled the island, leaving the prisoners to their fate. As recently as 1944, a colony was established on **Isabela** to which increasingly hardened criminals were sent. It was dissolved following a riot and mass escape, and in 1959, the islands were declared a national park.

There are 13 major islands, six small islands and 42 islets spread over an area of 80,000 sq km (30,000 sq miles). The land consists of lava resting on a

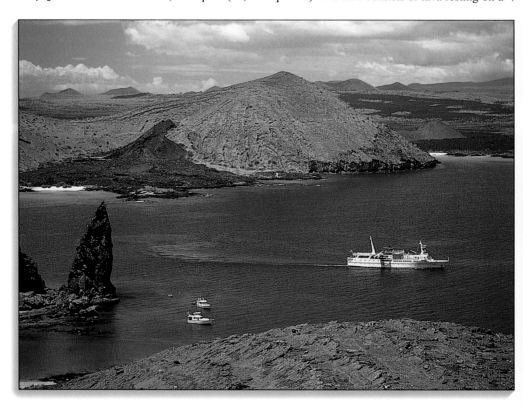

basalt base, volcanic refuse produced by successive underwater eruptions which continue today. The islands have never been connected with the mainland, but emerged from the water individually over a million years. The violence of the geological past is most evident on **Isabela** with its chain of five volcanoes as high as 1,700 meters (5,600 ft). One of them, the **Sierra Negra**, has the second largest crater in the world, measuring 10 km (6 miles) in diameter.

Seeds were transported accidentally by birds and aboard ships. Today the islands support almost 900 plant varieties, the most revered of which is the *palo santo*, found in abundance on **Isla Rábida ㉒**. There are six distinct vegetation zones ranging from low level desert to the uppermost *pampa*; a walk up to the old sugar mill on San Cristóbal passes most of them.

On **San Bartolomé**, two sparkling horseshoe beaches are separated by a narrow strip of semi-tropical forest. From the island's summit, one of the best vantage-points in the archipelago, the uninhabited volcanic wasteland of **Santiago** stretches away to the west. Within this desert is a freshwater spring which quenched the thirst of many a pirate docked in **Buccaneer Cove**. Doubtless these early visitors watched the flamingoes dance around the nearby lagoon, buried each other up to the neck in the coffee-colored sand of **Espumilla Beach** and, near **Puerto Egas ㉓**, were confounded by the fur seals that swam through an underwater tunnel between the open sea and two small, clear pools.

Creatures of the sea

Some of the best snorkeling is done off far-flung islands like **Española ㉔**, the only place in the world that the endemic waved albatross breeds. In **Gardner Bay**, flapping manta rays probably think you are just another sea lion, but the

Map on page 216

Author Herman Melville had a rather unromantic vision of the Galápagos Islands: "Take five-and-twenty heaps of cinders dumped here and there in an outside city lot; imagine some of them magnified into mountains, and the vacant lot the sea..."

BELOW: one of the famous iguanas.

real sea lions know better, and an aggressive bull should be given right of way. The females and young are playful; they can recognize the 290 varieties of fish in the water, but a pale figure with a mask and flippers is still a curious sight.

The Galápagos are home to the world's only marine iguanas, and the island of **Fernandina** ㉕ holds the largest colony. As inquisitive as the two related land species, they are much more dragon-like with their scaly skin – which turns from black to blue and red during mating season – and the row of spines along their back. Originally land-dwellers, they can submerge for only a few minutes at a time, searching for algae; and upon re-surfacing, snort a salty spray into the air. Watching their antics beneath the smoldering **Volcán La Cumbre**, which erupted in September 1988, is a truly primal experience.

Directly opposite Fernandina is **Urbina Bay**, and one of the few coral reefs in the archipelago. Fish of every color steer clear of the Galápagos penguin, the world's northernmost species, whose clowning routines indicate its delight in the equatorial sun. The entrance to nearby **Elizabeth Bay** is protected by a cluster of islands which penguins share with nesting pelicans. En route to Floreana, schools of sperm and killer whales cruise the deep waters, and bottle-nosed dolphins surf the bow waves of boats. At **Devil's Crown** ㉖, named after the jagged, truncated volcanic cone rising from the ocean, sea lions glide along strong currents, which make for adventurous snorkeling.

The beach on **Point Cormorant**, Floreana's most beautiful location, is dotted with olivine crystals, while the adjacent lagoons teem with flamingos. Around the point is the **Bay of Sharks** – its ring of pristine white sand is popular with nesting tortoises. The name refers to the relatively harmless white-tipped shark, which is found mainly here and off San Bartolomé. It is, along with

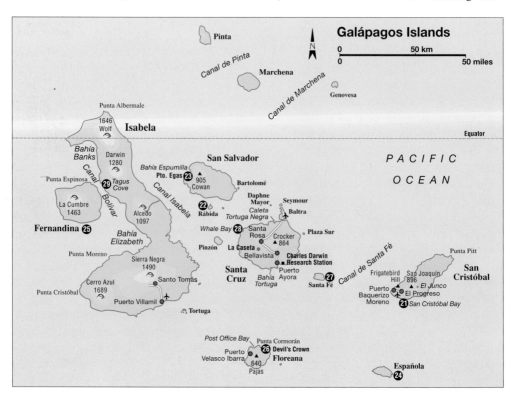

the enormous and equally docile whale shark, the only kind in these waters. On land, the unchallenged king of the islands is the giant tortoise, which can live 200 years and weigh up to 300 kgs (600 lbs). On rocky, sparsely vegetated islands like Isabela and Española, its longer neck and legs and saddle-shaped carapace enable it to reach higher to obtain food. These features are absent from the more cumbersome species inhabiting fertile islands like **Santa Cruz**.

The **Charles Darwin Research Station** was established on Santa Cruz in 1959, on the centenary of the publication of *The Origin of Species*. One of its most important programs is the controlled hatching of tortoise eggs, a necessary step since the introduction by early settlers of feral dogs, cats, goats, pigs and rats. On **Pinzón**, not one young tortoise has been sighted for nearly 50 years. The feral species also destroy vegetation, but have participated in the evolutionary miracle of the islands in at least one respect: the goats on **Santa Fe ㉗**, in the absence of freshwater, have developed a taste for the sea, and now live on it.

Scattered among the coves and hills are remnants of commercial ambition and military adventurism, which underline the inhospitable loneliness of these shores. In **Whale Bay ㉘** on Santa Cruz, ceramic fragments conjure images of the famous buccaneer Henry Morgan with a blue-footed booby squawking on his shoulder. Pirates and whalers recorded their passage on the cliff faces of **Tagus Cove ㉙** on Isabela: today the graffiti is read mainly by flightless cormorants. A more recent ruin is the incongruous skeleton of an abandoned salt mine dating from the 1960s which sits above Puerto Egas on Isla Santiago.

The Galápagos Islands are one of the few places in the world where animals still live undisturbed, and nowhere are the forces of evolution more clearly displayed. Visitors should leave no scars. ❑

Map on page 216

Darwin encountered a "strange Cyclopean scene" on a San Cristóbal beach – two tortoises munching on cactus. One "gave a deep hiss, and drew in its head"; the other "slowly stalked away". Darwin became fascinated with the beasts, noting numerous sub-species.

BELOW LEFT: Sally Lightfoot crab.
BELOW RIGHT: stairway to heaven.

BIRDS OF THE GALÁPAGOS ISLANDS

From the marbled godwit to the black-necked stilt, the birdlife on the Galápagos Islands, which taught us about evolution, is still rich, rare and rewarding

Where else, but on these small islands off the coast of Ecuador, will birds come out to greet you? Life with no native predators has made the birds of the Galápagos fearless, which means that many of them are easy to spot. There are 58 resident species, of which 28 are endemic, as well as about 30 migratory birds. The seabirds are the most often seen: in the dry coastal areas you are likely to spot species of the booby family, the waved albatross – only found on the island of Española – and the world's only flightless seabirds, the Galápagos penguin and the flightless cormorant. The best time to come is in winter (October to February) when most migrants are visiting, and birds are reproducing.

Then, a serious ornithologist might see 50 species in a week, and even a dilettante should be able to spot two dozen.

There are dangers in paradise, however: the introduction of domestic animals has been bad news. Some prey on the birds, others destroy or compete for their habitats. Farming on the inhabited islands also destroys habitats, and a natural phenomenon, the *El Niño* current, brings mosquito-carried disease and disrupts the food chain.

△ **PEREGRINE FALCON**
The peregrine falcon (*Falco peregrinus*) is a migratory bird frequently seen on the islands of Española, Isabela, Baltra and Santa Cruz from November to March. The falcon can reach very high speeds when it is swooping to attack prey.

◁ **GALÁPAGOS HAWK**
The female Galápagos hawk (*Buteo galapagoensis*) mates with up to four males in order to ensure that breeding will be successful.

◁ **BLUE-FOOTED BOOBY**
The blue-footed booby (*Sula nebouxii excisa*) has a wonderful courtship ritual, in which the male ostentatiously displays his brightly colored feet in order to attract a mate. Two or three eggs are laid and both of the parents share the task of incubating them. Once they have become independent, the young birds leave the islands and do not return to breed until some three years later.

THE SECRET OF DARWIN'S FINCHES

The finches of the Galápagos were vitally important in the development of Charles Darwin's ideas about evolution and the formation of species.

When he set off on his voyage around the world on HMS *Beagle* (1831–36), he believed, like most people of his time, in the fixity of species. But on the Galápagos he observed that 13 different species of the finch had evolved from a single ancestral group, and it was this (together with his observations of the islands' tortoises) which led to his contention that species could evolve over time, with those most suited to their natural environment surviving and passing on their characteristics to the next generation.

The main differences he noted between the finches was the size and shape of their beaks, leading him to conclude that the birds which survived were those whose beaks enabled them to eat the available food.

The 13 species of finch are divided into two groups: ground finches (pictured above is the large ground finch, *Geospiza magnirostris*) and tree finches, of which the mangrove finch, found only in the swamps of Isabela Island, is the most rare. You are unlikely to see all of them on a short visit, but it's an enjoyable challenge to see how many you can spot.

◁ VERMILLION FLYCATCHER

The vermillion flycatcher (*Pyrocephalus rubinus*) is an attractive little bird and quite unlike any other bird to be seen on the Galápagos Islands. It has a high-pitched, musical song and builds a distinctive cup-shaped nest, on which the female incubates the eggs.

△ FRIGATE BIRDS

The magnificent frigate bird (*Fregata magnificens magnificens*) and its close relation, the great frigate bird, can be seen near the coasts of many islands. Both males and females have long forked tails and the male is remarkable for the red gular pouch which puffs in the mating season.

◁ LAVA GULL

The lava gull (*Larus fuliginosus*) is believed to be the rarest species in the world. It roosts on the shores of saltwater lagoons and builds solitary nests along the coast.

△ BROWN PELICAN

The brown pelican (*Pelecanus occidentalis urinator*) is a huge, cumbersome bird which can often be seen following fishing boats in search of food.

THE TROPICAL GIANT

*Laid-back tropical paradise, economic miracle,
or home of the hedonistic carnival – Brazil is
a heady mix of them all*

Nearly half the South America continent can be described in one tantalizing word: Brazil. Almost as big as the United States and home to 145 million people, Brazil is a world in itself – a sensuous giant that invariably becomes a part of everyone who experiences its pleasures. Brazil the geographic colossus is also a state of mind, one that loosens up even the most cautious of spirits who venture there. That's the power of the Brazilian *jeito*, or way. Relax, hang loose, improvise, and *nao esquente a cabeça*: don't get hot-headed, come what may.

There is a vibrancy to Brazil unparalleled elsewhere in Latin America; the country's cutting-edge innovations and penchant for fads have led some to call it "the California of South America". But for all its laid-back ethos, Brazil is also a dynamo of economic activity. The world's eighth largest population produces the planet's 10th largest economy. Virtually everything one buys in Brazil is made in Brazil. Cars crafted in São Paulo run on lead-free sugar cane fuel (home grown naturally), and their compact disc players made in the duty-free Amazon port of Manaus play tunes from the recording studios of Rio de Janeiro.

As the major port of entry, Rio (*see page 233*) is where most visitors get their first dazzling impressions of Brazil, with its beautiful beaches, sensuously rounded peaks, and world-famous carnival. But like the iceberg below its tip, there's much more to Brazil than Rio. Nearby is South America's largest metropolis, São Paulo (*see page 238*), with 13 million people under its towering skyline, this is the country's powerhouse, the center of its massive commercial and industrial output. To the northwest lies Brasilia (*see page 239*), the pristine architectural wonder that sprang up from the wilderness to become the national capital. Beyond the triangle of political, cultural and economic power formed by these three cities are slightly more subdued wonders: the stately colonial cities of Minas Gerais (*see page 241*), living monuments of the gold and diamond booms; the inviting beaches and rich Afro-Brazilian culture of the Northeast (*see page 243*); the immense rainforests of the Amazon jungle that still cover more than half the country (*see page 254*); the vast marshlands of the Pantanal, a naturalist's paradise (*see page 251*); and the enormous waterfalls of Iguaçu (*see page 253*)   ❑

PRECEDING PAGES: coastal splendor, Costa Verde, west of Rio de Janeiro.
LEFT: Christ the Redeemer statue, Rio.

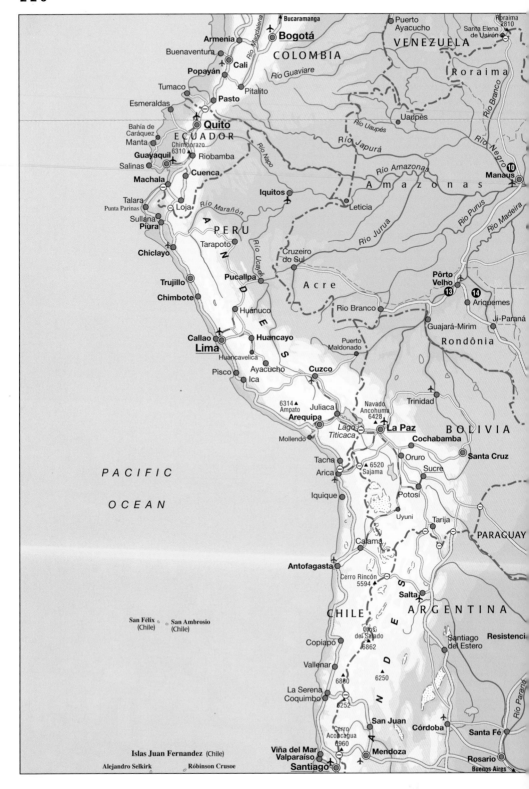

Bucaramanga

Puerto
Ayacucho

Roraima
2810

Santa Elena
de Uairén

VENEZUELA

Armenia
Bogotá

Buenaventura
Cali

COLOMBIA

Popayán

Pitalito

Pasto

R o r a i m a

Tumaco

Esmeraldas

Uaupés

Río Guaviare

Río Uaupés

Río Japurá

Río Branco

Río Negro

Quito

Bahía de
Caráquez

Manta

E C U A D O R

Chimborazo
6310

Riobamba

Río Napo

Río Amazonas

Manaus

10

Guayaquil

Salinas

Cuenca

A m a z o n a s

Machala

Iquitos

Leticia

Río Purus

Río Madeira

Talara
Punta Parinas

Loja

Río Marañón

Sullana

Piura

P E R U

Río Juruá

Chiclayo

Tarapoto

Río Ucayali

Cruzeiro
do Sul

Trujillo

Pucallpa

A c r e

**Pôrto
Velho**

13

14

Chimbote

Huánuco

Rio Branco

Ariquemes

Ji-Paraná

Guajará-Mirim

R o n d ô n i a

Callao
Lima

Huancayo

Puerto
Maldonado

Huancavelica

Pisco

Ayacucho

Ica

Cuzco

A
N
D
E
S

6314
Ampato

Juliaca

Navado
Ancohuma
6428

Trinidad

Arequipa

*Lago
Titicaca*

La Paz

B O L I V I A

Mollendo

Cochabamba

Tacna

6520
Sajama

Oruro

Sucre

Santa Cruz

Arica

P A C I F I C

O C E A N

Iquique

Potosí

Uyuni

Tarija

PARAGUAY

Calama

Cerro Rincón
5594

Antofagasta

Salta

San Félix
(Chile)

San Ambrosio
(Chile)

CHILE

A R G E N T I N A

Ojos
del Salado
6862

Copiapó

Santiago
del Estero

Resistenci

Vallenar

6880

6250

N
D
E
S

La Serena
Coquimbo

6252

Río Paraná

Cerro
Aconcagua
6960

San Juan

Córdoba

Santa Fé

Islas Juan Fernandez (Chile)

Viña del Mar
Valparaíso

Mendoza

Rosario

Santiago

Buenos Aires

Alejandro Selkirk

Róbinson Crusoe

Brazil

BRAZIL

This vast country literally pulsates with life, from the rampant
fertility of the Amazon to the sensual delights of Rio and the
modern sophistication of São Paulo and Brasília

Map
on page
226–7

Visitors can only hope to scratch the surface of this huge land, which still has vast unpopulated areas, and reveals its secrets reluctantly. It's worth making the effort, for there is much to discover, from the excitement of Rio de Janeiro and the gastronomic highlights of São Paulo to the majestic forests of the Amazon, scarred red by long, twisting rivers; the abundant wildlife of the Pantanal, or the solitude of the arid northeastern "backlands". The past comes to life in the gold towns in the south of Minas Gerais, such as Ouro Prêto, Tiradentes and Congonhas. Harder to get to, but worth the effort, are places like the high plateaux of Bahia State, the Chapada Diamantina, where Brazil's second highest waterfall tumbles from a mist-clouded plain.

Brazil is the world's fifth largest country, and the distance from the Andes to the Atlantic Ocean is almost 4,500 km (2,800 miles). Most of Brazil's attractions are a long way from the big cities, as well as from each other. The famous Iguaçu Falls in the far south is thousands of kilometers away from balmy Belém in the north. But traveling around Brazil has, almost at a stroke, become easier and cheaper, due to a price war between the country's leading airlines which broke out in 1998. Tourist facilities have in general improved due to Brazil's recent economic boom, though in many areas finances don't yet run to providing the kind of public facilities some tourists might take for granted at home. Until recently there were very few good hotels, and there is still only one hotel room per 10,000 inhabitants, compared with one per 70 in the United States. But new hotels, like other tourist facilities, are now opening almost daily.

PRECEDING PAGES:
Sugarloaf Mountain
dominates Rio's
Guanabara Bay.
LEFT: exhibitionism
at the Rio *Carnaval.*
BELOW: Ouro Prêto.

Conquering the interior

Brazil's interior was first penetrated by Europeans in the late 1600s. The first pioneers were Jesuits proselytizing to Guaraní Indians, followed by Portuguese immigrants too poor to acquire land in the sugarcane-dominated coastal regions. These settlers pushed into what is now the state of São Paulo to raise cattle and plant subsistence crops. Like the wealthy sugar planters whose labor force was mostly black slaves, these farmers also sought bonded workers, so they organized expeditions to abduct Guaraní Indians who inhabited the region. The Indians sought refuge in the Jesuit missions where Guaraní people lived in educated, highly productive communities.

Despite their barbaric raids, the *bandeirantes* (so named because of the banners they marched under), have gone down in Brazilian folklore as brave pioneers who opened up what has become the country's most productive economic region.

Just when the world market for Brazilian sugar started to go soft around 1700, a new boom shook the

Brazilian society showed a penchant for partying from its colonial start. An exasperated 17th century Jesuit instructor, José de Anchieta, wrote that the country was "relaxing, slothful and melancholic, so that all the time is spent in parties, in singing, and in making merry."

country. This time it was gold and diamonds, discovered by the *bandeirantes* in the rugged hill country of Minas Gerais. Most of the gold was sent to the Portuguese crown, but enough remained to build the baroque cities of Ouro Prêto, São João del Rei and Sabará. The new treasures were shipped to Europe through Rio de Janeiro, putting the backwater port on the map, and by 1763 Rio had become so important that the Portuguese crown moved the capital there from the sugarcane and slave entrepôt of Salvador.

Other booms followed, such as cotton. The biggest and most lasting boom, coffee, started in the late 18th century. The state of São Paulo was covered with coffee plantations as the craze for drinking coffee spread around the world. But coffee prices tumbled in 1930, and with them fell the government. Getulio Vargas, governor of Rio Grande do Sul, then seized the presidency and won Brazilians' hearts with his populist rhetoric and championing of organised labor. He established a corporate state apparently modeled on Mussolini's fascism, losing support after the fall of Hitler and Mussolini. Vargas resigned in 1945.

Eighteen years of constitutional rule and steady economic growth followed, until the early 1960s. With the number of landless peasants increasing dramatically, land reform became an explosive political issue. The military responded to the growing unrest by seizing power in April 1964.

Birth of the "Brazilian Miracle"

The military's crackdown on leftists (many of whom were tortured and killed) and generous fiscal incentives combined to attract a flood of foreign investment. The Brazilian economy boomed, mainly enriching those who were already wealthy. Disenchantment with military rule grew as the economy took a nosedive in 1980, crippled by enormous bills for imported oil and public works projects, such as a rarely used Amazon highway. The last of a series of military dictator presidents stepped down in March 1985.

Tancredo Neves, the man chosen by an electoral college to head the new civilian government, was a longtime opponent of the military. But Neves fell fatally ill on the eve of his inauguration, and his vice-president, José Sarney, was sworn in as president. The Sarney government inherited a foreign debt of more than $100 billion, the largest in the Third World. Sarney, closely allied with the military, quickly lost political support as inflation, which reached 1,000 percent in 1988, continued to ravage the economy.

Economic woes were accompanied by growing street crime. Such anti-social behaviour is relatively recent in Brazil, and is widely considered a product of the huge influx of rural Brazilians into large cities since the 1960s. Some were attracted by jobs, but many arrived as refugees from droughts in the Northeast.

Progress for the poor is often limited by racial discrimination. Although Brazil has often been called a racial paradise because of the high number of inter-racial marriages and an absence of open racial conflict, to be black in Brazil almost always means to be poor, and 40 percent of the country's population is black. But whatever their color, there is little chance of a poor Brazilian becoming a rich one.

From bust to boom

Few countries can have changed as much as Brazil since mid-1994, when inflation, then running at more than 4,000 percent a year, was halted in its tracks by some drastic measures, including the introduction of a new currency and the rescheduling of interest payments on Brazil's foreign debt. This released a huge amount of energy and set off a chain of events which are still transforming the country. Twelve to 15 million Brazilians joined the consumer society for the first time, causing food sales to surge and the demand for many other goods and services – notably tourism – to explode. Credit, absent for three decades, became accessible again, and millions went on a shopping spree. The number of new cars sold has doubled in the past three years, but as road building has not kept pace, there is widespread chronic congestion.

The pace of change has been fastest in Brazil's poorest region, the Northeast, as textile and footwear factories relocate in search of cheaper labor. Long stagnant state capitals such as Fortaleza, Recife and Salvador, which tend to have more character than the upstart cities of the south, are being given a new lease of life, and long neglected architectural gems are being tastefully restored.

Huge natural resources secure this country's future, but they also bring responsibilites towards the environment, particularly in the Amazon region, where destruction has occurred on a massive scale. The Rio Earth Summit was a recognition of these responsibilities, but there is a long way to go, tragically emphasized by the terrible rainforest fires of 1998. Indigenous people, particularly in the Amazon regions, where their lifestyles have been sustained over centuries, still suffer daily threats and invasions of their homelands not only by fire and logging, but from settlers looking for homes away from Brazil's

Map on page 226–7

Monument to Kubitschek, Brasília.

BELOW: crowded hillside *favela*, Rio.

southern cities. Rising unemployment in the cities has sent more people back to rural areas, adding to the pressure for land reform, which has become a source of intense conflict in the past few years.

Trouble in the rainforest

This conflict is exemplified in the remote western region of Rondônia (*see page 250*), where settlers are pushing back the rainforest – and the people who have lived there for centuries. Two factors set off the land rush: firstly, changes in agriculture in Brazil's prosperous south made many peasants landless in the 1970s. Frequent freezes combined with soaring world prices for soybeans convinced many coffee farmers to cut down their bushes and plant soybeans. Peasants who had sharecropped at the edges of the coffee plantations – assuring growers a stable workforce to harvest the beans – were no longer needed for the mechanized soybean harvest, and were forced to abandon their plots.

Secondly, the extension of the roadway BR 364 from the coffee regions of São Paulo state to Rondônia, the new Brazilian frontier, put into action the formula for peopling the Amazon enunciated by the Brazilian military, which then governed the country: "A land without people for people without land." Wealthy land speculators cashed in, buying up enormous tracts for cattle ranches. Such enterprises were subsidized by the Brazilian government until international concerns about the disastrous effect on the ecology forced them to abandon the policy. Not for nothing was the 1992 Earth Summit held in Brazil.

BELOW: the glorious church of Glória, downtown Rio.

Brazil's economy is now the 10th largest in the Western world, and nearly 70 percent of its exports are industrial goods – but the gap between rich and poor is still greater than almost anywhere else in the world. In most of the cities,

Rio de Janeiro

unemployment has led to rising crime, and muggings are a serious problem. Tourists can be targeted, and great caution is needed, but most crimes occur well away from city centers, and things are not as bad as is often made out. A special police force guards tourists on many of the beaches.

Despite the pace of change, most Brazilians are well aware that the most important things in life are personal relationships, having fun and making the best of what is available. Visitors will be impressed with their courtesy and friendliness, as well as their unflappable equanimity. Maybe it's because they have so many opportunities to let off steam, in carnival, music and football.

Rio de Janeiro, city of fun

Brazilians call **Rio de Janeiro** ❶ *a cidade maravilhosa* – the marvelous city – and they have ample reason to do so. There's the city's stunning setting: flanked to the east by the enormous **Bay of Guanabara** Ⓐ and to the south by the Atlantic Ocean, Rio sprawls around and even up the sides of enormous granite peaks and down to wide sandy beaches. The result of this topsy-turvy topography is a city sculptured around the whims of nature, giving the urban landscape a look that can only be described as sensuous. An Italian statesman gazing over Rio was moved to exclaim, "She's as beautiful as a woman."

And then there are the 10 million people who live in and around Rio. They're known as *cariocas*, and they epitomize the casual, good-natured disposition associated with all Brazilians. Part of the *carioca's* sunny outlook may derive from the smug satisfaction of living in a place most people only dream of, where it's possible to join the fun on the beaches for the price of a local bus fare. Another reason for the *carioca's* friendliness could be the open social scene of Rio. Unlike other big cities, where exclusivity heightens the appeal of social gatherings, in Rio people of all classes throng to public places for fun. The beaches are the biggest attraction, followed by soccer stadiums and carnival street parties. Bars are not dark, enclosed watering holes – in Rio, it's sociable to down a *chopp* (draught beer) out on the sidewalk and perhaps even bang out a samba tune with friends on nearby parked cars.

When it comes to sex, *cariocas* have a reputation for few inhibitions and tremendous appetites. That image developed in part from the bacchanal bashes of carnival, in part from the tantalizingly tiny beach attire favored by both genders. In Rio, you don't have to be gorgeous to be on display – just uninhibited. *Cariocas* are extremely tolerant (gay men seeking open minds flock to Rio from the rest of Brazil) and everyone can indulge in a little – or a lot of – exhibitionism. Pleasure became Rio's main money-maker after 1960, when the seat of government was moved from the seaside capital to landlocked Brasília. Rio went from being the center of the Brazilian universe to a mere tourist attraction, and it took a long time for the city to come to terms with its new identity. For the *cariocas,* tourist service is a long way from the past glories of inhabiting Brazil's capital, but they take comfort in knowing that the politicians who moved to Brasília left their hearts in Rio.

Maps
Area 226–7
City 232

TIP

Tourists can be targets for crime, so try to blend in as much as possible. Dress soberly, keep cameras and valuables out of sight, and carry only what you can afford to lose.

BELOW: carioca women are renowned for their tiny bikinis.

Guanabara Bay from Sugarloaf Mountain.

BELOW: snorkeling, one of the many outdoor sports available in Rio.

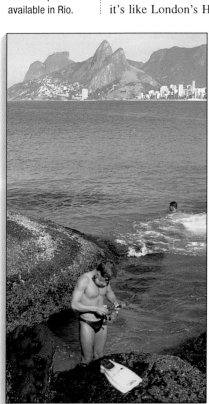

From the airport to the city center

Most visitors' first encounter with Rio takes place at **Galeão International Airport** ❸, a sleek modern complex famous for the purring sex kitten voices that announce arrivals and departures. Galeão is built on a man-made island north of Rio, and to the west is a massive swampy area known as the Baixada Fluminense, or Fluvial Lowlands, where two-thirds of the city's inhabitants live. This poor, featureless area is home for most of the city's bus drivers, maids, construction workers and salespeople.

The drive into the city from Galeão Airport passes Rio's port and soon after takes you into the heart of the downtown area. The main thoroughfare, **Avenida Rio Branco**, is lined by skyscraping banks, tourist agencies, and finally the ornate 19th-century buildings of the **Teatro Municipal** (which has a splendid ground floor café replete with mosaic tiles). Then there's the **Municipality** (whose steps often serve as bleachers for evening concerts), and across the street, the **Biblioteca Nacional** (library, with neo-classic and art nouveau paintings on display) and the **Museu Nacional de Belas Artes**, the country's foremost repository of classic Brazilian artwork, with regular exhibitions of contemporary art. Modern art is permanently on display in the exciting **Museu de Arte Moderna** in Avenida Infante D Henrique.

The **Museu Nacional** in the Quinta da Boa Vista was the palace of the emperors of Brazil, and their throne room and reception rooms remain among an eclectic ethnographic and natural history collection.

One of the best places to watch downtown action is on the open plaza in front of the **Teatro Municipal**, an area known as **Cinelândia**. Come nightfall it's like London's Hyde Park, with political campaigners, *capoeira* performers, guerrilla theater, and transvestites. This is the downtown's only movie theater district. On the other side of the Teatro Municipal is a wide pedestrian mall, the **Largo da Carioca**, a favorite redoubt of snake-oil vendors and leather artisans.

For a flavor of what Rio was like before the skyscrapers crowded its skyline, wander down the sidestreets off Largo da Carioca. Don't miss the stately **Confeiteria Colombo** at Rua Gonçalves Dias 32, with a mirror-lined tea room downstairs and elegant dining room upstairs. *Belle époque* furnishings evoke the late 19th century, when Rio's intelligentsia used to gather here. Stroll down Rua da Carioca for hearty German food and *chopp* at the lively **Bar Luiz**, a downtown fixture for more than a century.

Rising high above Largo da Carioca to the west is the **Santo Antônio Convent**, a complex of religious buildings built between 1608 and 1780. Beside the baroque main church is the lovely **São Francisco da Penitencia Chapel**. To the south stands Rio's cone-shaped **Catedral de São Sebastião** on Avenida Republica do Chile, finished in 1976. Nearby is the **Arcos da Lapa**, a towering 18th-century aqueduct that now serves as a bridge for streetcars, or *bondes* (pronounced "bon-jees") – so named because the original tickets looked like government bonds – that shuttle between a station next to the cathedral and the steep streets of **Santa Teresa** ❻, to the west of the

Map on page 232

center. Known for its precipitous topography and grand views, Santa Teresa is for many the most attractive of Rio's neighborhoods. Many of its residents are artists and musicians who moved there to take advantage of the views and location high above the mosquito-infested coastal strip. Be sure to see the **Chácara do Ceu Museum** on Rua Martinho Nobre, with splendid views and a lovely collection of Brazilian and European paintings.

Much of the shoreline between downtown Rio and the Bay of Botafogo, including **Santos Dumont airport ➊** (where Lockheed Electra turboprops shuttle to São Paulo), is the result of *aterro* (landfill). South of the business district is a tall stone monument built to honor Brazilians who died in World War II. Across the road, on a cliff, is the church of **Glória**. Then comes **Flamengo Beach ➋**, with adjoining large park. The polluted state of Guanabara Bay makes the water less than inviting. The next bay going south is **Botafogo ➌**, a lovely expanse with a marina and several movie theaters near the beach.

Emerging like a gigantic granite knee 400 meters (1,300 ft) from the waters of the entrance to Guanabara Bay is **Pão de Açúcar** (Sugarloaf Mountain) ➍. Cable cars leave Praia Vermelha beach every half hour to sweep visitors up the mountain via the Morro da Urca, with restaurant and amphitheater.

Suburbs on the sand

To the west of Sugarloaf begin Rio's legendary beaches. The first wide arc spans the neighborhoods of Leme to the east and Copacabana to the west, with a naval station at the western point. **Leme ➎** is mostly residential and quiet. Rua Princesa Isabel, which divides Leme from Copacabana, is a favorite with prostitutes, and nightlife in the area tends towards the seedy side. **Copacabana ➏**,

TIP

The best way to see the elegant 19th-century homes of Santa Teresa is to take one of the yellow streetcars that leave from the cathedral. Leave valuables behind, since the open-sided cars are vulnerable to pick-pockets.

BELOW: garlic for sale in a Rio market.

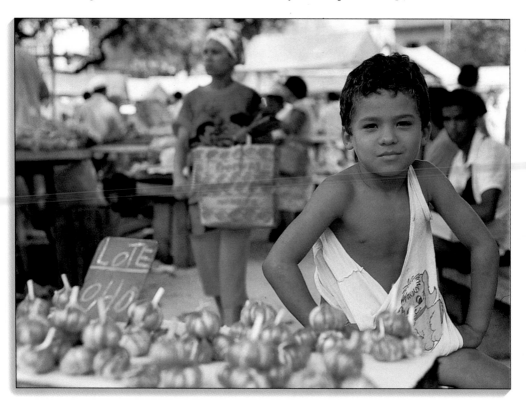

Carnaval!

Nothing else merits more preparation, more prolonged and devout attention, and a more lavish outpouring of private resources than the annual convulsion that has come to symbolize Brazil, for better or for worse. Extravagance, self-indulgence, exhibitionism and a kind of gleeful innocence are the basic elements – qualities that color life in Brazil, albeit less intensely, the rest of the year. Streets normally clogged with vehicles are reclaimed by revelers on foot; macho men lasciviously parade in drag; laborers masquerade as 18th-century royalty; mothers dress up like babies; the wealthy watch the poor perform; people stay up all night and sleep all day.

Carnaval arrived with the Portuguese, a re-invention of the late winter festivities of Europe. The celebrations are ostensibly the last shot at merry-making before the 40 days of fasting that precede Easter (the name is believed to be a derivation of the Italian *carne vale*, or farewell to meat). *Carnaval* in Brazil began as an aggres-

sive spree of throwing water, mud and flour at passers-by. This unpleasantness, which still characterizes *Carnaval* in Bolivia and Argentina, was banned in Brazil in the 19th century.

But the *Carnaval* that Brazil is renowned for – the opulent street parades of Rio de Janeiro – did not become a tradition until the 1930s, when neighborhood groups began to compete and became known as *escolas de samba*, or samba schools. Samba (*see page 57*) has become the signature music of *Carnaval*. Today the competition between samba schools is akin to the rivalry between top sports teams. Most of the members come from the humblest of Rio's neighborhoods, including the *favelas*. Samba schools hold practice sessions for months before *Carnaval*, which are often open to the public. The moment of glory comes at the gates of Rio's mammoth samba stadium, the Sambódromo, designed by Oscar Niemeyer. Eighty-five thousand spectators can be seated along this kilometer-long parade strip to watch the samba schools go dancing by. If you can't get a ticket, you can see the schools line up outside on Avenida Presidente Vargas.

The best street dancing is in Salvador, where carousing hordes follow deafening sound systems. As is the case everywhere during *Carnaval*, it's best to dress minimally (shorts or bathing suits) to blend into the crowds and not attract thieves. Many travelers prefer *Carnaval* in the Northeast. In Recife the preeminent *Carnaval* music is *frevo*, which ignites passions, while Bahian *Carnaval* features *afoxé*, monotonous music often sung in African languages by subdued participants in flowing satin robes.

Less frenetic *Carnavals* are held in the cities of Olinda and Ouro Prêto, and in Rio's outlying suburbs. Dancing is also held in Copacabana and Ipanema. Class lines seem to dissolve as elated revelers hop together down the streets in camaraderie fueled by generous amounts of beer and *cachaca* (sugarcane brandy). *Carnaval* has increasingly moved off the streets and into the clubs recently, and this is where the most intense debauchery and exhibitionism goes on.

Not everyone in Brazil is wild about *Carnaval*. Many intellectuals sneer at the kitsch, wanton drinking and lewdness. But for outsiders, there is probably no better time to see the Brazil of everyone's fantasies. ❑

LEFT: clothes serve a purely decorative purpose at Rio de Janeiro's *Carnaval*.

with 300,000 residents, is Rio's most densely populated highrise neighborhood, and can be quite hectic away from the beach. But it's a lively place to enjoy street celebrations during *Carnaval* and New Year's Eve. The magnificent beach stretches out almost a block to the water. It's floodlit at night, but stay close to the crowds on the sidewalk to avoid getting mugged. Tourists wandering by the water are considered "papaya with sugar" by petty thieves.

After Copacabana comes **Ipanema Beach 🛈**, which connects at its western end with another beach called **Leblon 🛈**. Both Ipanema and Leblon are largely residential, with fewer hotels than Copacabana. The beaches of these more exclusive neighborhoods are more in vogue with the *carioca* fast-set than traditional Copacabana. Behind them to the north is the freshwater **Lagoa Rodrigo de Freitas**, a large natural lagoon surrounded by highrises and restaurants.

Map
on page
232

South to the most unspoiled beaches

North of the lagoon are the **Jockey Club** race track and the **Botanical Garden** on Rua Jardim Botanico. Some 5,000 species of Brazilian plants cover the garden's 100 hectares (250 acres), and though some of the grounds have gone to seed, a visit there is still a pleasure. Another nature adventure is the ride up the proverbially hunchbacked **Corcovado Mountain 🛈** on the impressive steep cog railway that leaves from Cosme Velho. At the top, 700 meters (2,340 ft) above the ocean, towers Rio's trademark statue of **Cristo Redentor** (Christ the Redeemer). The road coming down from the statue wends through the tropical Tijuca National Forest, with several breathtaking lookout points.

South of the sands of Leblon, sprawling up the sides of granite slopes, are two of Rio's biggest *favelas* or hillside shantytowns – **Vidigal** and **Rocinha**. Their

Trendy boutiques with artistic signs like this are plentiful in Brazil's many coastal resorts.

BELOW:
flying down to Rio.

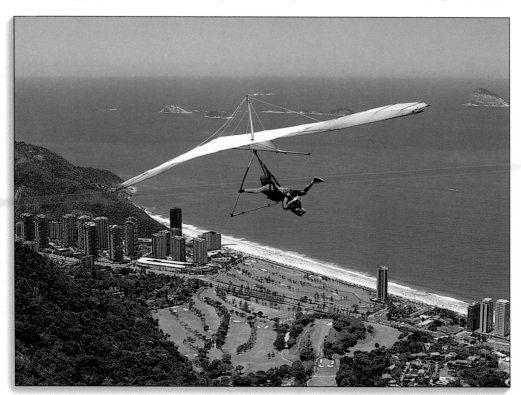

residents, who number hundreds of thousands, often endure such precarious circumstances in order to live close to their jobs on the south side of the city.

Further to the south is **São Conrado Beach** , a fast-growing suburb still free of the congestion that's endemic to the rest of Rio. Hang-gliders swoop down from the slopes above to wide sand expanses below. The cleanest beaches lie even further south beyond the primordial plains of **Barra de Guaratiba.** These are the areas not yet fully conquered by "the marvelous city". To see them is to understand the awesome beauty that gives Rio its enduring magic.

São Paulo: Brazil's workhorse

Colonial Parati, on the Costa Verde between São Paulo and Rio de Janeiro.

BELOW: São Paulo.

The first thing that strikes most visitors to the city of **São Paulo** ❷ is its sheer enormity. "I had no idea you had things like this down here," exclaimed then-US President Ronald Reagan as he flew over São Paulo by helicopter in 1982. Home to 13 million *paulistanos*, as the city's natives call themselves, São Paulo's phenomenal growth shows no signs of abating. Already the city covers nearly 2,600 sq. km (1,000 sq. miles), and it is ringed by mushrooming suburbs.

São Paulo is a center of trade and industry. Two-thirds of the country's industrial goods are produced in São Paulo, including nine out of ten automobiles. "São Paulo works so that the rest of Brazil can play," *paulistanos* will tell you. Since its foundation in 1554, São Paulo has always attracted self-reliant individualists – it was Brazil's equivalent to the Old West, and today proudly honors its old trailblazers, the *bandeirantes*. Those who followed came from all over the world, especially in the 19th century, bringing those industrious work habits. More recent immigrants have come from the drought-stricken states of northeastern Brazil. Poorly educated and unskilled, they often end up in the festering slums that hold half the city's population.

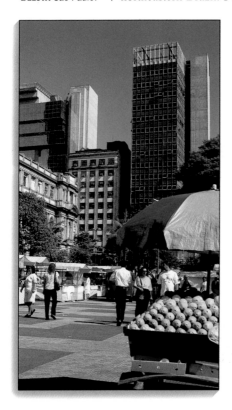

São Paulo is not a place to spend one's whole vacation, but it is well worth a visit. Its enormous array of restaurants are as diverse as they are numerous – a reflection of the city's varied ethnic makeup. The predominant cuisine is Italian, but there are also Japanese, German, Lebanese and French restaurants.

Paulistanos have cosmopolitan tastes, and they consider themselves trailblazers in the arts as well as industry. The pride and joy of the city is the MASP, or the **São Paulo Museum of Art**, with more than a thousand exhibits. And every odd-numbered year, São Paulo hosts one of the world's largest periodic art shows, the Bienal, featuring modern art from around the world. The pavilion where the Bienal is held is connected to a permanent collection of modern Brazilian art, housed in the sleek **Museum of Modern Art**.

Beneath the chaos

Perhaps the best way to explore São Paulo is by its clean, fast subway network. Stop off at **Liberdade**, home to the largest ethnic-Japanese community outside Japan. There are many inexpensive sushi bars in this area, and on Sundays there's a food and crafts fair at **Praça Liberdade**.

Neighborhoods such as **Jardim Paulista** or **Jardim America** have tree-lined streets and mansions that provide respite from the downtown rush. Another favorite oasis is the lovely **Parque Ibirapuera**, São Paulo's Central Park, designed by Oscar Niemeyer to celebrate the city's 400th anniversary in 1954. Its attractions include art museums, the striking **Legislative Assembly** and a **planetarium**. For a relaxing stroll, head for the leafy **Praça da República** with nearby shops at Avenida São Luiz, Rua Augusta and Rua Barão de Itapetininga. Watch for pickpockets.

Whether you like snakes or not, the **Butantã Snake Farm** should not be missed. Some 80,000 snakes there are milked for venom daily, and serum is prepared for distribution throughout Brazil. There is a museum as well, located at Avenida Dr. Vital Brasil 1500, in the Pinheiros district.

At night, São Paulo has a wide variety of clubs and cafés to while away the hours. Live music is even more plentiful here than in Rio. There's also a counter-culture quarter, the **Bixiga**, centered on Rua 13 de Maio. There are few old buildings left in the city, but the **Teatro Municipal**, which has resident opera and dance companies, evokes the elegant days of 19th-century coffee barons. The city frequently hosts world-class performers – *paulistanos* may be workaholics, but they demand the best when they knock off for some play.

Brasília: futuristic capital

Rising out of the great scrubby expanses of Brazil's central *cerrado*, **Brasília ❸** looks more like a gleaming extra-terrestrial settlement than Brazil's national capital. Absent are the red-tile roofs, intimate passageways and panache of pastel hues typical of Brazilian cities. Brasília is a cool, regimented architectural wonder, a "city of the future" that Brazilians are still trying to reconcile with the present. At 1,150 m (3,773 ft) above sea level and more than 800 km (500 miles)

Maps
Area 226–7
City 232

Medical researcher and friend, Butantã snake farm.

BELOW: Butantã snake farm.

from the coast, Brasília was built precisely because of its isolation from the great coastal cities. When Juscelino Kubitschek was elected President in 1955, he vowed that before he left office Brazil would have a new capital in its unpopulated interior, and he firmly believed that this capital would be a magnet to pull Brazilians away from their beloved coastline.

According to a popular joke, there are three great things about Brasília: its cool air, its enormous sky, and its air shuttle to Rio.

By 1956, work had already begun on Brasília. The city plan, drawn up by Lucio Costa, consisted of a central line of government buildings crossed by a curved arc of residential buildings – a layout that resembled the shape of an airliner. The architect chosen to design the structures was the Brazilian Oscar Niemeyer, a onetime student of the great modern Swiss architect Le Corbusier. Work proceeded at a furious pace, and by its inauguration in April 1960, Brasília already had 100,000 inhabitants.

At this time, Brazil's automobile industry was quickly expanding, so Brasília was designed with the certainty that everybody would get around in cars in the future. Wide thoroughfares sweep through the city, oblivious to the needs of pedestrians. With no sidewalks and few cross-walks, Brasília has the country's highest pedestrian mortality rate. Its grassy knolls are crisscrossed by red earth paths created by Brazilians who still depend on their feet to get around.

Modern wonder

Brasília is characterised by the graceful, pristine architecture of its public buildings. Niemeyer's designs are around the **Praça dos Tres Poderes** – the cockpit of the "airplane": headquarters of the government's executive, legislative and judicial arms. The low, white **National Congress** building has two towers rising from the middle, one occupied by the Senate, the other by the House of Deputies.

BELOW: Brasília's Foreign Ministry.

A huge inverted dish crowns the lower building on the Senate side, symbolizing the senators' lower susceptibility to voters' pressure due to longer terms in office. The Deputies' side is crowned by an open dish, representing the receptivity of congressman who face voters more frequently.

The presidential offices are in the **Palácio do Planalto**, which may be visited in office attire. The **Supreme Court**, with columns bathed by artificial waterfalls and a blindfolded sculpture of Lady Justice, is also open for visitors. Nearby is Brasília's most celebrated building, the **Foreign Ministry**, or Itamaraty, which appears to float in the pool of water surrounding it, and is highlighted by a sculpture known as the **meteor**. The roads leading to the "cockpit" are flanked by tall, identical office blocks housing the ministries. The commercial district lies where the two south and north residential wings intersect with the civic and commercial axis. All this can be seen from the observation platforms of the television tower located near the intersection of the axes.

Brasília has the overall feel of an enormous housing project built with little concern for its occupants. Residents are segregated according to their income levels, making Brasília more rigidly class-structured than any other Brazilian city. Those who built Brasília – poor migrants from the coastal states – now live on its peripheries in enormous shantytowns. Many work in the city as servants, taxi drivers and restaurant workers. Brasília's 400,000 residents are now only one-fifth of the population in the larger metropolitan area.

A generation of Brazilians has grown up in Brasília, and many are content to stay. Cultural life has broadened in recent years, and family ties are no longer exclusively with cities far from the capital. For all its technocratic veneer, Brasília has established an organic place in the society, remaining a symbol of audacity and the still unfulfilled dream of populating the hinterlands.

Minas Gerais: treasure trove of the Portuguese

Nestled in the steep hills north of Rio de Janeiro are some of Brazil's most beautiful colonial-era cities, in the large state of **Minas Gerais**, a mining region. In the 18th century it was the world's principal source of gold and today more than half the country's minerals and nearly all its iron ore come from here.

Belo Horizonte ❹, today's capital city of Minas Gerais, is neatly planned and a good base from which to explore the region. A hundred kilometers (60 miles) to the south lies the most prized creation of Brazil's Golden Age, the beautifully preserved city of **Ouro Prêto**. Its name comes from the gold encrusted with black iron oxide that was discovered nearby, early in the 18th century.

The find set off a gold rush, and Ouro Prêto soon became the colonial capital of Minas Gerais. The gold lasted more than a century, during which time Ouro Prêto and several nearby cities acquired sumptuous baroque churches and mansions, the only lasting heritage of 1,200 tons of gold extracted during that era. Thanks to the Brazilian government's decision to declare the entire city a national monument in 1933, much of its colonial treasures are intact, and it has retained its pleasant old-world atmosphere. Cobbled streets wend through hilly

Map on pages 226–7

Congress building, Brasília.

BELOW: Brasíia, a monument to mid-20th century urban planning.

Watching the world go by, Ouro Prêto.

quarters lined by well-kept colonial homes. Thirteen baroque churches gild the city of 24,000, many displaying the genius of the sculptor and architect Antônio Francisco Lisboa, better known as *Aleijadinho*, or Little Cripple. Afflicted as an adult by a crippling disease, Aleijadinho sculpted some of Brazil's most beautiful and expressive statuary – with his hammer and chisel strapped to his wrists.

The self-taught artist almost single-handedly shifted the aesthetics of the Golden Age from the boxish forms of mannerism to the sensuous curves of baroque. The most striking example is the exterior of the church of **Nossa Senhora do Rosario dos Prêtos**, built by black slaves (there were insufficient funds to complete the interior). Nearby is the church of **Nossa Senhora do Pilar**, whose interior is a profusion of baroque carved angels and gilded walls.

Off the main square, named after the 18th-century revolutionary Tiradentes, is the Church of **São Francisco de Assis**, an exquisite example of Aleijadinho's artistry and a repository of some of his most moving wood and soapstone figures. The interior was painted by high baroque master Manuel da Costa Athayde.

Ouro Prêto has an important mining school on Praça Tiradentes, and there is an interesting gem museum in the imposing **Governor's Palace** nearby, which has information about the gold and diamond mining that continues in the region.

Treasures of stone

The colonial town of **Mariana**, just east of Ouro Prêto, is another treasure left by gold barons who expressed gratitude for their good fortune by building extravagant churches. Work by Aleijadinho and Athayde can be found there, as well as a former beating post for slaves marked by a stone monument to Justice.

Thirty kilometers (20 miles) west of Ouro Prêto is **Congonhas do Campo**, the

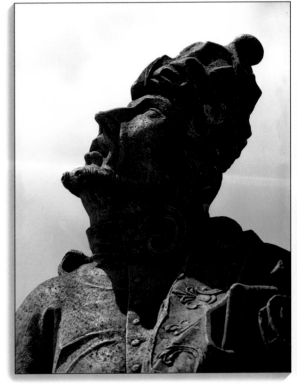

site of Aleijadinho's greatest feat: his hauntingly beautiful soapstone carvings of twelve Old Testament prophets outside the majestic church of **Bom Jesus do Matozinho**, a shrine for pilgrims. There are also 66 expressive carvings in cedarwood of Christ's Passion by Aleijadinho and his students.

Map on pages 226–7

A hundred kilometers (60 miles) to the south is **São João del Rei**, a colonial city of 50,000 with three striking 18th-century churches. There is also beautiful pewterware made at a local factory run by Englishman John Somers. Nearby is the silversmith village of **Tiradentes**, named after the man who agitated for independence from Portugal and was hanged in Ouro Prêto. **Sabará**, 22 km (14 miles) east of Belo Horizonte, has fine examples of Aleijadinho's work in its church, as well as Oriental influences, brought by Portuguese Jesuits.

The least commercialized of all the colonial towns is **Diamantina ❺**, 284 km (175 miles) north of Belo Horizonte. Once the center of a diamond boom, Diamantina was the birthplace of President Kubitschek, founder of Brasília. There are black statues carved in one of its churches, and instruments of torture are displayed, adding insight into how so many treasures were extracted.

Salvador and the Northeast

Brazil's Northeast is quite different from its prosperous south. The accent is different, the people are different, the food is more fiery and the barren *sertão* is more like an African desert than tropical Brazil. For the essence of the Brazilian mystique, one must go to where it all began: legendary, lustful **Bahia**, the state where Pedro Alvares Cabral established contact between Portuguese and native cultures in 1500. **São Salvador da Bahia de Todos os Santos ❻** is Brazil's first capital and is still the richest source of the country's cultural

BELOW: the colonial charm of Ouro Prêto.

identity. Salvador – also known as Bahia, the name of the surrounding state – is where much of the food, religion, dance and music that characterize Brazil originated, where Catholic Portuguese culture blended with the beliefs and aesthetics of the slaves who were brought from West Africa.

Brazil's party capital

The 2.2 million inhabitants of Salvador, known as *baianos* (pronounced bye-*ah*-nooz) are known throughout Brazil for their laid-back, festive temperament, which has made Salvador a favorite destination for vacationing Brazilians.

The city is convulsed by street celebrations almost every month of the year. *Carnaval* is the biggest – it officially begins a day before carnival in the rest of the country. Unofficially, preparations start in late November, agitated by commemorations of several religious holidays. Salvador's carnival is entirely participatory – frenzied hordes of minimally clothed dancers revel behind *trios elétricos* – floats laden with live bands and deafening sound systems. It is not for the faint-hearted, as the crowds often get unruly and are worked by petty thieves.

The backdrop for all this revelry is a city with a rich heritage and a beautiful natural setting. Salvador is built mostly on a high escarpment overlooking the Bay of All Saints. The upper level of the city, where almost all the ancient buildings are found, is known as **Cidade Alta**.

The **Pelourinho** neighborhood is full of pastel-hued 17th- and 18th-century buildings, considered the best representatives of such architecture in the New World. Here you'll find practitioners of *capoeira*, a kind of foot-fighting martial art originally brought by slaves from Angola, performed to the rhythm of a tambourine and the throbbing sound of a *berimbau*, whose single steel string

Baiana girl.

BELOW LEFT: canoes on the Recife coast.
BELOW RIGHT: Largo do Pelourinho, Salvador.

stretched across a bowed stick resonates in a hollowed gourd attached to the stick. *Capoeiristas* perform on the street for donations, but they also give shows during the evening at a cooking school and restaurant called SENAC along Pelourinho's plaza. It's best to visit Pelourinho in daylight, though, since street crime flourishes after dark. Pelourinho is also home to a famous black men's fraternal association named Filhos de Gandhi. This is a benevolent group connected to the syncretistic Afro-Brazilian religion of *Candomblé*. They assemble near the plaza for feast days and carnival, dressed in turbans and togas. Visitors will notice numerous women street vendors wearing flowing white lace dresses. They are known as Baianas, and they sell spicy and sweet specialties of Bahian cuisine.

An elevator near Pelourinho connects the Cidade Alta to the lower, more recently constructed **Cidade Baixa**, which has a big handicrafts marketplace called the **Mercado Modelo**. The white, lace-decorated garments sold here are typically Bahian. For a more typical market, and a compelling slice of local life, visit the **Mercado São Joaquim** further down the shoreline.

Cidade Baixa is the departure point for schooners taking tourists around the bay, and for passenger boats to small towns in the vicinity, as well as the island of **Itaparica**, where Club Med built its first installation in Brazil. Most of the island's 10,000 inhabitants make their living fishing, and the simple restaurants serve delicious seafood. Be sure to try the marinated fresh oysters.

Pristine beaches

Like Rio, Salvador is a city that lives at its beautiful beaches. The most accessible from downtown is **Barra**, small but extremely popular. Bars near the

Map on pages 226–7

TIP

Bahian cooking is considerably more spicy than elsewhere in Brazil, and generous amounts of coconut oil – *dêndé* – are used. Seafood predominates, and is often prepared in succulent stews called *moquecas*.

BELOW: *Baiana* lace dresses, Salvador.

beach are often jammed, and the fun continues long after sundown. Barra is at the tip of a long scalloped shoreline of beaches, most shaded by palms and with grassy areas. The best are the farthest out from the city, **Itapoán** and **Piatã**. It's best to hit these beaches on weekends when there are crowds, both for safety and because there will inevitably be live music performed at local *al fresco* bars.

Some 80 km (50 miles) north of Salvador is **Praia do Forte** a pristine stretch of 11 km (7 miles) of white sand beach bordered by 100,000 coconut palms. There is a sea turtle preservation project in the area.

Ilheus, a coastal city 390 km (240 miles) south of Salvador, is a mixture of modern and ancient architecture. The city is renowned for its lively carnival and the lovely beaches nearby, and is the center for 95 percent of Brazil's cocoa production. Further south down the coast is **Porto Seguro**, the fishing village where Cabral and his explorers first set foot in Brazil. In the past few years this has become one of the most popular destinations for Brazilian tourists.

Inland from Salvador begins the enormous scrub region called the *sertão*, frequently parched by drought and a tableau of human misery. The *sertanejos* who live there are often forced to leave to avoid starvation, but many return when the rains come, the others swelling the slums of the big cities.

Porto Seguro is the home of the sensual lambada dance, which is taught by curvaceous ladies at a host of waterfront bars.

Beyond Salvador

Bahia is the southernmost part of a nine-state region collectively known as the Northeast, home to a third of Brazil's population. The *nordestinos* have, until very recently, benefitted least from Brazil's material progress. Those who live along the coastal regions of Bahia are predominantly of African descent, while those living inland and to the north are a Portuguese/Indian mixture.

BELOW: the blood of a slaughtered chicken drips on an initiate's head during a *Macumba* ritual.

RELIGIOUS SPIRIT

Street intersections and meeting halls are places where you may see *Macumba*, voodoo-like rituals practiced with variations throughout the country. Macumba came with the West Africans on slave ships, and its phalanx of deities belongs to the traditions of the Yoruba-speaking peoples. The imposition of Christianity simply resulted in each of the new, European saints taking a corresponding identity with one of the Yoruba deities.

Because street intersections form a cross, they are thought to be centers of power. Visitors are usually welcome to watch Macumba rites, although photography is forbidden. *Candomble* is the kind of Macumba practiced around Salvador, where slaves first disembarked. Drumming is always an element and its hypnotic rhythms frequently plunge participants into wild gyrating trances. This happens at the sacred meeting places called *terreiros*. Devotees wear white to honor Oxalá, Candomble's equivalent to Christ and the highest of the deities.

In the south of Brazil, another kind of Macumba flourishes, *Umbanda*, from the Sanskrit aum-bandha: "limit of the unlimited". It is a kind of white magic – good deeds and generosity are asked of the gods. It blends Catholicism, Candomble, and a cult called "Spiritism" which started in France in the mid-19th century and soon made deep inroads in Brazil. People are believed to be visited by the spirits of deities during Umbanda sessions.

The Northeast has wonderful white sand beaches where you can still find fishermen using *jangadas*, an ancient precursor to the windsurfer. The city of **Maceió** has the most spectacular beaches nearby. North of Maceió is **Recife ❼**, the principal city of the Northeast, with 1.2 million inhabitants. Recife's beaches are protected by coral reefs, and the most popular is in the well-to-do **Boa Viagem** sector of the city. Just to the north is **Olinda,** a beautifully conserved colonial gem that is a popular destination for carnival revelers.

Further up the coastline is **João Pessoa**, the Americas' easternmost city. It's very pleasant and brightly painted, with a wealth of baroque churches. Huge sand dunes distinguish the beaches of **Natal ❽**, capital of the state of Rio Grande do Norte. Outside the city are other oceanside enclaves, such as delightful **Touros** (95 km/60 miles to the north), shaded by coconut groves.

Fortaleza ❾, the capital of Ceara, once drab and utilitarian, has benefited from the huge amount of capital which has flowed into the region in the past few years, using some of it to completely rebuild the seafront area, which now rivals Recife's Boa Viagem for elegance and liveliness. The city has become a very popular destination for tourists from Argentina and neighbouring countries.

Map on pages 226–7

The river ports: Manaus to Belém

The last thing you might expect in the middle of the Amazon jungle, 1,600 km (1,000 miles) from the sea, is a thriving port city. But **Manaus ❿** was cut from the wilderness in the 19th century: where mad conquistadors once searched in vain for gold, Brazilians found a modern El Dorado of rubber. Today, this strange outpost is enjoying a new boom as a tourist destination and one of the duty-free capitals of South America. Arriving in Manaus by boat is dramatic, not

Hammock room only on the deck class of an Amazon steamer.

BELOW: sunset over the River Amazon.

The great rubber boom ended almost as quickly as it began: tradition has it that a British gent smuggled rubber seeds out of the country saying they were for Queen Victoria's orchidarium, and soon plantations in Malaya were producing rubber more cheaply than Brazil.

because of the city, which is spread out on low bluffs – but because it is the meeting place of two Amazon tributaries at an 8-km (5-mile) wide junction. The dark River Negro, which looks like fizzy coca cola when riverboats churn it up, hits the yellowish River Solimoes, and the two vast currents run together, side by side without mingling their differently-coloured waters.

The chaotic bustle of modern Manaus is a dim reflection of its past glory. In 1888 the pneumatic tire was invented, and Amazon rubber suddenly became very valuable. For a brief, dazzling period, Manaus became the richest city in the world. Pioneers flooded into the jungle, creating the boom town of fast fortunes and grand gestures portrayed in Werner Herzog's film *Fitzcarraldo*.

Thousands of rubber tappers collected latex from isolated trees found deep in the jungle, working as virtual slaves along the sinuous waterways of the Amazon, and the newly-rich rubber barons, quaffing champagne and lighting their cigars with $100 bills, earned Manaus a name for extravagance and decadence. When the rubber boom collapsed, Manaus fell into a torpor that was only broken in 1967, when it became a duty-free zone.

The most famous and bizarre monument to the boom days is the grand opera house, the **Teatro Amazonas**. Materials for this temple of art in the jungle were wholly imported from Europe: white marble from Italy, iron pillars from England and polished wood from France. The sumptuous interior has four levels of Corinthian-columned balconies with red velvet chairs. The original house curtain remains, painted with Grecian nymphs lolling in the Amazon River. In its heyday, the opera house attracted such greats as the Italian tenor Caruso and today, fully restored, it can still pull in international names.

The old **port area** of Manaus is thriving. Wooden riverboats dump their

BELOW: opera in the jungle: Teatro Amazonas.

exotic cargoes, then grunting men lug the bananas or crates of soft drink among ankle-deep garbage, while overhead circle black urubu birds. Out on the river is a more modern floating dock for ocean-going cargo ships. Ramshackle houses have been thrown up around the port on precarious stilts. A more imposing construction is the stone **Customs House**, built by English engineers in 1906.

Map on pages 226–7

For a glimpse of the lost Indian cultures of the area, head for the **Museu do Indio** (corner Avenida Sete de Setembro and Rua Duque de Caxias), full of wooden blowpipes, feather headdresses and unexplained artefacts. Next door is one of the rubber factories still in operation, and it can be visited for free. There is even a "beach" near the **Hotel Tropical**, where braver swimmers can prove that the river is free of piranhas and electric eels which can so spoil a holiday.

Many tour companies head deeper into the jungle, but need a few days to get past the disordered "development" before finding virgin territory with animals. Jungle lodge stays are also on offer, with nature-watching canoe trips.

Toucan in the Amazon.

Beyond Manaus

Further down the Amazon is the port of **Santarém ⓫**, at the confluence with the Tapajós River. Once a colonial fortress, Santarém today is a kind of Dodge City for half a million jungle gold prospectors, or *garimpeiros*. On the south side of the mouth of the Amazon stands proud, stately **Belém ⓬**, 145 km (90 miles) from open ocean. A city of a million inhabitants, Belém retains the graceful airs of its rubber-boom heyday. Belém has an old town with colonial-era homes and churches. There's a fort nearby commandeered by Círculo Militar – try the mouth-numbing duck soup at its restaurant.

Belém's striking cathedral, **Basílica de Nossa Senhora de Nazaré**, was built

BELOW: sunset over Manaus dockside.

SLOWLY DOWN THE AMAZON

Nothing quite matches the romance of taking a slow boat down the world's greatest river. This vast waterway is still plied by hundreds of vessels: from ocean-going cargo ships to passenger boats. Tourist services run between the Amazon's two major ports, Manaus and Belém, but for the "authentic" Amazon experience, go for one of the smaller, wooden vessels. Known as *gaiolas*, or "birdcages", after the crowded mid-deck levels where passengers pile over one another in hammocks, these often antique boats still work the smaller tributaries from Manaus to Benjamin Constant, on the border of Colombia, then onward into Iquitos in Peru, and back. The Amazon is narrower here, allowing you to see more of the river life – from fishermen paddling in canoes to frolicking dolphins. Finding a boat is a matter of patience and luck. The smaller companies have no fixed schedules, and the only way to arrange a booking is to wander around the port and talk to people. Boats can be relatively comfortable or crowded, noisy and somewhat unhygenic. Those who can afford a few extra dollars often pay for a miniscule "cabin". Food is basic and bottled water should be taken. Stops are made at jungle villages, where the whole population turns out to watch the boat unload beer, pass out a few letters and take on a cargo of bananas. Gently swinging in your hammock to the rhythmical chug of the engine can be a very pleasant way to pass the time.

Anaconda crossing!

in 1909 with rubber boom money, and is as luxuriously baroque as those built two centuries earlier in Minas Gerais. Not far away is the dockside municipal market *Ver-o-Peso* ("check out the weight"), where fishermen bring their impressive catches. Another landmark is the **Emilio Goeldi Museum**, with exhibits of crafts made by Indians from nearby **Marajó Island**. Adjacent is a small zoo. Excursions leave Belém for Marajó Island, in the mouth of the river.

Rondônia: Brazil's wild west

If you thought the days of the Wild West were over, consider **Rondônia**. At the beginning of the 1970s this Brazilian state was tree-tangled wilderness on the southern flank of the Amazon jungle, bordering Bolivia. It was home to just a few thousand hardy rubber tappers. Today, settlers have pushed their way pell-mell into almost every corner of Rondônia, hacking down the jungle and frequently enforcing their land claims with the squeeze of a trigger. In the 1980s, nearly one-quarter of the Rondônian rainforest was destroyed, mostly by burning, to clear land for planting and cattle pastures. In the dry season, from May to October, a blanket of smoke hangs over the state as forests are incinerated.

With the extension of roadway BR 364 from São Paulo to the capital of Rondônia, the riverport of **Porto Velho** ⑬, express buses carried peasant migrants directly to the new frontier. A ride up BR 364 in one of the buses that ply the paved highway provides a revealing view both of frontier life and rainforest devastation. Along the highway are vast pastures cluttered with charred stumps and tall naked trunks of once-mighty rainforest trees. On the horizon looms the high dense wall of jungle that once covered the pastures.

BELOW: rough and ready in Rondônia.

A boom town called **Ariquemes** ⑭ along BR 364 gives a taste of the free-for-all world of the frontier. At the bus station, or *rodoviária*, sleek buses pull in from the south, discharging loads of dazed migrants clutching their possessions in feedsacks and battered suitcases. Some are met by relatives. A shop at the station sells T-shirts proclaiming "Rondônia – you have to see it to believe it."

In town, the dusty streets are lined by weather-beaten storefronts and filled with homesteaders shopping for provisions. Many have blond hair and blue eyes, legacies of their German forebears who settled in Brazil's south. As they wander the streets, snake-oil vendors compete with bible-thumping evangelists for their attention. Inside noisy bars, men shoot pool and talk about the latest confrontations between squatters and well-armed land barons.

Determined settlers

Despite endemic malaria, periodic shoot-outs, and poor soils, few of these people ever have second thoughts about having left the south behind. They are proud of their tenacity and are determined to make it on this quickly-expanding frontier. Discussions about ecological destruction fail to move them; short-term survival is their top priority. Those who occupied the rainforest before the land rush – the rubber tappers and Indians – have been forced further west as the frontier encroaches on their way of life. Rubber tapping has all but been abandoned in Rondônia as the trees have disappeared, despite laws enacted for their protection. Some 300,000 Brazilians still survive collecting the fruits of the forest – wild rubber, Brazil nuts and resin. They now live mostly in the state of Acre, west of Rondônia on the borders of Bolivia and Peru. Key to their survival is their isolation and international pressures to protect their benign co-existence with the rainforest. Some protected areas called "extractive reserves" have been established for these jungle harvesters. But as Brazil's population continues to grow faster than the new jobs, the pressures to clear the forest that have transformed Rondônia are likely to keep moving westward.

Map on pages 226–7

The Pantanal: bird paradise

An enormous marsh called the **Pantanal** is perhaps the most exquisite gallery of all for observing Brazilian fauna – "a bird-lover's paradise" in the words of Brazilian geographer Osvaldo Valverde. Spreading 100,000 sq km (40,000 sq miles) east of the Paraguay River on Brazil's western border with Bolivia, the Pantanal is home to more than 600 species of birds, 350 kinds of fish, and an abundance of reptiles and animals. Many of these are also found in the Amazon, but seeing them there is much more difficult because of the dense forest cover.

Ilha de Maracá, near Boa Vista.

The Pantanal's menagerie of birds is mostly waterfowl and waders. There are white ibises, egrets, blue herons, ducks, green parakeets, pheasants, and the 2-meter (6-ft) tall white Jabirú or Tuiuiú stork. During the rainy months of October to April, when waters are high in the north of the Pantanal, the birds feed on fish in the southern sector. From May until September, when the waters from the north flood down to the south, the birds move to the more shallow

BELOW LEFT: snappy sunbathers.
BELOW RIGHT: a red-necked Tuiuiú.

*Unfortunate
piranhas, Pantanal.*

waters in the north. The best time of the year to visit is during the cooler and dry winter months of June, July and August; January and February are infernally hot and humid. The Pantanal can be noisy in the dry season, since that's when birds are nesting by the hundreds in swamp trees. When the waters recede from the northern Pantanal in winter, wide sandy riverbanks are exposed. Brazilians like to camp on the banks during that season, but this is also when large alligators called jacarés like to sun on the sand. There are also ocelots, pumas, wild boars, jaguars, red lake deer, tapirs and a large furry rodent called the capivara.

Exploring the swamps

Access to the Pantanal's edge is quite easy, but getting around inside is another matter. **Cuiabá** ⓰, capital of Mato Grosso, is an attractive city that once enjoyed a gold boom, though it gets intensely hot here. Some 70 km (45 miles) northeast of Cuiabá there are cool waterfalls at **Chapada de Guimarães**, the source of much of the water that enters the northern part of the swamp. There are also some striking rock formations along the escarpment.

Just south of Cuiabá is **Santo Antônio de Leverger**, on the edge of the marshland. From there it's possible to fly to hotels and cattle ranches, or *fazendas*, within the Pantanal. You can obtain ground transport, boats, airplane flights, and even hot-air balloon rides at these lodges for observing the wildlife. Fishing is permitted – piranhas are prized for their supposed aphrodisiacal powers – but not hunting. Poachers have already made off with many alligators and capivaras, and the many conservationists in the area keep a close lookout for human predators. The main attraction of the area is **Baia Chacorore**, a huge shallow water basin flocked with roseate spoonbills. Its banks literally crawl with alligators.

BELOW: wildlife watching at the Caiman Ecological Refuge, Pantanal.

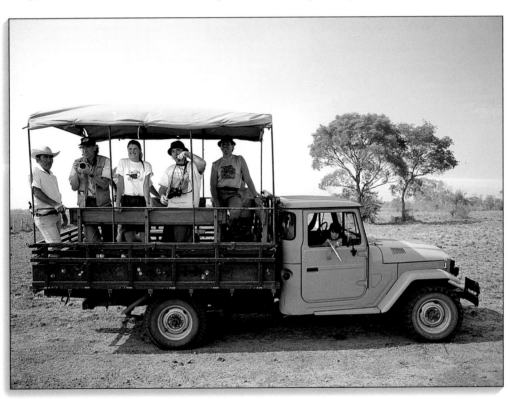

It is possible to drive into the Pantanal along the partially completed **Transpan-taneira Highway**, which starts just outside the small town of **Poconé**, 102 km (63 miles) from Cuiabá. Vehicles can be hired here. The road is often rough and it sometimes floods, but it crosses many rivers (there are 126 bridges) and provides a close-up view of the wildlife. The road ends 145 km (90 miles) into the Pantanal at Porto Jofre. Accommodation is available en route and at the port.

If the Transpantaneira were completed (which appears unlikely because of opposition from environmentalists), it would connect Cuiabá to **Corumbá ⑯**, a border town on the southwest flank of the Pantanal. Although the Pantanal reaches up to the city limits, local tours reveal little – much of the wildlife has fled to more remote areas. The best way to see the swamp from Corumbá is to arrange passage on cattle boats that penetrate more deeply into the area or organize a trip to one of the ranches on the highway linking Corumbá to Campo Grande.

Iguaçu Falls and the Itaipú Dam

The famous falls, which link the Brazil, Paraguay and Argentine borders, are described fully in the Argentina chapter (*see page 336*). The closest Brazilian city to the falls is **Foz do Iguaçu ⑰**, near the junction of the Paraná and Iguaçu rivers. This frontier town has grown phenomenally in the last two decades, largely due to the construction nearby of the world's largest hydroelectric dam. This facility, called **Itaipú** (Guaraní for "singing rock"), is well worth visiting, and guided tours are available. Built jointly by Brazil and Paraguay, it is powered by the waters of the Paraná River, which divides the two countries. The dam, which provides electricity mainly for far-off São Paulo, is an impressive sight, and a short film at the visitor center tells the story of its construction. ❑

Map on pages 226–7

Armadillo, caught for the cameras only.

BELOW: twilight flight, Pantanal.

THE RICHES OF THE AMAZON RIVER

The world's greatest river and largest rainforest, in the heart of Brazil, is estimated to contain one-tenth of the plant and insect species on earth

The Amazon River is one of the greatest symbols of Brazil. It rises in the snows of the Peruvian Andes just a short distance from the Pacific Ocean. It then travels across the heart of South America – a distance of 6,570 km (4,080 miles) – before it flows out into the Atlantic Ocean at the equator. It has about 15,000 tributaries, some of which, like the Araguaia and the Madeira, are mighty rivers in themselves. Just past Manaus, one of the most spectacular river sights is the meeting of the "black waters" of the Negro river with the "white waters" of the Solimoes river, two other Amazon tributaries. The Amazon has a heavier flow than any other river, depositing in the ocean each year about one-fifth of the world's fresh water.

At its mouth the Amazon is 300 km (185 miles) wide, a labyrinth of channels and islands, one of which has a greater land mass than Switzerland. The water flows with such force that it is still fresh 180 km (110 miles) out into the ocean.

RAINFOREST AND INDIANS

The Amazon's network of dark, dense jungles has often been referred to as The Great Green Hell. In the west of the Amazon basin, it is still possible to fly for several hours and see nothing below but a carpet of tropical forest, broken only by rivers snaking their way through the trees. The Amazon has remained virtually unchanged for the past 100 million years, for it did not pass through the same ice ages that altered other parts of the world's landscapes. Some areas are still inhabited by Indian groups who have descended down the centuries and have never had contact with the world outside their own jungle.

△ **AMAZON CRUISES**
A river trip along the legendary Amazon, taking in the sights, sounds and smells of the verdant jungle, is one of the highlights for many visitors to Brazil.

▷ **BLACK SPIDER MONKEY**
This delightful animal uses its tail to swing from branch to branch in the forest.

◁ **POISON ARROW FROG**
The poison from this brightly colored frog used to be extracted by local Indians to use on the tip of arrows.

△ **RIO MADEIRA**
Though just a tributary of the Amazon, the Madeira river itself flows over a distance of more than 1,600 km (1,000 miles).

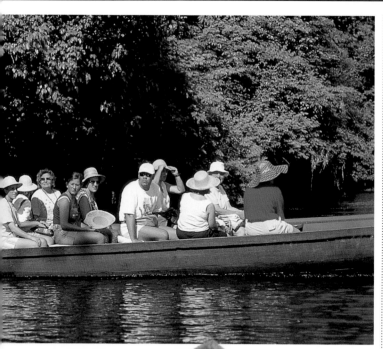

DEFORESTATION IN THE AMAZON

About 14 per cent of the Amazon forest has already been cut down, almost all within the last 30 years. Most of the destruction has taken place in the east of the basin, "opened up" in the 1960s and 1970s when the Brazilian military government built a vast network of roads. Cattle companies then moved in, burning the forest to sow pasture. But ranching was not successful, for the soils, once deprived of protective cover, leached and became barren.

Despite the rise in ecological awareness, new threats have emerged. Foreign timber companies want the Amazon's hardwoods, now that the rest of the world's hardwood forests have been destroyed; and big grain farmers, cultivating genetically engineered soya beans, are moving in here from the south of Brazil.

△ **JUNGLE LODGING**
At the eco-friendly Ariau Hotel guests can hear the bewitching sounds of the tropical forest at night.

▽ **VICTORIA REGINA**
The indigenous water lily has enormous, circular leaves that can be up to 2 meters (6 ft) across.

◁ **URUCU BERRIES**
Amazonian Indians treasure the Urucu tree. Its berries contain a red-colored dye the Indians use to paint their bodies and faces.

△ **RUBBER TAPPING**
Thousands of families, living deep in the rainforest, still tap rubber trees for the latex.

▷ **TOUCAN**
This striking looking bird, a recognizable image of the Amazon forest, uses its huge yellow bill to crush the seeds it feeds on.

THE SOUTHERN CONE

*Often considered the most European part of South America,
this region contains some of its most cosmopolitan
cities and starkly stunning scenery*

El cono sur – the "southern cone" of Paraguay, Argentina, Uruguay and Chile – makes up a geological and cultural unit quite apart from the rest of South America. Sparsely populated in pre-Columbian days by nomadic tribes, these countries today form the most ethnically and climatically European part of the continent.

European settlement came late to the south, with many areas unexplored until the late 19th century. The newcomers were from many places besides Spain, Portugal and Italy. Small colonies remain here of Germans, Boers, Britons and Swiss, all descendants of these pioneers. The attraction was the prospect of sudden wealth: several decades ago these countries were relatively affluent, riding on booms of agriculture and minerals.

Isolated Paraguay (*see page 265*) has no access to the sea, but its capital, Asunción, has become a bustling duty-free center – although horse-drawn carts still clatter through its streets, beneath statues of long forgotten generals. Most of the country is made up of the vast, sparsely-populated Chaco lands (*see page 272*).

Squeezed between the Pacific Ocean and the Andes mountains, ultra-narrow Chile (*see page 279*) covers a huge range of latitudes. Heading south from the northern Atacama Desert – one of the driest in the world – you pass through the moderate climate of the capital, Santiago (*see page 281*), with its surrounding vineyards (*see page 284*), to the snow-covered forests of the Lake District (*see page 290*). Beyond that are glaciers, peaks and windswept fishing villages of Chilean Patagonia (*see page 295*).

The republic of Uruguay (*see page 311*), once dubbed "the Switzerland of South America", for its progressive political tradition, had enough money from beef to build a powerful social welfare state. Today, the country seems frozen in the 1920s. The capital, Montevideo (*see page 313*), is a quaint city where hand-cranked automobiles still groan through the streets, while the country's beautiful beaches are mostly used by the wealthy from elsewhere in the world.

The second-largest country on the continent, Argentina (*see page 321*) was at the turn of the century its richest by far. Things haven't gone quite as expected since then, and the elegant capital Buenos Aires (*see page 325*) is crowded with the crumbling Parisian relics of the boom days. Argentina sprawls over every climatic zone, with arid northern plains where gauchos still ride (*see page 338*), the subtropical province of Missiones (*see page 336*), lush forests around Bariloche (*see page 339*), the windswept, sheep-strewn plains of Patagonia (*see page 341*), and at the southern tip of the continent, the chilly, mountainous island of Tierra del Fuego (*page 344*).   ❑

PRECEDING PAGES: huge chunks of ice broken from the glacier melt in the Canal de los Tempanos (Channel of the Icebergs) at Glacier National Park, Argentina.
LEFT: traditional chaps: gauchos of northwest Argentina.

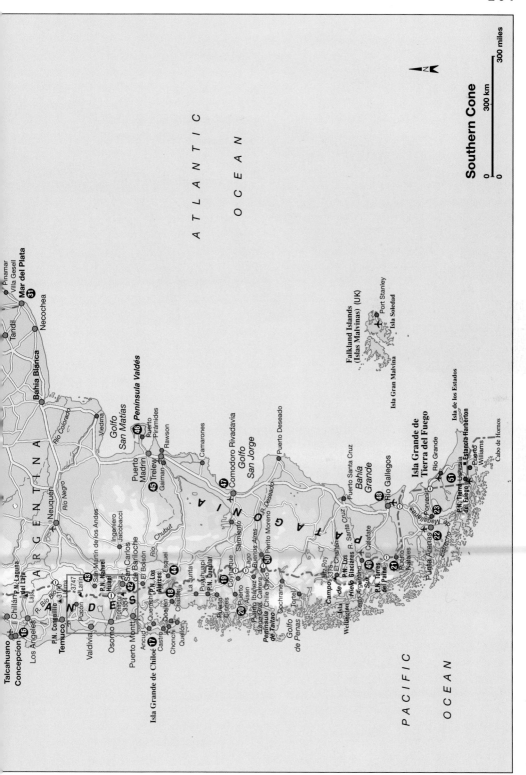

Southern Cone

0 300 km
0 300 miles

ATLANTIC OCEAN

PACIFIC OCEAN

Falkland Islands
(Islas Malvinas) (UK)

Port Stanley
Isla Soledad
Isla Gran Malvina

Isla de los Estados

Isla Grande de
Tierra del Fuego

Estancia Harberton
Río Grande
P.N. Tierra
del Fuego
Ushuaia
Puerto
Williams
Cabo de Hornos

Punta Arenas

Río Gallegos

Puerto Natales

El Calafate

Comodoro Rivadavia

Golfo
San Jorge

Puerto Deseado

Camarones

Puerto Santa Cruz
R. Santa Cruz
Perito Moreno

Puerto
Madryn
Puerto
Pirámides

Península Valdés

Golfo
San Matías

Trelew
Gaiman
Rawson

Viedma

Río Colorado

Neuquén

Río Negro

Bahía Blanca
Necochea
Tandil
Mar del Plata
Pinamar
Villa Gesell

P.N. Laguna
del Laja
Chillán
Los Ángeles
Concepción
Talcahuano
Temuco
P.N. Conguillío
Laja
R. Bío Bío
Lanín
P.N. Nahuel
Huapi
San Martín de los Andes
Ingeniero
Jacobacci
Pucón
Valdivia
Osorno
Puerto Montt
Ancud
Castro
Chonchi
Quellón
Isla Grande de Chiloé

San Carlos
de Bariloche
El Bolsón
Esquel
P.N. Los
Alerces
El
Maitén
La Junta
Chaitén
Río
Chubut

Puerto
Cisnes
Puyuhuapi
P.N. Queulat
Coyhaique
Puerto
Aysén
Puerto Ibáñez
Chile Chico
Cochrane
Tortel
Golfo
de Penas
Península
de Taitao
Isla
Wellington
Lago Gral. Carrera/
Lago Buenos Aires
Río Senguerr

Bajo
Caracoles
Gobernador
Gregores
Lago
Cardiel
Lago
San Martín/
Lago
O'Higgins
Campo de
Hielo
Sur
Campo
de Hielo
Norte
Lago Argentino
El Chaltén
P.N. Los
Glaciares
Mte. Fitz Roy
P.N. Torres
del Paine

Bahía
Grande

P.N. Magallanes

Porvenir

Cabo Vírgenes

3747
3194

ARGENTINA

A N D E S

P A T A G O N I A

16
17
31
43
42
1
18
44
20
19
45
46
47
48
49
50
51
21
22
23

PARAGUAY

One of the continent's most intriguing nations, this is a land of Utopias and experimental communities, where the language of the original inhabitants shares pre-eminence with that of their colonists

Map on pages 260–1

Surrounded by Bolivia, Brazil and Argentina, the small subtropical nation of Paraguay lies at the heart of South America. The River Paraguay divides the country into two distinct halves: the lush, fertile east, where most of the population lives, and the barren Chaco tablelands to the west, home to a few scattered settlements, Mennonite farmers, and nomadic Indians. The River Paraguay eventually feeds into the River Plate, linking the country historically and geographically to the other River Plate nations of Uruguay and Argentina.

"An island surrounded by land" is how exiled Paraguayan novelist Augusto Roa Bastos has described his landlocked native country. The phrase refers not only to Paraguay's physical remoteness but to a kind of psychic solitude brought about by wars, dictatorships and a profound sense of ethnic unity. A visitor to the capital, Asunción, can't help noticing the profusion of monuments commemorating military rulers, crushing defeats and Pyrrhic victories. Yet one is also struck by the tropical prettiness of the colonial city, and by the soft-spoken, gentle manners of Paraguayans, reminders that the Spaniards who first settled this region dreamed not of plunder but of founding an earthly paradise.

In a country where almost everyone is of part Guaraní descent, schoolbooks devote considerable space to pre-Columbian Paraguay. The Guaraní were the original inhabitants of what is now Asunción. Principally farmers, they were also accomplished warriors who bore suffering stoically. Early Spanish chroniclers reported with horror that the Guaraní were cannibals, although this custom was apparently limited to the ritual eating of prisoners of war. Their language, in the words of one Spanish priest, was "one of the most copious and elegant on the globe," and it was used as a *lingua franca* throughout the region.

PRECEDING PAGES: the Itaipú Dam. **LEFT:** guards at the Panteón de los Héroes, Asunción. **BELOW:** young Paraguayans.

Arrival of the Spanish

Asunción was founded on August 15, 1537, by Domingo de Irala, a man of letters who came seeking refuge from the miseries of the settlement at Buenos Aires and the rigors of the conquest. The Guaraní, who were also anxious for Inca gold, were eager to form an alliance with the Spaniards and gave them their daughters as tokens of good faith. The discovery that the Incas had already been conquered and plundered by Pizarro, and the lush life in Asunción, far from the sea and the watchful eye of the Spanish crown, induced Irala and his men to stay. The colonial farms were organized in a feudal manner, although intermarriage evened out the social hierarchy.

Fulgencio Yegros declared Paraguay's independence on May 14, 1811, and ruled along with a civilian lawyer named Doctor José Gaspar Rodríguez de Francia. Soon after independence Francia seized

*Steam train waiting
to depart from
Asunción station.*

BELOW: 19th
century etching of
General Urquiza's
Palace, San José.

power, and Congress named him supreme dictator for life in 1816. To protect Paraguay from the danger of annexation by Argentina or Brazil, Dr Francia closed the borders: no one was allowed in or out during his 24-year reign.

"El Supremo", as Francia was called, ruled by absolute decree. A learned man, initially a frugal and honest ruler, he grew deranged by power and isolation. At one point he ordered all the dogs in the country killed; he also decreed that none of his subjects could look at him in the street. At his death in 1840, no Paraguayan priest was willing to say a funeral Mass, and a priest was finally imported from Argentina. Paraguay was plunged into political chaos until the next dictator, Carlos Antonio López, was proclaimed in 1844.

López was an enlightened despot who re-opened the country to progress and sent students to Europe to study. But his son and designated successor, Francisco Solano López, was a weak and spoiled young man. Feeling that Paraguay's neighbors did not take his country seriously, he decided to intervene in Uruguay's civil war, and quickly found himself at war with Brazil and Argentina as well. The ensuing War of the Triple Alliance was disastrous for Paraguay.

The country was further ravaged by a cholera plague, and López, at this point seriously unhinged, ordered the executions of hundreds of people, including his own two brothers and scores of officers. Abetted by his famous Irish mistress, Elisa Lynch, he also executed his childhood sweetheart and other society ladies who had snubbed Madame Lynch. On March 1, 1870, he was shot by one of his own generals after refusing to surrender. "I die with Paraguay," he exclaimed, which was almost literally true. After the war and the carnage that followed, more than half the population of 525,000 were dead; of the survivors, only 29,000 were adult males. Paraguay was rebuilt mostly by women, who resigned themselves to a polygamous society as the Church looked the other way.

Between the fall of Solano López and Paraguay's bloody Chaco War with Bolivia, the country changed presidents 32 times and endured two assassinations of presidents, six *coups d'état*, two revolutions and eight attempted revolutions. Paraguay won the Chaco War of 1932 and 1935, fought over a piece of barren land that was believed to contain oil and other mineral deposits (*see page 38*), but once again the male population was devastated. A succession of dictators followed, until in 1954 the son of a German brewmeister, Alfredo Stroessner, seized power and ruled with an iron fist for nearly 35 years.

Winds of change

Stroessner played off one political faction against another while providing a sanctuary for fleeing Nazis and exiling, imprisoning, torturing and killing rivals and opponents. In the all-pervading climate of corruption, Paraguay became notorious as a haven for smuggling, much of it in narcotics. Human rights activists and some of the country's artists and writers, notably the novelist and poet Augusto Roa Bastos and the artist Carlos Colombino, provided a moral centre for resistance. Stroessner's regime brought some notable innovations, but in 35 years these developments may well have occurred without him. In the 1970s, the construction of a Brazilian-Paraguayan hydroelectric dam at Itaipú in eastern Paraguay stimulated land investment, expanded financial services, and provided thousands of jobs. The giant Paraguayan-Argentine hydroelectric project at Yacyreta, proposed in 1973, began operating in 1997.

On February 3, 1989, Stroessner was overthrown by General Andrés Rodríguez, his right-hand man and father of his daughter-in-law. Rodríguez promised a free press and a gradual return to democracy after the coup and his Colorado Party was elected into office in 1991. Gleeful Paraguayans took down the photographs of Stroessner, exiled to Brazil, that graced every shop window, changed the names of streets and towns, and decapitated statues of the former president. Since then Paraguay has been experiencing a process of democratic transition, marked by a new constitution, political and press freedoms and regular elections. Paraguay has also joined the Mercosur common market, a development that upsets some of the more extreme nationalists.

Offsetting these achievements are continuing wide disparities in wealth and a notable absence of land reform, not to speak of a pervasive military presence in national politics that surfaced in May 1996 in an attempted coup by the popular General Lino Oviedo. Despite these blemishes, democracy in Paraguay seems to be here to stay. The Colorado Party has continued to dominate political life, winning the presidency and most of the congressional seats in the elections of May 1998.

Asunción: elegance and neon lights

Today, **Asunción ❶** matches the dynamism of most South American cities while retaining a sleepy elegance, with elegant colonial mansions rubbing shoulders with luxury boutiques, duty-free shops and neon

Map on pages 260–1

The atmosphere of rather seedy militarism of the Stroessner years is brilliantly captured in Graham Greene's novel Travels With My Aunt.

BELOW: musicians perform with the traditional Guaraní harp.

A Bilingual Land

Spanish explorers in Paraguay, unlike other colonies, did not clash with the local indians but blended to form a homogeneous, bilingual society. This was possible mainly because the local Guaraní had nothing the Spanish conquistadors wanted to steal. What the Guaraní did have to offer was a peaceful life in a fertile country.

It is difficult to say how much the notorious Guaraní "harems" kept by the Spaniards were fact and how much exaggeration for the benefit of their miserable compatriots in Buenos Aires, but it was true that a great deal of social mobility was achieved by marriage, and that the mestizo offspring, as in Portuguese Brazil, were not considered marginal citizens.

Sociologists also cite the relatively high position of women in Guaraní society as a factor in the continuing status of the mother tongue. But perhaps the most decisive element in Paraguayan bilingualism was the missionary work of the Jesuits. Although the Jesuits imposed Spanish on the indians, they were impressed by the complexity and musicality of Guaraní, and produced catechisms and hymns in the native language. Ironically, as a result, the Guaraní neglected much of their original music. Nevertheless, Guaraní music still has a distinctive sound.

In 1624, the Jesuit priest Antonio Ruiz de Montoya created the first Guaraní dictionary and grammar, giving the language a written form and thus a better chance of survival.

During the dictatorship of Doctor Francia (1814–40), Paraguayans of pure Spanish descent were forbidden to intermarry. This attempt to dilute the country's ruling class increased contact between the two cultures and their languages. Guaraní was considered a sort of homely argot rather than the speech of educated people, but its use became more widespread during the War of the Triple Alliance, as a symbol of national pride and unity. On the battlefields of the Chaco War (1932-35) Spanish was banned and Guaraní was spoken, as a secret language. As a result, many older Paraguayans with little or no indian heritage speak Guaraní more fluently than Spanish.

In urban areas today, more than 70 percent of the population is completely bilingual; less than 12 percent speak only Spanish. In rural areas, the use of Guaraní still supersedes that of Spanish; 60 percent of the population speak only Guaraní. Before the 1970s it was rare for teachers to use Guaraní in the classroom, but changing ideas about bilingual education have made the new generation not only fluent but literate in Guaraní.

Novels and poetry are published in Guaraní translations; there are also theater productions, television and radio shows in the language. The influence of Guaraní on the language of the conquistadors is notable even to those who don't understand Guaraní: the musical tones, the penchant for modesty and understatement – none of which are characteristics of Spanish.

But despite the ever-presence of Guaraní melodies, and the 1981 Law of Native Communities which guarantees indians rights over their lands and cultures, the social position of full-blooded indians remains inferior. ❏

LEFT: A Guaraní woman sells handicrafts outside the Guaraní Hotel in Asunción.

lights. The **Plaza de los Héroes** is bright with butterflies and birds of paradise. Many passers-by seem to have come directly from central casting: fruit vendors with baskets on their heads, furtive black-market money-changers, the cluster of helmeted military police investigating a broken water pipe.

Gone are the bright yellow electric streetcars which Stroessner revived after the oil crisis of the 1970s. Gone too is the neon sign which flashed STROESSNER: PEACE, WORK AND WELL-BEING over the square, but its focal point is still the ornate **Pantéon Nacional de los Héroes**, which was built as a copy of Les Invalides in Paris. Inside are the tombs of the two López presidents, of two unknown soldiers, and a small urn containing what remains of the dictator Francia. It's said that his bones were dug up and flung into the river by an angry mob.

But no matter how Paraguayans feel about their military governments, this is a country that reveres soldiers; it's not at all unusual for passers-by to stop at this shrine and make the sign of the cross before the heroes' crypts. Diagonally across from the pantheon are shop windows that permanently display Chaco War memorabilia and accounts of battles. Across the street, on the corner of Chile and Palma, is a pleasant café called the **Lido**; a good spot to stop for fresh orange juice and a dish of rich cornbread called *sopa paraguaya*. West of the Plaza de los Héroes, on Presidente Franco, is the **Casa de la Independencia**, where independence was declared in 1811 and which nowadays houses a museum.

The historic old town

The oldest part of the city can be reached by following Calle Chile down towards the River Paraguay. On a small bluff is the pastel **Palacio del Gobierno**. It was built in the style of the Louvre by Francisco Solano López, who imported

Map on pages 260–1

The Palacio del Gobierno was designed by a British architect, Alonso Taylor. Having fallen out with his patron, Taylor was tortured in the palace basement but escaped with his life, unlike numerous other victims of El Mariscal.

BELOW: stormy sky over Asunción.

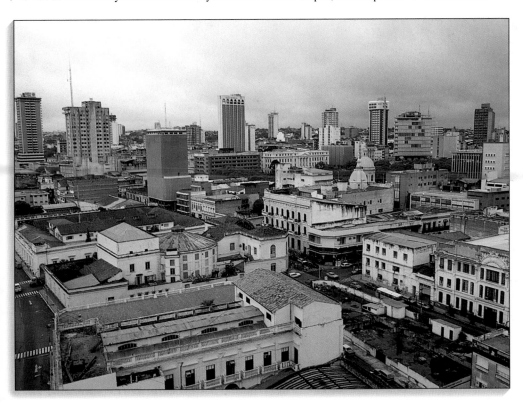

much of the building's beautiful interiors and furniture from Paris. He did not have much time to enjoy the palace since its construction was interrupted by the War of the Triple Alliance. Further along El Paraguayo Independiente are the tree-lined **Plaza Constitucion**, the **Congressional Palace**, and the newly renovated **cathedral**. Opposite the Palacio is the 18th-century **Manzana de la Rivera**, or Casa Viola. Once the headquarters for Strossner's elite forces, the Casa is now an innovative cultural center incorporating a museum of the history of the city. A short distance further on are the **Aduana** (Customs House), the port buildings and the barracks, naval headquarters and old fortifications that provide eloquent testimony to the one-time status of Asunción as a frontier city with only the river separating its inhabitants from the wild lands of the Chaco. From a pier by the palace a tiny ferry takes passengers across to the island of **Chaco-i**.

Parks and plazas

East of the Plaza de los Héroes is another large and pleasant square, the **Plaza Uruguaya**, which was once the site of a famous convent and was renamed in tribute to the Uruguayan government when they returned Paraguayan flags captured in the War of the Triple Alliance. There are two interesting bookshops in pavilions in the plaza, which also has stalls selling leather work, paintings and other crafts. Handicrafts made by the indigenous Maca people in their settlements on the outskirts of the city can be bought here.

A short distance away is the **Estación San Francisco**, a relic of the López years which was designed by Alonso Taylor. Now being restored courtesy of the Spanish government, the building is a Victorian gem, built largely of wood, but with cast iron supports and a tower that was once the home of the stationmaster. The station used to be the terminus for the British-run line to Encarnarción in southern Paraguay that ultimately linked to Buenos Aires. Nowadays occasional trains run to nearby Areguá on Lake Ypacaraí, pulled by wood-burning locomotives.

The Itaipú hydroelectric dam has given Paraguay the cheapest electricity in South America. World Bank loans for the project also enriched some Paraguayans beyond their wildest dreams. Some of their splendid new houses can be seen if you take a trip along Avenida España. There are also some beautiful old colonial houses with wide verandahs and gardens of bottlebrush and banana trees on this road, as well as the American Embassy, the library, and Stroessner's former home, now a museum.

Parque Carlos Antonio López, on the Avenida of the same name, provides a good view of the city from the Antonio López and Rio Gallegos intersection. The **Jardin Botánico**, 7 km (4 miles) outside Asunción, which has its own zoo, is well worth a visit, as are the nearby **Museo de Historia Natural** and the **Museo Indigentista**, both former residences of the two López presidents.

Across the river is a reservation of the Macá people, who were brought here from their home in the Chaco as a tourist attraction. They live in rather dismal conditions. Ironically, the best handicrafts are to be found in the middle-class suburb of **San Lorenzo**, along the

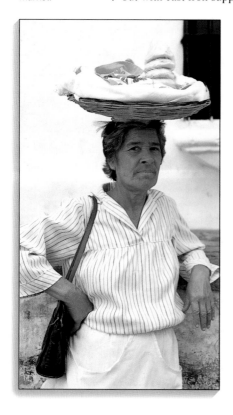

BELOW: Guaraní woman selling *chipas,* small cakes made from maize, in an Asunción market.

eastern highway, where the shop of the **Museo Boggiani** offers authentic and very beautiful artefacts made by indigenous people of the Chaco.

Traveling east

The Mariscal Estigarribia Highway crosses Paraguay to the Brazilian border town of Ciudad del Este, formerly Cuidad Presidente Stroessner. By express bus the trip takes about four hours, but there are interesting stops along the first half of the journey. About 20 km (14 miles) east of Asunción is **Capiatá**, which was first settled by the Jesuits in 1640. It has an interesting church, which contains a 17th-century sculpture made by the Guaraní under Jesuit instruction. Ten kilometers (6 miles) east is **Itagua**, famous for its production of *ñandutí*, or spiderweb lace, which is woven by hand into handkerchiefs, tablecloths and hammocks and displayed by the weavers in stalls along Route 2. There is a museum and an annual festival in July.

The resort town of **San Bernardino**, 55 km (35 miles) from Asunción on **Lake Ypacaraí**, is a favorite retreat of prosperous Paraguayans and a center for watersports. The lake, immortalised in a hauntingly beautiful Guaraní song, measures 5 by 24 km (3 by 15 miles) and is an idyllic spot, surrounded by tropical vegetation. The resort town of **Areguá**, on the southern shore of the lake, terminus for the short steam train journey from Asunción, has many shops and stalls selling earthernware. **Caacupé ❷**, 24 km (15 miles) down the road from San Bernardino, is another popular resort and religious shrine. On December 8, pilgrims come to this town from all over Paraguay carrying heavy stones on their heads as penance. Nearby are the villages of **Tobatí**, which has pottery and wood carvings, and **Piribebuy**, which has a fine church and an interesting museum. There are some lovely small resorts in the hilly, verdant country between Piribebuy and Paraguari near **Chololó**, where bathing is possible in refreshing streams.

Ciudad del Este ❸, on the Brazilian border, has been called South America's biggest late-night shopping center. It's a bustling, rather unattractive city with a makeshift boomtown air. Brazilians arrive by the busload to buy electronics, watches and other imported goods in the huge air-conditioned malls. The city is also a magnet for con artists, who hawk everything from imitation perfume to "musical" condoms. More impressive is the nearby **Itaipú Dam**, the world's largest hydroelectric project. Ciudad del Este is connected to the Brazilian counterpart city of **Foz do Iguaçú** (*see page 253*) by the **Puente de la Amistad** (Friendship Bridge), and is a portal to the famous falls of Iguazú (*see page 336*). There are tours and public transport to Iguazú and Itaipú, but the Salto Monday Falls, 10 km (6 miles) out of town, are only accessible by taxi.

On the trail of the Jesuits

Most of the Jesuit *reducciones* were set up in the fertile High Paraná, southeast of Asunción along Route One. In **Yaguarón**, 48 km (30 miles) south of the capital, there is a Franciscan mission, built in 1640. The church is a jewel of the Hispano-Guaraní baroque.

Map on pages 260–1

A Paraguayan witticism has it that every sentence starts in Spanish and finishes in Guaraní. Another saying is that Spanish is the language of the head and Guaraní of the heart.

BELOW: shop till you drop in Ciudad del Este, Paraguay's consumer capital.

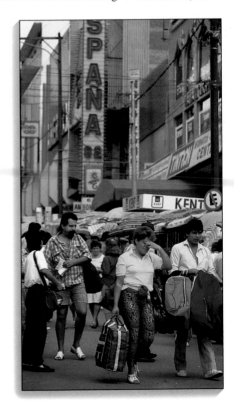

A Jesuit Utopia

In colonial times Paraguay encompassed parts of what are now Bolivia, Brazil and Argentina. Within this vast area the Jesuit order created an administrative unit or province that achieved a semi-independent status. Like the Franciscans who preceded them, the Jesuits' primary mission was conversion. They insisted on the human value and dignity of the Indian peoples and offered an alternative to the Spanish *encomienda* system (*see page 28*) that sought only to exploit their labour.

The Jesuits' first efforts at conversion started in 1587, one of the fathers being Thomas Fields, an Irishman from Limerick. The decision to gather the indians into settlements was made at a synod in 1603 and confirmed by Philip II of Spain in 1609. The following year, small parties of Jesuits began to travel into what was still largely unknown territory to Europeans. In the wild lands of the Chaco the Jesuits did no better than the

Spanish military expeditions that occasionally sallied forth from Asunción. With the Guaranís to the south and east of the city, they succeeded.

In the early years the Jesuit *reducciónes* (missions) were threatened by the *mamelucos* or *bandeirantes*, slave raiders from Brazil. In 1629 thousands of Guaranís were forced to flee from the upper Paraná, but 12 years later a Jesuit-led army, drawn from the missions, put the mamelucos to flight. The missions then flourished. Ultimately the Jesuits gathered in around 150,000 Guaranís to 30 missions in a broad belt of territory on either side of the River Paraná, living by theocratic-socialist principles.

By the early 18th century the missions were flourishing and were acquiring a reputation amongst European travellers as micro Utopias. The Guaranís were farmers, herding cattle and sheep, and cultivating crops such as *yerba maté* (herbs for maté tea – see page 315). Some developed skills as fine craftsmen and sculptors. The Jesuit priests also found the Guaranís to be highly musical and introduced them to European idioms, to the harp and the guitar.

But the grand experiment in communal living was not to last. The Jesuits always had their enemies, and by mid-18th century these included royal advisers in far-away Madrid. In 1767 the Jesuits were expelled from the country and the Guaranís were left to fend for themselves, at the mercy of the slave raiders or absorbed into the encomienda system. Most of the greatest Jesuit churches were destroyed or fell into ruin, but the remains of the missions (some still in ruins and some restored) bear testimony to the achievements of the Jesuits in this region. This whole historic episode has also been powerfully reconstructed in the recent film *The Mission*, starring Jeremy Irons and Robert de Niro.

Eight of the Jesuit missions were in what is now southern Paraguay, with the remainder in the neighboring Argentine province of Misiones (*see page 336*) and Brazil. The missions are accessible from Asunción by Route 1 running SE to Encarnación. ❑

LEFT: the imposing remains of a Jesuit mission in Southern Paraguay.

Nearby is a museum dedicated to Doctor Francia. The first Jesuit ruins are at **San Ignacio Guazú ❹**, at Km 226. The **Museo Jesuitico** houses a fine collection of indigenous art from the missionary period. Another museum has some interesting exhibits on the Chaco War. Route 4 runs west to **Pilar** and ultimately to **Humaitá**, near the junctions of the rivers Paraná and Paraguay, and whose garrison held out for three years during the War of the Triple Alliance.

To the northeast of San Ignacio is **Santa Maria de Fé**, established in 1669. It has a new church and a museum which houses dozens of Guaraní-made carvings of saints and apostles. Sixteen kilometers (10 miles) south is **Santa Rosa**, founded in 1698. The church was destroyed by fire in 1883, but wooden carvings, a tower and frescoes remain. These include a figure of the Annunciation, which is one of the great works of the Hispanic-American baroque. To reach the Jesuit ruins of **San Cosmé y Damian**, turn off Route 1 at Km 306 and travel 30 km (20 miles) south. Of particular interest is the sundial, which is all that remains of what was once a world-renowned astronomy center, built by Father Buenaventura Suarez and Guaraní laborers.

"Guazú" in Guaraní means big – hence the name of Iguazú Falls (note that they are spelt Iguaçu in Portuguese, and Iguassu in English!)

The city of **Encarnación ❺** was founded by the Jesuits on what is now the Argentinian (southern) bank of the River Paraná, and transferred to the present site on the northern bank in 1621. There is nothing left of the original Jesuit mission of Itapúa. The city, which is close to the **Yacyretá dam**, is a good centre for exploring the Jesuit missions at Trinidad and Jesus de Tavarangue. Nearby are Japanese colonies which produce soybeans, vegetables, timber, maté and cotton. About 30 km (20 miles) northeast of Encarnación is Paraguay's most splendid ruin, **Trinidad**. The sheer size of the mission, which has been declared a world heritage site by UNESCO, gives some idea of the scope of the Jesuit project in the New World. It was founded in 1706, relatively late in the Jesuit era, and the church was only finished in 1760, a few years before the expulsion of the Jesuits. There are many interesting features including a pulpit, carved in great detail. In addition to churches, Indian houses and crypts, there is a baptismal font and an impressive carving of the Holy Trinity, which was hollowed at the back so that a priest could hide inside and give an echoing rendition of the voice of God. Ten kilometres (6 miles) along a road north of Route 6 is **Jesus de Tavarangue**, founded by the Jesuits in 1685. Much of the site remains unfinished, as the Jesuits embarked on a massive building programme seven years before their expulsion. The most remarkable surviving features are the three arched doorways built by Catalan architects in the Spanish *mudejar* style.

BELOW: detail of Jesuit architecture.

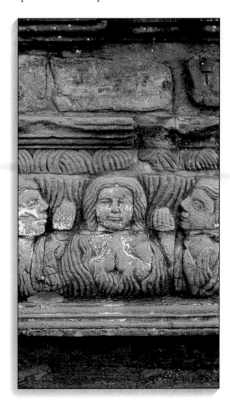

Traveling northeast

Less frequently visited than the populous eastern region, the northeast of Paraguay has a number of interesting and remote places. Accessible by taking Route 2 from Asunción to Coronel Oviedo, then heading northwards by Routes 3 and 5, is **Pedro Juan Caballero ❻**, a town on the Brazilian border. From here travelers can cross into Brazil, or travel southwest to **Parque Nacional Cerro Corá**, scene of the last battle in the War of the Triple Alliance and the death of "El Mariscal" Lopez. There are monuments to him in the park, as well as caves with pre-Columbian petroglyphs.

The River Paraguay provides an important route to the north. Three hundred kilometres (200 miles) upstream from Asunción is **Concepción**, which is a significant port for trading with Brazil and has a good market. There is boat traffic further upstream which, depending on river conditions, may be used by adventurous travelers to reach some of the more remote places. Some of these places are also accessible by four-wheel drive from the Chaco, again depending on weather conditions. The ports on these stretches of the river, such as Puerto Casado and Fuerte Olimpo, can be reached by air or boat. Only the most intrepid travelers, who are prepared to ask around for accommodation on arrival, are advised to visit these intriguing but isolated small towns.

The vast expanses of the Chaco

This desolate region, which is extremely hot in summer and waterless for months at a time, covers 60 percent of Paraguayan territory but holds only four percent of the population. It was once the preserve of indigenous groups, including the Nivaclé and Lengua people, who now share the region with military personnel, Mennonite colonists and other assorted migrants. There are a number of Catholic missions and large *estancias*, for this is cattle rearing country. Unlike most of the Chaco, the Mennonite areas have good roads and facilities. Hotel accommodation is available in the Mennonite towns. It is also possible to camp in the Chaco, as long as you take everything with you – especially water. The Chaco is a paradise for ornithologists, with immense gatherings after rains.

BELOW: Mennonite furniture shop.

The **Low Chaco**, the region nearest Asunción, is a primeval terrain of marsh

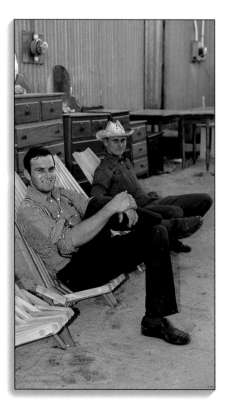

NEW SOCIETIES

The Chaco, like many remote regions, has attracted a number of unusual immigrant communities. Best known are the Mennonites, a strict Protestant Anabaptist sect, who began to arrive from 1927 onwards. They run their own banks, schools and hospitals, and subsist on a co-operative farming system, and they can often be seen in 19th-century dress at markets in Asunción. Most speak a variety of old German known as Platt Deutsch. Less well-known is the settlement of Nueva Germania, north of Coronel Oviedo.

This was the site of a very different experimental community founded in 1886 by Elisabeth Nietzsche, the fanatic sister of the philosopher Nietzsche, and her equally fanatical anti-semite husband. Their plan was to found a pure Aryan colony, but the venture foundered as the colonists came up against the unforgiving realities of dense vegetation, intense heat and torrential rains combined with a perplexing absence of ground water. Undaunted either by the rage of the duped colonists or by the suicide of her husband, Elisabeth returned to Germany where eventually she was able to greet Hitler as her true leader. The bizarre story is told in the book *Forgotten Fatherland: The Search for Elisabeth Nietzsche* by Ben Macintyre.

and palm forest, and is used for cattle ranching. It is easily accessible by traveling over the river bridge from Asunción and then up the first few kilometres of the Trans-Chaco Highway to **Villa Hayes**. This small town is named after the 19th-century American president Rutherford B Hayes, who arbitrated in Paraguay's favor in a territorial dispute after the War of the Triple Alliance.

At about Km 250 is **Pirahu**, which is a good place to stop and find out about road conditions. About 20 km (12 miles) further on is **Pozo Colorado**, the turning for Concepción, and at Km 415, **Cruce de los Pioneros**. All these places have restaurants and service stations, and Cruce also has a supermarket and a good hotel with an excellent restaurant. The proprietor is a mine of information about everything to do with the Chaco, from wildlife to politics.

About 50 km (30 miles) further along the highway, and off to the right, is **Loma Plata**, largest of the Mennonite towns. Further on, and also off to the right, is the Mennonite town of **Filadelfia ➐**, capital of the **Central Chaco**. Further north along the Trans-Chaco Highway, at Km 540, is **Mariscal Estigarribia**, a military post with facilities for the traveler. The paved road stops here. Further on, conditions can be very difficult, although the road does go all the way to Santa Cruz in Bolivia. It is possible to travel from Asunción to Bolivia by bus, especially in winter when road conditions tend to be better.

Further north is the **High Chaco**, a desert of thorn forests and military outposts. The roads are unpaved, and the land is rich with wildlife: jaguars, pumas, tapirs and poisonous snakes, as well as a kind of wild hog, discovered in 1975, that was thought to have become extinct in the Pleistocene Era. The large, remote **Parque Nacional Defensores del Chaco** is not easy to reach – enquiries should be made to the Dirección de Parques Nacionales in Asunción. ❑

Map on pages 260–1

BELOW: puma on the prowl in the High Chaco.

CHILE

Map on pages 260–1

This is a geographically diverse land, where you can experience the blistering heat of the Atacama Desert and chilling Patagonian winds, as well as beaches, lakes, mountains and city delights

Snaking down the Pacific coast of South America from latitude 18 to 56, Chile covers a huge range of temperatures and landscapes. Squeezed between the Andes and the Pacific, never more than 180 km (110 miles) wide, this spaghetti-like strip of land extends over 4,300 km (2,700 miles) of coastline. Within its borders are the world's driest desert, lush expanses of forest and a spectacular array of glaciers and fiords. Stretched directly along the Pacific "ring of fire", Chile also has some 2,085 volcanoes, of which 55 are active. In parts of the country, earth tremors are an almost weekly occurrence.

In the north of the country is the arid and mysterious Atacama Desert, rising to more than 4,500 meters (14,760 ft) above sea level as it meets the Bolivian altiplano. The northwest coast is distinguished by a range of expansive Pacific beaches and resorts. Chile's eastern boundary runs along the Cordillera de los Andes, which provides a mountain setting for Santiago, the capital city, placed right in the middle of the strip. South of Santiago the land becomes cooler, greener and more "alpine". Chile's Lake District has 12 great lakes and most of the country's active volcanoes. Further south, the coastline breaks up into islands, the largest being Chiloé, a rainy location steeped in regional folklore. In the far south of the country lie the remote territories of Chilean Patagonia, the glaciers and mountains of Torres del Paine National Park and the subarctic regions of Tierra del Fuego.

PRECEDING PAGES: Torres del Paine National Park. **LEFT:** harvest time in the Lake District. **BELOW:** Santiago's business center.

The wild geography hasn't stopped Chile from becoming one of the continent's most developed nations. Travelers are often surprised by the efficiency of Chile's banking system, public transport and services, though behind the affluent surface are social and economic imbalances waiting to be redressed.

Chileans are renowned among Latin Americans for an unusual creative flair: Chilean folk musicians, poets, painters and theater groups are followed in every country on the continent. And their reputation for legalizing (new laws are hawked in the streets of Santiago alongside chocolates and newspapers) and business acumen has earned Chileans a somewhat facetious label as "the English of South America".

The traditional hospitality of Chileans, noted by travelers from the 18th century on, is even more evident today. After years of dictatorship, Chileans have welcomed the influx of foreigners as a sign of support for their democracy.

Socialism to Fascism

Chile made few headlines on the world stage until 1970, when the country's first ever elected socialist government came to power under Salvador Allende, in spite of efforts by the right and the United States to subvert the process. The narrow margin of victory limited Allende's power, but the reforms which he implemented, designed to improve the standard of living for the poor, initially worked. Wages increased, land was redistributed, and the state created jobs. But opposition mounted from the middle and upper classes, terrified of revolution, and from the radical left, who considered Allende too soft on the middle class. Fearing nationalization, local and foreign capital fled. Production declined while demand increased, spurring rampant inflation and shortages. Long lines at markets are one of the most vivid memories of the Allende years. The right and the US government plotted to overthrow Allende, financing a 1972 truckers' strike. The truckers were soon joined by shopkeepers and professionals. Even so, Allende's Unidad Popular won 44 percent of the seats in the March 1973 congressional elections.

But in the early hours of September 11, 1973, tanks and troops surrounded the presidential palace, congress, newspapers and party headquarters. Some working class *barrios* were strafed from the air. Allende died when the air force bombed the Presidential Palace. Thousands of "subversives" were herded into stadiums which were quickly turned into concentration camps. Within hours, the Allende government had fallen in a bloody storm, and a four-man military junta took over, banning political activities and declaring a state of siege. Marxism, they declared, would be eradicated from Chile. At least 2,500 people (some estimates run as high as 10,000) were killed, and over the years many more would die as Chile's much-heralded democracy was crushed.

The leader of the coup, General Augusto Pinochet Ugarte, consolidated his power through repression and unmatched political cunning. Opposition was relentlessly and ruthlessly crushed. Dissidents – and many innocent people – were imprisoned, tortured, exiled or murdered. In 1988 the tide began to turn

Museo de Bellas Artes, Santiago.

BELOW:
General Pinochet.

against Pinochet. A referendum on his presidency was announced for October 5, and a series of reforms was conceded. Voters were registered, exile was abolished, and a state of emergency in effect since 1973 was lifted. When seven million Chileans went to the polls that day, the majority voted "No", bringing a resounding defeat to the General. Pinochet accepted his defeat, announcing that elections would be held at the end of 1989.

The new government took office on 11 March, 1990. But Pinochet did not relinquish all power. He kept cronies in eight seats in the Senate and stayed on as head of the army, ensuring that no revenge was taken on either himself or those who might have perpetrated injustices during his dictatorship, when some 2,000 people "disappeared." Bit by bit, however, confidence and democracy returned, helped by what some saw as an "economic miracle", which made debt and hyper-inflation seem like two more bad dreams from the past. Events came full circle at the end of 1993 when the center-left Democratic Coalition's Eduardo Frei, son of the 1960s president, was elected president. In March 1998, Pinochet retired as head of the army. As a former president, he is entitled to a life seat in the Senate, which he took up amid a wave of street protests.

Map on pages 260–1

Santiago, Chile's sophisticated center

The conquistador Pedro de Valdivia is said to have forgotten his tortuous journey to Chile from Peru when he gazed upon the valley at the point where the Mapocho and Maipo rivers descend from the Andes on their journey to the Pacific Ocean. Surrounded in all four directions by peaks rivaling the Alps, Valdivia knew he had found the right place for a settlement. Today, the conquistadors might not recognize **Santiago** ❽, the smoggy home to a third of the

BELOW LEFT:
colonial reflections, Santiago.
BELOW RIGHT:
shoeshine break, Plaza de Armas, Santiago.

Fortunes for sale, Santiago.

country's 12 million people, but it has a charm unmatched in South America.

Valdivia marked the center of colonial Santiago with the **Plaza de Armas** (1541). It served as a market and it was the place where criminals were hanged. Today, this clean, tree-lined square is a haven for old men, shoe shiners, vagrants and lovers. The pink **Correo Central** (1882), which houses the most efficient postal service in South America, has an impressive iron skylight that illuminates the central corridor. Next door, the excellent **Museo Histórico Nacional** in the Palacio de la Real Audiencia traces Chile's history from its pre-Columbian roots to the present. On the west side of the square is the country's largest church, the **cathedral** (1748-89), with an impressive baroque interior.

Two blocks away on Calle Catedral is the **Congreso Nacional** (1876) a neo-classical structure, home to Chile's legislative branch until it was closed in 1973. The federal courts are across the street. The **Palacio de la Moneda** (1805) is four blocks south on Calle Morandé. It is an imposing structure that originally served as the mint, but later became the presidential palace. President Salvador Allende died there when the junta bombarded "La Moneda" during the 1973 military coup, and bullet holes still mar buildings facing the palace.

Paseo Ahumada, a pedestrian mall linking Plaza de Armas to the **Alameda Bernardo O'Higgins** is the heart of Santiago, offering a human collage of business people, street vendors and money changers. Across the Alameda, the city's major east-west artery is the imposing, chalky-red **Iglesia San Francisco** (1586). The church has interesting touches of Arab influence, remnants of the Spanish. Alongside is **Barrio París-Londres**, where mansions from the 1920s border sinuous streets. Uptown from Ahumada, three blocks along Calle Augustinas, and past the 17th-century church of San Augustín is the **Municipal Theater**, built in 1857 and one of the finest on the continent. Plays, concerts and other cultural events are often held around the small, dimly-lit cobbled **Plaza Mulato Gil** (Metro Universidad Católica).

Green spaces beneath the Andes

Santiago's founders were careful to include trees and green spaces. In fact, Valdivia founded the city while standing atop one of its present-day parks, **Santa Lucía**, a small hill topped with terraces and a replica of a castle, which offers a view of the downtown area. **Parque Forestal** (1891) follows the course of the Mapocho River (corresponding to metro stations from Mapocho to Salvador). Tropical banana trees line winding footpaths which betray the confines of this narrow park. The **Museo de Bellas Artes** is here, an approximate copy of the Petit Palais in Paris, with a fine collection of works by Chilean artists.

The **Parque Metropolitano** covers four hills towering 800 meters (2,600 ft) over Santiago. A tram goes to a terrace on the peak, commanding a view of the whole city when the smog is not too thick. There is a statue of the Virgin Mary, two pools, a zoo, a botanical garden and a wine tasting center that offers the best of Chile's vineyards. A cable car descends half the length of the mountain, to Calle Pedro de Valdivia in *the barrio alto*. Strolls or horseback rides around the expansive **Parque O'Higgins** (Metro Line 2) became stylish for city dwellers when it opened in the late 1800s. **El Pueblito** is a replica of a typical southern village.

Bellavista is the cultural heart of Santiago, the night-time haunt of artists, writers and people who go to see and be seen. Dimly lit streets are sprinkled with raucous cafés, art galleries and restaurants, while roving theater troupes, musicians, and hippies peddle their work. At night, tables spill from bars along **Calle Pío Nono**, Bellavista's main drag. On the side streets, quaint homes with flowering gardens, eccentric details, and sculpted balconies weave an intriguing architectural quilt. The house where poet Pablo Neruda created many of his greatest works is on Calle A. Márquez de la Plata.

Mercado Franklin (four blocks east of Metro Franklin) is a weekend flea market that winds for several blocks through an abandoned slaughterhouse. Six blocks north of the Plaza de Armas along the Mapocho River is the fresh food center **Mercado Central**. Cafés at the seafood pavilion offer generous helpings of seafood at a low prices.

High fashion is also available in Santiago at a reasonable price. Uptown, the **Los Leones** area on Calle Providencia (Metro Los Leones), is an affluent neighborhood with several chic boutiques and swanky stores. **Parque Arauco** (Avenida Kennedy 5413) and **Apumanque** (Avenida Apoquindo/Manquehue) are fashion malls on the upper-east side of the city.

Around Santiago

The lofty Andes, the tranquility of rural valley communities and the cool breezes of the coast are all within a few hours of the capital by car or bus. On the eastern end of the city at the foot of the Andean mountains is **El Pueblito de los**

Map on pages 260–1

BELOW: vineyard harvest.

Wine Country

The conquistadors introduced vineyards in Chile in the 16th century, to supply the symbol of Christ's blood for the Catholic communion. Small wineries were nurtured on haciendas in the Maipo Valley throughout the colonial period by patrons doing their bit for the church. Today wine is one of Chile's finest products – its purpose rarely spiritual – and an increasingly popular export even to wine-soaked Europe.

The first commercial vineyard was established in 1851 when Silvestre Ochagavía brought French vine stock to the Maipo valley. Mining magnates began to build extensive irrigation projects, and the vineyards spread further from the river banks. The valley's lime-heavy soil, elevation and dry climate were ideal for producing world-class wines.

Chileans boast that when the French vines were decimated by a fungus in the late 19th century, their vines were rushed across the Atlantic to replenish the stricken vineyards.

The larger labels outgrew the confines of the valley in the early 1900s and new wineries sprung up near Los Andes and Rancagua. Today, the finest reserves carry the mark of *Cajón del Maipo,* near Santiago. The Maipo Vally comes alive in March during the *vendímia,* or harvest, when grapes are transported to the presses. Several wineries are open to the public, with informative tours and generous tastings.

The grounds of the Viña Cousiño Macul, on Avenida Quilin on the eastern outskirts of Santiago, are themselves a work of art, with a central lagoon stocked with waterfowl from around the world. It has been in the hands of the same family since 1856. The cellars are grand stone structures where bottles are available for purchase. Tours are available Monday to Friday.

Viña Santa Carolina, founded in the Ñuñoa neighborhood in Santiago (near the Estadio Nacional) in 1875, is named after the owner's wife. Though the vines have been transplanted to Molina and San Fernando, the stately colonial Casa Patronal remains, with the cellars nearby.

An hour's drive south of Santiago at Pirque, near to Puente Alto, is Viña Concha y Toro. Melchor Concha y Toro founded the winery in 1883, and it is now the largest in Chile with more than 10 vineyards in Maipo, San Fernando and Rancagua. The original vineyard and cellars are open to the public – a visit could be included in a weekend trip to the mountains.

About 32 km (20 miles) south west from Santiago, at Santa Ana, is Viña Undurraga, founded in 1885 by Francisco Ramón Undurraga, who imported vines from France and, a first for Chile, German stock from the Rhine Valley. Undurraga built his cellars and a magnificent colonial mansion to entertain guests, including royalty. The public is welcome, by reservation only (tel: 817 2346).

In 1927, José Canepa acquired choice parcels of wine country, and planted Cabernet Sauvignon, Sauvignon Blanc, and Rieseling vines in the Maipo Valley, Curicó and Lontué. Now the most modern winery in South America, its plant on Camino Lo Sierra is open to the public. ❑

LEFT: vats in a Chilean wine bodega.

Map
on pages
260–1

Domínicos. A creek meanders through the small village, around a cluster of adobe huts with thatched roofs. The sounds of craftsmen at work drift from the workshops where they produce leather, ceramics and metals. People still ride horses around the village of **Lo Barnechea**. Each weekend vendors set up an antique fair in the shadow of the town's adobe church.

Above Lo Barnechea, **El Arrayán** has become a refuge for city dwellers who have built comfortable and breezy homes on the Arrayán River valley. The **Santuario de la Naturaleza** is a park that follows the narrow Arrayán canyon.

Santiaguinos venture to the **Cajón del Maipo** on weekends to take afternoon tea, nibble on *empanadas* and *kuchen* (strudel) and relax in little towns and trails along the 40-mile canyon. The valley has distinct characteristics. A sinuous road leads from **Puente Alto** southeast, against the current of Maipo and its tributaries, to finally reach its source near the 5,000-meter (16,600-ft) extinct volcano **El Morado**. Arid peaks with names like **Punta Negra**, **Peladero**, **Lomo del Diablo** and **Yerba Buena** meld with the changing day's sun, turning from green and brown in the day, to blue, pink, orange and red before disappearing at dusk. The narrow valley floor is lush and intensively cultivated with vineyards and pasture land. Hiking, swimming, camping and climbing are practised in the area, and there are many picnic areas close to the road.

San José de Maipo, 25 km (15 miles) from Puente Alto, was founded in 1791 when miners discovered silver in the surrounding hills. Its adobe homes and central square pay homage to the past. At **San Alfonso** (Km 40) there is hiking and camping at **Las Animas Waterfall** facing the canyon wall. The road forks at **San Gabriel** (Km 47) where the mountains darken and the air grows thinner. **Lo Valdés** (Km 70) is on the southern fork of the road, a veritable oasis

Enjoying a beer at the rodeo.

BELOW LEFT: mud baths near the Argentine border.
BELOW RIGHT: skiing, Valle Nevada.

on the semi-arid slopes of the Morado volcano. The **Refugio Alemán** is a pleasant inn near extensive trails for exploring the snow-capped peaks surrounding the area. Nearby, **Baños de Colina** are natural hot springs in a small valley with magnificent views of the Andes and the valley below.

South of Puente Alto across the boulder-strewn Maipo River ravine is **Pirque**, birthplace of Chile's best wines. The **Reserva Nacional Río Clarillo** is in the midst of a semi-arid area where the best of indigenous cacti and flora flourish. In colonial times, Spanish aristocrats used to vacation on the sandy shores of **Laguna de Aculeo**. The lake fills a valley 60 km (37 miles) from the capital, in a wooded mountain setting. There are camping facilities, hotels and several restaurants along the shore. Twenty years ago the government built a dam where the **Tinguiririca** and **Cachapoal rivers** meet, forming the nation's largest man-made lake. **Rapel Lake** provides waterskiing, swimming and fishing.

Skiing in the Andes

Fit and healthy in Arica.

The omnipresence of dizzying Andean peaks makes Chile one of the finest ski centers in the world, with challenging runs that can be enjoyed from June to September. Three resorts are within sight of Santiago. **Farellones-Colorado** and **La Parva** are ski villages above El Arrayán, just 50 km (30 miles) from Santiago, along a sinuous road with 50 hairpin curves. **Valle Nevado**, set in a remote valley above Farellones, is a posh resort built in 1988 by the owners of Les Alps in France. There is a four-star hotel, and eight lifts go to slopes as high as 11,500 meters (37,700 ft) above sea level. **Portillo** is one of the most famous resorts in South America, located 9,000 meters (29,500 ft) above sea level in an Andean pass 7 km (4 miles) from the Argentine border at Mendoza.

BELOW: dry grape fields, Valle Elqui.

Pomaire, 60 km (35 miles) southwest of Santiago, has become a part of nearly every Chilean household. Dark clay scraped from Mallarauco Mountains is hand-shaped into pottery and sculpture, and fired in large rustic stone ovens to be sold in the dozens of adobe homes along the dusty main street.

The Pacific coast

Algarrobo, 110 km (70 miles) west of Santiago, became a resort in the late 1800s and is known for its calm seas and elegant vacation homes. It has also become an important yachting center, hosting international competitions. Nearby **El Quisco** is a tranquil town with wide beaches complementing a small fishing port and yacht club. **Isla Negra**, 4 km (2½ miles) south, is hidden within a cool pine forest, its rocky coast battered by great swells. Poet **Pablo Neruda's home**, the inspiration for many of his works, is on a bluff above the sea. It is now a museum (open Tues–Sun, 10am–2pm and 3–6pm; small entrance fee, including compulsory guided tour; phone first: 56-2-7378712).

The port of **Valparaíso ❾**, 120 km (75 miles) north of Santiago, is an enchanting town where a map is unnecessary and wandering is bliss. It is split between the geographically flat port area and 17 *cerros* (hills) that tower above the bay. The picturesque port is host to a strange brew of sailors, prostitutes, vagabonds and tourists. The *cerros* are an impressive maze of colorful homes, winding streets, narrow alleys, rickety *ascensores* (elevator trams), hidden plazas and treacherous stairways that cling delicately to the precipitous slopes. **Muelle Prat** is the oldest part of Valparaíso's port, dating to its foundation in the 16th century. To the west, at **Caleta El Membrillo**, fishermen unload their catch near weathered *picadas*, small shacks where the freshest seafood in the city is served. Nearby **Cerro Santo Domingo** is a spontaneous maze of streets and stately homes built by the emigrant merchants who founded Valparaíso.

Map on pages 260–1

Rickety rides

Valparaíso's *ascensores* are the best guide to the upper-city. For a few pesos, these romantic wooden trams make harrowing ascents to the neighborhoods high on the *cerros*. Ascensor Artillería (1893) first ran on coal, and goes to Avenida 21 de Mayo, providing a fantastic view of the bay. **Paseo Yugoslavo** is a promenade that winds along Cerro Alegre, among homes and gardens dating back to the early 1900s. Alegre is reached by the Ascensor El Peral.

Ascensor Concepción (1833) is the oldest elevator, reaching a neighborhood dating to the 19th century. Homes along **Paseo Atkinson** are simple, wooden structures that creep up the mountainside. **Iglesia Anglicana San Pablo** (1858) was built by British immigrants. Ascensor Barón serves the panoramic **Mirador Diego Portales** on the west side of the bay. **Convento and Iglesia San Francisco** (1845) was also used as a lighthouse to guide ships into the port.

A road along seaside cliffs leads 18 km (11 miles) south to **Laguna Verde**, a small fishing village set in a cove, with a long, unspoiled white beach. **Quintay**, 45 km (28 miles) from Valparaíso, is a fishing port surrounded by rocky cliffs.

BELOW: traveling in style, Viña del Mar.

It has an expansive beach, with fine white sand and provisions for camping.

Viña del Mar, the garden city, is a cosmopolitan Pacific resort, with a spicy mix of beaches, lush gardens and nightlife. Viña is taken over in the summer by Chileans and Argentines who crowd the expensive nightspots and bask on its golden, albeit polluted beaches. A century ago Viña was the retreat for affluent *porteños* (people of the port) from Valparaíso. They built mansions with large gardens that later became the city's parks.

The **Quinta Vergara** is Viña's most elegant park, filled with exotic plants from around the world. The **Palacio Vergara** (1908) was built by Viña's founders and today houses the **Museo de Bellas Artes**. The **Anfiteatro** hosts the International Festival of Song in February. **La Plaza** is the palm-filled center of old Viña with the neo-classic **Club de Viña** (1910), **Teatro Municipal** (1930), **Hotel O'Higgins** (1935), and the **Casa Subercaseaux** on its borders.

Pedestrian precinct **Calle Valparaíso** is the magnet to Viña's summer hustle, with cafés, shopping malls and an artisan fair. At the end of the street is **Cerro Castillo**, an opulent hill sprinkled with turn-of-the-century mansions and terraces overlooking the bay. Calle Alamos winds up the hill, past Castillo Brunet and the presidential palace. Avenida Peru is a misty promenade following the shore north of the hill. The **Casino Municipal** is the premier gambling house on the Pacific side of the continent, where South America's rich play for high stakes as tourists watch in awe. The promenade continues along Avenida San Martín, bordering long beaches mobbed by tourists in the summer.

Reñaca, 8 km (5 miles) north, is the chic place to be in the season. Its mile-long beach lies below rocky mountains speckled with fashionable apartments and smart hotels, which are accessible by little trams and stairways.

The sleepy fishing village of **Horcón** is the legendary center of Chile's counter culture. It is set on a rocky peninsula 90 km (55 miles) north of Viña del Mar, in the midst of a eucalyptus forest, with a small wharf and colorful skiffs. Tourists, hippies and gnarly fishermen provide a peculiar mélange in the village today.

Northern deserts

Northern Chile has a mysticism that sets it apart. The 1,900 km (1,100 miles) from Santiago to Arica seem silent, a landscape sprinkled with whitewashed adobe villages marooned in the **Atacama Desert**. Tradition bends the rules of Catholicism, and visits by extra-terrestrials find their way into the folklore.

Arica , in the far north, is right on the threshold of Peru. The downtown streets are filled with markets and stores catering to Peruvian and Bolivian smugglers. Arica is also known for its beautiful beaches and nightlife. **Plaza Aduana** provides cool respite from the desert sun. Nearby is **Iglesia de San Marco** (1876), a wrought iron sanctuary designed by Gustave Eiffel. The **Morro de Arica** is a huge mountain with magnificient views of the city, the Pacific, and the desert. A museum in an old fortress recalls the battle for Arica during the War of the Pacific (1879), when the city was won from Peru.

Several travel firms offer day trips east to **Lago Chungará**, near Bolivia, a magnificent if harrowing

TIP

On a visit to El Tatio Geysers, bring aspirin with you and lots of water to drink to ease the effects of altitude – headaches and nausea are common at this height. At the geysers, take great care not to tread on thin ground.

BELOW: Arica.

journey to 4,400 meters (14,500 ft). The emerald lake is surrounded by snowy peaks that rise high above the shoreline. Chungará is located in **Parque Nacional Lauca**, where alpacas, *vicuñas* (deer-like llamas), *vizcachas* (large hares) and white geese with black-tipped wings perambulate along the road.

Map on pages 260–1

Spectacular landscape

Calama ⓫, south of Arica, is a mining center servicing the massive Chuquicamata copper mine, 16 km (10 miles) away. Wisps of sulfur vapor from the mine linger among its bars, cheap hotels and restaurants. Tours of the open-pit mine are available. Three hours on the sinuous road to Bolivia is **Géiser del Tatío**, an impressive field of scalding geysers at an altitude of 4,500 meters (14,764 ft). The geysers are at their most exuberant at sunrise.

The pleasant village oasis of **San Pedro de Atacama** ⓬, 93 km (58 miles) southeast of Calama, was the most populated Atacamanian town in pre-Columbian times. It was conquered by the Incas in 1450, and by Pedro de Valdivia in 1540. The beautiful **Iglesia de San Pedro** (1641) is constructed of the same white adobe as most of the town. Next door is the impressive **Museo Arqueológico** (open daily; small entrance fee), with a fine collection of pottery, mummies, and ancient Indian vestments. Nearby is **Pukara de Quitor**, a mountainside stone fortress built by the Atacamanians during the Inca siege.

Iglesia de San Pedro de Atacama.

In the distance are lofty snowcapped volcanoes, including **Licancábur**, at 5,600 meters (19,300 ft) the highest in South America. Not far from the village is the enormous **Salar de Atacama** salt basin, as well as the **Valle de la Luna** (32 km/20 miles on a very bumpy road), a mysterious desert valley endowed with supernatural qualities and ringed by jagged, white peaks which contrast

BELOW: Valle de la Luna.

Church mural of the Crucifixion, depicting conquistadors as Roman centurions, San Pedro de Atacama.

with the ochre valley floor. At twilight its formations turn brilliant colors while salt crystals shimmer in the moonlight.

West of **Copiapó** ⓭ are **Caldera** and **Bahía Inglesa**, which comprise three successive bays with long, unspoiled beaches and year-round warm water. **La Serena** ⓮, a colonial city founded in 1543 as a trade link en route between Santiago and Lima, Peru, is known for its 30 distinctive churches. Remodeled in the 1950s, it is now one of the most attractive towns in Chile. The **Iglesia San Francisco** (1627) on Calle Balmaceda has a baroque façade, with interior mudejar details. The **Mercado La Recova** has a good selection of regional crafts.

Tongoy (61 km/38 miles south of La Serena) is a summer resort on a high peninsula overlooking the Pacific, with expansive, white beaches. Along the Elqui River is the narrow, serpentine **Valle del Elqui**. This lush refuge is famous for its clear blue skies, dry mountain air, steep arid mountains, and intensely cultivated pastures and vineyards that are the source of the national liquor, Pisco. **Monte Grande** ⓯ is a small village along the river where the Nobel prize-winning poet Gabriela Mistral spent her infancy. Her tomb is on the road to Cochiguaz. There are a number of communes in the area whose inhabitants practice meditation in what is considered to be a focal point of mystical energy.

South to the Lake District

The Lake District is a land of extreme beauty, a seemingly endless succession of lush alpine valleys surrounded by low Andean hills and snow-covered volcanoes. The outstanding scenery is reflected in the bitter-cold waters of the lakes, which were formed by the abrasive retreat of glaciers that once covered the region. Roughly half of the region's population lives in the cities, making a visit to the area a euphoric escape from the bustle of urban life. It's hard to believe that this natural paradise was once forbidden to outsiders. The Mapuche people wiped out every foreign settlement south of the **Bío Bío River** at the end of the 16th century, and remained undefeated until the 1880s.

Concepción ⑯, Chile's second largest city (pop. 368,000), on the banks of the mighty Bío Bío, was little more than a garrison town until 1818, when Bernardo O'Higgins declared Chile's independence there. The downtown area is best explored on foot on the pedestrian streets near the plaza. Four blocks south is **Parque Ecuador**, which winds up **Cerro Caracol** for a good view of the city. North is the **Universidad de Concepción**, founded in 1919.

About 29 km (18 miles) east of Los Angeles, deep within a wooded Andes valley is the town of **Salto del Laja**, the gateway to the Lake District. The frigid waters of the Laja River slice through some of the most beautiful scenery in Chile, before plunging 35 meters (115 ft) into a deep, rocky canyon, which is eternally bathed in a foggy mist. Within sight of the valley are four volcanoes that rise high above the forest.

The road east snakes through huge pine forests, nearing the mountains as the valley narrows and the terrain becomes semi-arid. Huge lava fields lie nearby, flanked by mountain cypress. **Parque Nacional Laguna del Laja** is located in a narrow valley. In the center is a 200-meter (650-ft) high volcanic cone that holds **Laja Lagoon**, and to the right is the desolate cone of **Laja Volcano**. Three of the four lakes in **Parque Nacional Conguillío** (110 km/70 miles east of Temuco) were formed by the depressions in lava fields spewed out by the **Llaima Volcano** (3,100 meters/10,170 ft) within the past 50 years. The narrow valley is covered with arucarias up to 1,200 years old, plus oaks and cypresses.

Map on pages 260–1

BELOW: Villarrica Volcano.

Turbulent landscape

Villarrica ⓐ is a major resort on the banks of the 1,140-sq. km (440-sq. mile) **Villarrica Lake**. Its blue waters change hue as the sun falls, reflecting the perfect cone of the Villarrica volcano. The lake is scarred by eruptions from the still-active volcano, which glows like the end of a giant cigar at night. The first European colony at Villarrica was beseiged by the Mapuche in 1598, and collapsed without survivors in 1602. The colony was not re-established until 1882. There is a Mapuche museum near the tourist office at Villarrica. The resort village of **Pucón ⓑ**, on the other side of the lake, is a summer haven for affluent Chileans, and its dirt roads are filled with bungalows and hostels run by the German immigrants who have settled in the area. **Parque Nacional Villarrica**, on the steep slopes of the volcano, is a bizarre mix of untouched forest and barren lava fields that seared through the woods during a recent eruption.

The slender **Lago Caburga ⓒ**, 24 km (15 miles) east, was formed when lava flows were blocked by the precipitous, densely-wooded valley. Foot trails lead to the **Eagle's Nest Falls** which are surrounded by lush ferns that thrive on the mist. Three pristine lagoons are hidden in the small valley, and several hot springs, fed by volcanoes, gush from the ground.

Lakes Calafquén, Panguipulli, Pellaifa, Neltume, Riñihue, Pirehueico, and, in Argentina, Lacar, are collectively known as the **Seven Lakes**. This little-known area wasn't really settled until the late 1800s, due to its remote setting and harsh winters. **Lican-Ray ⓓ** was built for tourists on a wooded peninsula overlooking Calafquén Lake. It is said to have the nicest beach in the area and is a magnet for vacationing Chileans in summer. **Panguipulli ⓔ** is a small, picturesque town on the banks of the lake, with an interesting Capuchin mission and church.

TIP

It is possible to hike to the 1,900 km (6,500 ft) peak of Villarrica Volcano and peer into the steamy crater, but take care, as the weather can turn stormy at a moment's notice.

BELOW: street musicians, Valdivia.

A road leads to the tip of a wooded peninsula, with sandy beaches on the lake. The nearby **Huilo Huilo Falls**, the highest in Chile, shoot into Neltume Lake through a lush fern-covered canyon, producing an eternal rainbow.

Map on page 292

German settlements

One of the first Spanish settlements in Chile was **Valdivia** ❺, located at the confluence of several waterways in the Valdivia Estuary. The area saw heavy Germanic immigration in the 19th century. The streets follow the sinuous rivers, and **Calle General Lagos** near the waterfront and lively port still has remnants of European architecture that the immigrants brought with them. The **Austral Museum** (open Tues–Sun) on **Teja Island**, chronicles the German migration. Nearby is the **Austral University**, with a large campus along the river. Valdivia was heavily fortified by the Spanish after 1600 to guard against Mapuche invasions. Tours are available to see the forts along the river.

The nearby city of **Osorno** ❻, 880 km (550 miles) south of Santiago, is the center of a cattle region. It lies east to west across the Rahue River, surrounded by azure-green pasturelands nourished by the area's abundant rainfall. The city was settled by German farmers, its shingled wooden homes and streets with names like Buschman, Amthauer and Matthei reminiscent of a distant past. **Calle Bulnes** has good river views. Try to catch the morning **Feria Ganadera**, Chile's largest cattle market, where burly *campesinos* haggle over animals.

Wooden boat and fishermen's houses, Puerto Montt.

Lago Puyehue ❼ (60 km/37 miles east) is a popular fishing and camping spot. The **Casablanca**, **Puyehue**, **Puntiagudo** and immense **Osorno** volcanoes are all within sight of the lake's waters. Near the eastern shore are the **Puyehue Hot Springs**, known for their therapeutic qualities. On the road to the

BELOW: Lago Negro.

Casablanca Volcano is **Aguas Calientes** (hot springs), through lush virgin forest.

Picturesque towns creep up to the edge of **Llanquihue Lake** and the perfect cone of the snowcapped Osorno Volcano is eternally reflected in its frigid waters. **Puerto Varas ❿** is an immaculate town created in 1854 to handle lake commerce to Puerto Montt, 19 km (12 miles) to the south. Today it is a thriving stop-off point for tourists who like to gamble in the casino at **Gran Hotel Puerto Varas** on the shore. **Frutillar ⓚ**, on the northern lakeshore, is filled with interesting German homes with meticulous gardens, and has a peculiar claim to fame: the world's southernmost palm tree. In February it hosts the **Semanas Musicales de Frutillar**, a music festival renowned throughout the continent.

On the eastern shore is **Ensenada ⓛ**, a tiny village set in the shadow of the Osorno Volcano and surrounded by lush forest cut by lava flows. Sixteen kilometers (10 miles) east, the rapids of the **Petrohué River** are broken by strange lava formations comprised of thousands of black volcanic stones, reminders of an ancient eruption. The Petrohué feeds into **Lago Todos Los Santos**. There are daily boat excursions along the length of the lake to **Peulla ⓜ**, a magnificent journey along shoreline mountains covered in dense virgin forest.

The unkempt gravel road south from Puerto Varas to Cochamó is a journey through an area of great wilderness beauty. **Cochamó ⓝ** is a tiny village on the estuary, a branch off to the Pacific through spectacular fiords that rise up to 1,500 meters (4,900 ft) straight out of the water. At Cochamó you can hire fishermen to give you a tour of the estuary in a skiff, where it's easy to spot seals, 30 kg (70 lb) groupers, and even whales.

Puerto Montt ⓟ was founded in 1853 by the adventurer Vincente Pérez Rosales, with a handful of German immigrants intent on settling Llanquihue

BELOW:
fishing boats,
Puerto Montt.

province. The area mushroomed when the railroad arrived, 60 years later. Today the city of 84,000 is a grimy port, gateway to Chiloé and the Patagonia frontier. Despite its size, Puerto Montt has a small-town feeling, with many homes of northern Germanic design: wooden, with pitched roofs, ornate balconies, and shingles well-weathered by the region's eternal drizzle. The cathedral in the central square is the city's oldest building, made of redwood.

Puerto Montt faces the Reloncaví Sound, and a walk along the waterfront is a good introduction to the city. **Angelmó**, a contiguous fishing port, is a jewel of indigenous maritime activity. Shacks on the pier offer fresh *erizos*, *locos*, and other cold water seafood, and burly fishermen mend their nets by the skiffs on the shore. The pier is lined with artisan shops that sell a wide selection of woolen goods and wood carvings. Young boys will row you across to **Isla Tenglo Q**, where you can walk around its fishing communities.

The rugged south: Chilean Patagonia

South of Puerto Montt, the land and sea become one as the country breaks into a maze of islands, fiords, rivers with myriad tributaries, lakes and wooded mountains with trees a thousand years old. Chilean Patagonia is a place of forbidding, intense beauty that has escaped the ravages of man.

The island of **Chiloé** ⓱ emerges just out of sight of Puerto Montt, a romantic place filled with picturesque villages, a hundred tiny enchanted islets, misty waterways, and little wooden homes. Chiloé is steeped in fishing tradition, and the magic of its culture attracts trekkers in search of the customs, legends and folklore of its friendly people. It is home to lively dances like the *cueca* and *vals*, local dishes like *curanto*, drinks like *chicha de manzana*, and myriad legends,

Maps
260, 292

Traditional wood-tiled church, Chiloé.

BELOW: chopping wood, Chiloé.

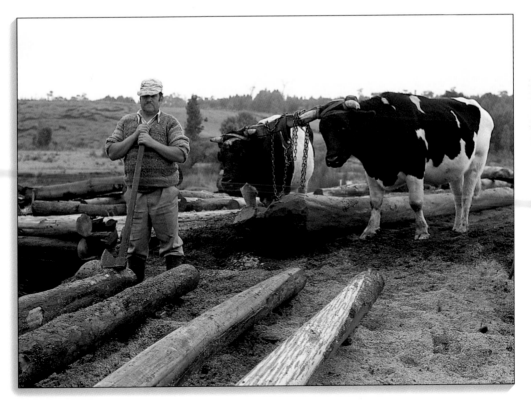

festivals and rituals all its own. Somehow it has held on to its oldest traditions.

The island is known for its 150 wooden *capillas* (chapels) with distinctive shingled steeples, porticos, glass-paned windows and three doors. Several times a year the island erupts with the largest religious festivals in Chile. But Chiloé's people cling to paradoxical legends that explain the unthinkable: *el trauco*, a mysterious old man who leaves young women unexpectedly pregnant during late night visits, or *caleuche*, a magical ship of endless party cheer that seduces fisherman who are lost forever on the high seas.

Ancud is Chiloé's largest town, with narrow streets packed with wooden commercial buildings from its heyday as a bustling port. The **Museo Regional** (open Tues-Sun) in an old fortress near the water, chronicles the history and culture of Chiloé. The road south to **Quemchi** snakes past an interesting eastern coastal area settled by European families.

Castro (founded in 1567), on the shores of a protected fiord, is one of the oldest cities in Chile. The **Iglesia San Francisco de Castro** is an unusual wooden cathedral on the plaza. The **Museo Municipal Etnológico** (open Tues to Sun) explains the island traditions. On the outskirts of Castro, the **Museo de Arte Moderno**, shows some of Chile's best contemporary art in a prizewinning farmhouse conversion (open Tues-Sun, free). In February the **Festival Costumbrista Chilote** is a marvelous display of island culture. At the waterside, fishermen park their skiffs beside rows of *palafitos*, houses on stilts.

Nearby **Dalcahue** is famous for its Sunday artisan fair, where the fine woolen sweaters for which the island is well-known can be found. **Chonchi** (26 km/16 miles south of Castro), known as the "three-floor city", is built on a cliff face overlooking the water. There is a nice church among several colorful *casonas*

(large houses) made of cypress with well-kept gardens. **Queilén** is a picturesque town situated on a narrow peninsula with long beaches at each end, and elegant old homes dating back to its founding as an immigrant colony in 1900. Ferries leave from **Quellón**, (not to be confused with Queilen), the southernmost port.

South to the end of the world

South of Chiloé lies the remote Region Aisén del General Ibáñez del Campo, where visits still give the sensation of penetrating a new frontier. The Carretera Austral road was finished in 1988 to open up new territory for expansion, but that has yet to happen. The region from Puerto Montt to Cochrane is still untouched by man, save a few fishermen and farmers. It is an amazing landscape where rocky cliffs drop into lush river valleys, dense jungles are bordered by glaciers, and turgid rivers lead to pristine lakes and the southern Andes.

Chaitén ⑱ is a coastal town with food, lodging and nice ocean and mountain views, which is accessible by a six-hour ferry from Chonchi or by the Carretera (56 km/35 miles). **Santa Bárbara**, 11 km (7 miles) north, is a picturesque fishing village along a wide beach.

The south is a contrasting mix of lush forest, waterfalls emerging from icy cliffs, glaciers and valleys flanked by the icy slopes of the Andes. The road passes the emerald waters of Velcho Lake, Michimahuida Volcano, Villa Santa Lucía, Futaleufú and Palena. From Santa Lucía the road follows the Río Frío along a wooded valley, reaching **La Junta** at the confluence of three rivers, from where there are excursions to the picturesque **Lago Rossellot**, and **Lago Verde**. The road continues to **Lago Risopatrón** and **Termas de Puyuhuapi**. Nearby **Parque Nacional Queulat** has amazing views of the *ventisqueros*

Visit the park, get the badge.

BELOW: wild scenery at the end of the world.

BELOW LEFT: a cargo boat in the Southern Ocean.
BELOW RIGHT: produce for sale, Punta Arenas.

(glaciers). **Puerto Cisne** is a small beachside village with hotels, restaurants and transport facilities. The town was colonized by Germans and Italians in the late 19th century. **Coyhaique** 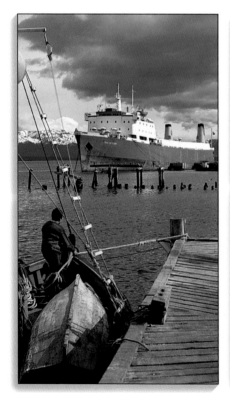 is a large town, and a good jumping-off point for exploring the region. Founded in 1929, it is largely a government and military center. The **Museo Regional de la Patagonia** (open Mon–Fri; small entrance fee) is a good introduction to the region's history. South of the city the land turns rugged, with trees giving way to weathered scrub. Steppe grasses begin to appear, buffeted by an incessant wind. The area was settled by ranchers who made their fortunes with enormous *fundos* (ranches).

   Puerto Aisén 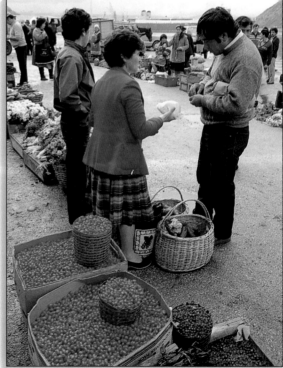 is a beautifully kept town, founded to service the ranches in 1914. In the region is **Laguna San Rafael**, a pristine lake which is only accessible after a journey through fiords and archipelagos. The lake is enclosed by the **San Valentine Glacier**, which sends huge blocks of 20,000-year-old ice crashing into the water as it makes its way to the sea. A few firms offer cruises there from Puerto Montt. About 95 km (60 miles) south of Puerto Aisén is **Lago General Carrera**, South America's second largest lake. It juts into Argentina, with views of the vast pampa to the east. On the Chilean side it is bordered by barren, rocky mountains eroded by glaciers. Several towns with lodgings are on the shore, including **Puerto Ibañez**, **Chile Chico** and **Cochrane**.

Torres del Paine

Down at the far south of the Andes mountain chain, **Torres del Paine National Park** is one of the newest nature reserves in South America, a 1,630-sq km (630-sq mile) uninhabited wilderness. Aficionados agree that the unique physical formations of the Paine (pronounced *pie-nay)*, crowded with glaciers, lakes and animals, offer the most magnificent walking in the world. The best time to be there is between December and April.

The jumping-off point for the National Park is **Puerto Natales ㉑**, a small, sleepy town set beside the Ultimo Esperanza Gulf, with a couple of hotels, and restaurants serving the local speciality, king crab. Tour boats head out from Natales to nearby glaciers. Not far away is a huge cave where a prehistoric Milodon sloth was found frozen several years ago. Today it's a picnic spot, with a plastic replica of the creature.

But most people visit Puerto Natales to arrange a trip to the Paine. Several times a week (every morning in summer), vans and buses make the three-hour drive along a rough dirt road to the park. The trail winds through mountain passes before descending to the foot of the Andes, providing the first view of the **Cuernos del Paine** (horns of the Paine): twisted pillars of grey granite dusted with snow, invariably surrounded by billowing clouds. As everywhere else this far south, weather in the Paine can be unpredictable, even in summer. The famous **Torres del Paine** (towers) are even more spectacular than the Cuernos, but are often obscured by the harsh, incessantly windy weather. Accommodation can be found at the **Hostería Pehoe** on a lake and the **Posada Rio Serrano**, an eccentricly converted *estancia* house.

Several day trips can be made from these bases, as well as more ambitious walks. The park has over 250 km (150 miles) of tracks, including a seven-day circuit. Along the way are *refugios* or shelters, often scanty wood and corrugated iron structures that barely keep out the elements – sleeping bags and cooking gear are essential. Those who complete the full seven-day circuit may be rewarded with extraordinary views of snow-covered peaks, turquoise

Map on pages 260–1

Freshly-caught centolla, *king crab.*

BELOW: tree bent in submission to the Patagonian wind.

Map
on pages
260–1

Bowsprit of the
Lonsdale, wrecked
near Punta Arenas.

BELOW:
Fuerte Bulnes, near
Punta Arenas.
RIGHT: guanacos in
Torres del Paine
National Park

lakes and lush valleys. The trails are lined with orange, red and purple flowers. Much of the park is lushly forested, although a recent worm plague has killed many trees. Walks pass the accessible **Grey** and **Dickman glaciers**.

Most routes allow walkers to see plenty of animals, most commonly the guanacos: unlike camelids in other parts of South America, they appear unafraid of people and can be easily photographed from up close. Condors cruise between mountain peaks, while hares and foxes dash about in the scrub. Although the weather can turn from fair to foul and back again within minutes, the memories of the park will last well after your clothes have dried. Many people who go for a day end up staying a week: the liberating sensation of being in one of the most remote and untouched wilderness areas on earth is worth savoring.

The remote Magallanes

The southernmost province of Magallanes is a solitary place with towns called Porvenir (Future) and Ultimo Esperanza (Last Hope) that try to shake the feeling that you have reached the end of the world. This is where the tip of South America has crumbled into myriad islands as the land, sea and ice mingle. The forbidding nature of the territory is reflected in the names of some of the islands, which include Madre de Dios and Isla Desolacion.

Punta Arenas ㉒ is a port city on the rolling hills above the barren, windswept steppe on the Straits of Magellan. This is a peculiar part of the world: the sky looks bigger here, and people seem distant and less open to outsiders, while the sun glares through the torn ozone layer. Punta Arenas is known for its monuments to the Yugoslav settlers and ranchers who pioneered the region. The **Magallanes Regional Museum** (open Tues-Sun; mornings only in winter) pro-

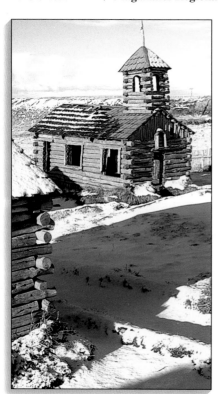

vides a fascinating trip back to the days before the Panama Canal opened, when the city boomed as ships called in on their journeys round the cape. **Cerro La Cruz** has good views of the city and across the straits to Tierra del Fuego.

Tierra del Fuego, an island of inhospitable territory across the straits from Punta Arenas, was discovered as Magellan struggled to make the passage to the Pacific in 1520. In the late 19th century the land was settled by a few immigrants from Yugoslavia and England who came to start huge sheep ranches, and cash in on the gold rush of 1881. The wooded mountains and swamps on the western side are cold and snowy in the long winter, and the rainforests to the east are warmer, though wetter. And the wind never ceases on the treeless pampas facing Punta Arenas, where hundreds of ranches prosper.

Porvenir ㉓ is the largest town (pop. 4,000) on the island, settled primarily by Yugoslavs. The **Provincial Museum** (open Mon-Fri; free) is recommended. You can take a ferry across the straits from Punta Arenas to the Porvenir docks, where a sign gives the distance to every port of Chile, as well as to Belgrade. The town itself is quiet and sleepy, apparently unchanged since the turn of the century. A road continues to the Argentine side of the island (*see page 344*) and the icy waters of Cape Horn, passing the southernmost piece of inhabited land on earth.   ❏

EASTER ISLAND

*Visiting this tiny Pacific outpost means a long flight from Chile,
yet each year many visitors make the journey to wonder
at its mysterious monolithic figures*

idden in the endless wastes of the Pacific, nearly 4,000 km (2,500 miles) from the coast of Chile, the small remnant of volcanic rock named Easter Island was once the most isolated place to live on earth. But in recent decades the Polynesian culture that left behind huge and inexplicable statues has drawn increasing attention from around the world. Where once only one ship a year made the visit to the island, today flights arrive regularly from Santiago. This tiny triangular south seas outpost measuring just 24 km (15 miles) across has a population of around 2,500, but there is a lot to explore. Easter Island has a wonderful raw, unspoilt beauty with windswept coastlines, gentle, treeless hills and a lush interior. Golden beaches and coconut palms are in short supply.

Archeologists now believe that Easter Island may have been first populated as long ago as AD 400. The Norwegian adventurer and archeologist Thor Heyerdahl argued in his famous book *Aku-Aku* that the inhabitants came from South America, noting resemblances between the island culture and that of Tiahuanaco in Bolivia (*see page 181*). But most academics today agree that the first settlers came from Polynesia, bringing sweet potato, sugar cane and bananas to the fertile ground of the island. Left in total isolation for centuries, the settlement prospered and spread. Its people created not only the remarkable stone *moai*, but also the *rongo rongo* script, the only writing system known in all Polynesia and the Americas.

The first Europeans arrived on Easter Sunday 1722, giving the island its name. Dutch Admiral Roggeveen spent a day ashore, recording that (unlike later accounts) the statues were upright, the lands were neatly cultivated and "whole tracts of woodland" were visible. The population may have been as large as 12,000.

LEFT: one of many *moai* statues.
BELOW: *moai* in the old volcanic quarry of Ranu Raraku.

Turbulent times

The picture changes in later descriptions. European explorers in the late 18th century noted that many of the statues had tumbled, little land was under cultivation and there were only a thousand people. The most likely explanation for the island's decline is that the population of Easter Island had outgrown its resources; the food supply failed, the forests were felled and soil began to erode. Without wood for canoes to escape from the island, fighting and cannibalism broke out, and the *moai* were toppled.

The people of Easter Island were to endure further suffering in the 19th century, when whalers and slave traders came to call. Of one thousand islanders taken as slaves to the guano islands off Peru in 1862, only a hundred were released alive, of which only 15 survived the return journey, bringing smallpox to wreak further havoc in the community. By 1871, only 175 islanders remained. Today over 2,000 people live on

How a typical Easter Island man might have looked before colonization.

the island, but about a quarter were born on the mainland, of Chilean ancestry. The airfield, opened in 1967, increased tourism, and in 1988 the airstrip was extended to become an emergency landing strip for the space shuttle, thrusting the island into the technological age. In the early 1990s Kevin Costner brought a Hollywood film crew to the island to produce the historically creative film *Rapa Nui*. Despite being a monumental flop, the film brought a surge of tourist traffic to the island in its wake. It is said that the Hollywood invasion pushed up prices and expectations – this may explain the fledgling nightclub scene, which is a little unexpected on an island where most tourists arrive equipped with binoculars and history books rather than swimwear and suntan lotion.

The mysterious moai

No one knows the true story behind the *moai,* but they are thought to have been symbols of gods and ancestors. They were carved from around 900 AD , out of the soft volcanic tufa of **Rano Raraku,** where some 400 incomplete pieces remain, many as high as 5.5 meters (18 ft) – the largest is 21 meters (69 ft) tall. Each probably took a year to complete. Once finished, the *moai* was cut out of the quarry and transported to a family burial platform called an *ahu,* some being given red stone "topknots". The family dead were usually placed in a vault beneath the *moai,* which was probably believed to transmit *mana,* or power, to the living family chief. All of the standing *ahu moai* that can be seen now have been re-erected in modern times. In the period of the tribal wars, all the *moai* were toppled, presumably to break the *mana* of the family chief they protected.

BELOW: the *moai* of Ahu Akiví.

The most famous of the *moai* are the standing sentinels embedded in the ground on the southern slope of Rano Raraku. These haughty-looking statues remain eyeless: *moai* were only given coral eyes once they were raised on *ahus*, at which time the *mana* began to work. Most of the sites can be reached on foot if you're happy to put in a couple of hours' walking through marvelous countryside, but don't expect to see everything on one walking tour.

The "Bird Man" cult

The most geologically spectacular place on Easter Island is the volcano **Rano Kao**, with its steep crater and multicolored lake. The ruined village of **Orongo**, sitting on steep cliffs above the crashing sea and three foam-washed islands, is surrounded by rocks with "Bird Man" carvings: a man's body is drawn with a bird's head, often holding an egg in one hand. Fortunately we know quite a lot about the Bird Man cult, as it continued up to 1862. It involved a strange rite that probably began in the period of the wars. The basis of the cult was finding the first egg laid by the *Manu Tara*, or sacred bird, each spring.

The chief of each tribe on the island sent one chosen servant to Moto Nui, the largest of the islets below Orongo. Swimming across the dangerous waters, the servants or *hopus* spent a month looking for the first egg. On finding the egg, the successful *hopu* plunged into the swirling waters with the egg strapped to his forehead, swam to the mainland, and climbed the cliffs to Orongo. The *hopu's* master, named Bird Man for the year, would be given special powers and privileges. Today there are more than 150 Bird Man carvings in the area, overlaid with fertility symbols. Nearby are markings and stones that have been interpreted as forming part of a solar observatory, where on the summer solstice the sun can be seen rising over Poike peninsula – one more mysterious attraction on this beautiful and fascinating island in the Pacific. ❑

Map on page 303

TIP

Motorbikes, jeeps and horses can be rented. Guided tours by four-wheel drive are highly recommended. You won't cover every single site in just one day's tour, but you'll see the most important ones.

BELOW: Easter Island women.

JUAN FERNANDEZ ISLANDS

*The location of the true story that inspired the fictional
Robinson Crusoe, these little known Pacific islands are also home
to some fascinating and unique species of plants and animals*

Named after Spanish navigator Juan Fernández, who discovered them in 1574, the Juan Fernández Islands owe their notoriety to a classic novel written by Daniel Defoe. Their place in history was set when Scottish mariner Alexander Selkirk was marooned on Isla Mas a Tierra, now officially known as Isla Robinson Crusoe, for four years in 1704. His experience provided the inspiration for Daniel Defoe's classic tale, *Robinson Crusoe*.

The three Juan Fernández islands – Isla Robinson Crusoe, Isla Alejandro Selkirk and Isla Santa Clara – lie 650 km (400 miles) off the Chilean mainland. Reaching them today can seem as complicated as it was for Selkirk to get off them 300 years ago. Unless you travel on a pre-arranged tour, flights to the islands from Santiago are irregular, to say the least. Winter rains flood the dirt runway, limiting air traffic to the months of October through April. Getting a seat and a confirmed departure date requires luck and dedication.

The flight to Isla Robinson Crusoe is followed by a two-hour journey in an open fishing boat to the township of **San Juan Bautista**. On a fine day, the water is clear and blue, with schools of fish zigzagging below and the obese Juan Fernández seals sunning themselves by the shore. The boatmen often smoke succulent lumps of freshly-caught cod and share them around with bread and water. The township of San Juan Bautista, where almost all of the archipelago's 4,500 inhabitants live, is located roughly where Selkirk spent his enforced leisure time. Set beneath forest-covered fists of stone with their peaks always lost in the grey mist, it consists of a few unpaved streets, a bar, a soccer field and a small cemetery with ship's anchors above many of the graves. With just a handful of automobiles, the only noise is the never-ending howl of the wind.

BELOW: the fictional Robinson Crusoe.

In Selkirk's footsteps

The classic hike from town follows Selkirk's path to **El Mirador** – the lookout used by the marooned sailor every day to scan the horizon on both sides of the island. Start early, at about 8am, to arrive before the mists roll in. The path runs through crops of introduced eucalyptuses into higher forests of indigenous trees. It also passes the remains of an old Spanish fort, as well as a turnoff to a rock bearing sailor's graffiti from 1866 – a ship and a giant fish.

The trail becomes a corridor through rainforest before revealing a knife-shaped peak. In the saddle of the mountain is the only place to see both sides of the island: lush, green Juan Bautista to the west; dry, brown swirls and jagged peaks on the northern side of the mountain. A plaque was erected here by a British warship in the 19th century commemorating Selkirk's ordeal. It has more recently been joined by a small memorial from one of the mariner's descendents from Largo in Scotland. On the return journey, call in at the **Caves of the Patriots**, where 300 pro-Spanish soldiers fled in 1814 after Chile's declaration of independence. Unlike Selkirk, they couldn't stand the wind and rain in their huge, damp caves, so gave themselves up. Back on shore, a number of other caves vie for the title of Selkirk's home, although for most of the time the mariner lived in his own handmade huts.

Within the town is Conaf, the island's national park service, financed mostly by European funds. The center operates to protect the unique flora and fauna of the area that put the island on the UNESCO World Heritage list. The plant life is unusually varied on the island, with 101 endemic varieties including a range of enormous ferns, many of which look as if they would be at home in Dr Seuss books. Of the unique animals, the red hummingbird is the most famous for its needle-fine black beak and silken feather coverage. Conaf spends most of its time trying to eradicate threats introduced by man: everything from mulberry bushes to the wild goats and feral cats descended from Selkirk's days. Rabbits were once a problem, but have been controlled by the simple solution of paying a trapper to catch and sell 150 a day (the islanders thought this a more humane solution than introducing the disease myxomatosis).

Biologists on the islands regularly turn up new finds: most recently, a fern called *dendroseries macranta* that had not been sighted since 1907 was found in a remote corner of the island.

But one of the real pleasures of any visit is just taking a seat by the wharf and watching the world go by, sipping on a beer and chatting with the islanders. Prepare to eat your fill of the local lobster too, as there may be little else on the menu – delicious for the first few days but palling by the end of your stay. ❏

The local delicacy is langosta de Juan Fernández *– a clawless lobster, which is also shipped to the Chilean mainland.*

BELOW:
Isla Santa Clara.

URUGUAY

This tiny nation, wedged in between Argentina and Brazil, was once a pioneer of social reform. It retains flavors of colonial opulence and rural frontier life, as well as elegant beach resorts

Map on pages 260–1

L ong known as the Switzerland of South America, due to its size, its democratic tradition and its dependence on the banking sector, Uruguay and its capital, Montevideo, are often seen virtually as one. This is not so surprising, given that the country covers an area of just 186,000 sq. km (72,000 sq. miles) and that more than half of its population of three million is located in Montevideo, the rest being spread among attractive coastal towns and the interior of the country, dedicated to cattle, sheep, rice and fruit production.

Successive colonial wars decimated Uruguay's indigenous Charrua population; the population today is made up principally of the descendants of Italian and Spanish immigrants who arrived in the late 19th and early 20th century, as well as a black or mixed-race minority descended from former slaves and Brazilian immigrants. Usually seen as less formal than the Argentines, the Uruguayans are of similar ancestry, though as a small and family-based society they are also less open in their social relations, in particular with foreign visitors.

Although Uruguayans tend to use Argentina as a reference point (they call themselves *Orientales*, or Easterners, as opposed to the Argentines to the west), there are some marked differences between Montevideo and Buenos Aires. One is Montevideo's racial mixture. In the 19th century, rumors of fair treatment attracted emancipated slaves from Brazil and Argentina. The army offered them a familiar regimented life, and many joined the infantry, which considerably reduced their numbers. Uruguayans claim to have no racial prejudice, but blacks tend to occupy the bottom rungs of the economic ladder.

Another difference with Argentina is Uruguay's strong secular tradition. The Catholic church plays no role in government, and holidays all have secular names: Christmas is Family Day and Easter or Holy Week is Tourism Week.

Uruguay claims to host the world's longest Carnival, held in Tourism Week (Easter) – it may be a little more sedate than the Rio version, but it is a good place to see *Candomblé*, which evolved from rituals and traditions brought by African slaves. The country also has a long tradition of tango, with many tango stars born in the country. Tango week is in October.

PRECEDING PAGES: house of the painter Paez Vilaró, Punta del Este. **LEFT:** *gaucho* with *maté* gourd. **BELOW:** Colonia del Sacramento.

Building a nation

The Portuguese were the first Europeans to settle the region, founding the city of Colonia in 1680. In 1726, Spain established a colony in Montevideo; the two countries battled over the area until Spain won possession in 1726. In 1815, José Gervasio Artigas led Uruguay to independence, becoming leader of the Uruguayan nation, but wars with Brazil postponed full independence for 10 years (*see page 31*). Artigas was eventually forced into exile in Paraguay. For the next 50 years, civil wars raged between two political forces: the Blancos (whites) and Colorados (reds). Initially feuding factions, they would eventually evolve into Uruguay's major political parties. In 1872, in the interest of beef exports, peace was established by ceding the Blancos' influence to the countryside and the Colorados' to the city, a division that remains to this day.

Montevideo is said to be a corruption of a Galician sailor's cry: "Monte vi eu!" (I saw a hill!).

The social revolution

José Batlle y Ordóñez is usually credited with forging the model of civic order that Uruguay became during the first half of the 20th century. Batlle (pronounced *Ba-zhay*) studied in Paris, and returned to Uruguay full of enlightened ideas. He became a political journalist, fearlessly attacking the country's dictators, founded his own newspaper, *El Dia*, in 1886, and gradually made his way into politics. He was elected President for the first time in 1903.

On a four-year sojourn in Europe between presidential terms, Batlle was impressed with the Swiss social legislation and state-operated industries. In his second term, Batlle introduced sweeping reforms, legalizing divorce, abolishing the death penalty, and establishing an eight-hour workday. He insisted that "God" be written in lower-case letters in his newspaper and forbade naming public buildings after saints. His 1918 Constitution provided for such basic rights as complete freedom of the press, the prohibition of arbitrary arrest, and decreed that prisons were for reform, rather than punishment.

BELOW: an early 19th-century view of Montevideo harbor.

After his death in 1929, Batlle's reforms had succeeded in liberalizing both parties. The widespread peace and prosperity of the past decades prevented even the conservative moneyed classes from objecting to the advance of social security and workers' rights. A coup d'état in 1933 temporarily halted progress, but a 1942 constitution provided explicitly for universal health, accident and unemployment insurance, and gave illegitimate children the right to inherit.

Map on pages 260–1

End of the welfare state

The collapse of Uruguay's wool and beef economic base in the late 1950s produced a crisis in the country's welfare system and a boom in poverty and unemployment. This in turn facilitated the rise of the guerrilla group Tupamaros in the 1960s and, in 1973, the rise of a repressive military government. During 12 years of dictatorship, one in every 50 Uruguayans was arrested at some point for presumed subversive activity. One in every 500 was sentenced to six years or more in prison, and some 400,000 fled into exile.

Uruguay has a median age of 47 – much older than in other Latin American countries. This is due partly to traditionally small families, but is also a result of the mass exodus of young people during the years of military government.

Following the return to civilian government in 1985, Uruguay enjoys comparatively high living standards and a relatively equitable distribution of wealth. But the country's banking system has become increasingly uncompetitive, and no industry has yet arisen to replace the increasingly limited demand for wool and beef exports, despite Uruguay's membership of the Southern Cone trade organisation Mercosur, where it is overshadowed by Argentina and Brazil. Some opening of the state monopolies of oil, energy and communications, and foreign investment may mark the road to growth in the largely stagnant economy.

Montevideo and the coast

To the visitor it can seem as if all roads in Uruguay lead to the beach – not so surprising given that the country has one of the most attractive coastlines in the continent. Even the capital, **Montevideo ㉔**, is noted for its long beaches, and virtually all the country's principal tourist destinations are on the coast, linked by the *ruta interbalnearia* (inter-beach route) running from Montevideo to Chuy, on the Brazilian border. Visitors who have had enough of the beach may want to head into the country and enjoy a slice of real rural Uruguayan life on an *estancia* (ranch), sampling Uruguay's famous beef and wine. Rural activities on offer range from horseback riding to wild boar hunting.

BELOW: make do and mend in Montevideo.

One of the most pleasant ways to travel to Uruguay is to cross the River Plate from Buenos Aires. There is a choice of hydrofoil, catamaran and ferry buses, taking between three and four hours to make the trip. From the decks, the low hill that gave Montevideo its name comes slowly into view.

Landing in Montevideo harbor and walking through the musty customs office may give you the sensation of going back in time. Old British Leyland buses and electric trolleys make their way down cobbled streets jammed with scooters, cyclists and pedestrians. Uruguay's high import duty on automobiles has filled Montevideo's streets with vehicles that would be considered antiques elsewhere. (Uruguayan auto mechanics are said to be among the best in the world.) The rural air is reinforced every August with a farm show, held in the **Parque Prado**.

With a population of 1.8 million, Montevideo is the only town of any size in Uruguay. Economic hard

Colorful hand-woven landscape.

times have given it an elegantly shabby look, although ceremonial occasions such as afternoon tea are as important as they are in Buenos Aires, as is the perpetual ritual of *maté* (*see page 315*) – you'll see people with their maté gourd and thermos of hot water on buses and in bank lines.

The best place to begin a tour of Montevideo is at the **Plaza Cagancha** (also called Plaza Libertad), on the main thoroughfare, Avenida 18 de Julio, named after the day in 1829 when Uruguay was finally freed of Argentine and Brazilian control. At Plaza Cagancha you'll find the main tourist office, offering brochures and free city maps. Av 18 de Julio runs downhill, past the **Gaucho Museum** at No 998 (open Mon–Sat), with its eclectic collection. The street leads to the city's main square, **Plaza Independencia**. To the left is an unattractive skyscraper known as the **Palacio Salvo**, which is, mysteriously, a beloved landmark for Montevideans. To the right is the art-deco **Hotel Victoria**, now owned by Moon's Unification Church. In the middle of the square is the subterranean tomb and equestrian statue of General José Artigas. Also worth visiting are the cream-colored **Government House**, now used only for ceremonial purposes, and the jewel-like **Teatro Solís**, an exact copy of the Maria Guerrero Theater in Madrid. The adjacent old-world **Aguila Restaurant** is a bit expensive, but the dark mahogany paneling, silver and elegant service give some idea of what Montevideo must have been like in its prosperous heyday.

Into the Old Town

BELOW: Plaza de la Independencia, Montevideo.

The archway at the west end of Plaza Independencia is part of the city wall that once protected Montevideo against its many invaders. It marks the entrance to the **Ciudad Vieja**, or Old Town, a neighborhood of narrow, winding streets

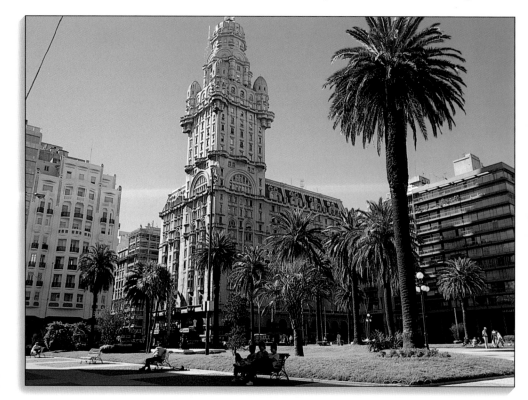

and turn-of-the-century buildings. The heart of the Old Town is **Plaza Constitución**. Here is the old *cabildo*, or town hall. Like the **cathedral**, also in the square, it's been renovated but retains its colonial appearance. The cathedral dates from the beginning of the 19th century and is the oldest building in the city. The cabildo has a good **Museum of National History** dedicated to the history of the city, containing clocks, furniture and portraits. **La Bolsa** (the Stock Exchange), the **Banco de la Republica** and the imposing **Aduana** (Customs House) are all north of the plaza and worth a look. Also intriguing is the **Palacio Taranco**, on the Plaza Zabala, the former home of a wealthy merchant who imported every stick of furniture and even the marble floors from France.

Following Calle Piedras down to the waterfront leads to the **Mercado del Puerto**, a lively fish market with a series of open-air restaurants at one end. Beef and seafood are both delicious in Montevideo; also try the *chivito* sandwich, served hot with melted cheese and bacon. Uruguayan beer is very good; it's made with spring water, not River Plate water, as in Buenos Aires.

From the old town there is a view across the port to the **Cerro**, the 139-meter (456-ft) hill which gave the city its name, topped with a lighthouse and fort.

A city of beautiful beaches

If the weather is good, try to visit one of the city's clean white-sand beaches. The city also has two lovely parks of historical interest. The **Prado** is located northwest of downtown (follow Agraciada north from 18 de Julio) in a neighborhood where some of Uruguay's grand old houses still stand. It was once the property of a 19th-century financier named José Buschental, who built a 40-hectare (175-acre) estate here and married the niece of Emperor Dom Pedro II

Map on pages 260–1

In 1939 the great German battleship Graf Spee was sunk a couple of kilometers off Montevideo, and its anchor can be seen in the port. The city stadium was built using metal plates from the leviathan's salvaged bulkheads.

BELOW: enjoying a cup of *maté* in the traditional way.

A CUP OF MATÉ

Everything stops for *maté* in Uruguay – in fact, so important is this stimulating brew that many Uruguayans carry their own DIY *maté* kit around with them at all times. This usually consists of a drinking gourd known as a *culha* or *maté*, sometimes decorated with silver, containing *yerba* (dried leaves); a *bombilla* (drinking tube), which has a strainer at one end, and a hot water flask.

Maté, or *yerba maté* is brewed from the leaves of an evergreen plant, *Ilex paraguariensis*, which is related to the holly and grows wild in Paraguay and southern Brazil. The drink was popular with the Guaraní people in pre-Columbian times, and the leaves were first cultivated on a large scale by the Jesuits.

Maté is now part of the culture of Uruguay, Paraguay, Argentina and Brazil, with the cup sometimes shared between friends or family. Each guest drinks from the cup and passes it back to the host to be refilled in turn. *Maté* is usually drunk plain, but sometimes lemon juice, sugar or even milk are added. Iced *maté* is increasingly popular. *Yerba maté* has diuretic and anti-rheumatic properties, and *maté* teabags are available in many northern hemisphere health shops.

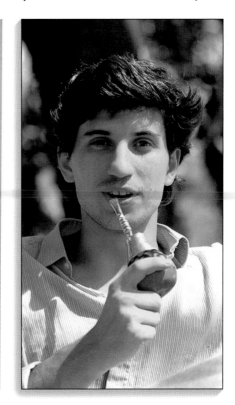

of Brazil. He brought fish from Asia as well as exotic plants and animals from around the world. This area has a statue of Buschental, as well as 800 varieties of roses. **Parque Rodó**, just behind the city's **Ramirez Beach** is resplendent with palms, eucalyptus and native ombú trees. It was named after José Enrique Rodó, one of the most prominent 19th-century South American writers, whose most famous work, *Ariel*, influenced a generation of intellectuals.

In summer, many Buenos Aires political news articles are datelined Punta del Este – Argentina's movers and shakers are all at the beach. The family of Paraguay's dictator Stroessner was vacationing at "Punta" when the General was overthrown.

Promenades and smart hotels

The metropolitan beaches stretch east as far as **Carrasco**, a fashionable suburb with streets shaded by big trees and houses that belong to the few well-to-do people left in Uruguay. This old casino still opens every season, though its glory days are long past. Montevideo's international airport lies just beyond Carrasco, 14 km (9 miles) from the city center.

Beyond Carrasco, the highway turns inland, but smaller roads branch off to the beaches. At Km 42, shortly before Atlántida, is the **Fortín de Santa Rosa**, an 18th-century fortress converted into a hotel with a virtually private beach and an excellent restaurant. **Atlántida**, 45 km (28 miles) from Montevideo, is surrounded by a windbreak of cypress and eucalyptus. The beach also has a casino, golf course and tearoom. Just beyond Atlántida is **Piriápolis**, a pretty town on a curving bay with an old-fashioned promenade dominated by the imposing Argentino Hotel, a 1920s spa with mineral baths, stained-glass windows and an elegant solarium where you may sip the curative sulfur-flavored water.

BELOW: an *asado* (barbecue) at the port markets.

The most famous beach on the Uruguayan coast is **Punta del Este ㉕**, a jet-set-studded peninsula that attracts well-heeled Argentines as well as a fair share of international celebrities and European royalty. Prices at "Punta" make this primarily porteño resort an exclusive one. The peninsula has two long and beautiful beaches: the Atlantic one is more windswept than the tranquil bay side. Those who don't share the Argentine herd instinct might find Punta more attractive off-season, when hotel rates go down and cool autumn breezes clear the sand of body-to-body sunbathers.

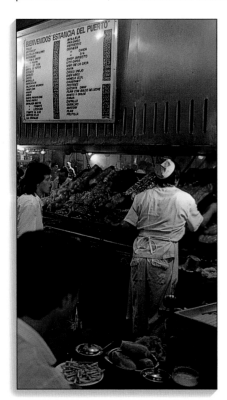

North of Punta del Este, the Uruguayan Atlantic coast is rich with gorgeous seascapes and deserted white-sand beaches. Along the coastal highway towards Brazil, it's worth stopping at the 18th-century Portuguese fortresses of **Santa Teresa ㉖** and **San Miguel ㉗**, now beautiful national parks and popular bird sanctuaries, and **Punta del Diablo**, an attractive fishing village with a number of small restaurants offering excellent seafood.

European communities

West of Montevideo are some interesting European settlements. **Colonia Valdense** was settled by Waldensians from the Piedmontese Alps, and **Colonia Suiza** is a small Swiss enclave, also known as **Nueva Helvecia**. Fifty kilometers (31 miles) west of Colonia Valdense is the 17th-century Portuguese town of **Colonia del Sacramento ㉘**. Colonia retains more of its original flavor than most cities in the region, partly because little has happened here since the Portuguese founded it as a rival to Buenos Aires in 1680. With a

population of only 10,000, Colonia can have the air of an Iberian ghost town.
Sights to see in the old quarter include the **Spanish Museum**, in a restored 18th-century viceroy's mansion, the **parochial church** and the **Portuguese Museum**, which has an excellent collection of mahogany and cordovan furniture. Narrow cobbled streets lead towards the river, where you can walk along the promenade to the remains of the colonial fortifications. A couple of miles further out stands a grandiose bullring, not used since Uruguay outlawed bullfighting at the beginning of the century. A hydrofoil connects Colonia with Buenos Aires; there is also the slower but more nausea-proof ferry.

Map on pages 260–1

North along the River Uruguay

For Uruguayans, a trip up the River Uruguay is the patriotic equivalent of an American tourist's pilgrimage to New England. The small, tidy villages where nothing appears to be happening were at one time the crucibles of Uruguayan independence. Thirty kilometers (18 miles) up the river from Colonia is **La Agraciada**, where the famous "Thirty-three Orientales" (*see page 31*) landed from Argentina and organized a battalion to expel the Portuguese from Uruguayan soil. A statue to General Lavalleja, the patriots' leader, is on the beach.

Browsing for bargains at the Sunday Tristan Narvaja fair.

The port of **Fray Bentos** comemmorates revolution of a different kind in its **Museo de la Revolución Industrial**. Fray Bentos was the site of the country's first meat extract factory. **Paysandú ㉙**, further upriver, is the town where Artigas led his followers when they fled Spanish rule in Montevideo. Today it's a popular spot for stalking the delicious *pez dorado* game fish. It's also where **Artigas Bridge** crosses the Uruguay River to Argentina. North of Paysanú are the remedial hot mineral springs of **Termas de Daymán** and **Arapey**. ❏

BELOW: the fashionable Parque Hotel, Montevideo, circa 1920.

LA

E
S
T
A
N
C
I
A

Z

EL
PALACIO
DE LA

PAPA
FRITA

ALISTA
RAMADOR

VALLE
951

SELECT

L
A
V
A
L
L
E

A
T
N
L
R
A
M
A
N
S
D

P
a
r
a
m
o
u
n
t

Coca Cola

Coca-Cola

ROMA

RESTAURAN

John Player Special

ARGENTINA

As the political strife of the past is replaced with economic growth, more visitors are being attracted to the furthest reaches of this mighty territory and to its stimulating capital, Buenos Aires

Map on pages 260–1

The second largest country in South America and the eighth largest in the world, geographical magnitude is not the only grand aspect of Argentina. The country is characterised by large cities, large ranches, large open spaces, even large steaks. In the mid-20th century, Argentina seemed set to become the Texas of South America. It was one of the richest nations on earth, and the Argentine rancher was a near-mythical figure of wealth comparable with the Texan oil baron or railroad king. But instead, the country became notorious on the world stage for political drama and military dictatorships.

Argentina has always been heavily orientated towards its capital, Buenos Aires, with the city sometimes described as a giant's head on a dwarf's body. Most of the country's economic, political, financial and industrial activity is focussed on the Buenos Aires area, implying that the distribution of wealth and resources is extremely skewed. Yet despite significant and rising poverty, Argentina has, with Uruguay, the highest standard of living in Latin America. It also has a population which likes to live well, and restaurants, hotels, resorts, museums and theaters abound. Throughout the country, the urban middle class has its nearby beach, lakeside resort, ski center or mountain village retreat.

Argentina covers a range of latitudes, from the sub-tropical northeast, with Jesuit ruins and the imposing Iguazú Falls, to the Andean northwest, changing abruptly from barren mountains to lush greenery, with the colonial architecture of Salta and the sugar-producing province of Tucumán. Central Argentina is characterised by spectacular mountain scenery, vineyards and impeccably tidy urban planning in Mendoza, green mountains and lakes in Córdoba, and attractive beach resorts in Buenos Aires province. In the south, bleak oil towns co-exist with Welsh communities, pseudo-Tyrolean architecture, pretty towns surrounded by snow-capped mountains and lakes, and magnificent glaciers in the far south. All these areas have a highly-developed tourist industry with good transport links, and all offer good accommodation and food, although prices reflect Argentina's relatively high standard of living.

PRECEDING PAGES: late afternoon on the pampa. **LEFT:** pedestrian mall of Lavalle, Buenos Aires. **BELOW:** tango hero Carlos Gardel.

The people of Argentina

Argentines are known for their strong localist tendency and their capacity to disdain those from the rest of the continent, tempered by a genuine instinct to be generous, helpful and hospitable. While the *porteños* (inhabitants of Buenos Aires – literally "people of the port") see their city as much more sophisticated and cosmopolitan than the rest of the country, many provincial cities also have large populations of second- and third-generation descendants of European and Arab immigrants, including Tucumán, Mendoza and Córdoba, cities which are also far enough away from Buenos Aires to have developed an exciting cultural, artistic and academic life of their own.

Very few pockets of indigenous population remain, except for small groups of Guaraní, Colla and Toba (or Witchi) people in the far north and Mapuches in the south, marginalised by the so-called "European" culture of Argentina.

Porteños, gauchos and caudillos

In the 18th century, when Buenos Aires was thriving as a smuggling center, fortunes began to be made in cattle hides and mule-breeding, and the indigenous people were forced back from the pampas. It was at this time that huge tracts of land were set aside for a few Spanish families, whose names would recur again and again as the power-brokers of Argentina.

For 70 years after independence in 1816, bitter civil wars raged, with Buenos Aires trying to impose a central rule over local strongmen, known as *caudillos*, and their armies of *gauchos*, wild mestizo horsemen who lived in the pampa (*see page 338*). The most famous *caudillo* was Juan Manuel de Rosas, who rose from the chaos of the civil wars in 1829 to become governor of Buenos Aires province and *de facto* ruler of Argentina. Rosas is remembered for his reign of terror, enforced by secret police, and his nationalist policies, giving Argentine goods the chance to compete against foreign trade. After 23 years, Rosas was thrown out and his supporters massacred. His protective tariffs were dismantled, flooding the country again with foreign goods, while the civil wars resumed.

It was not until 1886 that the final step towards nationhood was made, when Buenos Aires was separated from its province and declared the capital of Argentina. The country's leaders were eager to appear cultured and urbane, notably Domingo Sarmiento, who divided the world into "civilization" – represented by all things European – and "barbarity": the caudillos, gauchos and Indians. Codes were introduced to control the gauchos. General Julio Roca embarked on a "Conquest of the Wilderness" in the 1880s to open up the pampas and Patagonia, still controlled by Indians. Any native standing in his path was killed, the rest herded into reservations. Cultivation of the pampas exploded to keep up with the new demand for Argentine beef. Railways were laid across the country and Argentina was soon outstripping its rivals, Australia and Canada, in agricultural advances.

BELOW: a 19th-century painting of a *gaucho* and his *china*.

The immigrants arrive

Thousands of laborers were needed to keep the boom going. Before 1880, only a trickle of foreign workers stayed in Argentina. Overnight they became a flood. Most were poor peasants from northern Italy, with the next largest group coming from Spain. But Argentina's boom wealth was not shared among these new arrivals, and Argentina remained the property of around 200 close-knit families known as "the oligarchy". The result was a distortion in ownership that has stunted the country's growth and political life.

As the economy expanded, the new-found importance of Buenos Aires allowed it to shed the Hispanic colonial atmosphere and become an expression of all things French. The 16th-century street plan was cast aside and streets widened into grand avenues lined with marble footpaths, cafés and jacarandas. But political and economic inequalities began rising to the surface. Protest movements against the oligarchs' grip produced the middle-class Unión Cívica Radical, forerunner of today's party of the same name. While tensions grew in the 1920s, Buenos Aires became the cultural mecca of Latin America. The rich indulged in tango parties and balls rather than worry about social ills. Then the Great Depression hit. Nobody was surprised when, on September 6, 1930, the Argentine military marched into the Presidential Palace to take power under General José Uriburu. It was the first of many interventions.

The age of Perón

The military handed over to a series of conservative governments in the 1930s, allowing the oligarchy to run the country as if nothing had changed in 40 years. Then, in 1943, a group of young army officers staged a successful coup. One of the figures in the new government was a man who even today has a personality cult that dominates Argentine politics: Juan Domingo Perón. Perón joined the Army at 16, and became an ardent admirer of Mussolini while serving as military attaché in Italy. He chose to champion the disenfranchised and unprotected workers, many of whom were the children of immigrants. Perón took the post of Secretary of Labor and started to organize trade unions. He was later joined by the beautiful radio actress Eva Duarte. The daughter of a provincial peasant, Evita shocked high society but was worshiped by the working class for her passionate, if occasionally incoherent, speeches on their behalf. Thanks to her, women got the vote and a public health service was developed.
Perón fended off an attempt by a group of generals to unseat him and became

Map on pages 260–1

BELOW: Eva and Juan Perón.

Lighthouse, Buenos Aires harbor.

President. While he nationalized industries and started social welfare programs, Eva toured Europe in jewels and couture dresses as if she were a member of Latin royalty. Eva died tragically in 1952 of cancer, at the age of 33, but the Vatican resisted calls for her canonization. The magic quickly began to wear off. The cost of living was rising, government spending was out of control and corruption rife. When it was rumored that Perón would distribute arms to the trade unions, the military struck, bombing the Presidential Palace and forcing Perón to flee on a Paraguayan gunboat. His supporters were purged from every level of government, and even mentioning Perón's name in public was banned.

The "dirty war" and war with Britain

Despite the repression, Perónism lived on through 18 years of incompetent military and civilian rule. When full democratic elections were allowed in 1973, Perónist candidates won easily – and invited the aging founder back from exile in Spain to become President once again. Returning in triumph to Buenos Aires, Perón promptly died, leaving the presidency to his third wife, a cabaret dancer known by her stage name, Isabelita. The arrangement was a disaster. Argentina's economy nose-dived again, guerilla fighting began in the mountains in Tucumán, and terrorists began letting off bombs and kidnapping prominent figures. The military let the situation drag on until they had popular support for a coup in 1976. Then they began a "dirty war" to purge Argentine society of everyone it suspected of left-wing sympathies. As many as 30,000 people were kidnapped, tortured and secretly executed in the campaign.

But the officers seemed incapable of running the economy, with inflation reaching record levels and poverty growing. To distract attention, President

BELOW: jubilant Argentines took to the streets on the return of democracy in 1983 after seven years of military rule.

Galtieri decided to take the Falkland Islands, known as the Malvinas in Argentina (*see page 350*). The possession of these windswept rocks had been contentious since the British took them in 1833. It is unlikely that Galtieri expected British Prime Minister Margaret Thatcher to dispatch a task force to retake them. After a brief, bloody war, the Argentines were soundly defeated and the humiliated military were forced to call democratic elections in 1983.

Campaigning on a human rights platform, Radical candidate Raúl Alfonsin unexpectedly won the presidency. Although unable to raise Argentina from its economic slump, Alfonsin guided the country into a new democratic era. In 1989 the Judicialist (Perónist) party's flamboyant candidate Carlos Menem won the presidential elections by a landslide, after making wage increases his main campaign proposal. Menem imposed a series of draconian economic reforms and reformed the constitution to allow for his re-election. In 1998 he was proposing a new constitutional reform to allow him a third term from 1999, despite repeated allegations of corruption.

The unsmiling Argentines who populate the streets in the late 1990s know that the "fiesta" of a state-run economy with education, health care, job security and pension is over, as Menem warned when he took office in 1989 and set about undoing Perón's work. Meanwhile, Eduardo Duhalde, governor of Buenos Aires Province and Menem's would-be successor in 1999, waved the banners of social justice as he spoke of "re-Perónizing" the economy.

Maps, Area 260–1 City 324

Buenos Aires: sophisticated city with a passionate heart

Few countries are so gripped by their capital cities as Argentina is by **Buenos Aires** ㉚. Everyone and everything that passes through Argentina must at some stage come to "the Paris of South America." Sprawl-

BELOW: the Obelisk on Avenida. 19 del Julio, the widest street in the world.

ing over the flat, empty pampas, by the shores of the muddy Rio de la Plata (River Plate), Buenos Aires flaunts its European heritage and wistfully dreams of foreign shores. It is a city of immigrants who had always intended to return home, but still find themselves, somewhat uncertainly, in a strange and remote land. But it is also a city with a creative energy that can put New York to shame. Walk the streets at midnight, and you will see people of all ages just starting a meal in a restaurant, lining up for a movie theater session or discussing theater in a café.

The people of Buenos Aires are a special breed, renowned for their contradictions. Obsessed with style and appearance, the *porteños* turn their city into an open-air fashion parade. They are in love with the theater, public debates and the spectacle of politics in the street. Privately, the dramas of the mind exert an endless fascination: Buenos Aires has more psychiatrists per head of population than Manhattan.

A slice of Europe

Buenos Aires was founded more than 400 years ago, but it was virtually re-created at the end of the 19th century. Riding the beef boom of the 1880s, the city's Hispanic colonial buildings were leveled and replaced in the image of Paris. It was a time of tremendous wealth, when beef barons were sending their sons to

Beef and Red Wine

L ong before arriving, you will have heard that Argentina is a carnivore's paradise. Although it is exported to many parts of the world, the best beef is consumed at home with an almost religious reverence. Until recently Argentina's fine wine was one of the country's best-kept secrets, with very little being imported overseas, despite being the world's fifth largest producer. Today Argentine wines are being appreciated on dinner tables worldwide. Taken together, a cut of beef with a bottle of red are both a simple meal and part of a gastronomic ritual that goes to the heart of the country's traditions.

Steak preparation is regarded as an art, and the *parrillas* (steak houses) on every corner in Buenos Aires can seem more like temples to beef than restaurants. The most extravagant have meat in their windows being cooked in traditional *gaucho* fashion, with whole carcasses crucified on metal crosses around a mound of coals. Others have stuffed cows flanking the

doorways, and over the tables are posters illustrating the cuts. The most expensive and leanest cut is the *bife de lomo*, roughly equivalent to a sirloin steak in other countries. The popular *bife de chorizo* is cut from the rib near the rump, while a *bife de costilla* is a T-bone.

In a class of its own is the *tira de asado*, which is a strip of rib roast usually large enough to feed two. The *parrillada* is a portable grill of mixed cuts, including plenty of offal and sausages – for the most committed carnivores. *Vacio* comprises of the bottom part of what in the US is designated as sirloin, porterhouse and the flank, and is the juiciest of all cuts. *Matambre* is shaped like a Swiss roll with a vegetable and hard boiled egg filling. Often served cold, It can be an appetizer, or eaten inside French bread.

If you like your beef rare, order it *jugoso*; medium, a *punto*; and well done, *bien hecho*.

Steaks at an Argentine restaurant are unlikely to be sullied by vegetables, gravy or sauces. The most common accompaniment is a salad, which can vary from lettuce and tomato to a giant mixed extravaganza with artichokes and eggs. For those whose taste buds require a little more than salt and flesh, order the *salsa chimichuri*. This oregano and spice mix is traditionally a *gaucho's* favorite. The flavor is considered so strong that asking for it often gets a grunt of respect from the most sombre waiter – although the spices are unlikely to surprise most foreign palates.

Argentines drink around 12 gallons (48 liters) of wine per head each year. Grown near Mendoza and the drier stretches of the north near Salta, wines are both absurdly cheap and amazingly good. V*ino común*, served in jugs, is at the rougher end, but you will appreciate any of the inexpensive bottled *vino fino* on the wine list. There are around 50 varieties, and though many European grapes are used, Malbec and Torrentes are a local specialty. Continually reliable wineries include Navarro, Correas, La Rural, Escorihuela, Bianchi and Sant Elmo.

Argentines often drink their wine with soda water. Despite regular consumption, it is rare for an Argentine to be seen drunk. Few people go beyond a couple of glasses. ❑

LEFT: meat is rarely off the menu in the restaurants of Buenos Aires.

Europe, where they cut notorious figures in the local salons. Buenos Aires was a world center of fashion and high art, the cultural mecca of the Americas. But cracks were already appearing in the Argentine dream, and no sooner was the city built than the decline began. This sense of faded grandeur makes it a fascinating place to wander through. Buenos Aires is not so much a city of "sights" as of atmospheres, where the main pleasure is to stroll through the city's neighborhoods, stop for a cup of coffee, stroll on again and absorb some of the everyday flavor of a city that seems to exist in a world of its own.

Map on page 324

El Centro

The city center is carved up by wide avenues, lined by jacaranda trees and magnificent buildings that nobody has ever had the money to either knock down or restore. Bulbous cupolas protrude from their roofs, windows are framed by statues of Greek gods and hidden inside are marble stairways and chandeliers – all slightly tarnished and looking vaguely out of place.

The natural spot to start is at the pedestrian walkway of **Florida**, which is crammed at every hour of the day with *porteños* trying to catch glimpses of themselves in window reflections as they pass. It is lined with boutiques selling Argentina's famous leather goods, although shoppers should control themselves until reaching the cheaper **Avenida Santa Fe** at the **Plaza San Martín**, where a dramatic statue commemorates one of the only heroes in Argentine history that commands universal respect. The better shops in Florida are also at this end, between Avenida Cordoba and Santa Fe. Intersecting Florida is another pedestrian mall, **Lavalle**, with nothing but movie theaters, bingo and video game halls, restaurants and bargain stores. The street can clog with people every night, especially when movie sessions end.

The colorful houses of La Boca, Buenos Aires.

BELOW: presidential guards on parade, Buenos Aires.

The presidential palace is named **la Casa Rosada**, or "Pink House", for the tint of its masonry. It stands before the **Plaza de Mayo**, where guards in blue uniforms regularly strut and parade, surrounded by schoolchildren. Since 1980 an alternative procession has been mounted every Thursday by the white-scarfed Mothers of the Plaza de Mayo. They still demonstrate, as they did under the last dictatorship, for the return of their "disappeared" children.

On the port side of the Casa Rosada are the recycled 19th-century brick warehouses of the old port of Buenos Aires, now the new smart area for working and eating out. An oasis of sun and silence at the edge of the bustle of the banking district, the new **Puerto Madero** dockland development is an ideal place for a late afternoon drink on the promenade overlooking the water. At the other end of the plaza is one of Buenos Aires' few colonial buildings, the **cabildo** or municipal palace. Inside this whitewashed edifice, which now houses a museum, *porteños* argued for days before declaring the city's independence from Spain in 1810. Next door is the **Metropolitan Cathedral**, where General José San Martín is buried. The grand **Avenida de Mayo** stretches from here to the **Palacio del Congreso**, which looks like the White House in Washington DC. On the way, it crosses the **Avenida 9 de Julio**, which despite being the widest

TIP

San Telmo's major event is the Sunday antique market in the main square. Here you can scour hundreds of stalls for unique memorabilia of Argentina's more turbulent times while live jazz is played in nearby cafés and buskers tango in the streets.

avenue in the world manages to be clogged with traffic at most hours of the day. The street's crowning glory is the **Obelisco**, a rather tasteless phallic object around which the city revolves.

The nearby **Avenida Corrientes** is the showbusiness heart of Buenos Aires, lined with bright lights, art-deco theaters and movie theater palaces from the 1920s. Argentines prefer to eat dinner very late, and the restaurants along this street can be packed until 2am, while on Saturday nights, the last movie session does not even begin until 1.30am. Corrientes is also noted for its dozens of bookstores, which are crowded with browsers until the early hours of the morning. The **San Martín Cultural Center** holds art exhibitions, film festivals and photographic displays. A few blocks northeast, on Plaza Lavalle, is the sumptuous **Teatro Colón**, one of the world's great opera houses. A performance here should not be missed, if only for the experience of sitting back in wooden armchairs with plush velvet padding, looking out over six gilded tiers and gallery boxes. Guided tours are given daily to the theater's three floors of underground workshops and the small museum commemorating appearances by such greats as Melba, Nijinsky, Pavlova and Caruso.

Café society

To understand Buenos Aires, try to do as the *porteños* do: spend as much time as is humanly possible in the *confiterias* or cafés of the city, watching the world go by. To the *porteño*, Buenos Aires is mapped out not by streets, landmarks or *barrios*, but by key places to sit, write, think and observe.

Two of the city's oldest and most venerable *confiterias* are located within walking distance of this area. The **Ideal**, on Suipacha, near Corrientes, was

BELOW: looking for a gramophone? Try San Telmo.

where the once-sizable British community in Buenos Aires met for high tea every afternoon. These days you can still have tea and cakes surrounded by polished wood, brass and marble pillars while being serenaded with waltzes played on an ancient electric organ. Possibly the most famous of the *confiterias* is the **Tortoni**, on Avenida de Mayo and Piedras. In the 1920s it was the hangout of bohemians such as the writer Jorge Luis Borges, listening to tangos, experimenting with cocaine and debating poetics. Its red leather chairs, mirrors and chandeliers have changed little since that time, and every Friday night, older patrons gather in a back room to hear the tango again.

Remnants of the colonial city

For a taste of Buenos Aires as it used to be, head for the artistic barrio of **San Telmo Ⓐ**, south of the Plaza de Mayo. During the 1700s it was the riverside hub of the city, with one third of its population black. Its cobbled streets are lined by low buildings, tango bars and antique shops.

Colonial streetlight.

The most surprising thing about the working-class suburb of **La Boca Ⓑ** is the sudden splash of color in the otherwise reserved city. Coming to life in the mid-19th century as the home for Genovese dock workers, this barrio by the river is famous for its houses of corrugated iron, all painted in different dazzling tones. The 20th-century Argentine painter Benito Quinquela Martin was a leading influence in the suburb's use of color, and his home has been turned into a gallery for his paintings of dock workers. By night, La Boca has a series of gaudy restaurants where bands play renditions of kitsch classics.

The city's upper crust fled to the **Barrio Norte** in the 1870s when yellow fever hit Buenos Aires. Today it is the most elegant and refined of *barrios*,

BELOW: a night at the opera – the opulent Teatro Colón.

Map on page 324

A Dance of Passion

Loneliness and despair, jealousy and homesickness – all are themes of tango, Argentina's most famous musical tradition. The accompanying dance is a demonstration of strutting Latin *machismo*: passionate, erotic and flamboyant. So closely associated with the history of Argentina, tango is said to be a distillation of the national character. Where Brazil has the exuberant *samba*, *porteños* listen to the melancholy tango. True or not, the tango lingers throughout Buenos Aires like a perfume from another age.

The origins of tango can be traced to the slums of Buenos Aires at the end of the 19th century, where cultures from around the world were meeting – discharged soldiers from Argentina's civil wars, descendants of African slaves and boatloads of Italian and Spanish immigrants. Overwhelmingly male, the new arrivals gathered in the bars and brothels. They shared the loneliness of exiles, mixing their national music to create the haunting

tango sound. The dance was invented before lyrics were introduced, usually performed by two males waiting in line at the local bordello.

Before long, the tango was gaining popularity amongst the *porteño* working class. By the early 20th century, the wheezing sound of the *bandoneon* (concertina) had been added to the guitar, flute, violin and piano of tango ensembles. Writers even began putting their names to tangos. Only the snobbish upper classes kept aloof from the new rhythm, preferring to keep to their waltzes and polkas.

When the tango reached Europe, mothers in Edwardian England tried in vain to stem the popularity of the sensual dance, with its thrusting hip movements and intertwined limbs. Kaiser Wilhelm of Germany banned his staff from performing it. But for the rest of Europe, tango was the rage. And once the dance had succeeded in the salons of Europe, the Argentine upper crust accepted it wholeheartedly, agreeing with the French that it must be the very essence of Latin style.

In 1917, the little-known singer Carlos Gardel recorded the tango *Mi Noche Triste*. Almost overnight, the handsome figure became the first great tango star whose voice was heard around the world. Although arguments continue as to whether Gardel was born in France or Uruguay, he is remembered in Argentina as *El Pibe del Abasto* – the kid from the Abasto district of Buenos Aires. He became a movie star in Argentina, his place in the local pantheon assured when he was killed in an airplane accident in 1935 – as though Gardel were living out a tango himself. Today, new techniques are used to improve his old recordings, and in Buenos Aires they say: "Every day he sings better."

Tango fell into a lull in the 1950s until it was pushed in new directions by *tanguistas* like Astor Piazzola. Trained in classical and jazz music, he led a revival with his new, energetic arrangements. He can be heard in the hit 1987 film *El Exilio de Gardel* (The Exile of Gardel). Tango's renewed importance is clear, with university courses on offer, the FM Tango radio station and the *Todo Tango* television show, as well as the successful *Tango Argentino* touring company, which has filled theaters across Europe and the US. ❑

LEFT: singing tango on the street, San Telmo.

Maps
Area 260
City 324

where old ladies in minks sit under oak trees in outdoor cafés and business-men in European suits arrogantly order waiters about. The neighborhood is built around a giant walled cemetery, the **Recoleta** . Hundreds of ornate marble crypts contain the remains of the city's wealthiest families, with giant angels and grim reapers adding to the unsettling effect. The Barrio also boasts the city's range of *albergues transitorios* – hotels rented out by the hour – where, overlooking the Recoleta necropolis, local denizens can steal a few tense hours of sensory gratification.

When the urban rush becomes too much and you feel the need for a view and fresh air, head for the **Costanera Norte**. A promenade runs along the brown Rio de la Plata, where on a clear day you may be able to pick out the coast of Uruguay in the distance. Fashionable *parrillas* (grillhouses) line the road on the other side of the walkway, for when the exercise loses its charm. In October or November, a classic day can be spent at the *polo* by heading out to **Palermo** playing fields. An alternative day trip venue is the **Tigre Delta**, a weekend refuge for *porteños* of all ages for more than a century. Trains leave regularly from the cast-iron **Retiro** station in central Buenos Aires, taking passengers to the quiet, tree-lined rivers and canals within an hour. Wooden ferries leave for destinations further into the delta, where modern French restaurants and guest houses retain the atmosphere of the 1930s.

To the disgust of the Argentine old wealth, the Recoleta's most famous occupant is the daughter of a provincial nobody, Evita Perón. Thousands visit her tomb every year, in a crypt of black marble which has a single rose before it.

Beaches, lakes and mountains

About five hours' drive from Buenos Aires are the Atlantic coastal resorts of Mar del Plata, Villa Gesell and Pinamar. **Mar del Plata** ⓛ is also accessible by air in about 30 minutes from Buenos Aires. By far the largest of the country's sea-

BELOW: Mar del Plata.

side towns, it has an enormous quantity of hotels at all prices, all of which fill up from mid-December to mid-February. This very attractive city is the country's most attractive resort, and has a long *rambla* (pedestrian area) along the coast, beginning at its famous casino. The beach becomes heavily overpopulated in summer, but suburban areas are reasonably peaceful throughout the year. There are many *confiterias* and restaurants serving excellent seafood, and a good variety of movie theaters and nightclubs. Further north on the coast, **Villa Gesell** and **Pinamar** are much smaller and more peaceful. Both towns have more open spaces and wooded areas, in addition to their beaches, Pinamar being the more exclusive of the two, with more nightlife.

West to the land of wine and sun

The city of **Córdoba** ❷, some 700 km (435 miles) northwest of Buenos Aires, is one of the country's cultural and religious centers, known for the number of lawyers and seminaries it houses. The university is one of the oldest and most distinguished in Argentina, and the city offers both well-preserved colonial architecture – especially in religious buildings – and an active modern urban life.

The lakeside resort of **Villa Carlos Paz**, a former German enclave which still slightly resembles a Bavarian village, lies 36 km (22 miles) west, in the green sierras of Córdoba. Villa Carlos Paz is often crowded in summer, but has a wide range of hotels and restaurants, as well as beautiful scenery and access to the Sierra. To the north are **Cosquín**, a smaller town which hosts the National Folklore Festival in January, and **Rio Ceballos**, a quiet place to enjoy the mountains and rivers, and to walk in the Córdoba range, less rugged than the Andes. All these towns are easily reached by excursions from Córdoba city.

BELOW: ceiling of Córdoba Cathedral.

Southwest of Córdoba, on the Chilean border, **Mendoza** ❸ is more a tribute to hard work and ingenuity than to Argentina's natural scenery. An arid province at the foot of the Andes, Mendoza attracted Italian and French settlers in the late 19th century who, with encouragement from the progressive provincial government, installed irrigation methods which allowed the province to become one of Argentina's principal agricultural zones. Known as "the land of sun and good wine", Mendoza is the country's principal area of wine production and vineyards, although its prosperity is also based on its significant oil reserves.

Mendoza not as architecturally interesting as cities like Córdoba, due to earthquake devastation. However, it is by far the cleanest and tidiest city in Argentina, and full of trees planted to dispel the desert image. To the west of the city is the huge **Parque San Martín**, with hillside views of the city, a lake, horsedrawn carriage rides, the local university and a monument to San Martín, whose famous Andes crossing to Chile began at Mendoza. Public buses and organised tours go to the wine *bodegas*.

From the central plaza an attractive pedestrian precinct leads past the provincial legislature to **San Martín**, the main street, where the tourist office is located. The attractive **Plaza España** was donated to the city by the Franco government in the 1940s and displays a beautiful collection of Spanish tiles, as well as an example of the Mendozan obsession with fountains, lawns and trees. Mendoza is the base for a number of outdoor activities, including pony trekking and skiing, though the most exclusive center for skiing is the **Las Leñas** resort, roughly 400 km (248 miles) southwest of Mendoza.

Map on pages 260–1

Northern traditions

The north is the only part of the country where the indigenous people still survive in significant numbers. The region gives visitors a fascinating glimpse into Argentina's colonial past and the Andean countries just across the border. It was here that the first Franciscan monks settled, coming south from Peru and building whitewashed chapels in the desert.

Tucumán ③, one and a half hours from Buenos Aires by air or about 16 hours by bus, is known as the "cradle of independence", because Argentina's independence was declared in the **Casa de Tucumán** in 1816. Nightly *son et lumière* shows are held here. On the **Plaza Independencia** is the neo-French style government house and the cathedral. Nearby are the churches of **San Francisco** and the **Virgen del Rosario**. Half a block away is an open-air craft center run by the municipality, with several small restaurants offering excellent regional specialities. The **tourist office** and the **Museo Folklórico Provincial** are on Avenida 24 de Septiembre.

Jesuit church tower, Alta Gracia.

Leaving Tucumán by bus or car for **Tafí del Valle**, the road winds through mountainous terrain with sub-tropical foliage, rivers and waterfalls, as well as the **El Cadillal** reservoir near Tafí, an attractive mountain village favored by Tucumános for summer holidays. To the north of Tafí, the mountains become dry and moonlike before arriving at the ruins of **Quilmes**, the well-preserved

BELOW: Argentina's arid north.

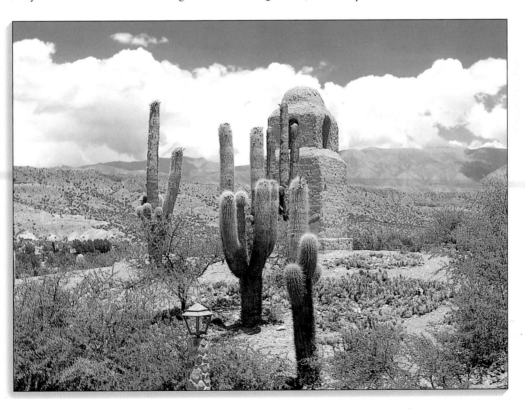

remains of an 18th-century Indian village. Some 20 km (12 miles) further north is **Amaicha del Valle**, the only village in Argentina in which the indigenous people hold the title to their ancestral lands. The Pachamama festival is held here in February. **Santa María**, 10 km (6 miles) away, is an attractive town turned boomtown by the nearby Bajo La Alumbrera gold and copper mine. About an hour beyond Santa María is **Cafayate**, a pretty town surrounded by wineries in Salta province. The scenery between Tucumán and Cafayate (about a six-hour drive) is among the most breathtaking and varied in Argentina.

Colonial churches and markets

Salta ㉟ is an open, relaxed town that can be used as a base to explore the surrounding provinces. Neo-colonial buildings line the straight streets that head towards the mountains, often little more than outlines obscured by dust. The center of town is an unexpectedly green plaza with well-preserved Spanish and Italian-style buildings. Most of the city's best old colonial buildings are on La Florida pedestrian mall and Caseros Street, which has the **Cabildo** (city hall), the home of the Uriburu family, San Francisco Church and San Bernardo Convent. The city is hot and glary by day – action begins at dusk, when the pedestrian malls turn into markets that are virtually monopolized by the Bolivians who have been pouring into Salta in recent years.

The north of Argentina is saturated by religion and any visitor to Salta will be surprised by the number of churches and statues of St Francis. In the **cathedral** are the town's pride and joy: the Virgin and Cristo del Milagro, statues carved in the 16th century and credited with miraculous powers. The ship carrying them from Spain was wrecked, but the figures washed up on the Peruvian shore.

BELOW: corn on the cob for sale.

Then in 1692, a sudden earthquake in Salta was dramatically halted when the statues were paraded in the streets. The simple, almost childlike figures are almost lost in the huge baroque altar of the church. Across the aisle, the faithful pray before a life-sized effigy of Christ fresh from the cross, complete with vast holes in his chest and a virtual fountain of fake blood. Depictions of suffering in colonial religious art had to be horrific indeed if they were to impress local indigenous people as worse than much of their own lives.

The museum in the **Cabildo** gives interesting insights into the last few centuries. Most of the rooms are devoted to European-Argentine heroes from the wars of independence, with paintings of their deeds alongside medals, vests and gloves. The Indian section, covering the Incas and customs still alive today, is a collection of pots and pans, dry and unexplained.

For a change of pace, one of the most exciting trips from Salta is to take *El Tren a las Nubes* – the Train to the Clouds. Fully equipped with a dining car, this poetically-named service leaves Salta for a spectacular journey through nearby mountains. In a major feat of engineering, it climbs through the barren **Quebrada del Toro** across steel span bridges to the small town of **San Antonio de los Cobres** at 4,000 meters (13,000 ft) in the Andes, on to its highest point at **Abra Chorrillos** (4,475 meters/14,682 ft) and then to the Chilean frontier at **Socompa** ㊱.

Towards the Bolivian frontier

A highway heads north from Salta to **Jujuy** 🟤. The population becomes more Indian the closer you get to the Bolivian border, while the road gets rougher, the houses poorer and the religious imagery stranger. Tiny chapels can be seen in the most remote villages. One of the most curious, in **Uquaia**, contains the *Angeles Caballeros*: a painting of angels dressed as 17th-century musketeers.

The road climbs to over 3,000 meters (9,800 ft) and the countryside dries out completely along the *quebrada* (gorge) of the **Rio Grande**. Odd land formations appear: some mountains are sharp triangles, others seem to spill like molten lava, while others look like decayed ants' nests. The small town of **Humahuaca** 🟤 is almost in Bolivia. In early afternoon it becomes an empty dust bowl, with winds sweeping from the valleys to cover everything with orange powder. The only sound comes from the 16th-century church. The town has several guest houses and restaurants, and is not far from the extensive archaeological site of **Coctaca**, whose mysteries are still being unraveled.

This small, poor town is dominated by a huge iron monument to Argentina's 19th-century war of independence. An artistic sleight-of-hand has given the fierce figures staring down over Humahuaca Indian faces, brushing over the memory of newly-liberated European settlers who spent the rest of the 19th century wiping out the indigenous people in the rest of the country. The local sense of history is also revealed by the old schoolhouse, which is emblazoned with the sign "Republic of Bolivia". Ask any of the students why and they look at the sign as if for the first time. The school masters are no more helpful. It was a long time ago, they might tell you, perhaps even a century.

"But I only teach European history," they will smile, and walk away.

Map on pages 260–1

BELOW: Jesuit ruins, San Ignacio Miní.

Misiones and the Jesuit ruins

Sticking out like a crooked finger from the northeast of Argentina, the subtropical province of **Misiones** boasts some unexpected associations. Graham Greene used its wet and steamy towns as the setting for his novel *The Honorary Consul,* where expatriate Britons and South American revolutionaries accidentally meet. More recently, the award-winning film *The Mission,* which was shot in the area, publicized the province's 18th-century Jesuit empire.

A linguistic note: we have used the Spanish spelling Iguazú here; but it is Iguaçu in Portuguese and Iguassu – usually – in English.

A visit to the region usually begins in the provincial capital of **Posadas ㊳**, which is accessible from Buenos Aires by daily flights. The town has a handicrafts market, four museums, two casinos and three discos. A highway escapes north from the town into the rich green countryside, kept lush by regular downpours. The road follows the flood-prone **Rio Paraná**.

It was in this same region in the 1600s that the teams of Jesuit priests began setting up their mission stations (*see page 270*). At their height in the 18th century, they housed 100,000 of the local Guaraní Indians, studying, growing grain and carving musical instruments which became renowned in the finest courts of Europe. Today, the ruins of the greatest Jesuit mission at **San Ignacio Miní ㊵**, just a two-hour drive from Posadas, are announced by the unfortunate marriage of a piece of Jesuit art caught in a concrete military bridge, designed by a former province governor. The grounds themselves are more tastefully kept. Busloads of visitors wander amongst the old Jesuit living quarters and cathedral, decorated with Indian carvings of angels and stars. Outside, the priests' gravestones bear simple messages: "Here Lies Father Juan, a good man."

BELOW: Jesuit ruins, San Ignacio.

Other Jesuit ruins can be found nearby, mostly overgrown by jungle. Sitting amongst these shattered relics of their religious empire, it is difficult to contemplate the unusual experiment that flourished here for over 150 years. While indigenous people in the rest of South America were being brutally exploited on plantations, here they were working and learning in a system which has earned the praise of many modern socialist writers. The Jesuit priests distributed grain according to need, and arranged standing Indian armies to keep out slave traders.

Only when the Jesuits were expelled from the Spanish colonies did the fatal flaw of the mission system reveal itself. The priests had ruled a paternalistic order, never training the Indians to run it themselves. With the Jesuits in exile, slave traders were more successful, the crops failed and the Guaraní people fled back into the jungle. Today, the descendants of those same Guaranís have returned to the ruins – this time to sell plastic flutes and feathers to tourists.

Iguazú Falls

The other great attraction of Misiones province is a few hours further up the highway to the border with Brazil: the magnificent **Iguazú Falls ㊶**. They can be reached from the commercial center of **Puerto Iguazú**. This spectacle is one of South America's most extraordinary sights. Millions of gallons of water thunder over the various cascades with such force that most visitors wear raincoats for protection from the violent spray. The falls are divided between Brazil and Argentina – while the Brazilian side is most spectacular, the Argentine side is more pleasant to explore – but to see them properly one must visit both sides. If attempting to do so in a day (which is possible, with some effort), it's best to start out on the Brazilian side. Though more removed from the falling waters, the Brazilian vantage point gives a much more panoramic view of the immense cascade. The light there is best in the morning for photographers.

This side also gives one the best views of the most spectacular section of the falls, the roaring **Devil's Throat**. Fourteen falls combine forces in their 100-meter (350-ft) fall, pounding the water below with such force that there is constantly a huge rainbow-spanned cloud of spray hovering above them. A catwalk on the Brazilian side, reached by a winding foot trail and an elevator, gives more intimate views. Helicopter rides are also available.

Crossing to the Argentine side requires no border formalities. A stop at the Argentine interpretive center can provide much useful information about the falls and surrounding flora and fauna, a service quite lacking on the Brazilian side. A series of catwalks explores the Argentine falls, including one rebuilt in 1988 that takes visitors over the water rushing into **Devil's Gorge**. There are areas where you can swim under the spray of the cascades, but cuticle parasites are sometimes a problem afterwards. It's also possible to climb down a series of trails and stairways to the river below, where a short boat trip takes visitors to the island of San Martin, making a pass close to one of the falls. The climb back up is strenuous, and should be attempted only by those in good shape.

The Argentines have created a national park adjacent to the falls, where there is a jungle trail posted with information, and a bird hide overlooking a swamp. A trek through the park can take most of the day. In the evening, catch a bus to

Map on pages 260–1

Cacique birds' nests.

BELOW:
Iguazú Falls.

The Gaucho

Scattered through the *estancias* of the Argentine hinterland are horsemen wearing a uniform from the country's distant past: black Spanish hats, woven Indian shawls, baggy pants known as *bombachas* and carrying wicked knives called *facónes*. They are the last descendants of a breed of South American cowboys, the *gauchos*. But apart from the visual effect, their lives are a pale shadow of their forebears'.

From the early days of Spanish settlement, individuals disappeared to the countryside and mixed with the indians. Fleeing criminals, escaped slaves and deserting militiamen lived at the fringes of society and were known as *la gente perdida:* the lost people. They developed their own harsh, nomadic lifestyle on the pampas, taming wild horses to ride and slaughtering escaped cattle, while learning how to hunt with the skilful use of lassoes and the *boleadores*: three balls connected by ropes that could wrap around the legs of any run-

ning target. Soon known as *gauchos* – the name may have derived from the indian words for "orphan" – they had a growing reputation for gambling, horsemanship and knife-fighting. Women, called *chinas*, played a subsidiary role in this macho lifestyle. Often kidnapped from settlements, they raised children in small huts indistinguishable from those of the indians.

But in the late 18th century, large tracts of pampas land was distributed to prominent *porteños*. Fences were put up in the grasslands and *gauchos* were seen as little better than cattle thieves. Many grudgingly signed up as ranch hands, working for subsistence wages on the lands they once roamed.

When the British took Buenos Aires in 1806, many *gauchos* were pressed into the army. After independence, they joined up with the private armies of provincial *caudillos*, who allowed them to indulge in their usual drinking, gambling and knife-fighting for several decades without undue molestation. But as the era of civil wars drew to a close, the days of the *gaucho* were numbered. New codes were introduced to regulate their movements, dress, drinking habits and diet. Thousands were pressed into military service.

Soon the *gaucho* was a symbol of the backward, chaotic Argentina that the statesmen of Buenos Aires wanted to destroy. *Gauchos* were described by Domingo Sarmiento as "biped animals of the most perverse stripe" whose carcasses were only good to fertilize the earth. Barbed wire fences hindered their movements still further – the *gaucho* was being eliminated as a distinct social grouping.

As this was happening in the 1870s, José Hernandez wrote in two parts his classic epic poem, *The Gaucho Martin Fierro*, which lamented the passing of the wild frontier past.

By 1926, when the second great literary work on *gauchos* appeared, *Don Segundo Sombra* by Ricardo Guiraldes, the *gaucho* was nothing more than a literary memory. This does not mean to say that there are not glimpses of the lost *gaucho* culture in the Argentina of today. In the furthest reaches of the country, on remote farms in Salta and Patagonia, hands still wear traditional *gaucho* dress – even if they are as likely to be driving a Land-Rover as riding a horse. ❑

LEFT: gaucho on a Buenos Aires *estancia*.

Puerto Canoas, where the day's dying light heightens the beauty of Devil's Gorge as swallows dive into their nests in the walls behind the tumbling water.

Iguazú Falls are best visited in autumn and spring – summers are intensely hot and the busiest time for tourists, while the water level drops considerably in winter. There are hotels on both the Brazilian and Argentine sides. Near the falls a marker shows the point at which Paraguay, Brazil and Argentina all converge.

The only sight capable of crowning the Iguazú experience is **Moconá Falls**, where the River Uruguay falls into itself in a fault more than a kilometer long, not far from the Brazilian town of **Tenente Portela**. For a panoramic view, take a ferry to Brazil from the Argentine town of **El Soberbio**. Boat trips are on offer in the same town for those craving a close-up white-water view.

Bariloche: Switzerland in the Andes

Strategically placed between the towering Andes and the plains of Patagonia, for six months of the year **San Carlos de Bariloche** ⓰ is a booming holiday resort with a unique alpine flavor. Summer brings hordes of travelers enjoying walks amongst the lush forests, spectacular glaciers and mountains of the surrounding Lake District. Later, the winter snows bring South America's select set of affluent skiers to the Andean slopes, filling Bariloche's restaurants by night with raucous fireside carousing. The remaining neglected months of the year are perhaps even more delightful: in spring, the valleys of the Lake District are filled with flowers and greenery, while autumn brings the slow shift of the forest colors to red, orange, cinnamon and ochre.

The alpine atmosphere attracted Swiss, German and Austrian settlers at the end of the 19th century. Today the town itself is a reproduction of a Tyrolean skiing village. Many of the buildings are designed like chalets, while the streets are full of chocolate shops and restaurants offering Swiss fondue, trout and roast venison. But the real attraction is the surrounding countryside. Bariloche's setting, by the shores of **Lake Nahuel Huapi**, surrounded by jagged brown mountains, is spectacular. In the distance you can spot the towering **Mount Tronador**, the highest peak in the region at 3,554 meters (11,728 ft).

Begin your visit by going to the **Patagonian Museum** near the **Civic Center**. It relates the region's history from the days when indigenous nomads roamed the countryside, covered from head to toe in animal grease for warmth, to the arrival of the first white pioneers. Outside in the square is a statue of General Roca, leader of the desert campaign which led to the virtual extermination of local tribes.

Dozens of tour companies offer visits to the surrounding attractions – alternatively, you can hire a car in Bariloche to explore the dirt roads and byways of this magnificent region on the border of Chile. The *circuito chico* or "short circuit" runs out along Lake Nahuel Huapi to the **Llao Llao Hotel**. Recently refurbished and reopened after years of neglect, it reflects the glory of its heyday in the 1940s. Boats run from the docks of Bariloche to **Isla Victoria**, whose myrtle forests are said to have inspired some of Walt Disney's advisers when drawing backgrounds for *Bambi*.

Map on pages 260–1

Iguazú means Great Waters in Guaraní – a fitting name for the most spectacular waterfalls in the western hemisphere. Taller than Niagara Falls by 20 meters and twice as wide, Iguazú Falls consists of 275 cascades over a gulf of nearly 3 km.

BELOW: St Bernard dogs in front of the Centro Cívico, Bariloche.

Ski school plaque, Bariloche.

Continuing around the circuit is the path to **Cerro Lopez**. In summer, the peak can be climbed to a refuge run by Club Andino, where hikers can stay overnight. On a clear day the Cerro offers spectacular views over the lakes and mountains of the region to Chile. Day trips can also be taken from Bariloche to **Cerro Tronador**, **Cerro Catedral**, **Cerro Otto** and the waterfalls of **Los Cesares**. The region is world-famous for its trout fishing from November to March, and in summer there is sailing and windsurfing on the lakes.

Exploring the wild countryside

Also passing through some of the world's most magnificent scenery is the so-called route of the seven lakes, which winds along the border with Chile. It leads to the small town of **San Martín de los Andes ㊸**, a more upmarket tourist destination than Bariloche, often used as a base for hikes, camping trips and skiing. The return trip over the **Córdoba Pass** runs through the lower regions of Neuquen province, much drier and closer to the Patagonian wastes. Fingers of stone protrude from thorny expanses, in what one English traveler in 1920 compared to the prehistoric *Lost World* imagined by novelist Sir Arthur Conan Doyle. Many of the *estancias* or ranches of the region are still English-run and worked by Chilean *peons* (farm hands) or weather-beaten gauchos, whose ponchos, knives and *bombachas* are definitely not worn just for tourists.

For a longer excursion, an overnight trip can be made to **El Bolsón**, once a hippy refuge of the 1960s, now a tourist and fishing resort with a twice-weekly handicrafts market. Further south, a road cuts through the serene **Cholila Valley** to **Esquel ㊹**. First settled by the Welsh, it is now the base for visiting **Los Alerces National Park** and the gateway to the **Chubut Valley**. Standing by the

BELOW: Lake Nahuel Huapi and Cerro López.

shores of the lake is **Estancia Nahuel Huapi**, founded by a Texan cowboy named Jared Jones in 1889. The house, which is still standing, was a refuge for Butch Cassidy and the Sundance Kid, on the run from the Argentine authorities, having brought their Wild West ways to the new frontier of Patagonia in the early 1900s. Today the pioneer's granddaughter runs horseback-riding trips into the remotest regions of her family property.

Wild, windswept Patagonia

Way down at the chilly southern end of South America, Patagonia has for centuries been a byword for the remote and the strange. But today Patagonia is linked to Buenos Aires with daily flights, and by bus for those with enough time to fully appreciate the size of this flat, empty plain that takes up one-third of the country's landmass. Heading south, the rich cattle country dries out and becomes divided into sheep stations. As recently as the 19th century some of these ranches were bigger than small European countries, with their owners ruling like royalty. Many are still run by the descendants of the original British owners, who continue to speak English in preference to Spanish.

First stop is the city of **Trelew** ㊺, surrounded by dry bluffs and dusty scrub. Thousands of Welsh colonists came here after 1865, fleeing their homeland, where their culture and language was being repressed by the English, to set up a "Little Wales" in the middle of nowhere. Despite some early disasters, the colony began to succeed. The Welsh used their irrigation skills to make the desert bloom, and soon Patagonian wheat was winning prizes at international shows. Welsh was spoken in the streets and taught in the schools.

But by the turn of the century, things were already going awry in Trelew.

Map on pages 260–1

BELOW LEFT: lady from the Welsh colony of Chubut. **BELOW RIGHT:** a Patagonian *peon* (farm labourer).

The Argentine government had imposed its authority on the town and many Spanish-speaking immigrants, attracted by the Welsh success, had arrived with their families. Floods devastated the area's crops. Many settlers left for Canada or Australia, but the core of the community stayed on, their Welsh nationalism slowly being diluted by intermarriage with Spanish speakers. Today, Trelew looks much like other provincial Argentine towns, although the street signs are still in Welsh. Echoes of its origins can be found in the old **Hotel Touring Club,** with cracked windows and an antique wooden bar full of old men playing chess on quiet afternoons. Many of the town's elders still speak in their native Welsh to one another, using Spanish when necessary. For a taste of the Welsh colony as it once was, take a half-hour bus ride to the village of **Gaiman**. Built around the irrigation canals that converted the desert into an oasis, Gaiman has a number of Welsh tea houses serving up Welsh cream pastries to passing visitors. A small museum is run by local historian Señora Tegai Roberts, who can chat just as happily in English, Welsh or Spanish.

The Portuguese explorer Fernando Magellan, the first European to see Patagonia, reported it to be full of dog-headed monsters and natives with steaming heads.

Whales and frontier towns

Easily reached from Trelew is the famous **Península Valdés** ㊻, which boasts some of the world's most peculiar wildlife. Charles Darwin spent weeks here on his famous journey in the *Beagle*, and today tourists come to watch the sealions yawning by the rocky shore and hundreds of penguins wandering in lines to the sea. During September and October, enormous right whales can be seen throwing up their tail fins as they mate dramatically off shore.

Flying south from Trelew, the Patagonian plain below looks increasingly desolate. Towns like **Comodoro Rivadavia** ㊼, once center of a brief oil boom, and

BELOW: rounding up sheep, Patagonia.

Río Gallegos ④ 3,000 km (2,000 miles) south of Buenos Aires, are devoid of rural charm. Unfortunately, because most flights pass through here, many travelers end up spending a night. Nothing much has happened since 1905, when Butch Cassidy and the Sundance Kid held up a bank on the main street.

Changing to a small propeller-driven plane in Río Gallegos, a one-hour flight cuts west across the plains to the foothills of the Andes and some of the most magnificent scenery in South America. The village of **El Calafate** ④ is surrounded with snowcapped mountain peaks and sits next to **Lago Argentino**, which seems to be full of turquoise milk rather than water. This remote village is enjoying a boom as the stepping-off point to the huge blue glaciers wedged in the forest-covered countryside nearby.

The most famous is **Perito Moreno** ⑤, a 160-ft (50-meter) high wall of ice which cuts through a lake. It cracks and growls throughout the day, with enormous chunks of ice regularly falling from its side to send waves of water thundering to the shore. The glacier is still advancing in four year cycles. Blocking off part of the lake, the water level rises until the glacial wall collapses in a spectacular scene that lasts for several hours.

From Calafate you can visit the sheep *estancias* of Argentina's deep south, where the occasional gaucho figure still works. Sheep-raising is a key industry in Patagonia, and between October and January, traveling teams of workers arrive for the shearing season. **La Anita** became notorious in 1921, when the whole of Patagonia was paralyzed by a strike of farmhands, known as *peons*. The organizer was a young Spanish anarchist named Antonio Soto, who had wandered through the Buenos Aires stage to Patagonia. The mostly British *estancieros* called on the government for help, and the army ended the strike,

Map on pages 260–1

Steaks for an asado.

BELOW: the Perito Moreno glacier.

with bouts of shooting followed by mass executions. One of the biggest of these was at La Anita – although it has since changed hands, and hardly anybody remembers where the 200 or so workers are even buried.

Located a few hours from Calafate is the **Fitzroy National Park**, where you can pass from the windswept plains to lush and wet forest amongst the snow-capped Andes. Hikes through the park cross mountain streams and landscapes reminiscent of Scottish moors. Clouds are constantly billowing overhead, but on a good day you can often catch a glimpse of Mount Fitzroy, a sheer knife of granite that is a favorite with fearless mountaineers.

Tierra del Fuego: last stop before Antarctica

It is the forbidding image of Tierra del Fuego that paradoxically lures travelers to the southernmost tip of South America. It was named "land of fire" by Magellan, who saw mysterious fires in the darkness when first passing the island.

For centuries afterwards, Tierra del Fuego was feared by sailors for the icy Antarctic winds that blew their ships towards jagged rocks. Few of them considered **Ushuaia** ➎, the world's most southerly town, an attractive refuge from the storms. Over the years it progressed from a primitive whaling station to a prison colony where Russian anarchists eked out their last days. Today, the land at the end of the world can be reached by daily flights from Buenos Aires. Ushuaia is no longer the wild outpost it once was, but an odd blend of modern tourist center, Klondike-style boomtown and the gateway to one of the world's last great wilderness areas.

The northern half of the island is flat sheep farming land – much like the rest of Patagonia – but the south is rugged and thickly forested. Approaching

BELOW: penguin colony at Punto Tombo, near Trelew.

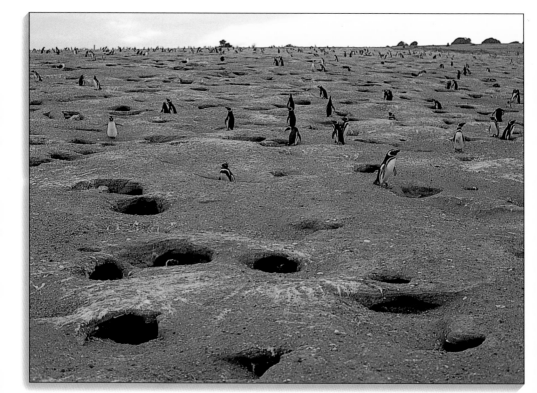

Ushuaia by plane is suitably dramatic, since the town is surrounded by snow-capped claws of granite. The dominating peak, **Mount Olivia**, would suit a Walt Disney wicked witch for its mist-shrouded and vaguely evil appearance. The weather lives up to Tierra del Fuego's reputation: even during the 20 or more hours of summer daylight, it shifts erratically from cold drizzle to perfectly cloudless skies, with the only constant being a gusty southern wind.

Ushuaia itself is far from being a picturesque pioneering town. The Argentine government has subsidized its development and new suburbs are being flung up everywhere. The main street is like an open-air department store, with duty-free electronic goods being offered from the new factories outside town. One of the town's claims to fame is the Bank of Tierra del Fuego, which is the world's first financial institution to have a branch in Antarctica.

This hubbub of development has created a new tourist infrastructure, with new hotels and restaurants, but the **Café Ideal** maintains the flavor of old Ushuaia. In a corrugated iron building, its walls are covered with photos of famous visitors, and next to the television set is a huge whale vertebra. Seafood is standard fare, with the local specialty being *centolla* or king crab. The **Beagle Channel**, on which the town sits, was named after the boat that carried Charles Darwin here in the 1830s for his famous wildlife studies. Boat trips can be taken on the channel past mountains dropping sheer into the water, circling islands populated by penguins or sea lions.

Windswept wilderness

The **Tierra del Fuego National Park** is now the main attraction of Ushuaia because of its easily accessible wilderness area. The walking here is simply

Map on pages 260–1

BELOW: Ushuaia, the world's south-ernmost town.

Map on pages 260–1

At one time Argentina had 80 million sheep and was one of the world's largest wool producers. Today only 30 million remain.

BELOW: a group of Ona Indians, before they were wiped out by settlers. **RIGHT:** sleepy elephant seal.

magnificent, following the spectacular coastline to lakes and glaciers. The park preserves the sense of being at the end of the world, with paths that wind around spongy moss oozing cold water, past tough shrubs and thorny bushes and trees which the wind has bent 45 degrees. The path to **Bahia Ensenada** passes an encouraging altar to the Virgin of Lujan, Argentina's patron saint of travelers. There is a camping ground at the rocky beach, where you can breakfast on sweet calafate berries, the mere taste of which is said to guarantee future return to Tierra del Fuego. Stepping stones lead to **Bahia Lapataia**, where you can pick fresh mussels from the sea. A picturesque narrow-gauge train will take you into the Tierra del Fuego National Park along a route formerly used to transport prison inmates to cut timber for houses.

Just three hours' drive from Ushuaia along a winding dirt road is the first *estancia* on Tierra del Fuego, **Harberton** (*see below*). Founded by the Rev. Thomas Bridges in 1888, it is open to tourists, with guides in English and Spanish. Harberton is worth visiting not just for its history but for the beauty of its setting. Surrounded by trees and flowers, perched above the blue Beagle Channel, the estancia seems like the calmest place on earth.

Back in Ushuaia, the bookshops are full of books on the local indigenous people, but they are dull, anthropological works written as if they were still wandering around the countryside. The rumors of murders are denied or forgotten, with only a few scraps suggesting the contrary: a ledger showing that only women and children were brought back from raids; a photo in a Liverpool newspaper showing a mass grave found by police.

The final certainty of the destruction of these tribes is that the only fires now burning in Tierra del Fuego are from the oil rigs off its coast. ❏

A GRISLY PAST

The good Reverend Thomas Bridges spent much of his time in Harberton in the late 19th century working with the local indians and writing a dictionary of the complex Yaghan language. To his dismay, he could see before his death that the lists of words would soon be the only monument to those who spoke them. As the British writer Bruce Chatwin noted, Darwin's theory of "survival of the fittest" was put into brutal practice in the 1890s. The indigenous people of the area, who had lit the fires that Magellan saw, occasionally killed and ate the sheep brought onto their land by European settlers. The newcomers decided to remove this "pest" en masse. Official records show that most of the indigenous people died of disease, but the folk memory persists of active resistance, battles and massacres.

The most grisly tale is of white bounty hunters being paid £1 sterling for each pair of Indian ears they brought back from the wilderness. Old-timers tell of such gruesome characters as the Scotsman Alex MacLennan, nicknamed the Red Pig, famous for his drunken ravings about killing indians. The Englishman Sam Hyslop, who is credited with gunning down 80 people of the Ona tribe, was caught by indians and flung from a cliff.

THE FALKLAND ISLANDS

These tiny, windswept islands in the South Atlantic were at the center of a violent international conflict less than two decades ago. Now peace has returned to the sheep pastures and penguin colonies

Some 500 km (300 miles) off the coast of Argentina, the Falkland Islands offer the type of treeless, windswept, austerely beautiful landscapes similar to the Orkney and Shetland Islands in Scotland. Like Scotland, the islands offer all four seasons in one day, with sun, wind and rain coming and going in a matter of minutes; also similar to Scotland are the hills and valleys uncharacteristic of flat Patagonia. There are southern desert-like landscapes, tall grass and wild flowers, though in places the scenery is marred by signs warning of minefields left over from the 1982 war (some 17,000 mines remain in certain areas).

With a total area of some 12,000 sq. km (4,633 sq. miles), the islands have a population of around 2,600 *kelpers*, or residents, with 500,000 sheep, as well as penguins, geese, whales and seals for company. Some 1,500 *kelpers* live in the capital, **Port Stanley**, known as Puerto Argentino to the Argentines who claim sovereignty over the islands. The few hundred youngsters who live outside the capital attend school by radio, with teachers visiting two weeks each year.

Disputed territory

The Falklands and South Georgia Islands have been in British hands since 1833, although Argentina has been firm in demanding sovereignty for over a century, on the grounds that the islands were taken from Spain by the British and that after Argentine independence from Spain, they should technically have reverted to their perceived position as part of Argentine territory. Claims by various European powers had always been doubtful and frequently shifting since the first reported sightings of the uninhabited islands in the late 16th century, although since its independence Argentina has never wavered from its claim that "las Malvinas son Argentinas". The area became strategically important to the rest of the world only in the latter part of the 20th century, given that the islands offer a claim both to Antarctic territory and to offshore oil deposits which have become increasingly exploitable with modern technology.

The horrendous 1982 war between the UK and Argentina followed an invasion first of South Georgia and then of the Falklands by troops sent by alcoholic Argentine dictator Leopoldo Galtieri. The war brought about the deaths of 655 Argentines, many of them conscripts, and 255 British troops. Thereafter, the attitude of the *kelpers* (universally of British origin) to Argentine sovereignty claims hardened still further, not unnaturally, with distrust of Argentine politicians reaching new heights. Communications with Argentina were cut off, and to date the islands are inaccessible from Argentina, or to anyone who holds an Argentine passport. Exceptions are made for

PRECEDING PAGES: Windswept solitude in the Falkland Islands.
BELOW: Magellanic penguins.

occasional visits organised for the relatives of dead Argentine soldiers buried in the islands at Darwin Cemetery, near the site of the battle of Goose Green. The remains of an Argentine fighter aircraft also lie at Goose Green.

Despite the traumatic experience of the invasion and the strong rejection of post-war Argentine overtures by the *kelpers*, the economic life of the islands improved after the war, not just because of oil exploration. A permanent garrison of some 2,000 troops has been based in Mount Pleasant since that time, a new airport, hospital and secondary school have been installed, and average annual income is now around US$20,000, a 700 percent increase over pre-war levels. Economic life centres on fishing (this includes fishing licences to foreign ships operating in the islands' 150-mile exclusion zone), agriculture and services, especially tourism, which benefits from spectacular wildlife. Agricultural lands were sub-divided and sold by the Falkland Islands Development Corporation after the war, and are now in the hands of some 90 farmers.

The islands cannot be reached from Argentina, but flights are available on Figas (Falkland Islands Government Air Service) and other services from Punta Arenas in southern Chile. Cruises are also available from Uruguay in spring and summer. The Falklands have only one paved road, from Mount Pleasant airport to Port Stanley, a picturesque town noted for its Englishness, with neatly painted houses framed by lawns and flower beds, and three churches. Port Stanley has one hotel, plus restaurants and bars, though there are no theatres for plays or movies. It also has virtually the only trees in the islands, brought from abroad and laboriously protected from the winds which constantly batter the islands. The port, with its windbreak hill backdrop, steadfastly faces the treacherous Southern Ocean and the still visible wreckage of old fishing vessels. ❑

The islands took their English name from the Falkland Sound, named after a British peer in 1690. Seventeenth-century French seafarers named the islands Les Isles Malouines ("Malvinas" in Spanish) after their St Malo home.

BELOW: Carcass Island settlement, Falklands.
OVERLEAF: heading for home, Ecuador.

Travel Tips

Insight Guides portray destinations in depth, providing the complete picture and the top photography

Insight Pocket Guides *focus on the best choices for places to see and things to do and include large fold-out maps*

Insight Compact Guides *portability makes them the perfect books to carry with you for on-the-spot reference*

Three types of guide for all types of travel

INSIGHT GUIDES Different people need different kinds of information. Some want *background information* to help them prepare for the trip. Others seek *personal recommendations* from someone who knows the destination well. And others look for *compactly presented data* for on-the-spot reference. With three carefully designed series, Insight Guides offer readers the perfect choice. Insight Guides will turn your visit into an experience.

The world's largest collection of visual travel guides

CONTENTS

Getting Acquainted

In South America, temperature depends greatly on altitude above sea-level, and temperate climates can be found among mountain landscapes away from the coast. Hot temperatures tend to prevail throughout the year in the lowlands, mainly along the coast. The **Colombian highlands**, for example, has moderate weather all year round, while the coast is tropical. The only seasons here are wet and dry, varying per region.

Venezuela has a tropical climate with average temperatures of 27°C (80°F). Four climatic zones are represented within its boundaries: hot, mild, cool and cold.

The rainy season lasts from mid-May until the end of October, but showers may fall in December or January. In Caracas, the January average temperature is 18.6°C (65°F), rising to 21°C (70°F) in July.

Peru's coastline has average temperatures of between 14°–27°C (58°–80°F), while in the highlands – or sierra – it is normally cold, sunny and dry for much of the year, with temperatures ranging from 9°–18°C (48°–65°F). The rainy season in the sierra is from December to May. The jungle is hot and humid with temperatures ranging from 25°–28°C (77°–82°F).

Lima alone suffers from the climatic condition the Peruvians call *garua* – a thick wet fog that covers the city without respite for the winter.

Ecuador's regions each have a distinct climate. The coast is hottest and wettest from January to April. The mountains are driest, and clearest between June and September, and in December. The

Oriente is usually inundated with rain between June and August, followed by a drier season until December. As on the coast, however, a torrential downpour is never out of the question.

In **Bolivia**, the average temperature in the highlands – the most popular area to visit – is 10°C (50°F). Rain falls heavily from November to March here, but May to November is very dry. The average temperatures in La Paz are between 6°–21°C (42°–70°F) during summer and 0°–17°C (32°–63°F) in winter.

In **Brazil**'s jungle region, the climate is humid equatorial, with high temperatures and humidity, and heavy rainfall all year round. The eastern Atlantic coast of Brazil, from Rio Grande do Norte to the state of São Paulo, has a humid tropical climate, also hot, but with slightly less rainfall than in the north and with summer and winter seasons. Most of Brazil's interior has a semi-humid tropical climate, with a hot, rainy summer from December to March and a drier, cooler winter (June to August).

Part of the interior of the northeast has a tropical semi-arid climate – hot with sparse rainfall. Most of the rain falls during three months, usually March–May. The average temperature in the northeast is 24°–27°C (75°–80°F).

Brazil's south, below the Tropic of Capricorn, has a humid subtropical climate. Rainfall is distributed regularly throughout the year and temperatures vary from 0°–10°C (30°–40°F) in winter, with occasional frosts and snowfall (but the latter is rare) to 21°–32°C (70°–80°F) in summer.

Paraguay has a subtropical climate. Summers (December to February) are very hot and humid; spring and fall are milder. In winter (June to August) temperatures can drop to 5°C (41°F) but it never snows.

Chile's central valley (Santiago, Valparaíso, Viña del Mar) has a Mediterranean climate with summer (January and February) averaging 28°C (82°F), and in winter 10°C (50°F). Evenings are cool and it

rains in winter but the weather is generally pleasant.

On the coast, it is humid, cloudy and windy, so it feels colder than inland. The lake district has a pleasant temperate climate, but winds can be chilly. The mountains are cold and it rains a lot. Patagonia is almost always cold. Fog, rain and high winds are not uncommon even in the summer.

In **Uruguay** fertile grasslands alternate with wooded hill country and lush river valleys. The climate is temperate. June, July and August can be quite cold and damp. Spring (September, October, November) and fall (March, April, May) are pleasant; summers (December, January, February) are hot but tempered by the cool Atlantic breezes.

Most of **Argentina** lies within the temperate zone of the southern hemisphere. The northeastern part is very humid and subtropical but has a mild winter. The pampas are temperate while the southern part of the country has colder temperatures and rain most of the year.

Rainfall varies in the humid pampas (which comprises the province of Buenos Aires, and some of the Córdoba and La Pampa provinces) from 99 cm (39 inches) in the eastern parts to about 51 cm (20 inches) near the Andes.

Consult your local public health service before leaving and be sure to get a certificate for any vaccination you have. The most common illnesses are picked up from contaminated food and water, so you should pay particular attention to what you eat and drink.

The quality of tap **water** in much of South America is unreliable, though it is probably safe to drink in most cities. As a rule, however, you are advised to drink only bottled water, or to take purifying tablets.

Hepatitis, picked up from contaminated food and water, is common, and all travelers should get immunized against the disease.

Malaria occurs in jungle areas of South America, so you should take anti-malaria tablets if you are visiting any part of the Amazon.

Yellow fever, transmitted to humans by mosquitoes, is prevalent in the whole of South America except Chile, Argentina and Uruguay. You are therefore advised to seek immunization. A yellow fever shot protects you for 10 years, but is effective only after 10 days, so plan ahead. You may be asked to show your yellow fever vaccination certificate if arriving from a country where yellow fever is endemic.

Your doctor should be able to advise you about other tropical diseases that may be endemic in the area you are visiting – such as dengue fever and Chaga's disease. All travelers should check that they are inoculated against tetanus, typhoid and polio.

You should take some form of remedy for **stomach upsets** and **diarrhoea,** which is likely to be the main complaint of most travelers. Immodium is a popular travel companion, but note that this medication treats the symptoms and not the cause. The other main cause of illness is the **heat.** Have respect for the power of the tropical sun: wear a hat and be sure to drink plenty of fluids.

Altitude sickness Travelers planning to spend time in the Andes should be aware of the dangers of altitude sickness. Anyone arriving by air in La Paz, for example, is likely to need several days to acclimatize.

Acute mountain sickness (called *puno*) is totally unpredictable – even the fittest people can be affected – and the only solution is to go back to a lower altitude as fast as you can. If you must continue, rest for a few days, drink lots of fluids but do not smoke or consume any alcohol.

Security and Crime

The crime rate is generally high in South America, although risks can be minimized by taking a few basic precautions. Jewelry should not be worn and large amounts of money and expensive watches should be kept out of sight. Keep an eye on your possessions at all times and make use of hotel safes whenever possible. Do not leave valuables in cars. Avoid walking alone and in deserted areas after dark.

Colombia is part of a major drug-smuggling route. Do not carry packages for other people without checking the contents.

The crime rate in **Venezuela,** particularly in Caracas, is high. You should not walk alone in narrow streets in downtown Caracas after dark and it is strongly recommended that you do not travel by car at night, particularly in the countryside where, should you have an accident or breakdown, the risk of robbery and other crimes is much greater.

Petty crime is now rife in the urban centers of **Peru.** Pickpockets and thieves are common in Lima and Cuzco and are amazingly adept at slitting open shoulder bags, camera cases and knapsacks. Officials also warn against dealing with anyone approaching you in the hotel lobby or on the street, allegedly representing a travel agency or specialty shop.

A special security service for tourists has been created by Peru's Civil Guard. They are recognizable by a white braid worn across the shoulder of their uniforms and can be found all over Lima, especially in the downtown area. In Cuzco, all police have tourism police training. The tourist police office in Lima is at Avenida Salaverry 1156, tel: 714-313.

There has been much publicity about terrorism in Peru. It is recommended that tourists avoid areas where there are terrorism alerts or border disputes with Ecuador or Bolivia. For specific inquiries, contact your embassy.

Money Matters

Travelers' checks in US dollars are the safest and most convenient form of currency, acceptable all over South America. Sterling and other currencies are not worth bringing (except if you are visiting French Guiana, whose currency is the French franc, or the Falkland Islands, where sterling is used).

Photography

Film is much more expensive than in the West, so stock up before you go. If you need to buy some once traveling, check the expiry date first.

Note that it is forbidden for military sites (including ports, transport terminals and bridges) to be photographed. It is best to ask permission, if you are unsure.

Many people, particularly from indigenous cultures, are sensitive about having their portraits taken, so ask first.

Changing money You can change money in banks, *casas de cambio* (exchange bureaus) and larger hotels; *casas de cambio* usually give the best rate of exchange. Take checks and cash in a variety of large and small denominations since exchange rates in some countries can change dramatically overnight; and bring only notes in optimum condition as some exchange bureaus can be sniffy about old notes. It is worth bringing a pocket calculator as some rates of exchange run into the thousands.

Cash You will always need to carry some cash with you, of course, and should think ahead of you are traveling into a rural area for some time. But try not to exceed the amount of cash covered in your insurance policy.

Credit and debit cards are also widely accepted, with ATMs (cash machines) in most cities. Before leaving home, check your PIN number, handling fees and cover in the event of loss or robbery. Many establishments also add their own supplementary charges.

Safety Great care should be taken with your money; try to carry it out of sight under your clothes when traveling. If your hotel is trustworthy, leave your money and valuables in the hotel safe (but always take a verified list of what you have deposited).

See the separate Money section under each country for more

details; rates of exchange given are correct in late 1998.

Finally, it is worth remembering the much-quoted advice: pack half the clothes you think you'll need, but twice the money.

Shopping

Much of South America's best bargains are still to be found in the local markets, particularly in the Andean countries, where prices are low and the choice of goods extensive. Jewelry, textiles, jumpers, ponchos and leather goods are all widely produced. A certain amount of haggling is expected but be careful not to go too far. Only too often you hear tales of people stomping off in a huff because a trader refused to cut the price of an item by the equivalent of $1.

Venezuela's craftsmen hold a prestigious position because of the variety and quality of their workmanship. Outstanding Quibor ceramics have pre-Hispanic origins, molded using styles and techniques handed down through the generations. Baskets, hammocks, hats and other products made from vegetable fibers are to be found in the towns and villages along the Easter Coast. Beautifully woven ponchos, colorful blankets and caps are sold by the Andean people while craftsmen of the *llanos* (prairies) sell four-string guitar-like musical instruments called *cuatros* as well as harps and mandolins.

Bolivia likewise produces a wide range of craft work, including tapestries, woolen clothing and wooden sculptures. And **Peru** is also known for the quality of its handicrafts, as well as its bargain gold, copper and silver items.

Colombia specializes in emeralds and leather goods, but if you're looking for a number of different gemstones, **Brazil**'s tremendous variety is unmatched, and prices are low. If you're not an expert gemologist, it's wise to buy from a reliable jeweler. The three leading jewelers operating nationwide are H. Stern, Amsterdam Sauer and Roditi,

but there are other reliable smaller chains. The top jewelers have shops in the airports, shopping centers and in most hotels. Leather goods are another good buy in Brazil; the finest leather comes from the south.

Chile's open, import-oriented free market economy offers a selection of just about anything you want to buy, but also produces some fine copper ornaments and lapis lazuli jewelry.

Ecuador is reknowned as the home of the Panama hat and also for its colorful balsawood carvings, while **Paraguay** is famous for its *Ñandutí* (*guaraní* for cobweb) lace, used to decorate bedcovers, tablecloths, mantillas, etc. Other good buys are guitars and harps, gold and silver filigree jewelry, tooled leather, and ponchos of cotton and wool.

Be careful when buying wool as *vicuña* is an endangered species and selling its wool is against international law.

Planning the Trip

Getting There

BY AIR

There are many flights from North America and Europe to all destinations in South America. Many European airlines operate connections from other European cities to link up with the long-haul flight from their own gateway, and the same applies within the US and for the major Latin American airlines (particularly Aerolíneas Argentinas, Avianca and Varig).

Argentina
From Europe: with British Airways, Iberia, Aerolíneas Argentinas, KLM, Swissair, Air France, Alitalia, Varig (via Rio or São Paulo), Avianca (via Bogotá), Vasp (via São Paulo), Cubana (via Havana).
From/via US: American Airlines and United Airlines.
From Australasia: Aerolíneas Argentinas (from Sydney and Auckland).

Bolivia
From Europe: Varig (via Rio or São Paulo), Aerolíneas Argentinas (via Buenos Aires), Vasp (via São Paulo).
From/via US: Lloyd Aéreo Boliviano (LAB), and American Airlines fly direct from Miami and New York to La Paz.
Within South America: AeroPeru flies regularly from Lima to La Paz. LanChile flies from Santiago and Arica, LAB from Caracas. Some flights also call at Santa Cruz or Cochabamba.

Brazil
From Europe: you can fly to Rio and São Paulo with British Airways, Iberia, KLM, Air France, TAP, Alitalia, Swissair, Transbrasil, Varig, Vasp,

Air Passes

If you are planning to cover large distances and time is short, consider buying one of the air passes that most Latin American airlines offer, covering one or a combination of countries. These passes usually work out cheaper than buying individual flights locally. They must be bought outside the country concerned, in conjunction with your transatlantic flight. Airpasses are currently available for Argentina (Aerolíneas Argentinas), Bolivia (Aerosur), Brazil (Transbrasil, Varig, Vasp), Chile (LanChile), Colombia (Avianca), Peru (Aeroperu) and Venezuela (Avensa/Servivensa).

Avianca (via Bogotá) and Cubana (via Havana). Varig, TAP and Transbrasil also fly to Recife and Salvador (via São Paulo on Transbrasil and Varig).
From/via US: to Rio and São Paulo with American Airlines, Continental Airlines, Delta, United Airlines, Transbrasil and Varig. To Manaus with LAB and Varig, and to Belo Horizonte with American Airlines.

Chile
From Europe: with British Airways, Air France, Iberia, KLM, Swissair, Alitalia, LanChile, Aerolíneas Argentinas (via Buenos Aires), Cubana (via Havana), Varig (via Rio or Sao Paulo), Avianca (via Bogotá).
From/via US: with American Airlines, Continental Airlines and United Airlines.
From Australasia: with Aerolíneas Argentinas from Sydney and Auckland (via Buenos Aires); with LanChile (via Easter Island).

Colombia
From Europe: with Air France, KLM, Alitalia, British Airways and TAP.
From/via US: American Airlines, Continental, United and Avianca.

Ecuador
From Europe: with Air France, KLM, Iberia and Lufthansa, Avianca (via Bogotá) and Cubana (via Havana).
From/via US: American Airlines and Continental Airlines.

French Guiana
From Europe: with AOM (via Paris).
From/via US: with Air France. Also via San Juan, Puerto Rico; Port au Prince, Haiti and Fort de France, Martinique.

Guyana
From Europe and US: British West Indian Airlines (via Port of Spain).

Paraguay
Aerolíneas Argentinas, American Airlines, Iberia, Air France, Ladeco, Lapsa (Paraguay's state airline), Lloyd Aéreo Boliviano (the cheapest), Pluna and Varig all travel to Paraguay.

Peru
From Europe: with Aeroflot, Alitalia, Iberia, KLM and Lufthansa; also Aerolíneas Argentinas (via Buenos Aires), Avianca (via Bogota), Varig (via Rio) and Cubana (via Havana).
From/via US: American Airlines, Continental Airlines, United Airlines, Aeroperú. Also to Cuzco with American Airlines, and to Iquitos with American Airlines and Aeroperú.

Surinam
From Europe: with Surinam Airlines (via Amsterdam).
From/via US: with Surinam Airlines.

Uruguay
From Europe: with Iberia, Varig (via Rio/Sao Paulo), and Aerolíneas Argentinas (via Buenos Aires).
From/via US: with American Airlines and United Airlines.

Arriving by Boat

An unusual alternative to flying is to travel by boat. You can join a cargo ship in either England or the US. For further information contact Strand Voyages, Charing Cross Shopping Concourse, London WC2N 4HZ, tel: 0171-836 6363, fax: 0171-497 0078.

Venezuela
From Europe: with British Airways, Air France, Alitalia, Iberia, KLM, Lufthansa, TAP and Avianca.
From/via the US: with American Airlines, Continental Airlines, United Airlines and Servivensa.

Tour Operators

In the United Kingdom:
Encounter Overland, adventure group tours. Tel: (0171) 370 6845; e-mail: www.encounter.co.uk
Exodus, adventure group tours, tel: (0181) 673 0859; e-mail: www.exodustravels.co.uk
Explore Worldwide, adventure group tours. Tel: (01252) 344161; e-mail: www.explore.co.uk
Journey Latin America, flights and tours. Tel: (0181) 747 3108; fax: (0181) 742 1312; e-mail: sales@journeylatinamerica.co.uk
South American Experience, flights and tailor-made itineraries. Tel: (0171) 976 5511; fax: (0171) 976 6908; e-mail: sax@mcmail.com
STA, specialists in student and under 26 fares, tours and hotels. Tel: (0171) 361 6114; e-mail: www.statravel.co.uk
Trailfinders, Longhaul and trans-atlantic flights, tel: (0171) 938 3366/937 5400.
Trips Worldwide, specialists in tours to the Guianas. Tel: (0117) 987 2626; fax: (0117) 987 2627; e-mail: post@trips.demon.co.uk.

In the United States
South American Explorers Club 126 Indian Creek Road, Ithaca, NY. Tel: (607) 277-0488; e-mail: explorer@samexpo.org

What to Pack

Take light summer clothes if heading for tropical zones. Note that shorts are frowned on in churches. In the highlands, a sweater should suffice in the evenings. Take a thick raincoat and woollen clothing if heading up into high mountain areas.

Rechargeable batteries and the recharger are useful for electrical equipment.

Argentina A – Z

Getting Acquainted

Area 1,074,000 sq. miles. (2,780,400 sq. km).
Capital Buenos Aires.
Population 35 million.
Language Spanish.
Currency Peso; US$1 = 1 peso, £1=1.6 peso.
Weights & measures Metric.
Electricity 220 volts.
Time zone GMT –3hrs, EST +2hrs.
Dialing code 54 (Buenos Aires +1).

Government & Economy

The Republic of Argentina is made up of 24 provinces. The government is a Federal Republic with a senate and chamber of deputies and a president as head of state.

Argentina is one of the world's richest farming economies: agriculture and livestock production provides over 50 percent of export earnings.

The manufacturing sector is also well-developed and the country is virtually self-sufficient in oil.

Embassies & Consulates

The following are in Buenos Aires:
Australia: Villanueva 1400, tel: 777-6580.
Canada: Tagle 2828, tel: 805-3032.
Ireland: Suipacha 1380 (2nd floor), tel: 325-8588.
Great Britain: Dr Luis Agote 2412/52, tel: 803-7070
United States: Colombia 4300, tel: 777-4533.

Public Holidays

- ● **January** 1
- ● **Easter:** Holy Thursday and Good Friday
- ● **May** 1, 25
- ● **June** 10, 20
- ● **July** 9
- ● **August** 17
- ● **October** 12
- ● **December** 8, 25

Visas

Tourists coming to Argentina must have their valid country passports; a visa is not necessary for citizens of the US and Western Hemisphere countries (excluding Cuba) and Japan, who can stay for three months.

In some cases a tourist card is all that is required which must be verified with a travel agent. Citizens of bordering countries of Brazil, Chile, Paraguay and Uruguay only need their ID cards.

Money

It is not a good idea to change money on the street – use *casas de cambio* where possible. There is no market rate, only an official exchange rate which is listed in the main daily newspapers. It is difficult to change travelers' checks in small towns, and the *casas de cambio* (exchange bureaus) charge large commissions.

Religious Services

St Andrew's Presbyterian Church at the corner of Belgrano and Peru has an English service at 10am. The community church in Acassuso also has an English service at 10.30am. A free bus leaves downtown at 9.30am from outside the Methodist Church at Corrientes and Maipú (opposite Teléfonica).

Getting Around

FROM THE AIRPORT

Ezeiza International Airport (EZE) is the arrival point for all foreign travelers. It is located about 30 minutes from downtown Buenos Aires. However, there is another airport, **Jorge Newberry**, located within the city and used mostly for domestic flights as well as for shuttling to and from bordering countries. Internal flights are available on Austral, Aerolíneas Argentinas and LADE.

BY AIR

Traveling by air in Argentina is done on the local airlines, which are Austral, Aerolíneas Argentinas and Lade. Jorge Newberry Airport, also known as "Aeroparque", is used for national traffic. For those tourists who wish to visit several cities, the Aerolíneas Argentinas 30-day "Visit Argentina" ticket can be used to stop off in towns.

The ticket is made up of four flight coupons which can be added to make up eight in total. Austral sells similar tickets called Jetpaq. They cost around US$450, (US$120 for extra coupons), must be purchased outside Argentina and in conjunction with an international flight ticket. Reconfirmation 24 hours before the time of your flight is strongly recommended.

BY SEA

Few **cruise ships** call at Buenos Aires. Traveling to Uruguay on the ferry is a pleasant trip, inexpensive and entertaining. A well-known company is **Ferrytur**, located on Cordoba 699, tel: 315-6800. There are boat connections between Uruguay and Argentina: Tigre to Carmelo and Montevideo to Carmelo. Ferry services run to Colonia from Daraena Sur and a hydrofoil service runs between Montevideo and Colonia four times a day during the summer. The English-language daily, *Buenos Aires Herald*, has listings of all sailings to Argentina.

BY BUS

The buses are a very good way to get around Buenos Aires, which is a very large city. They are one of the means of mass transportation that is usually prompt and very inexpensive. However, try not to get one during the rush hour as the queues are very long. Any part of the city can be reached. Bus stops are located throughout the city. The number and destination are clearly marked. Long distance travel on buses is also available.

A very large and modern bus terminal is located in Retiro. Information on bus destinations can be obtained at the terminal from the different companies.

Bus services are available from Chile, Bolivia, Paraguay, Uruguay and Brazil. Large air-conditioned buses are usually used for long-distance overland travel. But travelers must remember to be vigilant to ensure personal safety.

BY TRAIN

Most train services were suspended in 1994, when the government withdrew funding from Ferrocarriles Argentinos. For up-to-date information contact:
Ferrocarril Nacional Roca (southern) tel: 319-3900;
Ferrocarril Nacional Urquiza (north-eastern) tel: 553-7038;
Ferrocarriles Argentinos, tel: 306-1010.

BY ROAD

Traveling by automobile is possible. Most of the roads are paved but cautious driving is absolutely essential. Speed limits are posted and should be followed closely.

The Automobile Club of Argentina, located in Buenos Aires on Avenida Libertador 1850 (tel: 802-6061/7061), is very helpful

and can provide the traveler with maps and useful information.

BY TAXI

These can be easily recognized in Buenos Aires – black with a yellow roof – and are readily available 24 hours a day. The meter registers the amount of the fare. A bit of advice: be careful when paying and make sure the correct bill is given; quick exchanges of bills have been known to take place, especially with the tourist who doesn't know the language or the currency. A small tip (*propina*) is expected.

Car Rental

Remise taxis are private cars that can be rented, with a driver, by the hour, day or any other time period. Fares work normally work out much cheaper than those charged by ordinary taxis.

A list of *remise* offices can be found in the telephone directory, and staff in your hotel should be able to provide information, too.

BY SUBWAY

The subway system, better known as the **Subte**, is the fastest and cheapest way to get around Buenos Aires, and is the oldest in South America, bulit in 1913. Trains run daily from 5.30am to 10.15pm and tickets cost US$0.50 flat fare per journey. The rides are quick, taking no more than 25 minutes, and the waiting is between three to five minutes. The art work that can be observed at some of the stations is

quite unique and has an interesting background.

Many of these painted tiles were baked by artisans in Spain and France at the beginning of the century and around the 1930s.

Medical Services

Healthcare in this country is good. Hospitals have trained personnel, who have studied at home and abroad. There are excellent specialists in most of the medical fields, who make a point of attending international medical congresses to learn about recent advances in medical science and to bring them to Argentina.

Medical equipment is very costly, but all efforts are coordinated in order to maximize benefits. In some sections of the country, the hospitals may not have up-to-date equipment, but what is available is adequate for an emergency situation.

Emergency Numbers

For general emergencies, dial 101 for the **Police**, who can advise about other emergency services in the area. For medical emergencies in the Buenos Aires area, you can contact the following:
British Hospital, Perdriel 74, tel: 304-2051/1081.
Children's Hospital Pedro Elizalde, M.Oca 40, tel: 307-5553
Ricardo Gutierrez, Gallo 1330, tel: 962-9280.
Hospital de Clinicas, Cordoba 2351, tel: 961-6001.
Coronary Mobile Unit, tel: 107.
Poison Unit, tel: 962-6666.

Business Hours

Monday through Friday, the business hours are from 9am–6pm, and the banking hours are from 10am–3pm. Stores normally open 9am–8pm, but you'll often find that they close for several hours in the middle of the day for lunch and a siesta.

All government agencies as well as the banks close on public holidays.

Media

Several newspapers are available. The main local papers are *La Nación* and *Clarín*. The English paper is the *Herald*. There are newspaper and magazine stands throughout the city, where these and some foreign papers, as well as many international magazines, may be found.

There are five TV channels, and cable TV is also available. Most of

the programs are brought in from the US and some from Europe. Many drama series are locally made. Soap operas are also popular with afternoon viewers.

The radio stations carry a variety of programs. The BBC is on from 5pm to about 12.30am. A number of stations carry international top hits, local tango music as well as talk programs.

Postal Services

The main post office is located on Sarmiento 189, and operates Monday to Friday, 8am–8pm. Other small post offices are found throughout the city. Hotels are the best source of stamps.

Telecommunications

Telephone services are run by *Telecom* in the north and *Telefónica Argentina* in the south. Phone cards are available. Domestic calls can be made from public telephone boxes using coins or cards. In main cities the **Centros de Llamadas** offer good telephone and fax services. International public phones have a DDI sign. Many telephone offices send international faxes. In Buenos Aires you can make international calls and send faxes from the communications office on Avda Corrientes 705. Open 24 hours.

E-mail and the **Internet** can be used for US$5 an hour at The Internet Center, Maipú 24, tel: 343-1500; fax: 334-6283.

Useful Addresses

There are *casas de turismo* (tourist offices) in most big towns in Argentina. Buenos Aires also has the following offices and services:
The **National Tourist Office** is at: Santa Fe 883, tel: 312-2232, fax: 313-6834. Open Mon–Fri 8.30am–10pm, Sat 9am–7pm. There are also tourist information centers along Florida, the main city-center pedestrian boulevard. Here, in these booths, the traveler can obtain maps of the city and a bilingual (Spanish and English) tourist information newspaper called The *Buenos Aires Times*. It offers complete listings of what is happening in the city, as well as other pertinent and useful information. *Where*, a booklet giving a complete list of shopping, dining and entertainment, can be obtained in most hotels.
The provinces of Argentina have offices in Buenos Aires where the tourist can obtain valuable

information. Pamphlets about special events, attractions, lists of hotels, restaurants, etc. are readily available. All are located in the center of town and can be easily located. Look in the phone book.

Travel Agencies

ASATEJ, Florida 835, piso 3, Of.315, Buenos Aires, tel: 311 6953; fax: 311 6840. Aimed primarily at students, but there's no age limit. Useful noticeboard with items for sale, travel news, travelers seeking companions.
Cosmopolitan Travel, L. Alem 986, piso 7, Buenos Aires, tel: 311-6684/6695/ 2081/ 2474. 24-hour service available and many languages spoken.
Eves Turismo, Tucumán 702, Buenos Aires, tel: 393-6151. Helpful and efficient for flights both within Argentina and abroad.
Flyer Travel, Reconquista 621, piso 8, tel: 312-9194; fax: 312-1330.
Sooner Travel Agency, Avenida Santa Fe 780, Buenos Aires, tel/fax; 312 4954.
STO Travel, Hipólito Yrigoyen 850, Buenos Aires, tel: 34-0789.

Where to Stay

BUENOS AIRES
Buenos Aires Sheraton (luxury), San Martín 1225, tel: 318-9000; fax: 318-9353. Magnificent view of river and port.
Claridge Hotel (luxury), Tucumán 535, tel: 314-7700; fax: 314-8022. Old-fashioned British style.
Libertador Hotel (luxury), corner of Córboda & Maipu, tel: 322-6622; fax: 322-9703. Modern, central.
Marriot Plaza Hotel (luxury), Florida 1005, tel: 318-3000, fax: 315-3008. For the rich and famous with renowned Plaza Grill.
Carsson, Viamonte 650, tel: 322-3551. Faded, charming elegance.
Gran Hotel Colón, Carlos Pellegrini 507, tel: 320-3500, fax: 320-3516. Rooftop pool.
Gran Hotel Hispano, Avenida de

Mayo 861, tel: 345-2020. Housed in a colonial building and popular with budget travelers.
Hotel Phoenix, San Martín 780, tel: 312-4323; fax: 311-2845. Old world charm in beautiful building dating from the early 1900s.
Waldorff Hotel, Paraguay 450, tel: 312-2071; fax: 312-2079. Modern, near shopping streets.
Orly Hotel, Paraguay 474, tel: 312-5344.

PUERTO IGUAZU
Hotel International de Iguazú, Reservations in Buenos Aires, tel: 311-4259; fax 312-0488. Located in the National Park where the falls are, offering a magnificent view of its spectacular cascades. Very modern and with all the facilities.
Hotel Salta, Buenos Aires 1, tel: 211-011. Best hotel in Puerto Iguazú, in the main square.
Las Orquídeas, Ruta 12 at Km 5, tel: 20-472. Comfortable and inexpensive, outside the city in a beautiful location.

JUJUY
Hotel Termas de Reyes, tel: 0382; telex: 66130 NASAT. Located about 19 km (12 miles) from the city, offers thermal baths in all rooms, good facilities and heated pool.

MENDOZA
Hosteria Puente del Inca, Ruta 7, Las Heras, tel: 380-480; fax: 380-477. Secluded, within sight of Aconcagua.
Hotel Aconcagua, San Lorenzo 545, tel: 243-321. A few blocks from the main shopping area, with very modern architecture, pool and air-conditioned rooms. Good restaurant.
Plaza Hotel, Chile 1124, tel: 23 3000. Traditional establishment, in front of a beautiful plaza, with lovely antique furnishings.

BARILOCHE
Edelweiss Hotel, Avda San Martín 232, tel: (0944) 261-65, telex: 807-11 EDEL AR. A large five-star hotel, with up to 90 rooms plus several suites. Located in town and close to all amenities.

Hotel Tronador, Reservations in Buenos Aires 311-6684. A unique small lodge-type hotel with excellent food, offering fishing, horseback riding, hiking and beautiful surroundings for relaxation. Located in front of the Mascardi Lake, southwest of Bariloche. Open from November to April.

CARLOS PAZ

El Ciervo de Oro, Hipólito Yrigoyen 995, Carlos Paz, tel: 22498. A lovely, cosy lodge-type hotel right on the lake, with pool. Excellent food.

TUCUMAN

Hotel Garden, Crisóstomo Alvarez 627, tel: (081) 311-246. Clean and comfortable with reasonable rates including breakfast.
Hotel Corona, 24 de Septiembre 498, tel 310-985. Recently renovated, located on the Plaza Independencia.

USHUAIA

Del Glaciar, Camino Claciar Martial, tel: (0901) 306-036, fax: 396-38. A new four-star hotel above the city.
Malvinas Hotel, Deloqui 615, tel: 226-26.
Cabo Hornos Hotel, Avenida San Martín y Rosas, tel: 221-87. Clean and comfortable.

CALAFATE (LAGO ARGENTINA)

Hotel La Loma, B Roca y 15 Febrero, tel: 910-16. In the National Glacier Parks, has 27 rooms, centrally located with lovely views. Open from October to April. Several languages spoken.

What to Eat

Hotel breakfasts are rarely exceptional, and you'll do better to had for a local *confiteria* or bar. The most traditional breakfast includes *café con leche* (white coffee) and *medias lunas* (croissants, smaller and denser than the French variety). Other types of pastry (*facturas*) are usually also available. Good *confiterias* in the center of Buenos Aires include the Florida Garden (Florida and Paraguay) and the wood-panelled Richmond (Florida

near Corrientes). Breakfast is usually available from 8am onward.

Argentina is well known for its beef, and most visitors prefer this to other types of foods. The typical meal will be *empanadas* (meat pastries, although the filling will vary according to the region), *chorizos* or *morcillas* (pork blood sausages), an assortment of *achuras* (sweetbreads), and this is only the appetizer. For the main course, a good *bife de chorizo*, or *tira de asado*, or *lomo* are the most popular choices, accompanied by various types of salads. To finish off, try a *flan* (custard), topped with *dulce de leche* and some whipped cream. Enjoy now, worry about the calories later.

Eating in Buenos Aires

The scope of this guidebook does not allow a listing of restaurants from the all parts of Argentina, so the list below focuses just on Buenos Aires, where there is a vast choice. It is possible to eat out every day of the year and still not savor the cuisine of all the recommendable restaurants in the city. Dining out in Buenos Aires is a delightful experience. Food, wine and service are usually excellent.

Eating out is a favorite pastime of the locals (*porteños*), but the menu is not the only attraction. Restaurants are a place to socialize, to see and be seen, and share a bottle of wine until the early hours of the morning. Nevertheless, *porteños* take eating seriously. A list of recommended eateries follows, but don't be afraid to try any clean, well-lit place that catches your fancy. There are hundreds of good restaurants in the city, where the food is almost universally fresh and well-prepared in a simple Southern European style.

Restaurants in Buenos Aires open for lunch at noon, and for dinner around 8pm. But no one dines out in the evening before 9pm, with restaurants really coming alive between 10pm and 11pm. At weekends, restaurants stay busy long after midnight.

Regional Argentine

El Ceíbal, Güemes 3402, tel: 823-5807; Cabildo 1421, tel: 784-2444. Great place to try specialties from Northern Argentina, including *locro* (corn chowder), *humitas* (tamales) and *empanadas*. Inexpensive.

Parrillas (Steakhouses)

El Mirasol, Davila 202, tel: 315-6277. Upscale *parrilla* in posh Puerto Madero district, elegant atmosphere, reservations recommended. Expensive.
El Palacio de la Papa Frita, Lavalle 735. Inexpensive and popular.
La Cátedra, Cerviño 4699, tel: 777-4601. In the heart of the pleasant Palermo district. Nice atmosphere, excellent grilled beef but also interesting international cuisine and fresh salads. Moderate.
La Chacra, Avenida Córdoba 941, tel: 322-1409. Huge portions.
La Estancia, Lavalle 941, tel: 326-0330. Classic Asado-Restaurant in the heart of the city.
La Veda, Florida 1, tel: 331-8660. Dark wood paneling, excellent steak poivre, tango dinner show most evenings. Reservations recommended. Expensive.

Popular Eateries

Barbaro, Tres Sargentos 415, tel: 311-6856. A BA landmark, a charming, old world version of the hole-in-the-wall bar, a great place for a simple midday meal or for music, beer and bar food in the evening. Inexpensive.
Chiquilín, Sarmiento 1599, tel: 373-5163. One block from Corrientes, with the quintessential BA-restaurant atmosphere, serving very reasonable pasta and beef specialties. Fills up quickly on weekends. Inexpensive.
La Casa de Esteban de Luca, Defensa and Carlos Calvo. In the heart of San Telmo, in a restored colonial-style building, popular Sunday lunch after the San Telmo fair. Inexpensive.
Pippo, Montevideo 345. No frills but great atmosphere and unbeatable prices. Try a *bife de chorizo* (T-bone steak), or a bowl of vermicelli mixto

(pasta noodles with pesto and bolognaise sauce), washed down with the house red and seltzer. **Restaurant Dora**, L. Alem 1016, tel: 311-2891. An upscale version of a popular eatery with rave reviews on the enormous steaks and simple seafood dishes, a downtown "don't miss."
Te Mataré Ramirez, Paraguay 4062, tel: 831-9156. An excellent, original, international assortment of dishes, located in Palermo. Charming and ideal for either a romantic evening or a business dinner. Moderate to expensive.

Attractions

The Argentine people are extremely cultured and sport-loving. A wide range of activities are available, from the Buenos Aires Opera, to skiing in Bariloche. Museums, galleries, theaters, bookstores and several libraries are among the places to be visited. See the Places section of this book for descriptions of the most popular places in Buenos Aires and around the country.

A Rural Haven

Estancia Getaway: Visitors to Buenos Aires have the chance to get away from the buzz of the city, in the small town of San Antonio de Areco, about 70 miles (110 km) away. In this peaceful location, with beautiful scenery, the Aldao family has converted the Estancia La Bamba into a country inn, with all the facilities to make a stay comfortable and memorable. For more information tel: 392-0394 or 392-9707.

Theaters & Concerts

The theater season in Buenos Aires usually opens in March, with a large number and variety of plays on offer. The Argentines love a good drama and are highly critical. There is always something worth seeing. Check the local paper or with the hotel for the current and best ones

available. Recitals and concerts are promoted by the Secretary of Culture in an effort to bring culture to the people. The public responds enthusiastically by attending all events. Open-air concerts are very popular on hot summer evenings and are held in any one of the city's numerous parks.

Teatro Colón: Most of the renowned performers of the world are well acquainted with this magnificent theater. The building is in the Italian Renaissance style with some French and Greek influence. It has a capacity for 3,500 people, with about 1,000 standing. The acoustics are considered to be nearly perfect. Opera is one of the favorite programs for the season. In 1987, Luciano Pavarotti performed *La Bohème* here and tickets were sold out well in advance. Ballets are another favorite, performed by greats such as Nureyev, Godunov and the Bolshoi Ballet. The local company is very good and many of its members go on to become international figures. The Colón also has a magnificent museum, where all of the theater's history and its mementos are stored. It is an enlightening experience to have a guided tour of the theater and the museum. This can be arranged by calling 382-0554 for an appointment. Tours: Monday to Friday 11am–3pm, Saturday 9am, 11am and noon, closed Sunday. Tickets can be purchased at the box office located on Calle Tucumán. Closed January to February.

San Martín Theatre: Sarmiento 1551. Offers a variety of plays and musicals, and free music performances and exhibitions in the foyer. Check the local paper for performances.

Nightlife

The nightlife in Buenos Aires is certainly more lively than in many major cities of the world. Argentinians enjoy staying up late. People walk carefree in the late hours of the night, even though crime is on the rise.

Discos, nightclubs, cabarets and bars can be found in most of the city. Hear the latest hits from around the world and dance into the morning at, for example, **Cemento**, located on Estados Unidos 1238, or for a more formal crowd, dance at **Le Club**, on Quintana 111, or at **Hippopotamus**, Junin 1787. Other possibilities are:
Roxy, Rivadavia 1900. Reggae and rock.
New York City, Avda Alvarez Thomas 1391, tel: 552-4141. Popular with older clubbers.
El Dorado, Hipólito Yrigogen y 9 de Julio. Young and interesting crowd.

Tango Shows

A good tango show will be found almost everywhere, but the best shows are in Buenos Aires. Reservations are suggested for the following where such shows are staged:
Taconeando, Balcarce 725, tel: 362-9596 or 362-9599.
Casablanca, Balcarce 688, tel: 331-4621. Excellent show, prices include drinks.
El Caminito de San Telmo, Balcarce. Good show, price includes some drinks.
Michelango, Balcarce 4332, tel: 331-5392. In a converted monastery.
Armenonville, Alvear 1879, tel: 804-1033.

Sports

TREKKING
There are many tour operators in Las Heras, Mendoza, which specialize in climbing and trekking tours. One of the best is **Servicios Especiales Mendoza**, Amigovena 65, 5500 Mendoza, fax: (061) 244-721.

SKIING
The main ski resorts in Argentina are **The Cerro Catedral Complex**, located near Bariloche; **Valle de las Leñas**, in the south of Mendoza Province; **Los Penitentes**, a small resort near the town of Mendoza. There are also a number of small

facilities located throughout the southern provinces, including one in Tierra del Fuego and another near Esquel. Package tours tend to keep down the costs of a ski vacation.

Horseback Riding
Spend from half a day to a week riding under the open skies of the Andean foothills, near the town of Bariloche. Similar to dude ranching operations in the United States, but more rugged, with camping beneath the stars. Contact Carol Jones, **Estancia Nahuel Huapi**, Casilla 1436, Neuquen, Argentina, or **Hans Schulz**, Casilla 1017, Bariloche, Argentina, tel: (0944) 23835/ 26508, telex: 80772 POLVA AR.

Shopping in Buenos Aires

The best-known, and the most touristy, shopping street in the Argentinian capital is Florida, with Avenida Santa Fe coming a close second. You'll find the most expensive boutiques in Recoleta, the most exclusive part of Buenos Aires – primarily along Avenida Alvear, Quintana, Ayacucho and small side streets.

The city's finest jewelry stores are located at the beginning of Florida and on Avenida Alvear. Also, Sterns is located in the lobby of the Sheraton Hotel. The garment district is known as Once, and is accessible by taxi.

For antiques, the best-known area is the historic barrio of San Telmo. Every Sunday the San Telmo Fair takes place. The plaza is surrounded by stalls, which sell an array of objects, from cheap to outrageously expensive. Around the plaza are also many antique stores.

Buenos Aires also has a number of factory outlets (far from the city center), where a large selection of good-quality merchandise is available at low prices.

Bolivia A – Z

Getting Acquainted

Area 424,200 sq. miles. (1,100,000 sq. km).
Capital Sucre is the legal capital but La Paz is the effective capital.
Population 7.3 million. Seventy percent live in and around La Paz, Oruro and Lake Titicaca. About two-thirds are of pure Indian stock, most of the rest are *mestizos*, or mixed Spanish and local descent, locally referred to as *cholos* and *cholas*. About 1 percent are of African heritage, and a fraction of pure European and Japanese descent.
Language Quechua, Aymará and Spanish.
Currency Boliviano (US$1=B$5.6, £1=B$9).
Weights & measures metric.
Electricity 110 volts in La Paz, 220 volts elsewhere. Check first.
Time zone GMT –4hrs, EST +1.
Dialing code 591 (La Paz +2).

Government & Economy

The President is elected by popular vote every four years under the 1967 constitution. The country is divided into nine departments, each controlled by a delegate appointed by the president.

La Paz is the seat of the Government and Congress, although the Supreme Court sits in the small city of Sucre, the legal capital.

Bolivia is the poorest country in South America. More than half the population subsist on agriculture. Until the collapse of prices in 1985, tin was the major export earner for the country. Today, Bolivia still mines quantities of gold, silver and zinc. Natural gas is exported. The biggest money-spinner is coca growing, which the government hopes to curb – it employs thousands of peasants and contributes an undetermined but significant sum to the official economy.

Visas

Citizens of the United States and most European countries do not need visas; Australians, New Zealanders and most Asians do. At the border, the guards will grant entry for between 30 and 90 days. The immigration office for visa extensions: Avda Gonzalez 240. On departure, a US$20 tax is levied.

Embassies and Consulates

Canada: Avda 20 de Octubre 2475, tel: 375-224
Great Britain: Also representing Australia and New Zealand, Avda Arce casi Campos 2732, tel: 357-424, fax: 391-063.
United States: Avda Arce 2780, Consulate on Avda Potosí, tel: 350-251, fax: 359-875.

Money

Exchange your money in either banks or hotels as there is a lot of false currency in circulation. Ask for low value Bolivian banknotes and only carry small amounts on your person. Credit cards are not always accepted outside of major hotels and restaurants. Visa cash advances are possible from the Banco de La Paz in the capital.

Getting Around

FROM THE AIRPORT
El Alto, at some 4,060 meters (13,320 ft) above sea-level on the altiplano above La Paz, is the highest international airport in the world. Taxis to the center take about 30 minutes, US$8. "Cotranstur" minibuses also go to various points downtown, for about

US$0.50 (but allow about 1 hour because of all the drop-offs).

BY AIR

Domestic airlines LAB, TAM and AeroSur cover routes between most major towns and cities. Fares are comparatively cheap and, if time is short, it can be worthwhile to avoid a back-breaking bus journey, especially from La Paz to Potosí (on this route, it is necessary to fly to Sucre then take the four-hour bus journey to Potosí). **Crillon Tours** offers a comfortable minibus connection that can be arranged in La Paz – their office is at Avda Camacho 1223, tel: 374-566, fax: 391-039.

BY BUS

The bus network in Bolivia is well-developed, being the main form of public transport for most Bolivians. The quality of service however depends on the conditions of roads (of which only some 5 percent are paved), and the terrain covered. Luxury services run between La Paz, Cochabamba and Santa Cruz; quite rough services to Potosí. A wide choice of services are available to Coroico and Copacabana.

The great majority of travelers enter Bolivia via Lake Titicaca in Peru. Many companies offer minibus connections between Puno and La Paz. Crillon Tours (see address above) offers a luxury hydrofoil service both ways across the lake, allowing a stopover on the Island of the Sun, a meal in Copacabana and drinks on the water – as well as a visit to the Museum of the Altiplano with audio-visual displays, which gives an excellent introduction to Bolivia.

It is also possible to travel from Argentina by land, crossing the frontier at La Quiaca and continuing by bus or train – a slow but fascinating journey.

BY TRAIN

Trains run from La Paz to Oruro and Potosí. This is a long journey, worth paying for a pullman seat if available. Tickets can be bought in advance but schedules change frequently and delays are common.

From Brazil, the so-called "**Tren de la Muerte**" (Death Train) comes up from Corumbá on the edge of the Pantanal to Santa Cruz. It's not particularly comfortable but favored by more adventurous travelers, taking anything from 12–40 hours.

There are train and bus linksto and from Chile.

Tour Agencies

Most tour companies offer trips all over the country. For information on trekking and lists of recommended mountaineering guides, contact: **Club Andino Boliviano**, Calle Mexico 1638, tel: (02) 324-682.

For organized trekking and adventure tours, one specialist agency is: **Andes Expediciones**, Av. Camacho 1377, Edificio Saenz, Piso 3, Of. 1. La Paz. Tel: (02) 319-655/320-901; fax: (5912) 392344; e-mail: andesexp@ceibo.entelnet.bo

BY TAXI

For longer distances within La Paz, taxis are probably the best way to get around, either privately to go anywhere in the city for about US$1.40, or caught as colectivos, sharing with passengers along a fixed route for about US$0.25 each.

Medical Services

Make sure you have medical insurance that will provide you with private medical cover.

Major hotels have doctors on call. **The Clinica Americana** in La Paz (6 de Agosto 2821, tel: 323-023), or the **Clinica Santa Isabel** (opposite the Hotel Crillon) are competent and well-run. They can usually handle any problems that you may encounter.

Business Hours

Most businesses function from 9am–noon and 2–6pm, though banks generally close at 4.30pm.

Government offices invariably close on Saturdays.

Newspapers

In La Paz, you can choose from El Diario, Hoy and Ultima Hora, or the weekly, English-language publication the Bolivian Times. Other cities have their own local papers.

Postal Services

The main post office in La Paz is at Avda Mariscal Santa Cruz y Oruro, open Monday to Saturday 8am–10pm, Sunday 9am–noon. The outbound mail is quite efficiently posted to the rest of the world. The poste restante keeps letters for three months.

Telephones

Telephone calls can now be made by satellite to the United States and Europe. You can call from your hotel, which is the most expensive option, or the Entel offices in La Paz, Edificio Libertad, Calle Potosí and Ayacucho 267. Public telephones, found in all major cities, are the cheapest option. Phone cards can be bought for US$1/2/4/10.

Truck transport

To really get off the beaten track, trucks are the standard transport in the Andes. These are usually dilapidated, high-sided vehicles, with only a tarpaulin to protect you from the elements. They are used often by indians going to market, so you are likely to share your space with sacks of fruit and vegetables, or livestock (and in some cases slaughtered carcasses too). Most trucks leave early in the morning, from the market areas; timetables are unreliable and fares highly variable (though usually about half the equivalent bus fare); best to ask locally. A Bolivian truck journey may not be the quickest, but will be an authentic experience to remember.

Where to Stay

LA PAZ

Radisson Plaza Hotel, (5 star) Avda Arce 2177, tel: 316-161.
Sucre Palace Hotel, (3 star) Paseo El Prado 1636, tel: 363-453. Highly recommended.
Presidente, Potosí 920 y Sanjines, tel: 367-193, fax: 354-013.
Residencial Rosario, Illampu 704, tel: 326-531, fax: 375-532. Highly recommended mid-range hotel, lovely colonial building in the old market area, with a café and its own travel agency, running local tours and bus connections to Puno, Peru and Chile (*Turisbus*, tel: 316-156/ 369542; fax: 591-2-375532; e-mail: turisbus@caoba.entelnet.bo).
Andes, Avda Manco Capac 364, tel: 323-461. Said by budget travelers to be the cheapest in La Paz.

POTOSI

Hostal Colonial, Calle Hoyos 8, tel: 24265.
Hotel El Turista, Calle Lanza 19, tel: 22242.

SUCRE

Complejo Hotelero Mendez Roca, Francisco Argandoña 24, tel: 55-472.
Hotel Real Audiencia, Potosí 142, tel: 30-823.

COPACABANA

Hotel No me Olvides (known as the Centro Cultural Arco y Hamaca) Calle Michel Pérez 1–3, tel: 862-229.

What to Eat

Bolivian food varies by region. Lunch is the main meal of the day and many restaurants offer an *almuerzo completo* or three-course fixed menu. Staple foods of the highlands are potatoes, bread and rice. Meats are highly spiced. Trout from Lake Titicaca is excellent.

Where to Eat

It is best to eat food from restaurants and not street vendors. This is a small selection of recommended places in La Paz:

Los Escudos, Edif. Club de la Paz, tel: 322-028. Local food and live music.
Casa del Corregidor, Calle Murillo 1040, tel: 353-633. International and local dishes. Folk music.
Club de la Prensa, Calle Campero. Vienna, Federico Zuazo.
Wall Street Café, Calle Colón. Coffee, cakes and mouthwatering ice-cream sundaes.

Drinking Notes

The usual tea, coffee and soft drinks are readily available in restaurants and cafes, as is the *mate de coca* in tea bags.

Bolivian beer, brewed under German supervision, is surprisingly good. The favorite drink of everyday Bolivians is *chicha*, the potent maize liquor produced near Cochabamba. Keep in mind that altitude intensifies the effects of alcoholic beverages – both the intoxication and the hangover. Also remember that most Bolivians drink to get drunk.

Nightlife

La Paz has several *peñas* (folk clubs). Try the most popular, **Peña Naira**, on Sagárnaga, tel: 325-736, just above Plaza San Francisco, open every night with a US$5 cover charge. Others are at the **Casa del Corregidor** and **Los Escudos** restaurants (*see Where to Eat section above*).

Bars are not the most pleasant places to be in La Paz, frequented for inebriation rather than relaxation.

Where to Shop

The artisan's market in La Paz is along Calle Sagarnaga, between Mariscal Santa Cruz and Isaac Tamayo, and has a vast selection of Bolivia's craftwork. Most shopping takes place in the street markets. Vendors give a price and if buyers are not happy with it they are expected to offer an alternative.

Brazil A – Z

Getting Acquainted

Area 3,285,600 sq. miles (8,512,000 sq.km).
Capita: Brasília.
Population 154 million. Over half the population are white or near-white, 11 percent are Afro-Brazilians and the rest are of mixed race.
Language Portuguese.
Currency Real;US$1 = 1.18R$, £1= 1.9R$.
Weights & measures Metric.
Electricity Mostly 127 volts; 220 volts in Brasília, Florianópolis, Fortaleza, Recife and São Luis; 110 volts in Manaus.
Time zone Major cities and eastern half of country GMT –3hrs (EST +2hrs); Mato Grosso and the north GMT –4hrs (EST +1hr); Acre and western Amazonas GMT –5hrs (EST).
Dialing code 55 (Brasília +61, Rio de Janeiro +21).

Government & Economy

Brazil is a federal republic with 27 states, each with its own state legislature. Since the federal government exercizes enormous control over the economy, the political autonomy of the states is restricted. The overwhelming majority of government tax receipts are collected by the federal government and then distributed to the states and cities. The head of government is the president with executive powers and, in fact, exercises more control over the nation than the American president does over the United States. The legislative branch of the federal government is composed of a congress divided into a lower house, the Chamber of Deputies, and an upper house, the Senate.

In February 1987, however, the federal congress was sworn in as a national constitutional assembly to draft a new federal constitution for Brazil. The constituent assembly completely revised Brazil's constitution in 1987–88. The constitution approved in 1988 opened the way for direct presidential elections every 5 years.

Brazil is almost self-sufficient in food production and is the world's largest producer of coffee. It has huge reserves of metals and minerals and has seen expansion in technology-based industries in recent decades.

Visas

Most Asian, Australian, US, Canadian and French citizens are required to arrive with a visa; Britons and Germans are not. Your passport will normally be stamped for a 90-day stay.

Customs

You will be given a declaration form to fill out in the airplane before arrival. Customs officials spot check half "nothing to declare" arrivals.

Money

There is no significant difference between the bank rate of exchange and that offered by *casas de cambio* (exchange bureaus), at present, but check at your hotel as the economic situation is unstable. If you keep exchange slips, you can convert back into foreign currency US$100 worth of *reales*.

Holidays

January 1. New Year's Day (national holiday); Good Lord Jesus of the Seafarers (four-day celebration in Salvador da Bahía)
January 6. Epiphany (regional, mostly in the northeast)
January (3rd Sunday). *Festa do Bonfim* (Salvador da Bahía)
February 2. Iemanjá Festival in Salvador (the Afro-Brazilian goddess of the sea corresponds with the Virgin Mary)
February/March (movable). Carnival (national holiday; celebrated all over Brazil on the four days leading up to Ash Wednesday. Most spectacular in Rio, Salvador and Recife/Olinda)
March/April (movable). Easter (Good Friday is a national holiday; Colonial Ouro Prêto puts on a colorful procession; passion play staged at Nova Jerusalem)
April 21. Tiradentes Day (national holiday in honor of the martyred hero of Brazil's independence – celebrations in his native Minas Gerais, especially Ouro Prêto)
May 1. Labor Day (national holiday)
May/June Corpus Christi (national holiday)
June/July. *Festas Juninas* (a series of street festivals held in June and early July in honor of Saints John, Peter and Anthony, featuring bonfires, dancing and mock marriages)
June 15–30. Amazon Folk Festival (held in Manaus)
June/July. *Bumba-Meu-Boi* (processions and street dancing in Maranhao are held in the second half of June and beginning of July)
September 7. Independence Day (national holiday)
October. *Oktoberfest* in Blumenau (put on by descendants of German immigrants)
October 12. *Nossa Senhora de Aparecida* (national holiday honoring Brazil's patron saint)
November 2. All Souls Day (national holiday)
November 15. Day of the Republic (national holiday, also election day)
December 25. Christmas Day (national holiday)
December 31. New Year's Eve (on Rio de Janeiro beaches, gifts are offered to *Iemanjá*).

Getting Around

FROM THE AIRPORT

Most visitors arrive at Galeão International Airport, in Rio. There are official airport taxis here, for which you pay a fixed rate in advance according to your destination (approximately US$40 to Copacabana, for instance). If you decide to take a regular taxi, check out the fares posted for the official taxis so that you will have an idea of what is a normal rate. There are also regular air-conditioned "Alvoradas" buses, which leave from the 1st floor of the arrivals building, stopping at the city bus station and all central districts.

A tax of US$20, paid in local currency, is levied on international flights. Flight time from New York is around nine hours, from Europe around 12 hours. The largest airlines are Transbrasil, Varig and Vasp, which operate both international and internal flights.

BY AIR

For travel within Brazil, the major airlines are Transbrasil, Varig and Vasp, with other regional carriers which service the smaller cities.

Different lines have varying prices for the same routes. To get the best value call up for several quotes. There is a 30 percent discount for night flights (*vôo econômico or vôo noturno*) with departures between 10pm and 6am.

Transbrasil, Vasp and Varig also offer air passes which must be bought outside Brazil. Costing around US$440, they are valid for 21 days and limited to five coupons. Ask your travel agent about these – they are a good deal if you plan to travel extensively within Brazil.

The large airlines also cooperate in a shuttle service between Rio and São Paulo (with flights every half hour), Rio and Brasília (flights every hour) and Rio and Belo

Boat Trips

Short sightseeing or day-long boat tours are available in cities located on the coast or on major rivers. Many towns have local ferry services across bays and rivers and to islands. Schooners and yachts, complete with crew, may be rented for an outing.

Horizonte (usually about 10 flights per day). Although you may be lucky, a reservation is a good idea.

BY BUS

Comfortable and punctual bus services are available between all major cities, and even to several other South American countries, including Asunción (Paraguay), Buenos Aires (Argentina), Montevideo (Uruguay) and Santiago (Chile). While it is a good way to see a lot of the countryside, distances are huge, you sit in a bus for several days and nights, and the countryside is not continuously fascinating and varied. Nevertheless, buses on longer routes will stop for meals at regular intervals. Also, some luxury (*leito*) overnight services are available between large cities, with only three, reclining seats to a row, and including on-board service and blankets.

BY CITY BUS

Since just a small percentage of Brazilians can afford cars, public transportation is used a great deal. The larger cities have special air-conditioned buses connecting residential areas to the central business district including routes from airports and bus stations that pass by many of the larger hotels. You will be handed a ticket as you get on. Take a seat and an attendant will come around to collect your fare which is charged depending on the route.

The regular city buses are entered through the back door (often quite a high step up) and after paying the *trocador*, who will give you change, you move through the turnstile.

Robberies are committed on crowded buses, particularly in Rio and São Paulo, even in broad daylight. If you are bent on riding the regular city buses, try to avoid the rush hour when passengers on certain lines are packed tight. Don't carry valuables, keep shoulder bags in front of you and your camera inside a bag. Avoid calling attention to yourself by speaking loudly in a foreign language. In short, be discreet.

BY BOAT

Local boat tours and excursions are available in coastal and riverside cities. There are also options for longer trips.

Amazon River boat trips last a day or two to up to a week or more. These range from luxury floating hotels to more rustic accommodations. Boat trips can be taken on the São Francisco River in the northeast and in the Pantanal marshlands of Mato Grosso, popular for wildlife safaris and for angling. The Blue Star Line will take passengers on its freighters which call at several Atlantic coast ports. Linea C and Oremar have cruises out of Rio which stop along the Brazilian coast on the way down to Buenos Aires or up to the Caribbean. Book well in advance for the longer trips.

BY TRAIN

Except for crowded urban commuter railways, trains are not a major form of transportation in Brazil and rail links are not extensive. There are a few train trips, which are tourist attractions in themselves, either because they are so scenic or because they run on antique steam-powered equipment.

In the southern state of Paraná, the 66 mile (110 km) Curitiba-Paranaguá railroad is famous for spectacular mountain scenery.

In the Amazon region, you can ride what is left of the historic Madeira-Mamoré Railway – the 16 miles (27 km) of track between Porto Velho and Cachoeira de Teotônio in the state of Rondônia. The Madeira-Mamoré runs on Sunday only and strictly as a tourist attraction.

BY TAXI

Taxis are the best way for visitors to get around. It's easy to get "taken for a ride" in a strange city. Whenever possible, take a taxi from your hotel where someone can instruct the driver.

Medical Services

Should you need a doctor while in Brazil, the hotel you are staying at will be able to recommend reliable professionals who often speak several languages. Many of the better hotels even have a doctor on duty. Your consulate will also be able to supply you with a list of physicians who speak your language. In Rio de Janeiro, the Rio Health Collective (English-speaking) runs a 24-hour referral service, tel: (021) 325-9300 *ramal* (extension) 44 for the Rio area only.

Check with your health insurance company before traveling – some insurance plans cover any medical service that you may require while abroad.

Business Hours

Business hours for offices in most cities are 9am–6pm Monday through Friday. Lunch "hours" may last hours.

Banks open from 10am–3pm

Boat Excursions on the Amazon

The government-owned ENASA service for tourists ply the Belém-Manaus-Santarem-Belém run over 12 days. The modern boats have air-conditioned cabins, swimming pool, etc. Contact offices in Avenida Pres Vargas 41, Belém, and Rua Marechal Deoforo, Manaus for details.

Hammock space on the somewhat irregular ENASA passenger boats can be booked from Belém to Manaus and vice versa. Other services make the run, often in better condition than ENASA boats. They take five to six days from Manaus to Belém, as well as working along the more remote tributaries to Colombia and Peru.

Arranging passage on a boat is a matter of patience and luck in most cases as there are no fixed schedules for bookings.

Monday through Friday. The *casas de cambio* currency exchanges operate usually from 9am–5.30pm.

Media

The *Miami Herald*, the Latin America edition of the *International Herald Tribune* and the *Wall Street Journal* are available on many newsstands in the big cities, as are a selection of international weekly magazines.

Postal Services

Post offices generally are open from 8am–6pm Monday to Friday, 8am–noon on Saturday and are closed on Sunday and holidays. In large cities, some branch offices stay open until later. (The post office in the Rio de Janeiro International Airport is open 24 hours a day.)

Post offices are usually designated with a sign reading *correios* or sometimes "ECT" (for Empresa de Correios e Telégrafos – Postal and Telegraph Company).

Telephones

Pay phones in Brazil use tokens which are sold at newsstands, bars or shops, usually located near the phones. Ask for *fichas de telefone* (*ficha* pronounced "fee-sha"). Each *ficha* is good for three minutes, after which your call will be cut off. Insert several tokens into the slot and the unused tokens will be returned when you hang up.

The sidewalk *telefone público* is also called an *orelhão* (big ear) because of the protective shell which takes the place of a booth – orange for local or collect calls, blue for direct-dial long-distance calls within Brazil. The latter requires a special, more expensive token. You can also call from a *posto telefônico*, a telephone company station (at most bus stations and airports), where you can either buy tokens, use a phone and pay the cashier afterward, or make a credit card or collect call.

Phone cards, available from telephone offices, are being

introduced. For international calls, buy a 100 unit card at least; calls are rated either cheap or normal, depending on the time of day.

Tourist Information

Brazil's national tourism board, Embratur, has offices all over the world. You can also obtain information by contacting the head office in Rio. Write to: Embratur, Rua Mariz e Barros, 13, tel: 273-2212, 9° andar, Praça da Bandeira, 20000 Rio de Janeiro, RJ, Brazil.

Each state has its own tourism bureau. The principal offices are: **Manaus:** Emamtur, Rua Tarumã, 379, tel: (092) 234-2252. Information Center: Airport. **Rio de Janeiro:** Riotur, Rua da Assembleia, 10, 8–9° andares, tel: (021) 242-1947/242-8000; Flumitur, Rua da Assembleia, 10, 8° andar, tel: (021) 398-4077. Information Centers: International Airport, Bus Station, Corcovado, Sugar Loaf, Cinelândia Subway Station, Marina da Gloria. **Salvador:** Bahiatursa, Praça Municipal, Palácio do Rio Branco, tel: (071) 241-4333. Information Centers: Airport, Bus Station, Mercado Modelo, Porto da Barra. **São Paulo:** Anhembi Centro de Feiras e Congressos, Avda Olvayo Fontoura, 1209, tel: (011) 267-2122. Information Centers: Praça da República; Praça da Liberdade; Praça Ramos de Azevedo; Avda Paulista, at the corner of Rua Augusta; Shopping Center Morumbi; Shopping Center Ibirapuera.

Embassies & Consulates

Canada: Brasília: SES, Avda das Nações 16, Q 803, lote 16, s1. 130, tel: 223-7665. São Paulo: Avda Paulista, 1106, tel: 287-2122. **Great Britain:** Brasília: SES, Avda das Nações, Q 801, cj. K, lote 8, tel: 225-2710. Rio de Janeiro: Praia do Flamengo, 284, 2° andar (Flamengo), tel: 552-1422. São Paulo: Avda Paulista, 1938, 17° andar (Cerqueira Cesar), tel: 287-7722.

United States: Brasília: SES, Avda das Nações, lote 3, tel: 223-0120. Rio de Janeiro: Avda Pres. Wilson, 147, (Centro), tel: 292-7117. São Paulo: Rua Pe. João Manoel, 933, (Jardim America), tel: 881-7917.

Where to Stay

Tourist offices can provide lists of hotels in each state. The list below features mainly upscale hotels.

RIO DE JANEIRO (CITY)

Ambassador, Senador Dantas 25, tel: 297-7181, fax: 220-4783.
Caesar Park (luxury), Avda Vieira Souto 460, Ipanema, tel: 525-2525.
Copacabana Palace (luxury), Avda Atlântica 1702, Copacabana, tel: 584-7070, fax: 235-7330.
Intercontinental Rio (luxury), Rua Perfeito Mendes de Morais, São Conrado, tel: 322-2200, fax: 322-5500.
Luxor Copacabana (luxury), Avda Atlântica 2554, Copacabana, tel: 257-1940, fax: 255-1858.
Meridien-Rio (luxury), Avda Atlântica 1020, Leme, tel: 275-9922, fax: 541-6447.
Ouro Verde (luxury), Avda Atlantica 1456, Copacabana, tel: 542-1887, fax: 542-4597.
Rio Othon Palace, Avda Atlântica 3264, tel: 521-522, fax: 521-697.

SAO PAULO (CITY)

Caesar Park (luxury), Rua Augusta 1508/20, Cerqueira Cesar, tel: 253-6622, fax: 288-6146.
Maksoud Plaza (luxury), Alameda Campinas 150, Bela Vista, tel: 253-4411.
Moferrej Sheraton (luxury), Alameda Santos 1437, Cerqueira Cesar, tel: 253-5544, fax: (011) 289-8670.
São Paulo Hilton (luxury), Avda Ipiranga 165, Centro, tel: 256-0033, fax: 257-3137
.
BRASILIA

Brasília Carlton, Setor Hoteleiro Sul, Quadra 5, Bloco G, tel: (061) 224-8819, fax: (061) 226-8109.
Eron Brasília, Setor Hoteleiro Norte, Quadra 5, Lote A, tel: (061) 321-1777, fax: (061) 226-2698.

BELO HORIZONTE
Belo Horizonte Othon Palace, Avda Afonso Pena, 1050, Centro, tel: 273-3844, fax: 212-2318.

SALVADOR DA BAHIA
Bahia Othon Palace (luxury), Avda Presedente Vargas, 2456, Ondina, tel: 247-1044, fax: 245-4877.
Club Mediterrane (luxury), Estr Itaparica-Nazaré km. 13, Itaparica, tel: 880-7141, fax: 880-7165. Reservations in Salvador, tel: 247-3488.

OLINDA
Quatro Rodas Olinda, (luxury) Avda José Augusto, Moreira, 2200, Casa Caida tel: 431-2955, fax: 431-0670.

RECIFE
Boa Viagem, Avda Boa Viagem 5000, Boa Viagem, tel: 341-4144, fax: 341-1627.
Recife Palace Lucsim (luxury), Avda Boa Viagem 4070, Boa Viagem, tel: 465-6688/6767, fax: 326-8895.

MANAUS
Amazonas, Praça Adalberto Vale, Centro, tel: 622-3637.
Ana Cassia, Rua dos Andradas 14, Centro, tel: 232-6201, fax: 622-4812.
Tropical Manaus (luxury), Praia de Paula Negra, tel: 658-5000/5026, fax: 238-5221.

What to Eat

A country as diverse as Brazil naturally has regional culinary specialties: a result of varying geography, climate and, of course, immigration patterns. In parts of the south, the cuisine reflects the influence of its German community, while Italian and Japanese immigrants brought their cooking skills to São Paulo. Some of Brazil's most traditional dishes are adapted from African or Portuguese foods.

The staples for many Brazilians, however, are rice, beans and manioc. Although not a great variety of herbs is used, Brazilian food is tastily seasoned. Many Brazilians enjoy hot pepper (*pimenta*), and the

Brazil's National Dish

Considered to be Brazil's national dish (although not found in all parts of the country), *feijoada* consists of black beans simmered with a variety of dried, salted and smoked meats. Originally made out of odds and ends to feed the slaves, nowadays the tail, ears, feet, etc. of a pig are thrown in. *Feijoada* for lunch on Saturday has become somewhat of an institution in Rio de Janeiro, where it is served complete with white rice, finely shredded *couve* (kale), *farofa* (manioc root meal toasted with butter) and sliced oranges.

local *malagueta* chilis can be infernally fiery or pleasantly nippy, depending on how they're prepared.

The most unusual Brazilian food is found in Bahia, where a distinct African influence can be tasted in the dendê palm oil and coconut milk. The Bahianos are fond of pepper and many dishes call for ground raw peanuts or cashew nuts and dried shrimp. Two of the most famous Bahian dishes are *vatapá* (fresh and dried shrimp, fish, ground raw peanuts, coconut milk, dendê oil and seasonings thickened with bread into a creamy mush); and *moqueca* (fish, shrimp, crab or a mixture of seafood in a dendê oil and coconut milk sauce). Although it is delicious, note that the palm oil as well as the coconut milk can be a rich mixture to digest.

A favorite with foreign visitors and popular all over Brazil is the *churrasco* or barbecue, which originated with the southern gaucho cowboys who roasted meat over an open fire. Some of the finest *churrasco* can be eaten in the south. Most *churrascarias* offer a *rodizio* option: for a set price diners eat all they can of a variety of meats.

A few exotic dishes found in the Amazon include those prepared with *tucupi* (made from manioc leaves and having a slightly numbing effect on the tongue), especially *pato no tucupi* (duck) and *tacacá* broth with manioc starch. There are also many

varieties of fruit that are found nowhere else. The rivers produce many fish, including piranha.

Drinking Notes

Brazilians are great social drinkers and love to sit for hours talking and often singing with friends over drinks. Brazilian beers are really very good (note that *cerveja* usually refers to bottled beer, draft beer is *chope*.)

Brazil's own unique brew is *cachaça*, a strong liquor distilled from sugar cane, a type of rum, but with its own distinct flavor. Each region boasts of its locally produced *cachaça*, also called *pinga*, *cana* or *aguardente*.

Out of *cachaça*, some delightful mixed drinks are concocted. Tops is the popular *caipirinha*. It's really a simple concoction of crushed lime – peel included – and sugar topped with plenty of ice. Some bars and restaurants mix their *caipirinhas* sweeter than you may want – order yours *com pouco açucar* (with a small amount of sugar) or even *sem açucar* (without sugar).

Coffee Stop

Café is roasted dark, ground fine, prepared strong and taken with plenty of sugar. Coffee mixed with hot milk (*café com leite*) is the traditional breakfast beverage throughout Brazil. Other than at breakfast, it is served black in tiny *demitasse* cups, never with a meal (there are even little stand-up bars that serve only *cafezinho*). However you like it, Brazilian coffee makes the perfect ending to every meal.

Where to Eat

Lunchtime is usually noon–3 pm. For locals, this is the heaviest meal of the day. Dinner is 7pm–midnight (though locals eat late), but some restaurants stay open all afternoon and until 1 or 2am. Many restaurants in Brazil are closed Sunday evening and/or Mondays, so check before setting out. At the more expensive restaurants, it is advisable to make reservations. The following is a small selection of places to eat in the main cities.

RIO DE JANEIRO
Casa da Feijoada
Rua Prudente de Morais 10, loja B, Ipanema, tel: 523 4994.
Specializes in Brazil's favorite dish, made with black beans and various cuts of pork (see page 371).
Confeitaria Colombo
Rua Goncalves Dias 32 (Center).
Worth a visit for the fantastic art nouveau decor with mirrored walls and huge chandeliers. Afternoon teas a specialty.
Grottamare
Rua Gomes Carneiro 132, Ipanema, tel: 522 3186.
Popular and busy seafood restaurant.

SAO PAULO
Arabia
Rua Haddock Lobo 1397, tel: 3061 2203.
Wonderful Lebanese food in spacious restaurant; inexpensive.
Cheiro Verde
Rua Peixoto Gomide 1413, tel: 289 6853.
Cheap and cheerful vegetarian restaurant.
Koyama
Rua 13 de Maio 1050, Bela Vista, tel: 283 1833.
Excellent Japanese food in traditional surroundings.

SALVADOR
Tempero da Dadá
Rua Teixeira Mendes 55, tel: 331 4382.
Tasty regional cooking; inexpensive.
Trapiche Adelaide
Praça dos Tupinambas 2, Avenida do Contorno, tel: 326 2211.
International cuisine in a wonderful location right by the main bay.

RECIFE
Canto da Barra
Avenida Bernardo Vieira de Melo 9150, Candeias, Barra da Jangada, tel: 468 2624.
Tasty and inexpensive seafood.

BELEM
Lá em Casa/O Outro
Avenida Governador José Malcher 247, Nazaré, tel: 223 1212.
Delicious Amazonian specialties, including ice cream made from tropical fruits.

MANAUS
Paramazon
Rua Santa Isabel 1176 (Cachoeirinha). Tel: 233 7768.
Typical Amazonian dishes; inexpensive.

Museums

There are some beautiful museums and galleries around the country, listed in the Places section; São Paulo has some of the finest art galleries, while Minas Gerais and the Northeast are home to the best colonial buildings.

Music and Dance

Brazil is famous internationally for its music, and has exerted great influence on musical styles abroad, especially jazz. It is easy to buy and listen to Brazilian music abroad, but there is much more to discover on the spot.

A huge variety of musical forms have developed in different parts of the country, many with accompanying forms of dance. **Bossa nova**, **samba**, **choro** and **seresta** are popular in Rio and São Paulo, for example. And if you are visiting at Carnival, you'll see and hear plenty of music and dancing in the streets, mostly samba in Rio and *frevo* in the northeast. There are also shows all year long designed to give tourists a taste of Brazilian folk music and dance.

The classical music and dance season runs from Carnival through mid-December. Major Brazilian cities (mainly Rio, São Paulo and Brasília) are included in world concert tours by international performers. One of the most important classical music festivals in South America takes place in July each year in Campos do Jordáo in the state of São Paulo.

Chile
A – Z

Getting Acquainted

Area 292,100 sq miles (756,600 sq km).
Capital Santiago de Chile.
Population 14.6 million, 90 percent are mestizo.
Language Spanish.
Currency Peso (US$1=$463, £1= $741).
Weights & measures Metric.
Electricity 220 volts.
Time zone GMT –4hrs, EST +1.
Dialing code 56 (Santiago +2).

Government & Economy

Until 1990, Chile's government was a military dictatorship known for its horrendous human rights record, but a peaceful transfer of power to a civilian government took place when President Aylwin was elected.

Chile is a stable country with a solid free market economy. Travelers are impressed by the clean streets and amiable people. It is one of the safest countries on the continent.

Visas

Passports and tourist cards only are required for entry by all foreigners except citizens of New Zealand, China, India, Pakistan, all the ex Soviet countries and all African countries, who need visas. Tourist cards valid for 90 days are issued upon arrival, and can be renewed for another 90 days for US$8 at the immigration office on Calle Moneda in Santiago. To stay longer (than 180 days),go to a border country and return; a quicker method than the bureaucratic application procedure.

Customs

All bags are searched for agricultural products that may harbor disease. All food should be eaten or dispose of.

Clearance at border posts inland can be a bit more cumbersome. As at international entry points, bags here are thoroughly searched for agricultural products, and contraband searches are more frequent. Still, delays are not that long.

Embassies and Consulates

Canada: Nueva Tajamar 481 (12th floor), Santiago, tel: (56-2) 362-9660, fax: 362-9663.
Great Britain: El Bosque Norte 0125 (3rd floor), Santiago, tel: 231-3737, fax: 231-9771.
United States: Avda Andrés Bello 2800, Santiago. Tel 232-2600, fax: 330-3710.

Money

Changing money on the streets is not advisable anywhere.

ATM cash points, called *Redbanc*, are everywhere, even in some quite small towns. They accept most major credit cards and some bank cards. Hotels, restaurants and shops generally take most credit cards.

Getting Around

FROM THE AIRPORT

Santiago's main airport for international and domestic flights is Arturo Merino Benítez Airport, at Pudahuel, 26 km (16 miles) from the city. It is a relatively small airport and customs procedures are quick and easy. There are frequent buses from the airport, US$0.30–0.50; and the "Delfos" shuttle bus, US$6. A taxi should cost about US$15 to the center of town, but agree a price before starting your journey. There is a bank and *cambio* (exchange bureau), but the rates are not as good as in the city.

A national tourist service

(SERNATUR) office at the airport can book accommodation, as well as give general information.

Airport Taxes: a US$20 tax is charged on arrival in Chile by air. If you fly out of the country you must pay a US$18.25 exit tax. Domestic flights charge US$8 tax.

BY BUS

Chile's private intercity bus service is excellent and inexpensive. Roads are well maintained and buses are new, comfortable, and run on time. In Santiago, do check carefully which terminal your bus leaves from, as there are several, all on the main underground line. During offpeak times, you can bargain for a cheaper fare; always ask before you pay full fare.

Santiago's chaotic bus system is privately owned. Fares are cheap, but the system is difficult to use. The only way to find your bus is to look for the street on the marquee or ask the driver.

To and from Argentina: a number of bus companies go to Argentina from Antofagasta, Santiago, Osorno, and Punta Arenas. The main services are Cata, Tas-Choapa and El Rápido. A single ticket from Santiago to Mendoza costs around US$14 and Santiago to Buenos Aires around US$45. Pluma buses run through to Brazil

BY TRAIN

Chile has a passenger rail network of some 4,500 km (2,800 miles), stretching from Ollagüe (and on to Bolivia) in the north to its southern railhead in Puerto Montt.

Most of the system is state owned, trains are more punctual than in other South American countries, fares are reasonably priced (with some student discounts), but meals on board are expensive. A guide to the railways is published in several languages by the *Ferrocarriles del Estado*, available from larger stations.There are information offices in Santiago, at Bernardo O'Higgins 853 and Ahumada 11 (for the Antofagasta–La Paz line).

International routes: there are four lines linking with neighboring

Public Holidays

- **January** 1
- **May** 1, 21 (Navy Day)
- **August** 15
- **September** 11, 18 and 19 (Independence Day)
- **October** 12 (Columbus Day)
- **November** 1 (All Saints Day)
- **December** 8 (Immaculate Conception), 25

countries: two to La Paz, Bolivia, one via Arica and the other from Antofagasta via Calama; one from Arica to Tacna, Peru; and one from Antofagasta to Salta, Argentina.

Santiago Metro: three lines cross the city and provide fast, safe and inexpensive access to most places of interest. Trains run from 6.30am–10.30pm Monday to Saturday, and 8am–10.30pm on Sundays and holidays. Fares vary from US$0.25–40, according to the time of day; the simplest option is to buy a *boleto valor* – a charge card, for US$3.50,which deducts each journey automatically.

BY TAXI

Black taxis with yellow roofs can either be found at taxi ranks or flagged down in the street, and all run on meters. Tipping the driver is not customary.

Collective taxis (*colectivos*) have a fixed route similar to buses and may carry up to five passengers. The fare is displayed on the windshield. Tourist taxis are blue, but while in better condition than regular taxis, are more expensive and do not run on a meter. They can be found in front of hotels.

Emergencies

The police (*carabineros*) patrol regularly. They are friendly, generally helpful and do not expect to receive money.

Call **133** for all emergencies. For road conditions, dial 139.

There are several good hospitals in Santiago, such as **Clínica Las Condes** (Lo Fontecilla 441, tel: 211-1000), **Clínica Santa María** (Avda

Santa María 0410, tel: 777-6690) and **Clínica Aleman** (Avda Vitacura 5951, tel: 212-9700). Contact your embassy for a list of certified physicians.

Hitchhiking

Hitchhiking in Chile is safe, except for women on their own, and easier than in other South American countries. Truckers will pick you up sometimes, but motorists are reluctant to stop, so don't depend on it. Traffic is sparse in isolated regions.

Business Hours

Business hours change from city to city. In Santiago they are 9am–1.30pm, 2.30–6.30pm Monday to Friday. Banks open 9am–2pm, Monday to Friday. Exchange houses are open 9am–6pm Monday to Friday, and half a day on Saturday.

Newspapers

There are several independent dailies such as *El Mercurio*, *La Tercera* and *La Segunda*. For business and finance read *Diario Financiero* and *Estrategia*. International newspapers are also readily available.

Postal Services

Most post offices open 9am–5pm Monday to Friday, and until noon on Saturday. The system is more reliable than most in South America. The **Poste Restante** (*Lista de Correos*) in Santiago is in the main post office in the Plaza de Armas.

Telephones

Coin-operated public telephones for local and international calls are everywhere, and some take credit cards. The main phone companies, CTC, Entel, VTR and Bellsouth, have offices in most cities. Buy an Entel prepaid card so you can call from any phone booth.

Where to Stay

There is a high standard of hotels in Chile, especially in the main cities. These are some recommended places in the major tourist areas:

SANTIAGO

Hotel Carrera, Teatinos 180, tel: 698-2011, fax: 672-1083. Overlooking the presidential palace, this is Santiago's most traditional luxury hotel.
Hotel Foresta, Victor Subercaseaux 353, tel: 639-6262, fax: 639-6162. A beautiful place overlooking Santa Lucía Park.
Hotel Santa Lucía, Huérfanos 779, 4th floor, tel: 639-8201, fax: 633-1844. Cheap, clean and cheerful.
Sheraton San Cristobal, Avda Santa María 1742, tel: 233-5000, fax: 223-6656. This recently enlarged hotel is a bit out of the way, but remains popular.
Santiago Hostelling International, Cienfuegos 151, tel: 671-8532, fax: 672-8880, near the Los Héroes underground station. Members US$12 a night, US$14 for non-members.

There are several dives that cost a couple of dollars a night along General MacKenna, Amunategui, San Pablo and San Martin, but most of these *pensiones* and *residenciales* cost a certain amount of emotional toil. They include:
Hotel Caribe, San Martin 821, tel: 696-6681. This is the best, with clean rooms and communal showers.
Residencial Londres, Londres 54, tel/fax: 638-2215. Near the San Francisco Church on Alameda. In not a bad neighborhood, close to the subway and downtown.
Vegas Hotel, Londres 49, tel: 632-2514, fax: 632-5084. A clean and friendly place with large rooms and recommended for its breakfast.

VINA DEL MAR

Cap Ducal, Avda Marina 51, tel: 626-655, fax: 665-478. The best seafront view, with an excellent but expensive restaurant.
Hotel O'Higgins, Plaza Vergara, tel: 882-016, fax: 883-537. Viña's famous grand hotel.

Hotel San Martin, San Martin 667, tel: 689-191, fax: 689-195. Moderately priced.

There are a few *residenciales* near the bus station with rooms from $5 to $10, but they fill early, especially in the summer. The best bet is to stay across the bay in Valparaíso.
Garden Hotel, Serrano 501, Near Plaza Sotomayor, tel: 252-777. Decent rooms.
Hotel Reina Victoria, Plaza Sotomayor 190, tel: 212-203.
Residencial Lily, Blanco Encalada 866, tel: 255-995.

VALPARAISO

Hotel Brighton, Paseo Atkinson 151, tel/fax: 223-513. Overlooking the bay from Cerro Valparaíso. Moderately priced.

ARICA

Hotel El Paso, General Velásquez 1109, tel/fax: 231-965.
Hotel Lynch, Patricio Lynch 589, tel: 251-959, fax: 231-581. Inexpensive.
Residencial La Blanquita, Maipu 472, tel: 232-064. Clean rooms and good hot showers. Budget.
Savona, Yungay 380, tel: 232-319, fax: 231-606. With a laundry. Quiet and comfortable, inexpensive.

PUERTO MONTT

Colón Apart Hotel, Pedro Montt 65, tel: 694-290, fax: 264 293. Modern seafront hotel with self-catering suites.
Hotel Montt, Antonio Varas 301, tel: 253-651, fax: 253-652. Moderately priced.
Hotel Vientosur, Ejército 200, tel: 258-701, fax: 258-700. Moderate.
Hotel Vicente Perez Rosales, Antonio Varas 447, tel: 252-571, fax: 255-473.

CASTRO

Hotel Unicornio Azul, Avda Pedro Montt 228, tel: 632-359. Don't miss this delightful and inexpensive hotel. A good base to see the best of Chiloé Island.

EASTER ISLAND

Hotel Hanga Roa, Avda Pont, tel: 223-299. Expensive, as are nearly all on the island, but the most luxurious.

Rapa Nui Inn, Avda Policarpo Toro, tel: 223-228. Comfortable, with local hospitality.

What to Eat

Lunch is the main meal in Chile, and restaurants will have a cheap lunch menu for around three dollars. It starts with a simple salad with oil and lemon juice, followed by a hot bowl of *cazuela* or soup with meat, chicken or seafood, or *empanadas* (pastries stuffed with meat, onions, a boiled egg and a couple of olives), which may substitute the soup. In summer don't miss *humitas*, seasoned puréed corn wrapped in corn leaves, or *pastel de choclo*, a corn and meat pie.

Seafood is a hot favorite in Chile. Try *picarocos*, *jaiva* (crab) and *locos* (abalone) if you can find it. The main course usually consists of specially prepared rice and chicken, meat or fried fish. Dessert is a must, followed by a cup of instant coffee.

At night, sandwiches are popular fare: Chile is famous for its *churrasco* (steak sandwich with avocado), *chacarero* (steak with green beans), or *completos* (hot dogs with tomatoes, avocado and mayonnaise).

Where to Eat

SANTIAGO
For good, inexpensive eating, try the Bellavista neighborhood. At any of the places along Pio Nono, Constitución and Antonio López de Bello, expect to pay from US$15 per person. For Italian food, try **El Tallarín Gordo** or **El Siciliano**, and for seafood go to the **Azul Profundo**. Traditional Chilean food is served at **El Caramaño** while **Venezia** is the haunt of the bohemian crowd, but go to the dining rooms at the back.

In Providencia, non meat-eaters should try **El Huerto** (Orrego Luco 054), which serves excellent vegetarian dishes, or **El Café del Patio** (Providencia 1670), well-known for its organic vegetables. Nearby **Aquí está Coco** (La Concepción 236) and **Canto del**

Drinking Notes

Wine is by far the best alcoholic drink in Chile. *Undurraga, Concha y Toro, Carmen, Santa Rita, Pirque San Pedro* are among the more famous names. They are all worth sampling and most are inexpensive (*see page 284 for more details*).

Agua (Nueva de Lyon 0129) serve some of the best fish.

Uptown, El Bosque Norte and Isidora Goyenechea streets are full of high-class, sometimes expensive, restaurants. **Isla Negra** has the finest Chilean fare. **El Club** and **Publicity** offer excellent food in a relaxed setting.

VALPARAISO
Try *caldillo de congrio* or other typical seafood dishes in **El Bote Salvavidas**, on Muelle Prat, overlooking the port. The Ascensor Concepción is the best way to get to the **Café Turri**, Templeman 147, Cerro Concepción, with its marvellous view over the bay.

VINA DEL MAR
For cheap dinners, it is best to eat sandwiches and *platos del día* at Viña's innumerable cafés. **Cap Ducal**, the city's most famous waterfront restaurant, serves excellent seafood. For a reasonable lunch, try the daily menu at **Club de Viña** on the plaza. North of Viña, the coastal stretch between **Montemar** and **Cochoa** is happy hunting ground for small restaurants, serving local seafood: **El Pacífico** is particularly well known.

Culture in Santiago

Most **theaters** are downtown, including the Antonio Varas, La Comedia, Cariola, and the Centro de Extensión de la Universidad Católica. In Bellavista, El Conventillo, and in Ñuñoa, the Teatro de la Universidad Católica and Sala Arena add extra variety. Check the papers for listings, and book via individual box offices.

For **opera** and **classical concerts** in Santiago, try the Teatro Municipal, the Teatro de la Universidad de Chile and the Teatro Oriente.

There are **cinemas** in most neighborhoods, and "Ciné Arte" (quality foreign films) are very popular. Prices are reduced prices on Wednesdays in Santiago.

Nightlife

Santiago
Check out the cafés and bars along Constitución and side streets in Bellavista for Santiago's more bohemian crowd. In Providencia, people gather in **Brannigan's** and other pubs along Suecia and Generál Holley. Near Manuel Montt on Providencia is the English-style **Phone Box Club**. There is a choice of pubs and discos along Paseo San Damián in Las Condes.

For techno dancing, try **OZ**, on Chucre Manzur street in Bellavista, or, if you love tropical rhythms, go for salsa in **La Habana Vieja** (Tarapacá 755).

Viña del Mar
Here, try the crowded **Scratch** near the railway station. In nearby Reñaca, the best dancing is at **Kamikaze** (Vicuña Mackenna).

Art in Santiago

There are several art galleries worth visiting along Santiago's Avenida Nueva Costanera, including the A.M.S. Marlborough, Tomás Andreu and Plastica Nueva. On Alameda, try Arte Actual in the Centro de Extensión of the Universidad Católica.

Where to Shop

For the latest fashions, visit the department stores and boutiques on Providencia near Los Leones and Manuel Montt.

Stores open Monday to Friday, 10.30am–7.30pm and Saturday, 9.30am–1.30pm. Most, except for the malls, are closed on Sunday.

Colombia A – Z

Getting Acquainted

Area 439,600 sq miles (1,140,000 sq km), bordering Panama with coasts on the Caribbean Sea and the Pacific Ocean.
Capital Bogotá
Population 36 million. Colombians are of European, African and Amerindian descent. Nearly half a million belong to one of 60 tribes.
Language: Spanish.
Currency Colombian peso, US$ = 1,586 pesos, UK£ = 2,3258 pesos
Weights & measures Metric
Electricity 120 volts
Time zone GMT –5hrs, same as EST
Dialing code 57 (Bogotá + 1)

Government & Economy

Colombia's "limited democracy" is based on the Constitution of 1991. The president and members of the senate and house of representatives are directly elected. Indians have the right to two senate seats.

Colombia has one of South America's strongest economies and is self-sufficient in energy. Agriculture is the most important source of revenue, and Colombia is the world's second-largest coffee producer. Manufacturing comes a close second. Colombia produces 60 percent of the world's emeralds and 70 percent of the world's cocaine.

Business Hours

Generally Monday to Friday, 8am–noon, then 2–6pm. Banks are open from 9am–3pm, 9am–3.30pm on Friday. Many businesses shut on Monday.

Money

There are some legal *casas de cambios* (exchange bureaus) but generally you are advised to exchange cash and travelers' checks (in US dollars) at a bank. Since a photocopy of your passport is often required, you can speed up transactions by taking a supply of spare photocopies with you from home. Do not change money on the street and avoid carrying large amounts of cash.

Credit cards are widely used, but American Express is accepted only in high-priced establishments in Bogotá. Amex is represented in Colombia by the Tierra Mar Aire travel agency.

Getting Around

FROM THE AIRPORT

Bogotá's international airport is at El Dorado. Registered yellow taxi services run to the city center at a fixed rate of US$8. Elsewhere they are on a meter. Local buses also run to and from Bogotá airport during the day but luggage space is very limited. You can dial a taxi on 222-2222 or 311-1111.

Airport taxes: foreigners pay $25 departure tax when leaving Colombia by air. Make sure that your documentation is stamped with the date of your arrival, so that you don't have to pay double the exit tax on departure.

BY BUS

Bus transport along the main routes is generally good, often luxurious, but deteriorates when heading into the more remote areas. Normally, the rougher the road, the poorer the bus. The alternative on main routes is a *buseta* (minibus) or *colectivo* (a shared taxi that is more expensive but much quicker).

From Ecuador, buses go to and from the border at Tulcan/Ipiales. From Venezuela, you can choose between the coastal route from Maracaibo to Santa Marta, or the highland route from Caracas and Mérida to Cucuta via San Cristobal.

From Brazil, the only way to enter is via Leticia in the Amazon basin and then fly to Bogotá.

BY TAXI

Within the main cities, taxis are cheap and relatively reliable. Always try to take a taxi that uses a meter; if not, agree a price in advance (all taxis are legally obliged to display a list of additional charges). At night women should not travel alone in taxis. Be very wary of old-looking vehicles, and always keep an eye on your luggage.

Loss

Although most Colombians are honest and friendly, theft occurs in the larger cities and visitors should look after valuables at all times. The 24-hour **Tourist Police Service** in Bogotá is at Carreras 7, No. 27–42, tel: 283-4930 or 334-2501. If you have lost documents, contact the police at Calles 46 y Carreras 14; for loss of valuables, go to Calle 40, No. 8–09.

Medical Services

The main medical centers in Bogotá are **Cruz Roja Nacional**, Avenida 68, No. 66–31, tel: 250-66/231-9027/231-9008; or **Centro Medico La Salud**, Carrera 10, No. 21–36, tel: 243-1381/282-4021. Make sure you have health insurance.

Newspapers

Bogotá has several daily newspapers. Both *El Tiempo* and *El Espectador* are considered the most comprehensive in terms of news coverage.

The English-language *Colombian Post* is published twice a week but not widely circulated. **Drugstore Internacional**, Carreras 10, No. 26–71, sells US and European papers.

Postal Services

There are two postal systems in Colombia. The more reliable service is run by Avianca, the national

Visas

Visitors to Colombia need a passport but, according to the current regulations, do not require a visa. Check, however, since regulations may change. Visitors are given a 60/90-day stay on arrival. An onward ticket may have to be shown on arrival.

Extensions of 15 days for a maximum six-month period may be applied for. Exit stamps are necessary on departure.

airline. They have offices in most large cities often next door to the airline office.

The other system is state run and less reliable. The General Post Office in Bogotá is at the Avianca Building in the center of the city, opposite the Parque Santander. In small towns and rural areas use the Correos de Colombia.

Telephone & Fax

Telephone systems are automated and phone cards can be used. Fax services are available in large hotels, but it's cheaper to use Telecom offices.

The Telecom offices in all big cities have international communication facilities to enable you to dial home.

Parks & Reserves

Permits are sometimes required to visit Colombia's parks and nature reserves. For permits and information contact the **Ministry of Environment** (Ministerio de Medio Ambiente) Caja Agraria building, Carrera 10 No. 20–30, 8th Floor, Bogotá; tel: 283-0964, fax: 341-5331.

Useful Addresses

Tourist Offices

Bogotá: Fondo de Promoción Turística, Calle 90, Carrera 18–35, Oficina 203. They have offices in other cities as well. Limited information is also available at the

Edificio Centro de Comercio Internacional, Calle 28, No. 13A–15 and at the bus station and El Dorado Airport.

Tourist Agencies

Bogotá: Panamerican Tours, Carrera 11A Calle 93A–80, tel: 635-4000, or Eco, Guías, Carrera 3, No. 18–56A, Oficina 202 at the top of Avenida Jimenez.

Santa Marta: Reales Tours, Carrera 1A, No. 20–09, tel: 214-418, can arrange trips to Ciudad Perdida, Parque Tayrona, Cabo de la Vela and the Guajira Peninsula.

Cartagena: There are many tourist agencies in Bocagrande, the modern beach resort.

Embassies & Consulates

The following embassies and consulates are in Bogotá:

Canada: Calle 76, No. 11–52, tel: 313-1355.

Ecuador: Calle 100, No. 14–63, tel: 257-0066.

Great Britain: Calle 98, No. 9–03, 4th floor, tel: 218-5111 or 218-1867.

United States: Calle 37, No. 8–61, tel: 285-1300.

Where to Stay

Hotels in Colombia range from the luxurious at $130 a night to the basic at around $2 a night.

BOGOTA

Some of the 5-star hotels include:
Bogotá Royal, Avda 100, No. 8A–01, tel: 218-9911, fax: 218-3362.

Tequendama, Carrera 10, No. 26–21, tel: 286-1111, fax: 282-2860.

La Fontana, Diagonal 127A, No. 21–10, tel: 274-0200, fax: 216-0449. Recommended by many travelers.

For a hotel with some atmosphere and still perfectly comfortable though with less conveniences, try the **Hosteria de la Candelaria**, Calle 9, No. 3–11, which is in a converted colonial

mansion and furnished with beautiful antiques. Tel: 342-1727.
Budget hotels, often dismal, are located between Calles 13 and 17, and Avenida Caracas and Carrera 17, but this area is unsafe after dark.

CARTAGENA

Cartagena-Hilton. A luxury hotel in nearby El Laguito, tel: 650-666, fax: 650-661.

Hotel de Caribe, Carrera 1, No. 2–87, tel: 650-155, fax: 653-707.

What to Eat

Colombian cooking varies by region, although in the big cities any kind of international cuisine can be enjoyed. A few Colombian specialties worth trying are:
ajico: a soup of chicken, potatoes and vegetables, common in Bogotá.
arepa: a maize pancake.
arroz con coco: rice cooked in coconut oil, special to the coast.
bandeja paisa: a dish of ground beef, sausages, beans, rice, plantain and avocado.
carne asada: grilled meat.
cazuela de mariscos: seafood stew.
chocolate santafereño: hot chocolate accompanied by cheese and bread.
mondongo: tripe soup.
puchero: broth of chicken, beef and pork, typical of Bogotá.
tamales: chopped pork with rice and vegetables in a maize dough.

Where to Eat

In Bogotá, the **Casa Vieja** restaurants offer excellent regional food. They are at Avda Jiménez No. 3–73, Carrera 10, No. 26–50, and Carrera 116, No. 20–50. **Refugio Alpino**, Calle 23, No. 7–49, serves European food. Budget meals serving comidas corrientes, usually a fried piece of meat with beans and rice, are found in many of the restaurants.

In Cartagena, **La Fonda Antioqueña**, Carrera 2, No. 6–161, has traditional Colombian food, while **Paco's**, opposite the church of Santo Domingo, is also recommended.

Nightlife

Bogotá
In Bogotá, there are several good bars and salsa bars in the *zona rosa*, Calles 81 and 82, Carreras 11, 12, 13 and 14. Nothing gets moving until after midnight on Friday and Saturday. For taped tangos from Argentina, head for **El Viejo Almacén** at Carrera 5, No. 14–23.

Cartagena
In Cartagena, a Caribbean trio plays on weekends at **Paco's** opposite the Santo Domingo church – a good place to drink into the small hours. The bar attached to **La Quemada** has live salsa on Friday and Saturday nights, with dancing. For discos, head for the **Bocagrande** district.

Tours

Package tours, as well as travel within and beyond Colombia, can be arranged with **Interamerican Tours**, Calle 17, No.6–57.

Where to Shop

For Colombian handicrafts, the best place is **Artesanías de Colombia**, Carrera 3, No. 18–60 next to the Iglesia de las Aguas in Bogotá. Other shops are at Carrera 10, No. 26–50 and Carrera 7, No. 23–40.

Emeralds can be bought in the *joyerías* in Bogotá's **La Casa de la Emeralda**, Calle 30, No. 16–18 or in **Joyas Verdes Ltda**, Carreras 15, No. 39–15.

The best antique shop in Bogotá is on the Plaza Bolívar, next to the cathedral. Pre-Colombian pottery is sold in the **Centro Internacional**.

Ecuador
A – Z

Getting Acquainted

Area 104,500 sq miles (270,700 sq km), bordering Colombia in the north, Peru to the south and east and the Pacific Ocean in the west.
Capital Quito.
Population 14 million, 40 percent of which are of Quichua origin.
Language Spanish and Quichua.
Currency Sucre (US$1=S/6,300, £1=S/10,080).
Weights & measures Metric.
Electricity 110 volts.
Time zone GMT –5hrs, same as EST (Galápagos 1hr behind).
Dialing code 593 (Quito +2).

Government & Economy

There are 23 Ecuadorian provinces, including the Galápagos Islands. Democracy was established in 1979. The economy is based on oil, fishing, bananas, coffee and cocoa.

Visas

Visas are not required for a stay of up to 90 days. Permits (known as "T3s") for a 30-day stay are issued at the border or point of arrival and can be easily extended. For visa extensions, go to Avenida Amazonas 2639, open from 8am–noon and from 3–6pm. The immigration office in Quito is at Independencia y Amazonas 3149, tel: 454-122. The main police office dealing with tourist matters is on Calle Mantúfar.

Money

Travelers should bring US dollars for conversion as the dollar is highly valued and tends to fetch a higher rate of exchange. Travelers' checks are also acceptable. Diners and Visa credit cards are widely accepted for meals and purchases.

Postal Services

Postal services are unreliable, but better in Quito than in the provinces. The central post office and **poste restante** are located at Espejo 935 y Guayaquil in the old town.

Telephone & Telex

The main telephone and telex office (EMETEL) is on Avda 10 Augusto. The discount period is from 7pm–7am and at weekends. There is a shortage of phone lines but there are public telephones in the best hotels in city centers. Telex and fax services are offered by all major hotels.

Newspapers

The main daily newspapers sold in Ecuador are *El Comercio*, *Hoy*, *Tiempo* and *Ultimas Noticias*. Foreign papers and magazines are on sale in Quito.

Embassies & Consulates

Canada: Avda 6 de Diciembre 2816 y J. Orton, tel: 543-214.
Great Britain: Gonzáles Suárez 197 y 12 de Octubre, tel: 560-669.
United States: Avda 12 de Octubre y Patria, tel: 562-890.

Getting Around

BY AIR
Flights within mainland Ecuador are cheap. The local airlines SAETA, SAN and TAME run flights between main cities and the Galápagos.

From the Airport
Ecuador has international airports at Quito and Guayaquil. From Quito's Mariscal Sucre Airport there are buses to the old and new city center, and taxi fares are around US$5. Taxis from Guayaquil's Simón Bolívar International Airport

to the city cost US$4–5, and there are also buses. Ensure your carrier has arranged to get you to Quito if you are landing at Guayaquil.

BY BUS
Buses in Ecuador are cheap, plentiful and the most convenient way to travel: even though many roads are unpaved, and landslides are not uncommon in mountainous regions. Some air-conditioned, luxury buses cover the most popular routes.

International routes: Many travelers enter from Peru at the Tumbes–Huaquillas border post, changing buses at the frontier. Buses are frequent both ways. To Colombia, almost everyone takes the Quito-Ibarra, Tulcán–Pasto road.

Tours

Otavalo
Zulaytours offer cheap, comprehensive all-day tours of the villages surrounding Otavalo. The history and culture of the Indian people is outlined, and a visit to a pre-Inca cemetery is included. As each village specializes in a particular craft, the tour visits various homes to observe the different methods of production.

The Oriente
Metropolitan Touring offer luxury all-inclusive, 3–4-day tours down the River Aguarico from Lago Agrio to the Cuyabeno National Park aboard the Flotel Orellana (see box above). This area is excellent for wildlife. Cheaper and longer excursions can be organized in Misahualli. However wildlife is very limited, and trips can be disappointing. Dayuma Lodge is well established and reliable.

The Galápagos Islands
There are daily flights by the local internal airlines. Flights are heavily booked so you should confirm and reconfirm your seat and check in early at the airport.

All foreign visitors to the islands must pay an US$80 entrance fee to the national park on arrival at the airport. This can be paid in sucres

Excursions

Among Ecuador's snow-capped peaks, Chimborazo, Cotopaxi, El Altar and Tungurahua are certainly the most challenging, and 12 miles (20 km) north of Quito is **Mitad del Mundo**, where a monument and museum mark the equator. The road passes two dozen or so colorful billboards painted by prominent Latin American artists. On a clear day, a train or bus ride along the Avenue of the Volcanoes from Quito to Riobamba is a must.

Pasachoa is a refuge for native birds and plants and has been declared a protected forest. It is run by the Fundación Natura, which is based in Quito. Ideal for a day trip if staying in Quito.

or dollars. Keep the receipt, since you may have to show it again.

The Galápagos archipelago is almost entirely a national park, and no visitor is allowed to enter it without a qualified guide on an organized tour. The great bulk of visitors go on a cruise around the islands, taking at least three nights.

For many, a trip on one of the largest cruisers is the most comfortable and convenient way to visit the islands. The best two are the Galápagos Explorer run by SAN/SAETA from San Cristóbal island, and the Santa Cruz run by Metropolitan Touring. Both take around 80 passengers on three- or four-day cruises. You can also combine both trips to make a

River Transport

In the Oriente (Eastern lowlands), motorized dugout canoes are the chief form of public transport on Ecuador's main rivers. They can carry up to 30 passengers, as well as an unbelievable amount of cargo and livestock. Seating is on wooden boards (making your own cushion out of folded clothes will help on long journeys), and bags are usually stashed up at the front

seven-day cruise. Passengers visit the islands in groups of 10 on motorboats (pangas) accompanied by English-speaking naturalist guides.

The cost works out to between US$135 and US$225 per person per night on a twin-share basis (all inclusive, except for bar and airfare). In the United States and Europe, bookings can be made through: Galápagos Inc, 7800 Red Rd, S Miami, Fl. Tel: 1 (305) 665-0841, fax: 1 (305) 661-1457, toll-free in the US: 1 (800) 327-9854.

There are dozens of yachts operating cruises around the islands, most of which work out of Puerto Ayora, with a growing number are based in Puerto Baquerizo Morena to deal with the influx of tourists from san/Saeta flights. They can take anything from 6–20 people.

Galápago Sub-Aqua, Avda Charles Darwin, Puerto Ayora, Isla Santa Cruz, tel/fax: 593-4-314510, offers scuba diving tours and instruction.

Where to Stay

QUITO
Many budget hotels are in old Quito, the colonial heart of the city; however, crime is on the increase and it is safer to stay in the new town, which is where most of the shops and restaurants are located. In the new town, the cozy **Hostal Los Alpes**, tel: 561-128, has charming and tasteful rooms. The **Hostal Café Cultura** at Reina Victoria y Robles, is also highly recommended. The **Posada del Maple** on Rodriguez 148 y 6 de Diciembre is a good budget hotel,

end of the boat under a tarpaulin.

A much more comfortable (and expensive) alternative is the Flotel Orellana, a cruise ship which sails up the Aguarico River, close to the Peruvian border and the Cuyabeno Wildlife Reserve. Fully-inclusive packages can be booked through: **Metropolitan Touring**, Republica de El Salvador 970, Quito. Tel: 463-680; fax 464-702/465 868.

while **Hotel Carrión**, tel: 234-620, provides 5-star comfort.

GUAYAQUIL

The best area to stay is by the river, where the air is cleaner and cooler. **The Metropolitan Ramada**, tel: 565-794 and **Humboldt** hotels have good river views, while **Oro Verde**, tel: 327-999, is luxurious.

Where to Eat

QUITO

The main meal of the day is lunch (*almuerzo*), usually a soup followed by a main dish. There are many cafés for breakfast and snacks. Old Quito has little to offer but the streets surrounding Avenida Amazonas in the new town have many good restaurants. One recommended place is **La Viña**, behind Hotel Oro Verde at Isabel la Católica y Cordero, with excellent, although expensive, international cuisine. **Los Redes de los Mariscos**, on Amazonas y Veintimilla, is good (and safe) for seafood. A good vegetarian restaurant is **El Holandés**, Reina Victoria y Roca. For local dishes try **La Choza** at 12 Octubre 1821 y Cordero. For authentic Ecuadorian cuisine, try **El Campo Base**, Baquedano 355 y Juan León Mera, tel: 224-504. A popular meeting place for climbers.

GUAYAQUIL

In Guayaquil, the most pleasant place to eat is aboard one of the boats moored along the Malecón.

For cheaper and often more fiery seafood meals, the area just north of Parque del Centenario is good. Calle Escobedo has two popular street cafés serving breakfast. **Galeria El Taller Quisquis 1313**, and **Tertulia de Hilda, Huertado y Tunqurahua**, are recommended.

Nightlife

Nightlife in Ecuador often involves bars with astonishingly loud music. In **Quito**, the new town has its share of discos, as well as a reasonably authentic English pub, the Reina Victoria, on the street of the same

Public Holidays

- **January** New Year's Day (1)
- **January** Festival of the Three Kings (6)
- **March/April** Carnival (date variable, precedes Lent)
- **April** Holy Week; festivities on Good Friday and Easter Sunday (date variable)
- **May** Labor Day; workers' street parades (1)
- **July** Simon Bolívar's birthday (24)
- **August** Independence Day (10)
- **November** All Saints's Day (1), All Souls'Day (2)
- **December** Christmas Day (25)

name. The best *peña* (folk club) is the Taberna Quiteña, which has two venues – Avenida Amazonas and Calle Manabí in the old city.

El Pobre Diablo, Santamaria 338 y Juan Leon Mera, is an authentic Ecuadorian café-bar. Good for local snacks and drinks, with a friendly atmosphere.

In **Guayaquil**, countless all-night discos play the latest American and Latino tunes, and some good Colombian salsa. They are not places for the faint-hearted.

Otavalo has a couple of *peñas* which are lively at the weekend. In addition to excellent local music, they regularly feature groups from Colombia, Peru and Chile.

Where to Shop

Otavalan goods (including hand-knitted clothing, jewelry, wood-carvings, tapestries, leather goods and embroidered textiles) are the best buys in Ecuador, but there are also stores in Quito, Guayaquil, Cuenca and Baños where prices are reasonable.

Cuenca is perhaps the best place to buy quality gold and silver jewelry. Shops and stalls on Avenida Amazonas in Quito sell everything Ecuador has to offer.

French Guiana A–Z

Getting Acquainted

Area 35,135 sq miles (91,000 sq km).
Capital Cayenne.
Population 150,000. Seventy percent of people are of Creole (African/Afro-European) descent.
Language French (official language), French Guianese creole and English.
Currency French franc (Ff); US$1 = 6 Ff, £1 = 10 Ff.
Weights & Measures Metric.
Electricity 220 volts.
Time Zone GMT -3hrs, EST +2hrs.
Dialing code: 594.

Climate

The best time to visit the country is during August to December, the rest of the year, the rains are heavy and even during the dry period it is still very humid.

Government & Economy

French Guiana is an overseas department of the French Government. The country receives large subsidies from the French government and the EU. The economy is closely bound to that of France. Major sources of income in French Guiana itself include shrimp, mining, forest products and satellite launching.

Business Hours

Shop hours: Monday–Friday 8am–11.30am and 1pm–4pm. Saturday 8am–11.30am.
Banking hours: Monday–Friday 7.45am–11.30am and 3pm–5pm.

Visas & Customs

All visitors to French Guiana except EU nationals need a visa to enter the country.

There are no restrictions on the amount of currency visitors can bring in to French Guiana.

Money Matters

French Guiana is expensive as the standard of living is comparable to that of France. It is easy to change US dollars or travelers' checks into francs in Cayenne. Major credit cards are widely accepted and visitors can also get cash advances from ATMS at post offices.

Tourist Information

The **French Guiana Tourist Board** is at 12 rue Lalouette, BP 801, 97338 Cayenne, French Guiana; tel: 300 900; fax: 309 315. Information on accommodation is also available from the **Syndicat National des Agents de Voyage** (National Union of Travel Agencies), BP 513, 97300 Cayenne; tel: 382-781; fax: 325-700.

Tourist Offices Overseas

France has a tourist office devoted to distributing information about French Guiana. Contact the French Guiana Tourist Board, c/o Horwath Axe Consultants, 12 rue de Madrid, 75008 Paris, France; tel: 534-24139; fax: 438-73285.

Elsewhere, you should refer to the French tourist office.

Australia: French Government Tourist Office, BNP Building, 12th Floor, 12 Castlereagh Street, Sydney NSW 2000, tel: 231-5244.
Canada: French Government Tourist Office, 30 St Patrick Street, Suite 700, Toronto, ON M5T 3A3 tel: 593-4723; fax: 979-7587.
UK: French Government Tourist Offices, 178 Piccadilly, London W1V OAL, tel: 0891 244-123; fax: 0171 493 6594.
US: French Government Tourist Office, 610 Fifth Avenue, Suite 222, New York, NY 10020, tel: 212 757 1125; fax: 212 247 6468.

Embassies & Consulates

Canada: c/o High and Young Streets, PO Box 10880, Georgetown, Guyana, tel: 592 27 20 81; fax: 25 83 80.
UK: 16 avenue Président Monnerville, Cayenne, French Guiana, tel: 594 31 10 34/ 30 42 42; fax: 3040 94.
US: c/o 99–100 Young and Drake Streets, Georgetown, Guyana, tel: 592 25 49 00; fax: 25 84 97.

Media & Communications

Telephone and fax: IDD telephone services and fax facilities are available.
Newspapers: Daily newspapers include *France-Guyane* and *La Presse de Guyane*. There are no English-language newspapers available.
Radio: The BBC World Service broadcasts on MHz 17.79, 15.19 and 5.970. The Voice of America can be heard on MHz 13.74, 9.775, 7.405 and 5.995.

Getting Around

FROM THE AIRPORT

Cayenne-Rochambeau airport is 16km (10 miles) from Cayenne. There are no buses; taxis cost US$25 (more at night-time). Exit tax currently costs 177 francs.

BY AIR

Air Guyane has regular services to Maripasoula, Saül, Régina and St Georges from Cayenne.
Air Guyane: Roachambeau Airport, 97351 Matoury, tel: 594 29 36 30; fax: 29 36 31.

To rent a plane or book a charter flight contact: **Guyane Aero Services**, Zone d'aviation générale, 97351 Matoury, tel: 594 35 61 62; fax: 35 84 50. It is also possible to hire a helicopter contact: **Heli Inter Guyane**, Roachambeau Airport, 97351 Matoury, tel: 594 35 62 31; fax: 35 82 56.

By BOAT

Visitors can reach the interior of Guiana by boat. *Pirogues* are equipped with outboard motors. Wooden *pirogues* (dug-out canoes) can carry up to 12 passengers. Tours can be arranged, the average journey time is about five to six hours. Contact local tour agents in Cayenne or Kourou for details.

BY BUS

Buses: Cayenne and its suburbs are served by a regular bus network. Buses do not run on Sunday. Routes and timetables are available from: SMTC, 3 place des Palmistes. Tel:31 45 66.
Private coaches run between Cayenne and all the coastal towns to Saint-Laurent du Maroni. One daily service departs Monday–Saturday at 5.30am from Avenue Jean Galmot in Cayenne. It is advisable to book a ticket before departure. Bookings tel: 31 26 66 from 8am–noon and from 3pm–6pm.
Minibuses (*taxis colectifs*) run along the same route and are more comfortable than the coach. Departures start from the bus station, opposite the Laussat Canal in Cayenne. Information and bookings, tel: 30 73 05/30 52 25.

BY CAR

It is possible to hire cars in French Guiana but it is not a good idea unless you are used to driving in developing countries. Driving along dirt tracks is dangerous in the rainy season.

Car Hire

Most car hire agencies are open from 8am–noon and from 2.30pm–5.30pm, and from 8am–noon on Saturday.
AVIS, 77 rue du Lt. Goinet, Cayenne. Tel: 30 25 22; fax: 31 07 91; airport tel: 35 34 14.
Hertz, ZL de Collery, Cayenne. Tel: 35 11 71; fax: 35 10 48; airport tel: 35 60 69.
Europcar, ZL de Cllery, Cayenne. Tel: 35 18 27; fax: 35 15 57; airport tel: 35 62 69.

Tipping

At hotels and restaurants the service charge is usually included in the bill, if not, 10 percent is usually left as a tip. Taxi drivers do not receive a tip.

Accommodation Agencies

Club des Hôtelières (Hoteliers Club), Immeuble CTG, 12 rue Lallouette, Cayenne, French Guiana, tel: 293-931; fax: 299-621.
Syndicat des Hôteliers, Restaurateurs et Cafetiers de Guyane (Guiana Federation of Hotels, Restaurants and Cafés), PK 9, 2 Route de Rémire, 97354 Remire Montjoly, French Guiana, tel: 354-100; fax: 354-405.
Relais Départemental des Gîtes de France (Guest Houses of France, Departmental Office), Immeuble CTG, 12 rue Lallouette, 97300 Cayenne, French Guiana, tel: 300-900; fax: 30 93 15.

Where to Stay

CAYENNE
Amazonia (luxury), 26–28 Av de Gaulle, 97300 Cayenne, tel: 310-000; fax: 311-296. Some rooms have kitchenettes. Air-conditioning, restaurant and swimming pool.
Central (luxury), at the crossroads of rue Molé and Mecker, 97300 Cayenne, tel: 319-441; fax: 306-600. Swimming pool.
Phigarita (luxury), 42 rue Colomb, 97300 Cayenne, tel: 313-300; fax: 307-749.With air-conditioning, pool.
Hotel Ajoupa (moderate), Route du Camp du Tigre, 97300 Cayenne, tel: 303-308; fax: 301-282. With pool and garden.
Le Neptima (inexpensive), 21 Rue Félix Eboué, 97300 Cayenne, tel: 301-115; fax: 301-478.

REMIRE
Motel Beauregard (luxury), PK, 9,05 Rte de Rémire, 97351 Remire, tel: 354-100; fax: 354-405. With pool, horse riding, mini golf and tennis.

KOUROU
Mercure Ariatel (luxury), Lac Bois diable, 97310 Kourou, tel: 328-900; fax: 326-160. Luxury bungalows, with swimming pool.
Hotel des Roches (luxury), BP 814, 97310 Kourou, tel: 320-066; fax: 320-328. Restaurant, swimming pool and piano bar.
Le Ballahou (moderate), 2 and 3 rue a Martiel, 97310 Kourou, tel: 324-206; fax: 325-208.

REMIRE MONTJOLY
Motel du Lac (luxury), Chemin Poupon, 97354 Remire Montjoly, tel: 380-800; fax: 38 10 34.

MATOURY
Le Polygone (luxury), Carrefour du Larivot, 97351 Matoury, tel: 351-400; fax: 35 28 50. Bungalows, with pool, shop, tennis court.
Le Grillardin (luxury), PK 6 Rte de Matoury, 97351 Matoury, tel:356-390; fax: 35 86 05.
Lac Maran (budget), PK 1, 5 de Rouchambeau, 97351 Matoury, tel: 356-294.

ST-LAURENT DU MARONI
Hotel Star (luxury), 109 Rue Thiers, 97320 St Laurent du Maroni, tel: 341-084; fax: 34 25 19.
La Tentiare (luxury), 12 Av Franklin Roosevelt, 97320 St Laurent du Maroni, tel: 342-600; fax: 341-007.
Chez Julienne (inexpensive), Route des Malgaches, 97320 St Laurent du Maroni, tel: 341-153.
Le Toucan (budget), Bd. du Gal de Gaulle, 97320 St Laurent du Maroni, tel: 341-259; fax: 341-007. With terrace, restaurant.

ROURA
Auberge des Orpailleurs (luxury), 62 Route de l'Est, tel: 376-297. Meals available; hammock lodge.
Amazone River (budget), Bourg de Roura, Esplanade del'eglise, 97311 Roura, tel: 280-200. One carbet (wooden lodge) with hammocks, and café.

SINNAMARY
Hotel du Fleuve (luxury), BP 114, 97351 Sinnamary, tel: 345-400; fax: 345-303.

Sinnarive Motel (budget), Savane Manuel, 97315 Sinnamary, tel: 345-656.

Tourist Lodges

The following places offer traditional wooden lodges (carbets) located in areas of natural beauty, often deep in tropical forest:

Les Maripas (Guyane Excursions), PK 17, on the road to Degrad Saramaka, 97310 Kourou, tel: 320-541. Hammocks.
Degrad Cascades (La Marine), Cascades River, one hour from Tonnégrande by pirogue, tel: 399-365. Hammocks and beds.
Campement de Saut Sonnelle, 30 minutes by boat along the Inini River from Maripasoula, tel: 314-945. Hammocks.
Gite Quimbe Kio, village of Cacao, 97352, Cacao, tel: 270-122. Hammocks/beds.
Amazonie Detente, Valentin Falls, Mana River, tel: 325-288. Hammocks.
Eden des Eaux Claires, 7km north of Saül in remote "massif central", tel: 309-111. Camp in tropical forest; beds or hammocks.

Carnival

Carnival usually starts in January. While it's not the extravaganza of Rio de Janeiro or the Caribbean, it is a vibrant affair with a cultural mix of Creole, Brazilian and Haitian influences. Every weekend from Epiphany festivities are held until they reach a five-day non-stop partying climax before Ash Wednesday. In the colorful parades in central Cayenne, dancers dress in elaborate costumes, each day based on a different traditional theme.

What to Eat

As a département of France, French Guiana has an expectedly high standard of food, particularly in and around Cayenne, with added color and variety provded by its rich racial mix. There is a wide choice of restaurants, mostly serving French and international cuisine, but also Vietnamese, Indonesian, Creole and Chinese cooking can be found. Prices are relatively high at the best restaurants, but a decent, cheap meal can be had at one of the many Asian cafés or food stalls.

Where to Eat

CAYENNE

By the Canal Laussant are many Javanese and Creole cafes and food-stalls, although some are not particularly clean and it is not a safe area at night.

Deli France,
corner of Rue Justin Cayatée and Avenue du Général de Gaulle. Good snacks, pastries and coffee.

La Victoire,
40 Rue 14 Juillet.
Chinese and Creole cuisine served at outside tables; tasty and good value meals, friendly atmosphere.

Les Pyramides,
corner of Rue C. Colomb and Rue Malouet.
Inexpensive Middle Eastern dishes, such as couscous and grills.

Hostellerie Les Amandiers,
Pointe des Amandiers.
The best in the city, facing attractive park. Expensive but worth it.

KOUROU

Le Provence,
11 Passage G Monnerville.
French, best in town but pricey.

Ballahou,
Ballahou Hotel, 1 Rue Armet Martial.
Good fish and seafood.

ST-LAURENT DU MARONI

Restaurant Vietnam, 19 Avenue Félix Eboué.
Good value Asian dishes.

Chez Felicia,
Avenue du Général de Gaulle.
Creole cuisine, reasonably priced.

Restaurant La Saramaca,
Av Felix Eboue.
The best in town but expensive (also has accommodation at the back of the restaurant.)

Guyana A–Z

Getting Aquainted

Area 83,000 sq miles (215,000 sq km).
Capital Georgetown.
Population 758,000.
Language English (official language), Creole, Hindi, Urdu and Amerindian are also spoken.
Currency Guyana dollar; US$1 = G$147; UK£1 = G$235.
Weights & Measures Officially metric although imperial measures are widely used.
Electricity 110V (Georgetown), 220V (most other places).
Time Zone GMT - 4 hrs, EST + 1 hr.
Dialing Code 592.

Climate

The temperature remains warm with equatorial humidity all year round, but not excessively hot; average temperatures are between 24°C (75°F) and 31°C (88°F). The best time to visit is July–November, between the two wet seasons, which are from May through June and from December through January. Average annual rainfall is 230 cm (91 inches).

Government & Economy

Guyana gained independence in 1966 and became a republic in 1970. The government is democratically elected and the president is head of state.

The economy is based on four export products: bauxite, gold, sugar and rice. Gold production has increased in recent years. It is one of the poorest countries in the Western Hemisphere

Visas

Visas are required by visitors from all except the following countries: US, Commonwealth countries, Belgium, Denmark, France, Germany, Greece, Ireland, Italy, Luxembourg, Netherlands, Portugal, Spain, Norway, Finland, Sweden, Japan and Korea. Proof of onward travel is also necesssary.

Public Holidays

- **January:** New Year's Day (1)
- **February:** Republic Day and Mashramani Festival (23)
- **March/April:** Phagwah (Hindu Religious Holiday), Good Friday, Easter Monday and Eid-ul-Azha (Muslim Holy Day)
- **May:** Labour Day (1), Independence Day (26)
- **July:** Caricom Day (1)
- **August:** Freedom Day
- **December:** Christmas Day (25) and Boxing Day (26)

Customs

No duty charged on personal goods, but high charges on items brought in for commercial purposes.

Money Matters

The currency is the Guyanese dollar, available in denominations of 1, 5, 10 (coins), 20, 100, 500 and 1,000 (notes). The value of the Guyanese dollar (G$) is revised weekly.

Most banks and bureaux de change buy only US or Canadian dollars and UK sterling. It is possible to change travelers' checks at a few of the larger stores and travel agents in Georgetown.

Tourist Offices

Tourism Association of Guyana, 157 Waterloo Street, North Cummingsburg, Georgetown, tel: 250-807 (24-hr emergency hotline: 56699); fax: 250-817. E-mail: tag@solutions2000.net; web site: www.interknowledge.com./guyana

Specialist Tour Operators

Wilderness Explorers: 61 Hadfield and Cross Streets, Georgetown, Guyana, tel: 262-085.
Trips Worldwide, 9 Byron Place, Clifton, Bristol BSB 1JT, tel: (117) 987-2626; fax: 987-2627.

Media & Communications

Telephone: IDD is avaliable in most main towns and cities.
Fax: available from the Guyana Telephone and Telegraph Company, the Bank of Guyana Building in Georgetown and larger hotels.
Postal Services: post services are very good and cheap. The main Post Office is on Main Street in Georgetown.
Newspapers: *The Guyana Chronicle* is a state-owned daily newspaper. Other dailies include *The Mirror*, *The Kaieteur News* and *The New Nation,* and the independent *Stabroek News*, (daily except Mondays); and the respected and popular weekly *Catholic Standard.*
Radio: BBC World Service (MHz 17.79, 15.19, 11.75 and 9.915), the Voice of America (MHz 13.74, 9.775, 7.405, 5.995).
Television: there are 14 TV channels, broadcasting mostly US satellite programs but with increasing local productions.

Emergency Numbers

Police: 911
Fire: 912
Ambulance service: 913

Embassies & Consulates

British High Commission, 44 Main Steet, PO Box 10849, Georgetown, Guyana, tel: 265-881/4; 253-555/250671.
Canadian High Commission, corner of High St & Young St, Georgetown, tel: 272-081.
France, 7 Sheriff St, Subrayanville, tel: 275-435.

United States, Young St, Georgetown, tel: 254-900
Brazil, 308-9 Church St, Queenstown, tel: 257-970.
Surinam, 304 Church St, Queenstown, tel: 256-995/67-844.
Venezuela, Thomas St, Georgetown, tel: 260-841

Car Hire

Camex, 125 'D' Barrack Street, Kingston, Georgetown, Guyana. Tel: (592) 276-976.
Trident Auto Rentals, 215 Camp Street, Georgetown, Guyana. Tel: (592) 253-867; fax: 256-864.

Getting Around

FROM THE AIRPORT
Chedi Jagan International Aiport is 25 miles (40 km) from Georgetown at Timehri. Minibuses (No 42) to the center cost US$1, and will take you to your hotel for a small fee; taxis cost US$20–25 (double at night, cheaper to book a seat on a minibus on arrival). Departure Tax is G$1,500.

BY AIR
Internal flights are the best way to get around Guyana. Guyana Airways has scheduled flights from Georgetown to Lethem. Charter companies include Trans Guyana Airways and Kayman Sankar. An airstrip at Ogle, about 20 minutes from the centre of Georgetown by road, is used for domestic flights.

BY BUS
A series of minibuses and collective taxis run along the coast and to many destinations inland. This form of transport is cheap but slow. Taxis have an H in their number plates.

BY RIVER
Guyana has over 600 miles (965 km) of navigable waterways. There are frequent services but they tend to be erratic. *Ballahoos* are six-seater boats, *corials* are four-seater boats.

BY CAR
Most of the main roads are found in the coastal area. There is a highway being built between Bonfim in Guyana and Boa Vista in Brazil; when it is finished it will allow Guyana to connect with the network of roads on the continent.

Where to Stay

Most of the luxury and business hotels are in Georgetown; quality ranges from good to reasonable.

GEORGETOWN
Le Meridien Pegasus, Seawall Road, tel: 252-8539; fax: 260-532. Luxury, with pool, restaurants, tennis, gym (also owns **Timberhead Rainforest Reserve** - *see below*).
Hotel Tower, 74-75 Main Street, tel: 272–011/5, (800) 742-4276 for reservations; fax: 265-691/256-021. Luxury, with pool and very good restaurant.
Cara Lodge, 293 Quamina Street, tel: 255-301; fax: 255-310. Small and luxurious; converted 150-year old mansion, with good restaurant, bar and service.
Florentene's Hotel, 3 North Road. Lacytown, tel: 262-283. Clean and economical; highly recommended.
Rima Guest House, 92 Middle Street, tel: 257-401. Safe and central budget hotel, with good value restaurant.

NEW AMSTERDAM
Hotel Astor, 7 Strand, tel: 3578. Comfortable mid-range hotel, breakfast available, recommended.
Parkway Hotel, 4 Main Street, near

Security

Georgetown is a colorful and attractive city but you should take care in some areas (avoid Tiger Bay and Albouystown in particular) and do not walk around the streets at night. Violent crimes on the streets and highways are common, and there are many beggars, although most are harmless.

the mosque, tel: 3928.
Reasonable mid-range place; clean friendly and safe.

LETHEM

Savannah Inn, General Store. Tel (592 - Georgetown) 69716. Good and clean, mid-range. Can also be booked through Wilderness Explorers (tel: 262-085), and organizes jungle tours.

Jungle Lodges

There are an increasing number of lodges and camps in the tropical forest interior, catering for the growing eco-tourism market. These establishments, whose facilities range from basic to up-market, usually run their own treks and nature safaris. Some recommended places are listed here.
Timberhead Rainforest Reserve, two hours from Georgetown by air and boat up the Kamuni River. Reservations with **Le Meridien Pegasus** in Georgetown (see above). Three comfortable lodges with inclusive facilities, meals, and guided activities. Good bird-watching area.
Dadanawa Ranch, 60 miles (97 km) south of Lethem, is a huge establishment, which runs horseback riding and trekking expeditions. Can also be booked through Wilderness Explorers, above.
Rock View Ecotourism Resort, Annai, a village 70 miles (112 km) from Lethem, tel: 64210; fax: 57211 (or book through Wilderness Explorers, above). Small, with some cheaper rooms, bars, and a zoo.

Outdoor Activities

Guyana's most popular sport is cricket. The Georgetown Cricket Club, at Bourda, is one of the finest grounds in the Caribbean.
  The coastline is not ideal for water sports, but there are some good opportunities in the interior for trekking and river-rafting, which can be arranged by local tour operators.

What to Eat

Guyanese cuisine is good and varied, combining influences from the Caribbean, creole, African, European, North American, Amerindian and Asian populations. Seafood is particularly tasty. Some interesting creole dishes include the traditional Christmas dish, pepperpot (meat cooked with hot spices and cassava juice); cow-heel soup and saltfish. There is a wide range of tropical fruits (often served in some excellent juice bars) and vegetables. Locally produced rum is the favored tipple, and the beer, Banks, is quite palatable.

Where to Eat

Many restaurants close on public holidays; cheaper places are often open only for lunch. Formal dress may be demanded in some of the capital's upmarket restaurants.

GEORGETOWN

Browne's Brasserie Café,
Le Meridien Pegasus, Seawall Road.
International and creole cuisine, good English breakfast.
El Dorado,
Le Meridien Pegasus, Seawall Road.
International and creole cuisine, smart and upmarket.
Sidewalk Cafe and Jazz Club,
176 Middle Street, tel: (592) 261-416. Local and international cuisine; also has shows by top-name musicians.
The Coal Pot,
17 Hincks Street.
Good lunchtime menu, cheap and tasty seafood, popular.
Salt and Pepper,
Robb Street.
Recommended for cheap and authentic Guyanese dishes.

NEW AMSTERDAM

Brown Derby,
corner of Church and Main Streets.
Good East Indian and Chinese food.
Circle C,
Main and Charlotte Street. Good and cheap creole cuisine.

Paraguay A–Z

Getting Acquainted

Area 157,000 sq miles (406,800 sq km).
Capital Asunción.
Population 4.3 million. Eighty percent of Paraguayans are mestizo. There has also been heavy immigration from Korea, Japan and Taiwan.
Language Spanish and Guaraní.
Currency: Guaraní; US$1=G/2,810; UK£1 = 4,500.
Weights & measures Metric.
Electricity 220 volts.
Time zone GMT –3hrs in east, –4hrs in the west (EST +3hrs, EST +1hr).
Dialing code 595 (Asunción +21).

Government & Economy

General Alfredo Stroessner was overthrown in 1989 after 35 years in office, yet still today both the Colorado Party, founded in 1887, and the armed forces remain highly influential in national politics.
  Political reforms since the demise of Stroessner include the adoption of a new constitution in 1992, and a process of decentralisation of power to local departmental and municipal government.
  Agricultural products such as meat, soya and cotton still account for the main bulk of exports, although the economy still relies strongly on contraband and drug smuggling.

Customs

Alcohol, tobacco and electronic items for personal use are admitted to the country duty-free.

Visas

The entry requirement for most countries (including Great Britain) is a passport. Check with your local travel agent to see if you require a visa and accompanying papers.

Money

It is not possible to exchange guaraní outside the country – so only change what you will need. *Casas de cambio* will accept travelers' checks. ATM dispensers are fairly widespread and major credit cards are widely accepted.

Tourist Information

The *Dirección Nacional de Turismo* is at Palma 468 in Asuncíon. Information is available at the Touring & Automobile Club of Paraguay at 25 de Mayo y Brasil.

Emergencies

A satisfactory ambulance service is not available; it's best to transport the patient by private means or taxi. Have someone phone the hospital, stating the nature of the illness and asking that a doctor receive the patient in the emergency room. To contact the police in an emergency, dial **442-111**.

For emergencies, contact any of the Asunción emergency rooms: **Centro Paraguayo del Diagnóstico**, Gral Díaz 975 y Colón, Asuncíon, tel: 947-722.
Hospital Bautista, Avda Rep. Argentina and Campos Cervera, tel: 600-171 or 607-944.

Business Hours

Working hours are similar to those of Central America. Many shops and offices open at 6.30am.

The siesta, which is between noon–3pm, is observed during the hot season, and offices then open again until 7pm. Banks tend to be open from 7.30–11am and are closed Saturday, although some have longer hours. Dinner is served somewhat earlier than in neighboring countries, that is, 8.30–11pm.

Religious Services

The state religion is Roman Catholicism. There is a Sunday Mass in English at Padres Oblatos de María Chapel, on Gómez de Castro and Quesada. Other churches include the Anglican Church on Avda España 1261, the Mormon Church on Avda España and the Brasília Synagogue on Gral. Diaz 657.

Media

Radio is the most effective means of communication. One of the most popular is *Radio Ñandutí*, recently re-opened after being shut down by Stroessner's government. Two privately-owned television networks operate in Asunción; all TV drama programs are imported from the United States and the neighboring countries. Channel 8 shows CNN in English.

Newspaper quality has improved considerably since press censorship was lifted in 1989. The widest-circulating dailies are: *ABC Color*, *Noticias*, *La Nación*, and *Ultima Hora* (an afternoon daily).

Telecoms

It is wise to send important letters by registered mail. All mail must be deposited at a post office counter. Long-distance calls can be made from ANTELCO office on N.S. de Asunción and Presidente Franco. Telex and fax services are also available. International calls are called either *ordinario* or *urgente*, urgent calls costing twice as much.

Embassies & Consulates

Germany: Av Venezuela 241, tel: 24006/7.
Great Britain: Pte. Franco 706, p4 (Casilla 404), tel: 444-472/449-146. Will keep mail received.
United States: Av Mcal. Lopez 1776, tel: 213-715/210-489.

Public Holidays

- **January** 1
- **February** 3
- **March** 1, Maundy Thursday Good Friday
- **May** 1, 14, 15
- **June** 12
- **August** 15, 25
- **September** 29
- **October** 12
- **November** 1
- **December** 8, 25.

Getting Around

FROM THE AIRPORT

Asunción's Silvio Pettirosi Airport is 16km (10 miles) from the center; taxis can be booked at agencies' desks, approximately US$15; buses from outside the airport to the center, US$0.30, but luggage space is limited. There is an entry tax of US$12 and departure tax of US$4 (cheaper to pay in guaranís).

BY BUS

Buses are the main means of transport within Paraguay; the main terminal is a 20-minute cab ride from the center of Asunción at Rep. Argentina and Fernando de la Mora (tel: 552-154). "Executive" buses vary according to company.

There is a luxury international bus service that serves Asunción and Ciudad del Este, Pedro Juan Caballero and Encarnación by way of Argentina, Uruguay and Brazil.

BY RIVER

There are several boats that sail up the **Paraná River** to **Concepción** every 2–3 weeks, a journey of 27–30 hours ; the *Guaraní III*, Saturdays at 11am, US$8 plus US$7 for a cabin,; meals served on board; the *Cacique II*, Wednesdays at 7am, US$27 1st class, US$17 2nd class, US$11 deck space, basic restaurant on board. An irrregular passenger boat service shuttles downstream between **Buenos Aires** and Asunción. The journey takes five days and can be suspended during the dry season.

BY CAR

Petrol is cheap and car hire relatively inexpensive; contact Touring y Automóvil Club Paraguayo, Calle Brasil, tel: 210 550.

Taxis are inexpensive, averaging US$2 per journey in Asunción. Minimum charge is about US$0.80; more by night. One main taxi stand is in front of the Hotel Guaraní on the Plaza de los Héroes; or call RadioTaxi: 550-116/311-080.

Where to Stay

ASUNCION

Cecilia Hotel, Estados Unidos 341, tel: 210-033/034, fax: 497-111. Has a good restaurant.

Chaco Hotel, Caballero esq. Mcal. Estigarribia, tel: 492-066/9, fax: 444-223. Rooftop pool.

Excelsior Hotel, Chile 980, tel: 495-632/5. The best. Modern with conference facilities.

Guaraní Hotel, Ind. Nacional y Oliva, tel: 491-131, fax: 443-647. Central, tried and tested.

Hotel de Yacht y Golf Club Paraguay, PO Box 1795, tel: 361-17, fax: 361-20. Sporting, with all the trimmings.

What to Eat

Paraguayan specialties include surubí, a tasty fish dish; sopa paraguaya, a rich cornbread; soyo, a beef and vegetable soup; empanadas and fresh tropical juices. Paraguayan beef is excellent. Also make sure you try tereré, a local ice-cold drink.

There are also a number of excellent Brazilian restaurants with succulent barbecue grilled meats and large self-service buffets.

Where to Eat

ASUNCION

Bar San Roque, Eligio Ayala esquina Tacuary, near Plaza Uruguaya. Old-style café-restarant with an excellent selection of different cuisines. Closed Sunday.

Bar Asunción, Estrella y 14 de Agosto. Fast food and Paraguayan specialties.

Amstel, Avda Rep Argentina 1384. Expensive; good traditional food.

La Preferida, 25 de Mayo y Estados Unidos, tel: 491-126. Excellent international cuisine.

Sukiyaki, Avda Constitución near Brasil. Japanese.

Tallyrand, Mcal Estigarribia 932, tel: 441-163. Best and most expensive. French cuisine and game.

Drinking Tips

Paraguayan beer is made according to German methods and is excellent. The national wine is not recommended. The local sugar cane liquor, caña, is popular but just about any imported liquor is available here at low prices.

Theater Restaurants

A typical evening's entertainment is a restaurant floor show, with Paraguayan harp and guitar music, and sometimes the (indescribable and unmissable!) bottle dance. Prices vary according to the quality of the show, but are generally about $10 per person. Recommended spots include:

Hermitage, 15 de Agosto 1870.

Hotel Casino, Ita Enramada Cacique Lambare y Rio Paraguay, tel: 330-41. Out of town, also has casino.

Tours

Check with recommended tourist agencies such as: Inter Express, Luis A. de Herrera and Yegros, and Time Tours, 15 de Agosto y General Díaz, tel: 493-527.

Cinemas

Some of the best foreign films are shown here. Check the daily newspapers for what's on where.

Where to Shop

The street market in Calle Palma is pedestrianized on Saturday mornings and has a variety of goods; leather and lace are good value.

Peru A–Z

Getting Acquainted

Area 496,100 sq miles (1,285,000 sq km).

Capital Lima.

Population 22 million. Because of successive waves of immigration, Indian and mestizo citizens live side by side with Europeans and Chinese and Japanese. The country's coastal cities to the south include a cohesive black population.

Language The official languages are Spanish and Quechua, although all school children must also study English. Near Puno and Lake Titicaca, Aymara is spoken.

Currency Sol, US$1=S/3; UK£1 = S/4.8.

Weights & measures Metric.

Electricity 220 volts.

Time zone GMT –5, same as EST.

Dialing code 51 (Lima 1).

Government & Economy

Since 1979 Peru has been governed by a democratic government under a constitution. Presidential elections are held every five years and municipal elections are held every three years. The country is divided into 24 departments and the province of Callao which is where the country's main port is located.

Fishing, mining and tourism play important roles in the economy, although the government of Alan García gradually revitalized the farming sector. Petroleum is extracted from the Amazon jungle area, providing half the domestic demand.

A slump in the manufacturing sector, caused partly by the

nation's refusal to pay its huge foreign debt and the corresponding cut of new aid from lenders, resulted in a series of problems with foreign reserves, weakening the currency in the mid-80s.

In 1992, the manufacturing sector began to return to growth when consumption was stimulated by salary increases and successful negotiations by the Fugimori government with Peru's international creditors. Agriculture and the copper and fishing industries all reached record highs and Fujimori was re-elected in 1995.

Visas

Visitors from all European countries (except Spain), the United States and Canada, do not require visas to enter Peru. With a valid passport, citizens of these countries receive a tourism card which is usually good for 90 days. Australians and New Zealanders need visas. A 30-day extension is available upon payment of $20 and presentation of a return travel ticket. Contact the *Dirección General de Migraciones* in the Ministerio del Oficina de Migración, Avda España cda 7, Breña, tel: 330-4111.

Vaccinations are not required for entry to Peru.

Tax: on departure, a $20 exit tax on international flights must be paid in US dollars or the same amount in Soles.

Customs

It is illegal to take archeological artifacts out of the country. Special permits are needed to bring professional movie or video equipment into Peru. In Cuzco, a special tax is charged for professional photographers passing their equipment through the airport.

Money

Dollars in cash can be changed with the *cambistas*, authorized money changers on street corners, found in large cities. They generally wear a green jacket and carry a calculator

(it's worth having your own calculator handy, to check their sums.)

Most international credit cards are accepted. Credit card loss can be reported in Lima. Visa: 372-5808, or free call 0800-1-3333. Diners Club: 221-2050. MasterCard: 222-4242.

Useful Addresses

Main Tourist Office: PromPeru, Ministerio de Industria, Comercio Interior, Turismo e Integración, piso 13, San Isidro, tel: 224-3126. They also have a counter in the national departure area and international arrival area of Jorge Chávez Airport, Lima.

Tourist Police Office: Museo de la Nación, Avda Javier Prado Este 2465, piso 5, San Borja, tel: 476-7708.

Medical Services

Most major hotels have a doctor on call. Three clinics in Lima and its suburbs have 24-hour emergency service and usually an English-speaking member of staff on duty: **Clínica Anglo-Americana**, Alfredo Salazar s/n, San Isidro, tel: 221-3656/221-2240; the **Clínica Internacional** Jr. Washington 1475, Lima, tel: 433-4306 and the **Clínica San Borja**, Avda Guardia Civil 337, San Borja, tel: 475-4000/3141/4997. **Emergency Hospital Casimiro Ulloa**, Avda República de Panamá 6355, San Antonio, Miraflores, tel: 445-5096/8544. A recommended English-speaking dentist is Victor Manuel Aste. Tel: 441-7502.

Business Hours

Offices normally operate from Monday to Friday, 8.30am–6pm with a break from 12.30–3pm; or some open continuously from 9am–5pm. Banking hours are from 9am–12.30pm and from 3–6pm from Monday to Friday all year round.

Embassies & Consulates

The following diplomatic representation is all in Lima: **Canada:** Libertad 130, Miraflores, tel: 444-4015, fax: 444-4347. **Great Britain:** Natalio Sánchez 125, 4th floor, Lima, tel: 433-8923, fax: 433-4738. **Ireland:** Santiago Acuña 135, Urb. Aurora, Miraflores, tel: 445-6813, fax: 242-3849). **United States:** La Encalada, cda. 17 s/n, Monterrico, tel: 434-3000 (emergencies after hours, tel: 434-3032), fax: 434-3037.

Getting Around

FROM THE AIRPORT

There is a bus service, **Transhotel** (Logroño 132, Miraflores, tel: 448-2179), which runs to and from Jorge Chavez Airport, Lima. Make reservations beforehand.

A bit more expensive but reliable are **Lima Taxis** (tel: 476-2121). A normal taxi will charge about $10 to or from the airport (US$20 to Miraflores), and it's much safer than trying to flag one down in Avda Faucett, outside the terminal.

You can also **rent cars** at the airport, where Avis, Budget, Dollar, Hertz and National have offices open 24 hours a day. An international driver's license is needed and is valid for 30 days. For additional days, it is necessary to obtain authorization from the **Touring and Automobile Club of Peru**, located at César Vallejo 699, Lince, tel: 221-2432, fax: 441-0531.

BY AIR

Domestic airlines Aero Continente and AeroPerú serve most cities in Peru. **Aero Continente** is at Avda José Pardo 651, Miraflores, tel: 242-7638; fax: 241-8098. **AeroPerú**'s main office is at Avda José Pardo 601, Miraflores, tel: 241-1797, fax: 447-8862. For trips over the **Nazca lines** or special short flights, Aerocondor has an office at Jr. Juan de Arona 781, San Isidro, tel: 441-1354/440-1754.

BY ROAD

Lima has a multitude of city bus lines. Most are overcrowded, slow and not recommended for tourists.

Cab fares are generally so inexpensive by international standards that they are preferred.

For travel outside the city, cars may be rented, transportation can be arranged through travel agencies and buses are available to just about every part of the country.

Peru has borders with five other countries: Chile, Bolivia, Colombia, Brazil and Ecuador. The border crossing with Chile is at Tacna on the Peruvian side, Arica on the Chilean; taxis regularly make the crossing and some long distance buses operate between Lima, Quito, Santiago de Chile and Buenos Aires. Tickets sometimes include food and overnight accommodation in resthouses.

From Bolivia, efficient minibus services will take you from La Paz to Puno; alternatively, **Crillón Tours** in Bolivia offers a hydrofoil across Lake Titicaca. The journey from Ecuador is also straightforward: take a bus to the Huaquillas border and walk through to Tumbes. Other buses operate from there.

BY TRAIN

There are train services in the south to and from Arequipa, Puno and Cuzco. Make sure you have a guaranteed seat and a tourist (first-class) ticket. Tickets for the Puno to Cuzco journey can be bought in Puno, Cuzco or Copaca-bana in Bolivia.

The train depot for all departures in Lima is the **Desamparados Station** behind the Presidential Palace, tel: 276-620/289-440. The journey up to La Oroya and Huancayo has been suspended since 1991, although there is still a service in operation from Huancayo to Huancavelica.

Where to Stay

AREQUIPA

El Portal, Portal de Flores 116, tel: 215-530. Excellent views and rooftop pool.

Hotel La Casa de mi Abuela, Jerusalem 606, tel/fax: 224-585. Very popular budget place, idyllic garden setting; some mini-apartments; locals tours booked.
Libertador Hotel, Plaza Bolívar on Selva Alegre, tel: 221-5110, fax: 241-933. Reservations in Lima: tel: 442-1996, fax: 442-2988. The most traditional hotel in Arequipa. Expensive.

CAJAMARCA

Hostal Laguna Seca, Avda Manco Capac Baños Termales. Just outside the city at the thermal baths, the waters of which enter the bathrooms of this hotel; tel: 823-149, fax: 823-915). Expensive.
Hotel Sierra Galana, Lima 773, tel/fax: 922-470. Reservations in Lima, tel: 446-3652, fax: 445-1139. Very comfortable and central.

CUZCO

El Dorado Inn, Sol 395, tel: 231-232, fax: 240-993. Five-star hotel with pool and sauna.
Libertador Cuzco, Plazoleta Santo Domingo 259, tel: 231-961, fax 233-152. The best of the five-stars.
Corihuasi, Suecia 561, tel: 232-233. Cheap hotel two blocks from the Plaza de Armas.
Hostal Loreto, Pasaje Loreto (the famous Inca walled lane). Popular with budget travelers.

IQUITOS

Explorama Lodge/camp. Outside the city in virgin rainforest. To make reservations in Iquitos, check at the administrative offices on Avenida de la Marina 340, tel: 252-530, fax: 252-533.
Hostal La Pascana, Pevas 133, tel: 231-418. Basic but comfortable budget hotel, with garden.

LIMA

Gran Hotel Bolívar, Jr de la Unión 958, Plaza San Martín, tel: 427-2305. The doyen of Peruvian hotels.
Hotel Crillon, Comena 589, tel: 428-3290, fax: 426-5920. The hotel's Sky Room stages the best folkloric show in Lima.

Sheraton Lima Hotel & Towers, Paseo de la República 170, tel: 433-3320, fax: 433-6344. Deluxe hotel with 500 guest rooms, on the edge of town.
Hotel Europa, Jr Ancash 376, Plaza San Francisco, Lima, tel: 427-3351. Very cheap hotel in the heart of downtown Lima.
Hotel España, Jr Azángaro 105, Lima, tel: 428-5546, fax: 330-5412. Budget hotel in central area.
Miraflores Park Plaza, Avda Malecón de la Reserva 1035, tel 242-3000. The most luxurious hotel in Miraflores with ocean view.
Hostal El Patio, Diez Canseco 341, tel: 444-4884, fax: 444-1663. Colonial style hotel in the heart of Miraflores.

NAZCA

Hotel de la Borda, Km 447 off the Pan American Highway. Reservations must be made in Lima, tel: 440-8430. Friendly, renovated *hacienda* near the airport.

PUNO (LAKE TITICACA)

Hotel Libertador Isla Esteves, Isla Esteves, Puno, tel 368-577, fax: 7879. Reservations in Lima tel: 442-1996, fax 442-2988. Big, white modern building with an excellent view of the Titicaca. Expensive.

TRUJILLO

La Casa Suiza, Los Pinos 451, tel: 51 (044) 461-285. Situated in the nearby beach village of Huanchaco.
Libertador Trujillo, Independencia 485, Plaza de Armas, tel: 232-741/244-999, fax: 235-641. Good value.
Hotel El Golf, Urb. El Golf, PO Box 329, tel: 44-242-592, fax: 44-232-515 Luxury hotel with pools.

What to Eat

Peru's cuisine is just about as varied as its geography and ranges from scrumptious seafood to potatoes – the staple in a variety of highland dishes – to tropical fruits from the Amazon jungle.

Recommended dishes include *ceviche*, or raw fish and/or shellfish marinated in lemon juice and onions. A typical chicken entrée is *ajï de gallina* served in a lightly spicy creamed sauce. Also with a spicy sauce, but this one cheese-based, is *Papa a la Huancaina*. For the adventurous, *cuy* or guinea pig is available stewed or fried. Hot peppers (*ajï* or *rocoto*) are used liberally in many typical dishes.

As for desserts, the Peruvians have a variety of fruits including *chirimoya*, a large green fleshy fruit, or *lúcuma*, a small, tangy, nut-like fruit, or *tuna*, the sweet crisp fruit of the cactus. *Mazamorra morada*, a fruity pudding dating from colonial days, is another favorite at the end of a meal.

Where to Eat

LIMA
La Gloria Calle Atahulapa 201, Miraflores tel: 445-5705. Delicious Mediterranean-style food.
El Otro Sitio Sucre 317 in the suburb of Barranco, tel: 772-413. International and traditional dishes.
La Rosa Nautica Espigon No 4 Costa Verda, Miraflores, tel: 470-057. Lima's best seafood restaurant on an ocean boardwalk.

CUZCO
Café Bagdad Plaza de Armas. Serves good food and has balcony seats overlooking the square.
Pucará, Plateros 309, corner of the

Where to Shop

Jirón de la Unión in downtown Lima is the best place to find good-quality gifts made from precious metals.
Some of the best artisan work is found at the **Feria Artesanal** on Avenida de la Marina and Avenida Sucre, in Pueblo Libre. Handicrafts from all over Peru can be bought here, although prices are higher than in their place of origin.
Kunturwasi, Ocharán 182, Miraflores, tel: 242-9469/444-0557, has a very good selection of Peruvian crafts.

Plaza de Armas. Excellent home-made, international and typical Peruvian food, charming atmosphere. Reservations recommended.
Pizzería Chez Maggy Plateros 339, and **Trattoría Adriano**, Avda Sol 105 corner with Mantas. Excellent places to have a good pizza.
Quinta Eulalia, Choquehuanca 384. Serves typical food from the region. Lunch only.

Museums

Peruvian officials claim that the city of Lima alone has more than 75 museums. While there are museums of all types, it is in the categories of colonial and pre-Columbian art and history that Peruvian museums excel.

See the Places section for details of the best places. Most museums are closed on Mondays (as throughout South America).

Architecture

Of the dozens of colonial buildings still in Lima, some have been restored and are well worth a visit.
Casa de Riva-Aguero,
Camaná 459, Lima, tel: 427-9275. Owned by the Catholic University, the second floor of this mansion is a folk-art museum. Open Monday to Friday 1–8pm and Saturday 9am–1pm.
Casa de Aliaga,
Jr de la Unión 224, tel: 424-5110/7560. One of the first homes in the city, the same family has continuously occupied this mansion since 1535 until the present. Can be visited only through Lima Tours.
Casa Osambela,
Conde de Superunda 298, tel: 427-7987. Used by a collection of educational institutes, there are frequent lectures, documentaries and art exhibitions at this home.

Trekking

Preparation: The Peruvian dry season, May through September, offers the best views and finest weather. For safety reasons and for

greater enjoyment, parties of three to four or more should hike together. Groups are easily formed in Cuzco, and the Tourist Office on the Plaza de Armas provides a notice board for this purpose. In Huaráz, contact the Casa de Guías, Parque Ginebra 28 G, Huaraz, tel: 721-811, fax: 722-306.
Equipment: Supplies should include a backpack, sturdy hiking boots, sleeping bags, insulated pad, tent and a stove for trekking. This equipment can be hired at a number of highly-visible adventure travel agencies, specially in cities like Huaraz and Cuzco. The cost is minimal, but quality often suffers. Inspect hired equipment carefully before departure. It can get very cold at night, and by day, the Andean sun burns quickly. Have a hat handy. For the less adventurous, porters can be hired for the Inca Trail. In the Cordillera Blanca, *arrieros*, or mule-drivers, are quite inexpensive and readily available.
Food: All food should be brought from a major town. Very little is available in the smaller villages. Freeze-dried food is not available, but a variety of dried fruits, cheeses, fruits, packaged soups, and tinned fish can be easily acquired in a number of *supermercados*, *bodegas*, and open-air markets. Drinking water should be treated with iodine. Add instant drink mixes like Tang to offset the unpleasant taste.
High Altitude: The effects of high altitude can be significantly diminished by following a few simple precautions. Alcohol, overeating and physical exertion should be avoided for the first day or two. Drinking ample liquids helps the system adjust quickly. The sugar in hard candy stimulates the metabolism, and aspirin eases headaches. *Mate de coca*, tea brewed from coca leaves, is said to be the best remedy for any sickness.

Nightlife

Lima is full of colorful *peñas* where folk music and dance performances go non-stop into the early hours. Go about 9pm to get a good seat.

Brisas del Titicaca,
Walkuski 168, Llma, tel: 423-7405.
An authentic *peña* with Peruvian
dance shows. Popular with the
locals and cheap.

Manos Morenas,
Pedro de Osma 409, Barranco, tel;
467-0421/4902. Good Peruvian
food Wednesday to Saturday with a
criollo show at 10.30pm.

La Noche,
Avda Bolognesi 307, Barranco, tel:
477-4154. A good and lively bar to
go to for a beer.

Drinking Tips

As for liquid refreshment, Peru
has several **beers**, including
Cristal, Pilsen, Arequipeña and
Cusqueña, all of which are light
lagers. Its best **wines** are
Tacama and Ocucaje. The
national **cocktail** is *pisco sour* –
made from grape brandy, lemon
juice and egg white with a dash
of cinnamon (the Hotel Grand
Bolívar in Lima serves the
Catedral pisco sour, often
claimed to be the best in all
Peru).

It is recommended that
travelers drink only **bottled water**
(and specify "*sin hielo*" – "no
ice" in other cold drinks) and that
they refrain from eating food sold
by street vendors.

Surinam A–Z

Getting Acquainted

Area 163,265 sq km
(63,037 sq miles).
Capital Paramaribo.
Population 423, 000.
Language Dutch (official language),
Sranan Tongo, Hindi, Javanese,
English, Chinese, French and
Spanish are also spoken.
Currency Surinam Gilder (SG),
US$1 = SG401; UK£1 = SG642.
Weights & Measures Metric.
Electricity 110/220v AC, 60Hz.
Time Zone GMT - 3; EST + 1.
Dialing Code 597.

Government & Economy

Surinam has a democratically
elected government, with one
legislative house, the National
Assembly. The president is head of
state and head of government.
Major industries in Surinam include
the export of bauxite and
aluminium, palm oil, shrimp and
fish and bananas. The US is a
major trading partner.

Consulates & Embassies

British Honorary Consulate,
c/o VSH United Buildings, PO
Box 1300, Van't
Hogerhuysstratt 9–11,
Paramaribo, Surinam. Tel:
402 558; 403 515.

American Embassy, PO Box
1821, Dr Sophie
Redmondstraat 129,
Paramaribo, Surinam. Tel:
476 459; fax: 420 800.

Visas

Visas are required at present for
visitors from Australia, Canada, the
Netherlands, Germany, New
Zealand and the US. Two good
passport photographs, an
application form in duplicate and a
fee are necessary for the visa
registration process. Entry
requirements are becoming more
relaxed, however; contact your local
embassy for the latest situation.

Customs

All money should be declared on
entry. The import and export of
local currency is limited to SG100;
there are no restrictions on foreign
currency. Visitors to Surinam are
required to exchange US$177 or
SG 300 on arrival. Children
between the ages of 2–12 are
expected to change half this
amount.

Business Hours

Banking hours: Monday–Friday
9am–2pm. Shops and
businesses: Monday–Friday
9am–4.30pm; Saturday
9am–1pm.

Money

Most transactions should be made
in cash; checks are not accepted.
Inflation is high and it is difficult to
buy Surinam gilder abroad. Most
travelers take US dollars into the
country. The best place to change
money is at banks but there is also
a thriving (although illegal) black
market.

Credit cards: American Express
is accepted in most large hotels
and tourist restaurants and shops.

Public Holidays

1 Jan; Good Friday; Easter (2 days);
1 May (Labor Day); 1 July (National
Unity Day); 25 November
(Independence Day); Christmas (2
days). Hindu and Muslim holidays
are also taken, dates varying,

according to the lunar calendar: Holi Phagwah (March or April, Hindu New Year); Id ul Fitr (end of Ramadan); Id Ul Azah; Youm un Nabi; Deepavali (usually November).

Getting Around

FROM THE AIRPORT

All international flights land at Johan Adolf Pengel Airport which is about 31 miles (50 km) south of Paramaribo. There are several minibus companies, US$4 to the city center, or taxis US$20.

BY BOAT

There are various daytime ferry services up the rivers, such as a 4-hour journey up the Commewijne River, daily at 7am from Paramaribo with the Surinam Navigation Co.

International routes: it is possible to book a place on the passenger ferry from Springlands in Guyana or from St Laurent de Maroni in French Guiana.

BY ROAD

In Paramaribo public transport consists of taxis or buses. It is possible to rent a car, but there is a general shortage of car parts in the country and most are not in very good shape; driving is on the left-hand side of the road.

There are no major roads in the interior of the country except for the East-West highway which runs from Albina in the east to Nieuw Nickerie in the west. Buses operate on the coastal highway but they are a very uncomfortable way to travel. It is also possible to use taxis around the coastal regions.

There are road links from Guyana and French Guiana.

Communications & Media

Telephones: IDD is available. There are no area codes.
Telegrams: Offices of Telesur in Paramaribo and throughout the country can be used to send telegrams.
Newspapers: *De West* and *De Ware Tijd* are Dutch-language dailies.

Radio: The BBC World Service (MHz 17.79, 15.19, 9.915 and 5.970) and Voice of America (MHz 17.71, 13.74, 9.455 and 5.995).

Tourist Organisations

Surinam Tourism Foundation, PO Box 656, Dr JF Nassylaan 2, Paramaribo. Tel: 410 357; fax: 477 786; e-mail stsur@sr.net
Surinam Tourism Department, Ministry of Transport, Communication and Tourism, PO Box 656, Paramaribo. Tel: 471 163; fax: 510 555.

Specialist Agencies

Surinam Tourism Company, METS ltd, Rudielaan 5, Paramaribo. Tel: 492 892/497 180; fax: 497 062.
Trips Worldwide, 9 Bryron Place, Clifton, Bristol BS8 1JT, UK. Tel: (0117) 987 2626; fax: (0117) 987 2627.

Where to Stay

PARAMARIBO

Hotel Torarica, Kleine Waterstraat, tel: 471500; fax: 411682. The best in the city, with pool, restaurants and all facilities.
Hotel Ambassador, Dr. Sophie Redmonstraat, tel: 477555; fax: 477903. Very good budget hotel, with restaurant.
Graf van Zinzendorf Herberg, Gravenstraat 110, tel: 471607. Large rooms, popular.
Guesthouse Flair, Kleine Waterstraat 7, tel: 422455. Clean, recommended.

NIEUW NICKERIE

Hotel Ameerali, Maynardstraat 32, tel: 231212; fax: 231066. Clean, if small, rooms; comfortable.
Hotel Luxor, St. Jozefstraat 22, tel: 231365. Old-fashioned and friendly place; clean rooms with private bath.

What to Eat

The standard of food in Surinam is very high but so are the prices as

most produce is imported. The local cuisine matches the rich ethnic mix of the Surinamese people, and can be very good. Indonesian dishes, such as *bami* (fried noodles) and *nasi goreng* (fried rice) are spicy and served in cheap and cheerful food stalls. Manioc (cassava), sweet potato, plantains, chicken, prawns, and fish feature prominently in Creole cuisine; while amongst Hindustani specialties are *roti* (mixed curried vegetables and chicken wrapped up in a fried pancake) and *phulawri* (fried chick peas). Chinese cuisine is also plentiful and good value.

Parbo is the locally-produced beer, and is quite drinkable and cheaper than imported brands. The most popular spirit is rum.

Where to Eat

PARAMARIBO

Sarinah, Verlengde Gemenelandsveg 187. Far from downtown but excellent Indonesian cuisine.
Iwan's, Grote Hofstraat 6, off Watermolenstraat. Expensive but one of the best Chinese restaurants.
Natasha, opposite Torarica Hotel. Tasty and cheap Indian food.
Chalet Swiss, Lim-a-Po Straat. Good and cheap sandwiches (but more Dutch than Swiss-style).

NIEUW NICKERIE

Moksie Patoe, Gouverneurstraat 115. Good and varied menu in friendly bar and restaurant.
Incognito, Gouverneurstraat 44. Recommended for Indonesian food.

Tipping

If your restaurant bill does not include a 10 percent tip it is usual to leave this amount. It is not usual to tip taxi drivers.

Attractions

Much of Surinam's countryside is tropical forest, so the main appeal to visitors is to take guided tours into its rainforest and coastal reserves. As the road system is minimal, the most practical form of transport is by small plane, or by boat up one of the many rivers. Amongst the highlights for scenic and cultural interest are: the **Galibi Nature Reserve** on the Marowijne River near to the village of Albina (turtle-nesting site in July and August); **Marienburg**, the last remaining sugar estate in the country, in the Commewijne district; **Jodensavanne**, south of Paramaribo on the opposite bank of the Surinam River, where the remains of one of the oldest synagogues in the Western Hemisphere have been restored; and the **Natuurpark Brownsberg** in montane rainforest two hours from Paramaribo.

Surinam has an impressive national park system. Contact Stinasu (the Nature Preservation Foundation of Surinam) for more information and details of their inexpensive guided tours.

Uruguay A–Z

Getting Acquainted

Area 68,000 sq miles. (176,200 sq km).
Capital Montevideo.
Population 3.9 million.
Language Spanish.
Currency New Peso; US$1 = NP10.7, UK£1 = NP17.1.
Weights & measures Metric.
Electricity 220 volts.
Time zone GMT –3hrs, EST +2hrs.
Dialing code 598 (Montevideo 2).

Government & Economy

With the exception of the 1973–85 military dictatorship, Uruguay has enjoyed a liberal democratic system for the past century. Presidents are elected for five years, and cannot run for consecutive terms. The constitution, modeled on Switzerland's, has traditionally provided for a wide array of social services, but the current economic crisis has made many of these benefits seem quite theoretical.

Chief exports of the country are beef and wool, followed by rice, citrus and fish products, and some consumer goods. Current aims are to improve the country's infrastructure and to take advantage of a well-educated population to produce skilled labor and high-valued exports. With a population of nearly 4 million, it is the smallest Spanish-speaking country in South America.

Visas

A valid passport is required for most visitors. Exceptions are nationals of other American countries, who need to show identity documents.

Travelers must fill out a card at the customs counter that has to be surrendered on departure. The stamp on passports is usually good for three months and can be extended for a small fee at the Migraciones Office on Calle Misiones 1513, Montevideo, tel: 960-471.

Customs

There are no special restrictions on liquor, tobacco, or electronic goods brought in for personal use.

Getting Around

FROM THE AIRPORT
Montevideo's airport is at Carrasco, 20km (12.5 miles) away, 30 mins by taxi, approximately US$20; and various bus services, US$1–4.
Tax: International departure tax is US$12 (except for flights to Buenos Aires, for which US$6 is charged).

BY BOAT
International services: the most enjoyable way to travel to Montevideo is by **night ferry**, which leaves Buenos Aires at 9pm, arriving at 8am the following morning. The cost is around a third of the air fare, and includes a sleeping berth or, for a bit more, a private cabin.

There are also three daily ferries from Colonia. Hydrofoils run frequently between Buenos Aires and Colonia. The trip takes 50 minutes, and the ticket includes a connecting bus service for a three-hour trip to Montevideo. The journey can be rough on windy days.

BY AIR
Internal flights within Uruguay are quite inexpensive; the main airlines are *Pluna* and *Aviasur*. *Tamu*, the military airline, offers further reduced prices to most Uruguayan destinations.

BY ROAD
The nation's bus system is quite good with a number of competing companies whose rates can vary.

Religious Services

Most Uruguayans are nominally Catholic. There is a Methodist church (in Carrasco) and an Anglican church in Reconquista 522 which holds services in English. Montevideo has a synagogue.

In Montevideo, taxis are cheap though not always plentiful. The city bus system is a mixture of old British Leyland buses and ancient electric trolleys, but the service is fairly efficient. Bus no 104 (catch it on 18 de Julio) makes a slow but scenic tour of the beaches as far as Carrasco.

International services: There is a daily bus service from Buenos Aires to Montevideo. The trip takes 10 hours. Buses also run on the Pan-American Highway from Rio de Janeiro to Montevideo and on to Colonia.

BY TRAIN

The railway system was built by the British in the 19th century and hasn't been over-modernized since. In January 1988, all passenger services were withdrawn. Only lines between Tacuarembó-Rivera and Montevideo-25 de Agosto run, but check service details once you are in the country (the reintroduction of the line to the Brazilian border has been rumored).

Business Hours

Most shops are open Monday to Friday 9am–noon and 2–7pm. On Saturday they stay open from 9.30am–12.30pm. In Montevideo, banks are open between 1pm and 5pm and are closed on Saturday.

Money

Most banks and exchange houses make a small charge for changing US dollar travelers' checks into US dollars, which are widely accepted. Credit cards and travelers' checks are frequently not taken outside Montevideo.

Media

There are four television stations in Montevideo; one is state-run. A large percentage of programs come from Argentina. Uruguayans are avid newspaper readers; dailies include the prosaic El Día, El Observador and El País as well as the left-leaning República (good for film, theater and other social happenings) and the communist La Hora. There are also a number of interesting weeklies – Busqueda is considered foremost.

Postal Services

Postal services have improved since postal workers were forbidden to strike, but letters should be sent airmail. There is a convenient downtown office in the Intendencia.

Telephones & Telexes

The new telephone center (**Antel**) on San José between Paraguay and Ibicuy is the most efficient place to make international calls. Telex and telefax services are also available. Payphones require tokens (fichas) which may be purchased at Antel or at newsstands.

Public Holidays

Uruguay has a strong secular tradition whereby Christmas is known as Family Day; Holy Week is Tourism Week, celebrated with horse shows, etc. During Tourism Week, hotels must be booked in advance. Carnival is celebrated with lively parades of minstrels known as murgas, and businesses close on Monday and Tuesday of that week.

Other holidays are:
- **January** 1 and 6
- **April** 19
- **May** 1 and 18
- **June** 19
- **July** 18
- **August** 25
- **October** 12
- **November** 2
- **December** 8

Tourist Information

The main tourist office is on Plaza Fabini (Entrevero). It offers free maps, information on hotels, etc. The main bus company (Onda) and money exchange houses are also located here. The tourist office at the Terminal Tres Cruces bus terminal is open 7am–11pm.

The **Tourist Commission** is located at Lavalleja 1409.

For information on current hotel prices, go to the Centro de Hotelería at 1213. They also give away maps. There is an American Express office at Mercedes 942, which opens from 1–5pm, Monday to Friday.

Embassies & Consulates

Canada: Tagle 2823, tel: 623-630
Great Britain: Marco Bruto 1073, tel: 623-597.
United States: Lauro Muller 1776, tel 236-061.

Where to Stay

MONTEVIDEO

Columbia Palace, Rambla Republica de Francia 473, tel: 960-001, fax: 960-192.
Hotel International, Colonia 823, tel: 905-794. First-class modern hotel on a quiet street. Recommended for business travelers.
Hotel Lafayette, Soriano 1170, tel: 922-351. First choice for top business people.
Hotel Victoria Plaza, Plaza Independencia 759, tel: 989-565. Hotel owned by Rev Moon's Unification Church. Secretarial services, fax, roof-garden restaurant, nightclub.

PARQUE

Hotel Mediterraneo, Paraguay 1486, tel: 905-090. Small, charming hotel converted from a mansion.
Playa Ramirez, Old-fashioned resort hotel with 1930s décor. Pool, beach views, tearoom, ballroom, casino.

NEAR ATLANTIDA

Fortin De Santa Rosa, Ruta Interbalnearia, tel: 67-346. Charming converted old fortress, with a quiet beach a few meters away and an excellent restaurant.

PUNTA DEL ESTE

Hotels are invariably expensive, especially in season. Recommended include: **Americana** (tel: 807-94), **London** (tel: 419-11), **La Posada del Gobernador** (tel: 3108), **Peninsula** (tel: 415-33).

COLONIA

Recommended hotels include: **Rincón del Río** (tel: 3002), Esperanza (tel: 2922) , **El Mirador** (tel: 2004), **Italiano** (tel: 2103).

What to Eat

Most Uruguayans are of Spanish or Italian descent, and customs generally follow those of Southern Europe. Breakfast consists of coffee and croissants; lunch is the main meal and is served 1–3pm. Dinner tends to be quite late. On weekends restaurants are jammed at midnight. Restaurant portions, particularly meat, are often enormous; it's all right to order one dish for two.

Uruguayan cooking, like Argentine cooking, consists of two staples: beef and pasta. Uruguayans also like seafood. Try *calamares a la plancha* (grilled squid), *cazuela de mariscos* (seafood stew), and *lenguado* (sole) *a la provenzal*. Ice cream and pizza are excellent snacks as is *chivito*, a Dagwood-type sandwich. For dessert, try a kind of custard called *isla flotante*.

Where to Eat

MONTEVIDEO

Mercado del Puerto, Calle Piedras. Closed Sunday. Expensive grills, good atmosphere.
El Fogón, San José 1080. Grilled beef a specialty; seafood excellent.
El Aguila, Buenos Aires 694, next to Teatro Solis. Elegant service with a continental menu.

El Palanque, in the Puerto market complex. Grilled beef and seafood. Open Sunday.
Doña Flor, Artigas y Avda Espana. Classy French cuisine.
Punta del Este, te Mataré Ramírez, route 10. La Barra (near Galeria Manzione). High-class international menu. Open summer only.

Concerts

The **Teatro Solis** offers concerts from national and visiting companies. The season starts March through November. The **Teatro Circular**, on Rondeau behind the Plaza Cagancha, offers a series of theater productions.

Drinking Notes

For coffee or snacks, try the **Café La Pasiva** in the Plaza Independencia or the **El Lusitano** at 18 de Julio across from the Plaza Cagancha. **Cakes** on the pedestrianized Rambla has superb cakes, coffee and beer. **Sokos** on 18 de Julio, has good sandwiches and more substantial meals. Uruguayan wine is drinkable but nothing special. Beer is made with spring water and is very good, especially *Norteña*.

Bars & Nightclubs

Jazz is available at **Alianza Francés** and Brazilian music at **Clave de Fu**, Pocitos. For tango dance and music, try **Tangueria del 40**, Hotel Columbia, in the Ciudad Vieja. The most popular discos are **Caras y Caretas**, **Punta Gorda** and **San Telmo** on Maldonado 1194. Gambling is available at the Parque Hotel and the Hotel Carrasco in Carrasco.

Venezuela A – Z

Getting Acquainted

Area 352,00 sq miles (912,000 sq km), with a 1,700 mile (2,700 km) Caribbean coast, and 72 islands.
Capital Caracas.
Population 23 million. There is a mix of African and European descendants. The native population is fewer than 200,000. More than eighty percent live in the urban areas of the country's many, middle-sized cities, the largest of which are concentrated on or near the northern coast.
Language Spanish.
Currency Bolívar (Bs), USS$1 = Bs570; UK£1 = Bs912.
Weights & measures Metric.
Electricity 110 volts.
Time zone GMT –4hrs, EST +1hr.
Dialing code 58 (Caracas +2).

Government & Economy

Venezuela is a centralized federal republic formed by 22 states, one federal district and 72 federal departments (corresponding to Venezuela's islands in the Caribbean Sea). The government system is a representative democracy with three branches of government: legislative, executive and judicial.

Executive power rests solely with the president designated by direct, popular and secret ballot for a five-year term, with the possibility of running for one more term after a lapse of at least 10 years out of office. With the council of ministers, the president is answerable to the legislature, which is made up of two-chambers, of senators and deputies, also elected by direct vote every five years. Ex-presidents of the republic automatically become life members of the Senate. The judicial branch is under a Supreme Court of Justice.

There are numerous political parties, the most important and long-established being Copei and Acción Democrática, with others including MAS (the Socialist party) and Causa R (Revolutionary party).

Visas

Entry is by passport and visa or passport and tourist card. If arriving by air, tourist cards (valid for 60 days) can be issued to citizens of the United States, Canada, Japan and most Western European countries (except Spain and Portugal). If arriving by land, a visa must be obtained from a consulate before arrival – requiring a letter of reference.

It is a good idea to carry your passport with you at all times (be sure to have photocopies of all documents guarded in a separate location in case of loss) as the police mount spot checks and anyone without ID is detained.

Money

It's best to change travelers' checks or US dollars in a *casa de cambio*. Only accept US dollars if changing money in hotels.

The majority of banks do not change travelers' checks.

Getting Around

FROM THE AIRPORT

Simon Bolívar Airport handles international flights for Caracas; the adjacent **Maiquetía** is the main domestic terminal; they are on the coast 30km (18.5 miles) from the city center. The journey is highly scenic but also very prone to traffic jams – allow up to two hours during the daytime. Taxi fares are roughly US$15, but drivers are notorious for over-charging. The official taxi line at Simón Bolívar Airport charges roughly double the going rate. The alternative is to phone a taxi on

(02) 753-9122 /4155. An airport shuttle bus service (with Simon Bolívar International Aeropuerto written on the vehicles) departs from outside the Maiquetia terminal, to the left as you exit the international arrivals building, and costs US$2.

International departure tax (whether leaving the country by air, overland or by sea): US$25.

Porter services are available at major airports and hotels. The going rate is about US$1 per bag.

Venezuela has six international airports and 282 airdromes of which 250 are private, used mostly by small planes and helicopters.

The Subway

The Caracas **Metro** runs daily 5.30am–11pm. It is air-conditioned, clean (no-smoking), safe and quick, and probably the best way to travel around the city. There are three lines, running east to west and north to south. Single journey fares cost US$0.25, and there are also 10-journey (*multi abono*) books of tickets for US$3. Student discounts available with international ID card.

MetroBuses depart from each subway station, serving southern suburbs. Buy a transfer ticket (*integrado*), US$0.20.

BY BUS

There are 64,370 km (40,000 miles) of roads, 18,000 of which are paved, and there are many freeways. Long distance east-bound **bus lines** operate from a new bus station in Caracas, the Terminal de Pasajeros General Antonio José de Sucre, located on the eastern outskirts of the capital. Bus travel varies a lot in quality, with most companies liable to run bone-shaking wrecks of buses on the same routes as luxury coaches.

West-bound long-distance buses currently have no terminal so operate from streets around the Nuevo Circo.

Emergencies

The nationwide emergency telephone number, **171**, is for police, fire and ambulance services.

Medical Services

Better hotels have physicians on call. Check with the concierge. Every town has a rotating system to ensure a pharmacy is open 24 hours. These are marked with a *turno* sign.

In an emergency, contact **171** or, in Caracas (02):

Hospital Universitario (UCV), south from the Plaza Venezuela freeway exit, tel: 606-7111.

Clínica de Emergencia Infantil (children's emergencies) Edif Topacio, 4th floor, Avda Avila, between Avs Caracas and Gamboa, tel: 516-111

Business Hours

Business hours are generally 8am–noon and 2–6pm. Shops, even in malls, usually do not open until 9–10am and close for lunch (often until 3pm) but they do stay open until 7pm and sometimes 8pm.

Newspapers

The Daily Journal, founded in 1945 by Jules Waldman, is the country's only English-language paper, and every day publishes a calendar of cultural and community events, galleries and museums.

The most comprehensive list of the week appears in the Friday edition.

The very informative travel and leisure magazines *Escape* and *Entonces* are published with text in both English and Spanish.

The main Spanish-language papers published in Caracas with a national distribution are *El Nacional*, *El Universal*, *Economia Hoy*, *Reporte*, *El Mundo*, *Meridiano* (all sport), *Ultimas Noticias*, *El País*, *El Globo* and *Abril*.

Postal Services

The Venezuelan postal system is extremely inefficient, although much better for mailing abroad rather than locally. As a result, motorbike courier services abound in Caracas and other courier services are favored to other parts of the country.

Embassies & Consulates

Australia: Quinta Yolanda, Avda Luis Roche, entre 6ta & 7ma Transversal, Altamira, tel: 263-4033, fax: 261-3448.
Canada: 6ta Avda entre 3ra y 5ta Transversal, Altamira, tel: 264-0833.
Great Britain: Torre Las Mercedes, Piso 3, Avda La Estancia, Urb. Chuao, tel: 993-5528/4224, fax: 993-9989.
United States: Calle F con Calle Suapure, Colinas de Valle Arriba, tel: 977-2011, fax: 977-0843.

Where to Stay

Fairmont International, Torre Capriles, Planta Baja, Plaza Venezuela, Caracas, tel: 782-8433, fax: 782-4407, will book hotel rooms in Caracas and also in 102 hotels in the rest of the country. The airport tourist office is also very helpful and will make reservations.
The Venezuelan Hotel Association, Anahoven, tel: (02) 574-3994 or 574-7172 liaises with the state tourist authority to supervise hotel standards and to deal with all customer enquiries and complaints.

Hotels

CARACAS
Avila, Avda Washington, San Bernardinao, tel: 515-128, fax: 523-021. Traditional flavor in quiet residential neighborhood.
Caracas Hilton, Avenida Libertador y Sur 25, tel: 503-5000, fax: 575-0024. Well located and a favorite of the Japanese.
El Condor, 3rd Avda de Las Delicias.

Saban a Grance, tel: 991-115. Among the main shopping centers.
Tamanaco Inter-Continental, Avenida Principal las Mercedes, tel: 924-522, fax: 208-7004. Best hotel in Caracas.

CIUDAD GUYANA
Inter-Continental Guyana, tel 222-235, fax: 222-253. 5-star hotel overlooking Caroní River and Falls.
Rasil, tel: 233-025, fax: 227-703. Central location and all facilities.

MERIDA
Posada Luz Caraballo, Avda 2, No 13–80, tel: 525-441. One of three *posadas* in town (Veijo Tojado, Papa Miguel). Reliable, comfortable, economical and in the center of town.
Park, Calle 37, tel: 637-014, fax: 634-582. One of the best downtown hotels.

Tourist Information

Corpoturismo (the Venezuelan Tourism Corporation) is the state tourist authority with overall responsibility for matters relating to tourism. Their main office is in Torre Oeste, Piso 35–7, Parque Central, Avenida Lecuna, Caracas, tel: (02) 507-8815 or 507-8726, telex: 27-328 TURIS VC, fax: (02) 574-8489. They also have information desks at the Simón Bolívar international and national airports.
Free-phone number: (800) 43-328.
Email:
104721,2167@compuserve.com
Web site:
http://www.indecu.gov.ve

What to Eat

Venezuelan cuisine is of an excellent quality and reflects the diverse cultural influences of its melting-pot culture. In the principal cities every type of cuisine is represented.

At Christmas, *hallaca* is the most traditional dish. This stew consists of chicken, pork, beef, spices,

Public Holidays

- **January 1st** – New Year's Day
  Carnival on the Monday and Tuesday before Ash Wednesday **Holy Week** Thursday to Saturday
- **April 19th** – Anniversary of the National Declaration of Independence
- **May 1st** – Labor Day
- **June 24th** – The feast day of San Juan Bautista
- **July 5th** – Anniversary of the Signing of Venezuelan National Independence Act
  July 24th – Anniversary of the birth of the Liberator, Simon Bolívar
- **October 12th** – Columbus Day (Anniversary of the Discovery of America)
- **December 25th** – Christmas Day

olives, raisins and capers wrapped in banana leaves and steamed.

Pabellón is considered to be the national dish, combining rice, black beans, shredded beef and *tajadas* (sliced and fried ripe plantains).

The Andes are known for *pisca* (a rich and tasty soup with broth, eggs and bread), trout in all forms, and smoked cheese.

Coro is famous for its goat dish *tarkari de chivo* (curried, roasted, or prepared with coconut milk) and goat's milk cheese.

Zulia State has delicious coconut-based specialties like *conejo en coco* (rabbit cooked in coconut milk) and a selection of sweets and candies.

The coastal region is widely known for its tasty seafood specialties like *consomé de guacucos* (middle-sized clams) and *empanadas de cazón* (shredded shark meat turnovers), lobster and fish such as grouper.

A typical and very popular Venezuelan dish is *mondongo* (tripe stew with chickpeas). The *arepa* is traditional flat round bread made from corn meal or wheat flour.

The beef is excellent throughout the country.

Nightlife

Caracas is a swinging city by night and there are many and varied discos and nightclubs. Caraqueños usually eat at home at 8pm and in restaurants between 9pm and 11pm and the partying goes on until well into the early hours of the morning. There are many small clubs, restaurants and bars on **Plaza Altamira Sur** and along the **Sabana Grande**.

Where to Eat

Like any other great metropolis, Caracas has a huge variety of international restaurants.

The greatest concentration of restaurants are in: **Barquisimeto**, along Avda Lara between Paseo Los Leones and the Barquisimeto Country Club; **Maracaibo**, along 5 de Julio and Avda 4 Bella Vista; in **Maracay**, along Avda Las Delicias; in the city of **Mérida**, on Avda chorro de Milla or Calle 24 facing Plaza Los Heroínas; **Puerto La Cruz**, along Paseo Colón and in Valencia, along Avda Bolívar Norte.

The cheapest food is at **Fuentes de Soda** and the **Pollo a la brasa**, a no-frills place featuring spit-roast chicken. Most of the economical spots offer a daily *menú ejecutivo*, usually with soup, a main dish, dessert and a beverage for a low, fixed price ($2–$4).

Food in bars may cost 50 percent more and there is no need to feel reticent about asking for prices before you order as the price of a beer can often be as much as three times higher. You can save on the 10 percent service charge if you eat at the bar and not at a table. If in doubt consult the price list which by decree restaurants must put up on or near the front door. Restaurants may not charge for bread, butter or condiments.

CARACAS

Las Mercedes and the **Altamira–Los Palos Grandes** zone offer a huge variety of cuisines and

trendier, more upscale dining spots; Avda **Francisco Solano**, between Chacaíto and Avda Las Acacias, has a large concentration of Italian restaurants; **Candelaria** (recommended only for daytime visits) for Spanish food and *tascas*.

An excellent source of information is *Miro Popic's Guía Gastronómica de Caracas*, updated annually, in English/Spanish, available in most bookstores and hotels.

Arábica Coffee Bar: Avda Andrés Bello at Los Palos Grandes, tel: 285-3469. Best coffee in the city; the only place in the country offering estate-grown single-variety coffees from all over Venezuela, roasted daily. Also a great choice of distinct pastries.

Tambo: Avda Francisco de Miranda, Torre Europa, ground floor, Campo Alegre, tel: 952-4243/6995. Two distinctive offerings under one roof: Peruvian and Japanese, reflecting the dual roots of the owner. A place to see and be seen.

Urrutia/Casa Urrutia: Avda Francisco Solano, Esq Los Manguitos, Sabana Grande, tel: 710-448. Spanish cuisine with 30 years of tradition initiated by Adolfo Urrutia, with Basque–Navarrese specialties; consistent, and no one ever leaves disappointed.

Bar Basque: Between the corners of Alcabala and Peligro, Candelaria, tel: 572-4857. Tiny, friendly, inviting bar/restaurant in the same place in the heart of the Spanish zone of Caracas for some 30 years, with unwavering quality. One of the best restaurants at any price in the city. Open only for lunch.

El Buffet Vegetariano: Avda Los Jardines, La Florida, tel: 747-490. Half a century of consistent style and quality. Fixed vegetarian menu daily, abundant portions, no smoking, no liquor.

La Paninoteka: Avda El Empalme, La Campiña, tel: 748-321. Tiny place with excellent quality, honest home cooking, mostly traditional Venezuelan specialties; menu changes regularly based on requests of clients. Closed weekends.

Le Petit Bistrot de Jacques: Avda Principal of Las Mercedes, tel: 993-4093/910-975. A more authentic French bistro you couldn't find, even in Paris. Intimate setting, fixed menu written on the mirrors, classic bistro offerings – cassoulet, choucroute, steak frites, homemade pastries. Closed Saturday lunch and Sunday.

Le Gourmet: Hotel Tamanaco Inter-Continental, Las Mercedes, tel. 208-7242. Beautiful, formal setting with a recent facelift. Premium dining with excellence guaranteed in flavor, presentation and service. Live background music. Top chef prepares primarily French cuisine but with imaginative touches.

Via Appia: Centro Coinasa, ground floor, La Castellana, tel. 263-9923, 265-5348. Family-run Italian eatery with great attention to details, everything prepared fresh, extremely popular place among power people in town.

El Portón: Avda Pichincha, El Rosal, tel. 952-0027. Large place divided into various areas, with typical Venezuelan dishes and beef; live entertainment in the dining area with *música criolla* and *ranchera*, the equivalent to American country and western.

Papagallo: CC Chacaíto, next to the Chacaíto Metro. Long-time establishment with enormous menu and specials of the day, where one can always count on a fast, generously-served, economical

Where to Shop

In the Caracas area, **Hannsi** in El Hatillo has the largest and widest selection of Venezuelan arts and crafts of any place in the country, with items for every budget. The most exquisite of objects are found in **Casa Caruba**, Avda Andrés Bello entre 1ray 2da Transversales, Los Palos Grandes.

The **Sabana Grande Boulevard** is an excellent commercial artery with hundreds of boutiques, jewelry stores, bazaars and stores.

meal. Great place for people-watching; with its convenient location, a traditional meeting place; open from early morning 'til around midnight.

Verdelecho: Hotel Eurobuilding Caracas, Chuao, tel. 907-1111, 959-1133. Natural food, long on salads; vegetarian fare with a gourmet flair.

Concerts

The Venezuelan Symphony Orchestra and the Caracas Municipal Symphony give regular concerts in the **Sala Rios Reyna** of the **Teresa Carreno** on Paseo Colón, one of the most important architectural works in the city.

Theaters

There are several permanent theaters and many theatrical groups. Every night there is a different presentation somewhere. The most important theaters are: **Rajatabla**, **Ana Julia Rojas**, **Alberto de Paz y Mateos**, **Chacaito**, **Luis Peraza**, the **National Theater** (home of the National Theater Company), **Los Cedros**, **Santa Sofia**, **La Campina**, **Sala Cadafe** and **Las Palmas**.

Internet Cafés

Internet cafés can appear and disappear overnight, so if you have access to the Net and you're about to travel to a different country, you can keep up-to-date with news of the latest cybercafés on: <www.netcafeguide.com>.

ARGENTINA
Cybercafé
Maure 1886, Buenos Aires 1426
Email:
info@cyber.com.ar
Southern Internet
San Martin 2384, Rio Gallegos
Email:
southern@internet.siscotel.com

BOLIVIA
Ciber Café MoNET
Calle 11# 256 Obrajes, La Paz 112
Email:
rodasbun@mail.café-monet.com
Cibermania
Barrio Equipetrol, Paseo Comercial "El Chuubi" Oficina 5, Planta Alta Santa Cruz de la Sierra
Email:
café@cibermania.com

BRAZIL
Arrobacafé
Barra de Tijuca
(South of Rio de Janeiro)
Email:
cerf@arrobacafe.com.br
Tripp's.Bar
Avda Nossa Senhora Aparecida, 405, Seminário
80440-000, Curitiba, Paraná
E-mail:
gerencia@tripps.com.br

CHILE
Osorno
Email:
megapc@ctcreuna.cl
Café Virtual – virtual bar
Alameda 145, Santiago
E-mail:
webmaster@café-viryual.cl

COLOMBIA
Cafénet Pereira
E-mail:
wwwmngr@correo.cafenet.net.co

Punto Web Café-Bar Internet
Calle 43 Cra 69A Esquina, Medellin
E-mail:
puntoweb@col3.telecom.com.co

ECUADOR
CaféNet
Reina Victoria y Cordero, Local 14 Quito
E-mail:
dinosaur@mail.io.com

PARAGUAY
Patio de Luz
Mexico 650 c Azara, Asunción
Email:
pegaso@uninet.com.py

PERU
Internet Cusco
Avda El Sol s/n, Galerias UNSAAC Cusco,
E-mail:
soluciones@expreso.com.pe
Hostal Familiar Mami Panchita
Jirón Bolivar 206 – San Miguel Lima, Peru
E-mail:
raymi_travels@perusat.net.pe

URUGUAY
Cyber Planet – Centro Internet
Avda Italia 5775 loc 148/149 11500 Montevideo, Uruguay
E-mail:
cyberplanet@cs.cs.com.uy
El Cybercafé Luis de la Torre
11300 Montevideo, Uruguay
E-mail:
martinp@cs.com.uy

VENEZUELA
Puntocom c@fé
Prolongación A. 4 de Mayo, Centro Ejecutivo Tradimart Porlamar Isla de Margarita
Web Universe Internet Café
Valencia
E-mail:
internetcafe@webuniverse.com
NewsC@fé
4 de Mayo, Porlamar, Venezuela
Email:
xpress@enlared.net

Language

Making Contact

Whether you need to know what time the next bus leaves or whether your hotel room is quiet, with a shower and a view of the beach, making yourself understood in the local language will be the key to success of your stay in South America. The good news is that you can get by in the whole continent with just two languages: Spanish and Portuguese (with the obvious exceptions of the Guianas). While people in many tourist establishments will speak English, once you are off the beaten track, hardly anyone will, and just making the effort to speak a few words will gain you a lot of appreciation. There are idiomatic differences from one country to the next, but you will soon pick these up as you go.

It would be impossible for us to give a complete language guide here, but the following are some useful words, phrases and tips that will hopefully ease understanding and may even save you time and money.

Portuguese

Although Portuguese, and not Spanish, is the language of Brazil, if you have a knowledge of Spanish, it will come in handy. You will recognize many similar words, and most Brazilians will understand you if you speak in Spanish. If you like to wander around on your own, you might want to get one of the pocket dictionaries available in several languages to and from Portuguese. If you are unable to find one at home, they are on sale at airport and hotel shops and book stores

in Brazil.

First names are used a great deal in Brazil. In many situations in which English-speakers would use a title and surname, Brazilians often use a first name with the title of respect: *Senhor* for men (written *Sr* and usually shortened to *Seu* in spoken Portuguese) and *Senhora* (written *Sra*) or *Dona* (used only with first name) for women. If *João Oliveira* or *Maria da Silva* calls you *Sr John*, rather than *Mr Jones*, then you should correspondingly address them as *Sr João* and *Dona Maria*.

There are three second-person pronoun forms in Portuguese. Stick to *você*, equivalent to "you," and you will be all right. *O senhor* (for men) or *a senhora* (for women) is used to show respect for someone of a different age group or social class or to be polite to a stranger. As a foreigner, you won't offend anyone if you use the wrong form of address. But if you want to learn when to use the more formal or informal style, observe and go by how others address you. In some parts of Brazil, mainly the northeast and the south, *tu* is used a great deal. Originally, in Portugal, *tu* was used similarly to the German "Du," among intimate friends and close relatives, but in Brazil, it's equivalent to *você*.

If you are staying longer and are serious about learning the language, there are Portuguese courses for non-native speakers. Meanwhile, here are some of the most essential words and phrases:

Greetings
Tudo Bem, meaning "all's well," is one of the most common forms of greeting: one person asks, "*Tudo bem*?" and the other replies, "*Tudo bem.*" This is also used to mean "OK," "all right," "will do," or as a response when someone apologizes, as if to say, "that's all right, it doesn't matter." Other forms of greetings are:

Good morning (good afternoon) *Bom dia (boa tarde)*
Good evening (good night) *Boa noite*
How are you? *Como vai?*

Well, thank you *Bem, obrigado*
Hello (to answer the telephone) *Alô*
Hello (common forms of greeting) *Bom dia, boa tarde* etc.
Hi, hey! (informal greeting also used to get someone's attention) *Oi*
Goodbye (very informal and most used) *Tchau*
Goodbye (literally "until soon") *Até logo*
Goodbye (similar to "farewell") *Adeus*

My name is (I am) *Meu nome é (Eu sou)*
What is your name? *Como é seu nome?*
It's a pleasure *É um prazer*
Pleasure (used in introductions as "Pleased to meet you") *Prazer*

Good! Great! *Que bom!*
Health! (the most common toast) *Saúde*

Do you speak English? *Você fala inglês?*
I don't understand (I didn't understand) *Não entendo (Não entendi)*
Do you understand? *Você entende?*
Please repeat more slowly *Por favor repete, mais devagar*
What do you call this (that)? *Como se chama isto (aquilo)?*
How do you say ...? *Como se diz ...?*

Please *Por favor*
Thank you (very much) *(Muito) Obrigado (or Obrigada, for a woman speaking)*
You're welcome (literally "it's nothing") *De nada*
Excuse me (to apologize) *Desculpe*
Excuse me (taking leave or to get past someone) *Com licença*

Pronouns
Who? *Quem?*
I (We) *Eu (Nós)*
You (singular) *Você*
You (plural) *Vocês*
He (she) *Ele (ela)*
They *Eles (Elas)*
My (mine) *Meu (minha)* depending on gender of object
Our (ours) *Nosso (nossa)*
Your (yours) *Seu (sua)*

His (her or hers) *Dele* (*dela* or *deles*)
Their, theirs (*Delas*)

Getting Around
Where is the...? *Onde é...?*
beach *a praia*
bathroom *o banheiro*
bus station *a rodoviária*
airport *o aeroporto*
train station *a estação de trem*
post office *o correio*
police station *a delegacia de polícia*
ticket office *a bilheteria*
marketplace *o mercado*
street market *a feira*
embassy (consulate) *a embaixada* (*o consulado*)
currency exchange *uma casa de câmbio*
bank *um banco*
pharmacy *uma farmácia*
(good) hotel *um* (*bom*) *hotel*
(good) restaurant *um* (*bom*) *restaurante*
bar *um bar*
snack bar *uma lanchonete*
bus stop *um ponto de ônibus*
taxi stand *um ponto de taxi*
subway station *uma estação de metrô*
service station *um posto de gasolina*
newsstand *um jornaleiro*
public telephone *um telefone público*
supermarket *um supermercado*
shopping center *um shopping center*
department store *uma loja de departamentos*
boutique *uma boutique*
jeweler *um joalheiro*
hairdresser (barber) *um cabeleireiro* (*um barbeiro*)
laundry *uma lavanderia*
hospital *um hospital*

Taxi *Taxi*
Bus *Onibus*
Car *Carro*
Plane *Avião*
Train *Trem*
Boat *Barco*

A ticket to... *Uma passagem para...*
I want to go to... *Quero ir para...*
How can I get to...? *Como posso ir para...?*

Please take me to... *Por favor, me leve para...*
Please call a taxi for me *Por favor, chame um taxi para mim*
I want to rent a car *Quero alugar um carro*

What is this place called? *Como se chama este lugar?*
Where are we? *Onde estamos?*
How long will it take to get there? *Leva quanto tempo para chegar lá?*
Please stop here (Stop!) *Por favor, pare aqui.* (*Pare!*)
Please wait *Por favor, espere*

What time does the bus (plane, boat) leave? *A que horas sai o ônibus (avião, barco)?*
Where does this bus go? *Este ônibus vai para onde?*
Does it go by way of...? *Passa em...?*

Airport (Bus station) tax *Taxa de embarque*

I want to check my luggage (on a bus, etc.) *Quero despachar minha bagagem*
I want to store my luggage (at a station) *Quero guardar minha bagagem*

Shopping
Do you have...? *Tem...?*
I want... please *Eu quero... por favor*
I don't want... *Eu não quero...*
I want to buy... *Eu quero comprar...*

Where can I buy... *Onde posso comprar...?*
cigarettes *cigarros*
film *filme*
a ticket for... *uma entrada para...*
a reserved seat *um lugar marcado*
another the same *um outro igual*
another different *um outro diferente*
this (that) *isto* (*aquilo*)
something less expensive *a lgo mais barato*
postcard *cartão postal*
paper *papel*
envelopes *envelopes*
a pen *uma caneta*
a pencil *um lápis*
shampoo *xampu* or *shampoo*

soap *sabonete*
toothpaste *pasta de dente*
sunscreen *filtro solar*
aspirin *aspirina*

I need... *Eu preciso de...*
a doctor *um médico*
a mechanic *um mecânico*
transportation *transporte*
help *ajuda*

How much? *Quanto?*
How many? *Quantos?*

How much does it cost? *Quanto custa? Quanto é?*
That's very expensive *É muito caro*

A lot, very (many) *Muito* (*muitos*)
A little (few) *Um pouco, um pouquinho* (*poucos*)

At the Hotel
I have a reservation *Tenho uma reserva*
I want to make a reservation *Quero fazer uma reserva*
A single room (A double room) *Um quarto de solteiro* (*Um quarto de casal*)
with air conditioning *com ar condicionado*
I want to see the room *Quero ver o quarto*

Suitcase *Mala*
Bag or purse *Bolsa*
Room service *Serviço de quarto*
Key *Chave*
The manager *O gerente*

At the Restaurant
Waiter *Garçon*
Maitre d' *Maitre*
I didn't order this *Eu não pedi isto*
The menu *O cardápio*
The wine list *A carta de vinhos*

Breakfast *Café da manhã*
Lunch *Almoço*
Supper *Jantar*
The house specialty *A especialidade da casa*

Carbonated mineral water *água mineral com gás*
Uncarbonated mineral water *água mineral sem gás*
Coffee *Café*

Tea *Chá*
Beer *Cerveja*
White/red wine (red wine) *Vinho branco/tinto*
A soft drink (juice) *Um refrigerante (Suco)*
An alcoholic drink *Um drink*
A cocktail *Um cocktail*
Ice *Gelo*

Salt	*Sal*
Pepper	*Pimenta*
Sugar	*Açucar*
A plate	*Um prato*
A glass	*Um copo*
A cup	*Uma xícara*
A napkin	*Um guardanapo*
An appetizer	*Um tira-gosto*
A snack	*Um lanche*
Beef	*Carne*
Pork	*Porco*
Chicken	*Frango*
Fish	*Peixe*
Shrimp	*Camarão*
Well done	*Bem passado*
Medium rare	*Ao ponto*
Rare	*Mal passado*
Vegetables	*Verduras*
Salad	*Salada*
Fruit	*Fruta*
Bread	*Pão*
Butter	*Manteiga*
Toast	*Torradas*
Eggs	*Ovos*
Rice	*Arroz*
(French-fried) potatoes	*Batatas (fritas)*
Beans	*Feijão*
Soup	*Sopa*
Sandwich	*Sanduiche*
Pizza	*Pizza*
Dessert	*Sobremesa*
(Sweets)	*(Doces)*

The bill, please *A conta, por favor*
Is service included? *Está incluido o serviço?*
I want my change, please *Eu quero meu troco, por favor*
I want a receipt *Eu quero um recibo*

Money

Cash *Dinheiro*
Do you accept credit cards? *Aceita cartão de crédito?*
Can you cash a travelers' check? *Pode trocar um travelers' check?*

(cheque de viagem)
I want to exchange money *Quero trocar dinheiro*
What is the exchange rate? *Qual é o câmbio?*

Time

When? *Quando?*
What time is it? *Que horas são?*
Just a moment please *Um momento, por favor*

What is the schedule? (bus, tour, show, etc.) *Qual é o horário?*
How long does it take? *Leva quanto tempo?*

Hour	*A Hora*
Day	*O Dia*
Week	*A Semana*
Month	*O mês*

At what time? *A que horas?*
At one-o-clock *A uma hora*
(two-, three-...) *(duas, três...)*
An hour from now *Daqui a uma hora*

Which day?	*Que dia?*
Yesterday	*Ontem*
Today	*Hoje*
Tomorrow	*Amanhã*
This week	*Esta semana*
Last week	*A semana passada*
Next week	*A semana que vem*
The weekend	*O fim de semana*
Monday	*Segunda-feira*
Tuesday	*Terça-feira*
Wednesday	*Quarta-feira*
Thursday	*Quinta-feira*
Friday	*Sexta-feira*

(Monday to Friday are often written as *2a, 3a, 4a, 5a*)
Saturday *Sábado*
Sunday *Domingo*

Numbers

one	*um*
two	*dois*
three	*três*
four	*quatro*
five	*cinco*
six	*seis*
half a dozen	*meia*
seven	*sete*
eight	*oito*
nine	*nove*
10	*dez*
11	*onze*
12	doze
13	*treze*
14	quatorze
15	quinze
16	dezesseis
17	dezessete
18	dezoito
19	dezenove
20	vinte
21	vinte e um
30	trinta
40	quarenta
50	cinqüenta
60	sessenta
70	setenta
80	oitenta
90	noventa
100	cem
101	cento e um
200	duzentos
300	trezentos
400	quatrocentos
500	quinhentos
600	seiscentos
700	setecentos
800	oitocentos
900	novecentos
1,000	mil
2,000	dois mil
10,000	dez mil
100,000	cem mil
1,000,000	um milhão

Commas and periods in numbers take an inverted form in Portuguese: 1,000 is written 1.000 and one and a half (1.5) is written 1,5.

To help you understand the addresses in this appendix, here's what the Portuguese words mean.

Al or Alameda=lane.
Andar=floor, story.
Ave or Avenida=avenue.
Casa=house.
Centro=the central downtown business district, also frequently referred to as a cidade or "the city."
Cj or Conjunto=a suite of rooms or sometimes a group of buildings.
Estr or Estrada =road or highway.
Fazenda=ranch, also a lodge.
Largo (often written as *Lgo*) = square or plaza.
Lote=Lot.
Pça or Praça =square or plaza.

Praia=beach.
Rio=river.
Rod or Rodovia =highway.
R or Rua =street.
Sala=room.
Ordinal numbers are written with °
or a degree sign after the numeral,
so that 3° andar means 3rd floor.
BR followed by a number refers to
one of the federal interstate
highways, for example BR-101,
which follows the Atlantic coast.
Telex and telephone numbers are
given with the area code for long-
distance dialing in parentheses.
Ramal=telephone extension.

Spanish

There is quite a colorful variety of
local idioms and variations
throughout Spanish South America
An expression you will hear
everywhere in Ecuador, for
instance, and which is difficult to
translate, is *no mas*. *Siga no mas*
for example, means "Hurry up (and
get on the bus/move down the line
etc)." *Come no mas* means "Just
eat it (It'll get cold/it's nicer than it
looks, etc.)." In Argentina, the
Spanish "ll", as in "*llanos*", comes
out like something between a **j** and
zh; while the familiar "*tu*" is
replaced by the archaic sounding
"*vos.*" In Chile and to a lesser
extent Peru, they are notorious for
dropping the ends off their words,
particularly those that end in
"–ado", which become "ao"
instead, such as "*huevos pasaos* –
soft-boiled eggs". It may come as a
relief to know, however, that
Colombians pride themselves on
speaking the clearest and "purest"
Spanish in South America.
    In the Andes, the *indígenas* all
speak Spanish but you will hear
Quichua words which have crept
into the language: *wambras*
translates as "guys," and *cheveré*
means "cool."

VOWELS

a as in father
e as in bed
i as in police
o as in hole
u as in rude

CONSONANTS are approximately like
those in English, the main
exceptions being:
c is hard before **a**, **o**, or **u** (as in
English), and is soft before **e** or **i**,
when it sounds like **s** (as opposed
to the Castilian pronunciation of **th**
as in think). Thus, *cen*so (census)
sounds like senso.
g is hard before **a**, **o**, or **u** (as in
English), but where English **g**
sounds like **j** – before **e** or **i** –
Spanish **g** sounds like a guttural **h**.
G before **ua** is often soft or silent,
so that *agua* sounds more like *awa*,
and Guadalajara like Wadalajara.
h is silent.
j sounds like the English h.
ll sounds like y.
ñ sounds like ny, as in the familiar
Spanish word *señor*.
q is followed by **u** as in English, but
the combination sounds like **k** instead of like **kw**. *¿Qué quiere
Usted?* is pronounced: Keh kee-ehr-
eh oostehd?
r is often rolled.
x between vowels sounds like a guttural **h**, eg in México or Oaxaca.
y alone, as the word meaning and,
is pronounced **ee**.
Note that **ch** and **ll** are a separate
letter of the Spanish alphabet; if
looking in a phone book or
dictionary for a word beginning with
ch, you will find it after the final **c**
entry. A name or word beginning
with **ll** will be listed after the **l** entry.

If you have no Spanish, here are
some basic words to help you get
around:

My name is Mary	*Me llamo María*
Hello, how are you?	*¿Hola, que tal?*
I'm very well, and you?	*Yo, muy bien. ¿Y usted ?*
Very well, thank you	*Muy bien, gracias*
Good morning	*Buenos días*
Good afternoon	*Buenas tardes*
Goodnight	*Buenas noches*
Welcome	*Bienvenido*
Hello	*¡Hola!*
Bye	*Adios*
See you later	*Hasta luego*

How are you?	*¿Qué tal?*
Very well	*Muy bien*
Thank you	*Gracias*
Don't mention it	*De nada*
Please	*Por favor*
Excuse me	*Perdón*
Yes	*Sí*
No	*No*
What is this?	*¿Qué es esto?*
How much is this?	*¿Cuánto es?*
Good morning, where is the Tourist office?	*Buenos días, dónde esta el oficina de turismo*
Straight	*derecho*
To the left	*a la izquierda*
To the right	*a la derecha*
Town Hall	*Ayuntamiento*
Bank	*Banco*
Library	*Librería*
Art Gallery	*Sala de Exposiciones*
Pharmacy	*Farmacia*
Bus stop	*Parada de Autobús*
Train station	*Estación de tren*
Post office	*Correos*
Hospital	*Hospital*
Church	*Iglesia*
Hotel	*Hotel*
Youth hostel	*Albergue*
Camping	*Camping*
Parking	*Aparcamiento*
Sports ground	*Polideportivo*
Square	*Plaza*
Discotheque	*Discoteca*
Beach	*Playa*

Numbers

1	*uno*
2	*dos*
3	*tres*
4	*cuatro*
5	*cinco*
6	*seis*
7	*siete*
8	*ocho*
9	*nueve*
10	*diez*
11	*once*
12	*doce*
13	*trece*
14	*catorce*
15	*quince*
16	*dieciséis*
17	*diecisiete*
18	*dieciocho*
19	*diecinueve*
20	*veinte*

21	*veintiuno*
25	*veinticinco*
30	*treinta*
40	*cuarenta*
50	*cincuenta*
60	*sesenta*
70	*setenta*
80	*ochenta*
90	*noventa*
100	*cien*
101	*ciento uno*
200	*doscientos*
300	*trescientos*
400	*cuatrocientos*
500	*quinientos*
600	*seiscientos*
700	*setecientos*
800	*ochocientos*
900	*novecientos*
1,000	*mil*
2,000	*dos mil*
10,000	*diez mil*
100,000	*cien mil*
1,000,000	*un millón*

Days of the week

Monday	*lunes*
Tuesday	*martes*
Wednesday	*miércoles*
Thursday	*jueves*
Friday	*viernes*
Saturday	*sábado*
Sunday	*domingo*

Months of the year

January	*enero*
February	*febrero*
March	*marzo*
April	*abril*
May	*mayo*
June	*junio*
July	*julio*
August	*agosto*
September	*septiembre*
October	*octubre*
November	*noviembre*
December	*diciembre*

Further Reading

Colombia

The Politics of Colombia, by Robert H. Dix (Praeger, NY, 1983).

The Search for El Dorado, by John Hemming, (Bogotá, 1984) is an account of the Spanish conquest of Colombia.

Colombia, by Francois de Tailly, (Delachaux and Niestle, 1981) has photographs and text in Spanish and English.

Whitewash: Pablo Escobar and the Cocaine Wars, by Simon Strong, (Macmillan, 1995); the incredible story of the Medellin drugs baron.

Any traveler going to Colombia should read the works of Gabriel García Márquez. His short stories and classic work *One Hundred Years of Solitude* give an invaluable insight into Colombia's past and society.

Venezuela

In the Rainforest, by Catherine Caufield (Picador, 1985). A definitive report on the Amazon jungle.

The General in his Labyrinth, by Gabriel García Marquez (Aims Int'l Books, 1993). Traces the final days of Simón Bolívar.

Venezuela In Focus – a guide to the People, Politics and Culture by James Ferguson (Latin America Bureau, 1994).

Peru – Maps & Books

Maps are available from *Infotur* free of charge. Larger city maps are sold at newspaper kiosks, bookstores and the *Instituto Geografico National* at Avenida Aramburu 1190 in the suburb of Surquillo, tel: 759-960. One-time use of map room and files is available from the South American Explorer's Club or, for the $25 membership fee, unlimited use of the club's resources and its office (with storerooms, safe deposit boxes, library, kitchen, first aid materials) on Avenida Republica de Portugal 146, tel: 0051-14-250142.

Lost City of the Incas: The Story of Machu Picchu and Its Builders, by Hiram Bingham, (out of print). Bingham's famous account of his discovery of Machu Picchu.

The Conquest of the Incas, by John Hemming (Harcourt Brace, 1973).

The Bridge of San Luis Rey, by Thornton Wilder (Turtleback, 1986).

Ecuador

Galápagos: A Natural History Market, by Michael Jackson, 1987 (Univ of Calgary Press, 1994).

The Voyage of the "Beagle", by Charles Darwin, 1835–1836 (Penguin USA, 1989). Darwin's epic voyage around the coasts of South America which led, 20 years later, to his theory of evolution by natural selection.

Bolivia

Bolivia in Focus – A Guide to the People, Politics and Culture by Paul Van Lindert and Otto Verkoren (Latin America Bureau, 1994).

The Open Veins of Latin America, by Eduardo Galeano (Monthly Review Press, 1998). A study of South America's sad history of exploitation.

The Incredible Voyage, by Tristan Jones (Sheridan House, 1996). Including several months sailing about Lake Titicaca.

We Eat the Mines and the Mines Eat Us, by June Nash (Columbia Univ Press, 1993). On life and death in the Bolivian tin mines.

Brazil

Brazil and The Brazilians, by G. Bruce (New York, NY: Gordon Press Pubs., 1976).

The Cloud Forest, by Peter Matthiessen, (New York: 1961).

Chile – Maps & Books

Mapa Caminero de Chile is one of the best maps of the country.

For a history of pre-Colombian Chile, check out *Chile – The Legacy of Hispanic Capitalism*, by Brian Loveman (OUP, New York, 1979).

For stories about travels in the south, try *The Old Patagonian Express*, by Paul Theroux (Penguin Books, New York, 1980).

Argentina

In Patagonia, by Bruce Chatwin, (New York: Summit Books, 1977).

Idle Days in Patagonia, by W.H. Hudson (London: Everyman's Library, 1984).

Two Thousand Miles' Ride Through the Argentine Provinces, by William MacCann (William. Reprint of 1853 edition).

Peron and the Enigmas of Argentina, by Robert D Crassweller (WW Norton & Co, 1988)

Santa Evita by Tomás Eloy Martinez (Transworld, 1997).

Other Insight Guides

The *Insight Guide* series now has almost 190 titles, spanning every continent. Apa Publications has also created two companion series of guidebooks. *Insight Pocket Guides* provide short-stay visitors with a range of carefully selected itineraries and include full-size pull-out maps. *Insight Compact Guides* are handy mini-encyclopedias, ideal for on the spot use.

In the *Insight Guide* series, South America and Latin America are covered by books on *Argentina, Buenos Aires, Belize, Brazil, Rio de Janeiro, Amazon Wildlife, Chile,*

Costa Rica, Ecuador, Mexico, Mexico City, Peru and *Venezuela.*

These companion guides give detailed, practical information backed up by entertaining essays and stunning photography.

ART & PHOTO CREDITS

Map Production: Berndtson & Berndtson Productions

© 1998 Apa Publications GmbH & Co. Verlag KG, Singapore.

INSIGHT GUIDE
SOUTH AMERICA

Cartographic Editor Zoë Goodwin
Production Stuart A. Everitt
Design Consultants Carlotta Junger, Graham Mitchener
Picture Research Hilary Genin

Index

n

New Insight Maps

When you're on the road you sometimes need the big picture that only a large-scale map can provide. This new range of durable Insight Fleximaps has been designed to complement the books and meet that need.

Detailed, clear cartography
produces easy-to-follow route and city maps with main sites highlighted, plus full index

Informative and easy to use
with the top 10 sites listed, plus useful facts about the destination, addresses, handy tips

Laminated finish
makes the maps durable, easy to fold, and allows use of a non-permanent marker pen

INSIGHT GUIDES

The world's largest collection of visual travel guides

The Insight Approach

The book you are holding is part of the world's largest range of guidebooks. Its purpose is to help you have the most valuable travel experience possible, and we try to achieve this by providing not only information about countries, regions and cities but also genuine insight into their history, culture, institutions and people.

Since the first Insight Guide – to Bali – was published in 1970, the series has been dedicated to the proposition that, with insight into a country's people and culture, visitors can both enhance their own experience and be accepted more easily by their hosts. Now, in a world where ethnic hostilities and nationalist conflicts are all too common, such attempts to increase understanding between peoples are more important than ever.

Insight Guides:
Essentials for understanding

Because a nation's past holds the key to its present, each Insight Guide kicks off with lively history chapters. These are followed by magazine-style essays on culture and daily life. This essential background information gives readers the necessary context for using the main Places section, with its comprehensive run-down on things worth seeing and doing.

Finally, a listings section contains all the information you'll need on travel, hotels, restaurants and opening times.

As far as possible, we rely on local writers and specialists to ensure that information is authoritative. The pictures, for which Insight Guides have become so celebrated, are just as important. Our photojournalistic approach aims not only to illustrate a destination but also to communicate visually and directly to readers life as it is lived by the locals. The series has grown to almost 200 titles.

Compact Guides:
The "great little guides"

As invaluable as such background information is, it isn't always fun to carry an Insight Guide through a crowded souk or up a church tower. Could we, readers asked, distil the key reference material into a slim volume for on-the-spot use?

Our response was to design Compact Guides as an entirely new series, with original text carefully cross-referenced to detailed maps and more than 200 photographs. In essence, they're miniature encyclopedias, concise and comprehensive, displaying reliable and up-to-date information in an accessible way. There are almost 100 titles.

Pocket Guides:
A local host in book form

However wide-ranging the information in a book, human beings still value the personal touch. Our editors are often asked the same questions. Where do *you* go to eat? What do *you* think is the best beach? What would *you* recommend if I have only three days? We invited our local correspondents to act as "substitute hosts" by revealing their preferred walks and trips, listing the restaurants they go to and structuring a visit into a series of timed itineraries.

The result: our Pocket Guides, complete with full-size fold-out maps. These 100-plus titles help readers plan a trip precisely, particularly if their time is short.

Exploring with Insight:
A valuable travel experience

In conjunction with co-publishers all over the world, we print in up to 10 languages, from German to Chinese, from Danish to Russian. But our aim remains simple: to enhance your travel experience by combining our expertise in guidebook publishing with the on-the-spot knowledge of our correspondents.